TRAGEDY AND POSTCOLONIAL LITERATURE

This book examines tragedy and tragic philosophy from the Greeks through Shakespeare to the present day. Using postcolonial literature, it explores key themes in the links between suffering and ethics. Under the singular and fertile rubric of tragedy, Ato Quayson reconceives how we think of world literature. He draws from many key works – *Oedipus Rex, Philoctetes, Medea, Hamlet, Macbeth,* and *King Lear* – to establish the main contours of tragedy. Quayson uses Shakespeare's *Othello*, Chinua Achebe, Wole Soyinka, Tayeb Salih, Arundhati Roy, Toni Morrison, Samuel Beckett, and J. M. Coetzee to qualify and expand the purview and terms by which Western tragedy has long been understood. Drawing on texts such as the *Poetics* and *The Nicomachean Ethics*, and augmenting them with Frantz Fanon and the Akan concept of *musuo* (taboo), Quayson formulates a supple, insightful new theory of ethical choice and the impediments against it. This is a major book from a leading critic in literary studies.

ATO QUAYSON is the Jean G. and Morris M. Doyle Professor of Interdisciplinary Studies in the Department of English at Stanford University. He has previously taught at the University of Cambridge, the University of Toronto, and New York University, and has held fellowships at Oxford, Harvard, Berkeley, the Australian National University, and Wellesley College, among others. He is a Fellow of the Ghana Academy of Arts and Sciences, the Royal Society of Canada, and the British Academy.

TRAGEDY AND POSTCOLONIAL LITERATURE

ATO QUAYSON

Stanford University

CAMBRIDGE
UNIVERSITY PRESS

CAMBRIDGE
UNIVERSITY PRESS

University Printing House, Cambridge CB2 8BS, United Kingdom

One Liberty Plaza, 20th Floor, New York, NY 10006, USA

477 Williamstown Road, Port Melbourne, VIC 3207, Australia

314–321, 3rd Floor, Plot 3, Splendor Forum, Jasola District Centre,
New Delhi – 110025, India

79 Anson Road, #06–04/06, Singapore 079906

Cambridge University Press is part of the University of Cambridge.

It furthers the University's mission by disseminating knowledge in the pursuit of
education, learning, and research at the highest international levels of excellence.

www.cambridge.org
Information on this title: www.cambridge.org/9781108830980
DOI: 10.1017/9781108921992

© Cambridge University Press 2021

First published 2021

Printed in the United Kingdom by TJ Books Limited, Padstow Cornwall

A catalogue record for this publication is available from the British Library.

ISBN 978-1-108-83098-0 Hardback

To the memory of my family's dearly departed:
Maa Rosie, Maman Angeline, Agya Emmanuel, Tonton
Paul, Tantine Emilie, and Esi

Contents

Preface and Acknowledgments

The genesis of my interest in tragedy started in a somewhat indirect way during my undergraduate studies at the University of Ghana. Mr. Aloysius Denkabe (fondly called Alo by all) delivered classes on Practical Criticism and the History and Theory of Literary Criticism. It was in the second class that he first introduced us to Aristotle's *Poetics*. Alo spoke very slowly and softly and you had to listen really hard to learn from him. It was listening to him that first ignited my curiosity about the formal aspects of literary criticism but especially about how literary form might respond to sustained philosophical investigation. The tragedies we were exposed to at university were mainly of the Shakespearean variety. Of these there was no shortage, since the West African Examinations Council made sure that we had substantial doses of Shakespeare for both our Ordinary and Advanced Levels examinations. This was to continue at university but with the added attraction of a small sample of Greek tragedies, *Oedipus Rex* being the most memorable. On applying to Cambridge for my doctoral studies I wrote what must have struck the Faculty of English's graduate admissions committee as a somewhat peculiar reading of *Things Fall Apart* through Aristotle's *Poetics*. They let me in!

But it was only after completing my PhD and returning to join the English Faculty at Cambridge after a year as Junior Research Fellow at Wolfson College in Oxford that my full immersion in tragedy was to take place. I place this turn in my intellectual life squarely at the feet of Mr. Colin Wilcockson. Colin was then Director of Studies in English at Pembroke College and he called me in shortly after my arrival at the college to ask if I would mind sharing the supervision (tutorial) of the tragedy paper with him. I agreed enthusiastically without quite understanding what I was letting myself into. It was a complete and unmitigated nightmare! I recognized too late that what turned out to be my scanty grasp of Shakespeare and a few Greek texts was not enough to teach final-year students anything serious about tragedy. What I did have were the skills of slow and steady patience in the study of literary texts that I had gathered from Alo. And so began a desperate attempt to try and remain at least three pages ahead of my students each week and to listen to them very closely to see what I could learn about this capacious genre that encompassed not only literary texts, but also philosophy, religion, theology, anthropology, art, film, and much else. The ten years that I spent teaching tragedy at Cambridge were the most intellectually stimulating of my life. Their effect was to tinge my consciousness permanently with vague perceptions of tragedy everywhere. In fact, all of the books I wrote after my first – *Strategic Transformations in Nigerian Writing* – were about tragedy, without, however, consciously acknowledging them as such.

I was also, at the same time, developing as an Africanist postcolonial scholar, with my supervisor Mr. Tim Cribb insisting that to be an African was as much a choice and a vocation as was my identity as a Ghanaian. We had many, many long and meandering conversations about African literature and the state of Western theory on which we frequently disagreed. He did not much like theory, so any theory that I sought to apply in my dissertation (and I was wedded to the damned thing) had to be robustly argued at all times. But how better to think about the efficaciousness of theory than through the prism of tragedy and where better to see the workings of tragic ideas than through postcolonial writing? This book represents twenty-five years of worrying the point.

My mother taught me about tragedy long before I encountered the forms of its expression. She was a very religious person and had the gifts of healing and prophecy. Her prayers before meals struck us children as pointlessly lengthy disquisitions on all the small things that were bothering her, which we each often listened to with at least one eye open and lots of knowing winks and suppressed giggles. The formula of her prayers was always the same: heaps of praises on God's holy name, plaintive requests for our safety, then complaints about some bad behavior of the people she traded with at the market, and a few times with prayers for the safety of some major political figures, such as Nelson Mandela when he was in jail. There was always a note of suppressed and plaintive anxiety in her prayers, as if she wanted God to see that she really was trying, but that in spite of all her prayers and gift offerings He was not fully attentive to all our needs. It took me many years to figure out that what I thought was a cry to God came from a much deeper and complicated source. It came from the very depths of her soul for having walked out of a bad marriage and leaving us behind with my father when we were much younger. This was extremely bold and unusual for a woman of her generation, and she spent many years in acts of atonement that I could not really understand until I had had children of my own. The point of my mother's anxious prayers was what they expressed of the intractable ethical contradictions of making choices in a world that was far from ideal. And yet she undertook all things from a deeply held belief that her unbounded faith would ultimately vanquish all the ills that confronted us. She died in the year I started my job at Cambridge and before I could gather the tools by which to fully make sense of her predicament and to talk to her about what it must have felt like bringing up children who were blissfully oblivious to her deepest sorrow.

***

This book has benefited over the years from conversations with more interlocutors than I can possibly remember. Some of the most stimulating conversations had little or nothing to do with tragedy. I want to thank especially the much-missed Tejumola Olaniyan and Abiola Irele, as well as Adeleke Adeeko, Anjali Prabhu, Moradewun Adejunmobi, Neil ten Kortenaar, Ankhi Mukkherjee, Adwoa Opoku-Agyeman, Aloysius Denkabe, Colin Wilcockson, Tim Cribb, Karin Barber, Uzo Ensowanne, John Kerrigan, Kenneth Mills, and former students Christopher Warnes, Julian Murphet, Joanne Leow, Esther de Bruijn, Heba Jamana, and Noor Naga, among the many others I have had long and continuing conversations with.

The English Department at New York University provided the very receptive intellectual environment in which I began to write the book in the fall of 2017. It was there that I had the privilege of getting to know Richard Halpern, with whom I had lively conversations on his own fine book on tragedy and with whom I shared my own ideas. Tom Augst was a tireless advocate, while Wendy Lee and Elaine Freedgood were always on hand with wry insights about the exhilarating but sometimes fruitless work we did as laborers in the academic vineyard. I want to also thank Jini Kim Watson and Emily Apter for the diverse conversations I had with them on a variety of topics both personal and professional; Robert Young for his long-time friendship; and Lytle Shaw for giving me and my wife a magnificent tour of New York when we first arrived. Manthia Diawara provided invaluable advice and comradeship, while Frankie Edozien was always solicitous about our welfare. Stanford offered its own support for the completion of the manuscript. To Lanier Anderson, Alex Woloch, Blakey Vermuele, Margaret Cohen, Gavin Jones, Patricia Parker, Tom Owens, Mark Greif, Shelley Fisher Fishkin, John Bender, Roland Greene, Richard Roberts, James Ferguson, Liisa Malkki, Joel Cabrita, Paula Moya,

Ramon Salvidar, and Maritza Colon a very special thanks for welcoming us so warmly and also for the patient exposition of the intricate workings of Stanford.

I want to express very special thanks also to Noor Naga for being such a patient and altogether assiduous early copy editor, to Emma Sullivan for her more professional overview of the manuscript, and to Ray Ryan for his consistent support and encouragement throughout the writing of this book. To the anonymous readers of Cambridge University Press, warm gratitude for both seeing the value of my argument and also pressing me to improve it in various directions.

Grace Toleque has been my whispering companion from start to finish and has had to put up with more unprovoked disquisitions on tragedy at all times of day and night than any human being should ever be exposed to. I raise a full glass to her patience, her quiet capacity to discern what I am trying to get at even when I haven't got it myself, and to her gentle and abiding love. Noah and Kamau bore witness to the madness that afflicted me at different stages of the writing, and to them I also want to say many thanks for at least politely pretending that I was also a sane man among men.

To my dearly departed mother and to all those who have helped on this long and transformative journey, *medaase,* which means "thank you" in Akan but translates literally as "I prostrate myself before you."

The flaws in this book are, tragically, all mine.

CHAPTER I

Introduction
Tragedy and the Maze of Moments

The hanging of Ken Saro-Wiwa and eight of his colleagues in Nigeria by Sani Abacha's government in November 1995 had a most visceral impact on me. I was badly shaken. I had just started teaching the tragedy paper at Cambridge University when the news brought me forcefully to the blank futility of trying to align what I was doing in the classroom with what was taking place in a part of the world I was deeply invested in. And, moreover, to a writer who had stood up to "speak truth to power" on behalf of his community. What was more tragic than that? For those who do not know about him, a few words of introduction: Ken Saro-Wiwa was a writer and environmental activist who, for almost two decades before his untimely death at the hands of his own government, had been making forceful arguments about the devastation that oil companies such as Shell had inflicted upon the Ogoni community. The Ogonis are a micro-minority in Eastern Nigeria much less known than the Igbo, who themselves shot to international fame both through the writings of Chinua Achebe and also because of the ultimately unsuccessful secessionist bid they launched against Nigeria in the Biafra War of 1967–1971. There were many casualties of that war on both sides, but Saro-Wiwa argued that the pollution of his people's lands would have a more profound impact than anything that had ever happened in Nigeria's entire history. And he was right. There are oil-polluted lands in Eastern Nigeria that cannot be cultivated for food for the next thousand years. It represents an environmental devastation of near-apocalyptic proportions.

I remember at the time pacing up and down my office deeply upset and by turns shaking my fists in the air and holding my head in my hands. Raymond Williams's *Modern Tragedy*, which argued the imperative for us to not separate the domains of the literary from the historical in our scholarly definitions of tragedy, gave me only momentary satisfaction. Around the same time as the news of the hangings, the singer Enya released

her hit single "Anywhere Is." The song had what sounded to me like a
marching tempo that was somehow directly contradicted by its lyrics:

> I walk the maze of moments
> but everywhere I turn to
> begins a new beginning
> but never finds a finish
> I walk to the horizon
> and there I find another
> it all seems so surprising
> and then I find that I know
>
> You go there you're gone forever
> I go there I'll lose my way
> if we stay here we're not together
> Anywhere is

Is the repetition of new beginnings that never find a finish a product
merely of confusion or of fundamental chaos? And what is to be made
of the impression that if one person goes they go forever (death?), but
if the other goes they lose their way (alienation?). Why can they both
not stay in the here and now forever? And where or what is
"Anywhere"? Does it fold into itself an ontology of time composed
of iterations of circularity, or is "Anywhere" the product of longing
and bewilderment that can never be resolved? Is this a love song, or,
as I chose to interpret it at the time, a song about unrelieved tragic
nostalgia? For some reason that was never quite clear to me, Saro-
Wiwa's hanging and Enya's song became inextricably fused in my
mind such that their contradictory combination became the sound-
track of my emotional responses to the difficult task of working out
a feasible resolution to the confusing question of tragedy.

Enya's song, like the other texts I will discuss here, seems significant for
me in its ethico-aesthetic dimension that also reflects upon the event of
Saro-Wiwa's hanging.[1] And it is this subliminal impulse to respond to the
ethico-aesthetic entailments of both literature and real life that led me first
to write *Aesthetic Nervousness: Disability and the Crisis of Representation* and

---

[1] In the heat of the moment I wrote an essay trying precisely to do this, that is, to deploy the concept of
literary tragedy in order to read the life of the activist-writer. The results seem to me now to have been
uneven, partly because if the objective had been to marshal public sentiment against the Nigerian
government, then this was not the best way to go about it, and partly because the entire episode and
the history behind it transcended the capacity of any autonomous literary concept for explaining it
fully. See my "Anatomizing a Postcolonial Tragedy: Ken Saro-Wiwa and the Ogonis," *Performance
Research*, 1.2 (1996): 83–92.

now *Tragedy and Postcolonial Literature*.[2] *Aesthetic Nervousness* was in many ways the direct progenitor of the present book, except that there I referenced disabled characters and literary tropes of disability as surrogates for different forms of bodily impairments and examined how these unsettled existing protocols of representation. I argued there that the literature of disability helped to induct us into more complex ethical responses to the status of people with disabilities in real-life situations. I feel that *Tragedy and Postcolonial Literature* will allow me to do much more than I managed to accomplish in *Aesthetic Nervousness*. This is because I now delink the broad concept of suffering from any specific character type or existential condition and instead read suffering across different contexts, in works from a variety of cultural backgrounds in the postcolonial world. I also draw substantially on the large and varied history of tragic expression from the Greeks and Shakespeare and on to present times.

Notwithstanding all I have said of my inspirations so far, to attempt a fresh statement on tragedy at the present time still seems like a somewhat forlorn enterprise. There is already a vast and formidable range of scholarly work on the subject and many events that take place in today's world are taken to fall readily under the commonplace epithet of tragedy. The perceived relationship between tragedy and the historical phases of its emergence has been ever thorny, as is the question of whether it is the product of particular historical epochs or exclusively of individual acts of writing. On the one hand, the celebrated hallmarks of Greek and Renaissance tragedy seem remote and alien: the anguish of kings and high personages; the vicissitudes of the founding of nations; the ineluctable unfolding of fate and necessity; and the intensification of time as it veers toward catastrophe. On the other, tragedy's transposition from the theatre and into the novel, film, opera, painting, and other media has placed it in the vicinity of the everyday, to the point that, for some, its force as a literary expression has been utterly attenuated. This is the much-discussed view of George Steiner's *The Death of Tragedy*, which I pick up later in this Introduction. And if the elements of plot, pathos, conflict, suffering, self-discovery, and death have always guaranteed a celebration of tragedy's universality, then it is also true that tragedy has been subject to surprisingly variant interpretations. All of these have been sources of intense debate. And so, this book is proffered not simply to rectify a glaring absence in the

---

[2] Ato Quayson, *Aesthetic Nervousness: Disability and the Crisis of Representation* (New York: Columbia University Press, 2007).

field, which, of course, it also attempts to do, but as a means by which to rethink postcolonialism *through* the prism of literary tragedy and vice versa.

I would like to clear a misunderstanding that regularly comes up with usage of the term postcolonialism among nonspecialists. While the prefix "post-" in the term hints at its temporal inflection, that is, that it pertains to matters that occurred "after" colonialism; by the 1990s, the term was used without a hyphen to denote the field as an area of recognizable interests, debates, and controversies.[3] Understood not as limited to the implicit temporal marking of the "post-", but as the sign of a critical orientation toward colonialism and its legacies, postcolonial studies in general have been concerned with the representation of experiences of various kinds including those of slavery, migration, oppression, and resistance; as well as the intersections between race, gender, and sexual identities, and the responses to the continuing neocolonial discourses of Euro-America. Thus, unlike what pertains in commonplace understandings of the term, it is important to bear in mind that postcolonialism does not refer simply to colonial violence and the resistance toward it, especially as it might be illustrated from ex-colonial societies in different parts of the world, but to much more wide-ranging and multi-layered social, cultural, and political phenomena. It is also important to note that the term is used to shed light on a spectrum of colonial space-making practices and the sociopolitical relations that derive from them in different contexts. These include: a) the establishment of bureaucratic and administrative arrangements for the governing of distant territories (the British in India, the French in Mauritius, the Spanish and Portuguese in South America, etc.); b) plantation economies and post-plantation societies (Jamaica, Malaysia, Haiti, Barbados, the United States, etc.); c) white settler colonialism (Australia, South Africa, Canada, and for some commentators, also the United States); d) migration, refugees, diasporas, and the large populations of ex-colonials in Euro-America and elsewhere (Rohingyars in Myanmar, Somalis of Nairobi and Minnesota, Africans in China, Algerians in France, etc.). A growing concern among postcolonial scholars has also been the fate of racial minorities in the West, including Native Americans and African Americans in the USA and the Aboriginal and Métis populations of Canada and Australia, among others. The varying interests that fall under the rubric of postcolonialism allow for a wide range

---

[3] I provide a full account of the genealogies and multiple inflections of the term "postcolonialism" in "Introduction: Postcolonial Literature in a Changing Frame," the opening chapter of *The Cambridge History of Postcolonial Literature*, vol. I, ed. Ato Quayson (Cambridge: Cambridge University Press, 2012), 1–29.

of applications, thus designating a constant interplay and slippage between the sense of historical transition; a specific sociocultural location pertaining to colonialism and empire in past and/or present contexts; and an epochal configuration.[4] However the term is construed, a central underlying assumption is that a focus on the discourse and ideology of colonialism is as important as one on the material effects of subjugation and interracial relations under varying contexts and conditions. While occasional reflections on postcolonial tragedy have not been uncommon, a sustained analysis of the relationship between tragedy and specifically postcolonial representations is really only to be found in Timothy J. Reiss's *Against Autonomy: Global Dialectics of Cultural Exchange* and David Scott's much more elaborate *Conscripts of Modernity: The Tragedy of Colonial Enlightenment.*[5] However, both Reiss and Scott are interested mainly in outlining a philosophy of postcolonial history, so their remarks on tragedy, though highly insightful, do not focus predominantly on literary examples. Scott will be especially important to my discussion of colonial modernity as reflected in Chinua Achebe's rural novels and I shall be returning to him many times in the course of these pages. It is the generative quality of postcolonialism not as a temporal marker but as a mode of reading political, social, and cultural relations in different contexts and parts of the world that allows me to bring together in *Tragedy and Postcolonial Literature* writers with as varied provenance and thematic emphases as Chinua Achebe, Wole Soyinka, Tayeb Salih, Toni Morrison, Arundhati Roy, J. M. Coetzee, and Samuel Beckett, among various others. While I shall attempt in each chapter to explain how each writer illustrates features of postcolonialism, the underlining assumption in all of them is that these writers collectively give us an incremental and fertile view of what might pass for postcolonial tragedy. Many other writers could have been included in these pages (I think immediately of Jean Rhys, Gabriel

---

[4] There are many useful books and essays on postcolonialism. For a good range that pays attention to the various historical and more discursive usages of the term, see Ella Shohat, "Notes on the Postcolonial," *Social Text*, 31/32 (1992): 99–113; Anne McClintock, "The Angel of Progress: Pitfalls of the Term 'Postcolonialism'" in *Colonial Discourse/Postcolonial Theory*, eds. Francis Barker, Peter Hulme, and Margaret Iversen (Manchester: Manchester University Press, 1994), 253–256; Ania Loomba, *Colonialism/Postcolonialism*, 2nd edition (London: Routledge, 2005); Robert J. C. Young, *Empire, Colony, Postcolony* (Oxford: Wiley Blackwell, 2015). The different forms of colonial space-making and thus the different kinds of postcolonial theories that might be applied to them are elaborated more fully in Ato Quayson, "Introduction: Postcolonial Literature in a Changing Historical Frame."

[5] Timothy J. Reiss, *Against Autonomy: Global Dialectics of Cultural Exchange* (Stanford: Stanford University Press, 2002) and David Scott, *Conscripts of Modernity: The Tragedy of Colonial Enlightenment* (Durham: Duke University Press, 2005).

García Márquez, Isabel Allende, Junot Diaz, Naguib Mahfouz, Gayl Jones, Richard Wright, Ngũgĩ wa Thiong'o, and Michael Ondaatje as other worthy possibilities for inclusion in the discussion), but the point of this book is to show that our understanding of what falls under the definition of literary tragedy can and must be enriched from the many rich postcolonial examples now available to us.

From Aristotle Through the Akan to Fanon: A Psychoexistential Poetics

The argument of this book is essentially built on an Aristotelian foundation, which I shall elaborate incrementally throughout. But it is important to delineate this Aristotelian foundation from the very outset and to clarify in what ways it opens up avenues for a working definition of postcolonial tragedy. Aristotle suggests in the *Poetics* that a) plot is the soul of tragedy; b) plot depends on a structured sequence of incidents that flow inexorably from one to the next; c) complex plots are preferable to simple plots and that a complex plot aligns discovery/knowledge (*anagnorisis*) to reversal (*peripeteia*); d) the reversal of the hero's fortunes is triggered by an error of judgement (*hamartia*) that is symptomatic of an impasse of understanding; and e) for the audience, the tragic action has an educational and thera-peutic function, generating pity and fear the better to channel them (*catharsis*).[6] Each of Aristotle's concepts from the *Poetics* has been the subject of vigorous debates in the history of tragedy but of special interest to me are the concepts of *hamartia* and *anagnorisis*, which I elaborate upon and turn to slightly different uses in various chapters in this book. I also draw from Aristotle's comments on plot to elaborate the concept of causal plausibility (more on this presently), which I argue indicates the specific ways in which tragic plot structure is connected to the elicitation of our sympathy for the suffering of the protagonist. I shall raise a number of problems regarding causal plausibility in relation to the work of Samuel Beckett in Chapter 9.

If in the *Poetics* Aristotle focuses specifically on tragic plot in outlining for us its main elements and emotional effects, it is in *The Nicomachean Ethics* that he elaborates upon the nature of the good life, which in his view derives both from settled orientation and the exercise of ethical choice. The question as to whether the supreme good emanates from "the *possession* or in the *exercise* of virtue" is settled for him with reference to the latter, for as

[6] Aristotle, *Poetics*, ed. T. S. Dorsch (London: Penguin Classics, 1965).

he notes, at the Olympic Games, "it is not the best-looking or the strongest men present that are crowned with wreaths, but the competitors (because it is from them that the winners come), so it is those who act that rightly win the honours and rewards in life."[7] This emphasis on virtue as deriving from action is consistent with his installation of the principle of action at the core of his definition of tragedy in the *Poetics*: "The representation of the action is the plot of the tragedy; for the ordered arrangement of the incidents is what I mean by plot .... Of these elements [spectacle, character, plot, etc.] the most important is the plot, the ordering of the incidents; for tragedy is a representation, not of men, but of action and life, of happiness and unhappiness – and happiness and unhappiness are bound up with action."[8] "Nevertheless," as he continues to argue in the *Ethics*, "it seems clear that happiness needs the addition of external goods, as we have said; for it is difficult if not impossible to do fine deeds without any resources."[9] The resources Aristotle has in view here are of a material character, but will also later be shown by him to encompass the much broader ambit of worldly goods. Martha Nussbaum has glossed the category of worldly goods as implying the "interactions of *philia*, either familial or friendly" and good health, as well as the benefits of citizenship and communal belonging.[10] We might add to these the freedom of expressing one's identity with respect to racial, gender, and sexual orientations, as well as the capacity to revise these without fear of social condemnation. To go back to Aristotle: since "one swallow does not make a summer; [and] neither does one day," a man needs a whole and complete life to call himself "blessed and happy," and to exercise ethically meaningful choices.[11] At the same time, he recognizes that "in the course of life we encounter many reverses and all kinds of vicissitudes, and in old age even the most prosperous of men may be involved in great misfortunes, as we are told about Priam in the Trojan poems."[12] A good person cannot long remain good – that is, exercise ethically meaningful choices – if they have encountered great reversals of fortune: "For no activity is perfect if it is impeded, and happiness is a perfect thing. That is why the happy man needs (besides his other qualifications) physical advantages as well as external goods and the gifts of fortune, so that he may not be hampered

---

[7] Aristotle, *The Nicomachean Ethics*, trans. J. A. K. Thomson (London: Penguin, 2004), 1098b34–1099a6, also 1106b36, emphasis in the original.
[8] Aristotle, *Poetics*, 39.   [9] Aristotle, *Ethics*, 1099a32–34.
[10] Martha Nussbaum, "Tragedy and Self-Sufficiency: Plato and Aristotle on Fear and Pity'" in *Essays on Aristotle's Poetics*, ed. Amélie Oksenberg Rorty (Princeton University Press, 1992), 266.
[11] Aristotle, *Ethics*, 1098a19–22.   [12] Aristotle, *Ethics*, 1100a5–9.

by lack of these things."[13] The happy man, then, is one "who is active in accordance with complete virtue, and who is adequately furnished with external [worldly] goods, and that not for some unspecified period but throughout a complete life".[14] For Aristotle, ethical choice is an expression of *eudaimonia*, translated from the Greek variously as indwelling virtue, happiness, and also flourishing.[15] From his account in the *Ethics, eudaimonia* has a dynamic dimension related to the exercise of virtue-as-action and a contingent element pertaining to dependence on external or worldly goods. Aristotle's question regarding what constitutes the good life is also answered at different points in the *Ethics* with respect to practical reason as well as to the dictates of contemplation.[16] All these furnish the grounds for identification with the plight of a man of moral equilibrium and settled character orientation who falls into ruin, a man he describes in the *Poetics* as neither good nor bad, but who through an error of judgment and the interaction with unpredictable circumstances, suffers an ethically significant reversal of fortune. Negative or intractable conditions may be triggered either through character misjudgment or from chance and contingent circumstances, but the point to be lamented is that however these conditions occur, they may come to restrict the character's capacity to exercise ethically significant choices. In Nussbaum's various readings of Aristotle, the frustration of access to worldly goods serves to atrophy the character's self-perception, making it difficult or even impossible for her to draw upon the internal and external resources that would enable her to exercise ethically significant choices.[17] Her capacity for making ethically significant choices is impeded by the loss of external goods such that the atrophying of her capacities are the direct measure of such impediments. This is what for me unites Achebe's Okonkwo, Morrison's Sethe, Soyinka's Elesin Oba, Arundhati Roy's Ammu, and Coetzee's Magistrate, as we shall see later in the book.

[13] Aristotle, *Ethics*, 1153b16–20.   [14] Aristotle, *Ethics*, 1101a14–17.

[15] For Aristotle, *eudaimonia* and thus virtue is directly tied to action; *Ethics*, 1095a18–20, 1098a15–22, 1176a33–47.

[16] These are especially to be found in *Ethics*, X.7–8.

[17] My description of Aristotle's ethical propositions is heavily inspired by Martha Nussbaum's writings on the subject. See also, her "The 'Morality of Pity': Sophocles's *Philoctetes*," Rita Felski, ed., *Rethinking Tragedy* (Baltimore: Johns Hopkins University Press, 2008), 148–169; and *The Fragility of Goodness: Luck and Ethics in Greek Tragedy and Philosophy* (Cambridge: Cambridge University Press, 2001). See also, Julia Annas, *The Morality of Happiness* (New York: Oxford University Press, 1993), especially ch. 18; Sarah Broadie, "What Should We Mean by 'The Highest Good'," in *Aristotle and Beyond: Essays in Metaphysics and Ethics* (Cambridge: Cambridge University Press, 2007), 153–165; and Howard J. Curzer, "The Supremely Happy Life in Aristotle's *Nicomachean Ethics*," *Apeiron*, 24 (1991): 47–69.

When Aristotle notes in the *Poetics* that the plot of a tragedy must have a beginning, a middle, and an end, he is not simply calling for the mechanical temporal sequencing of the tragic action, but rather for the establishment of the terms of what Nussbaum glosses as causal plausibility. As she notes, whether with respect to literary tragedy or real life, for the victim of suffering to elicit sympathetic identification from the witness to their suffering, it has to be shown, first, that they were not culpable for the catastrophe that befalls them, second, that even if they were somewhat culpable, the scale of the catastrophe vastly outstrips their culpability, and third, that the catastrophe has undermined the sufferer's capacity to make ethically informed judgments. It is these three elements that collectively define causal plausibility for the audience and in the eye of the one that bears witness, thus triggering sympathy for the sufferer and perhaps an active response to their suffering.[18] And yet in the literary representation of suffering, causal plausibility entails a number of other elements, not all of which necessarily comply with Aristotle's notion of the ideal plot. At issue are the elements of circumstance and contingency, and sometimes even of the contrast between the human domain and that of the natural world, as we shall see amply illustrated in Arundhati Roy's *The God of Small Things* in Chapter 8. In contrast, unlike the work of the other postcolonial authors noted in the previous paragraph, in much of Samuel Beckett's work the randomization of causes and effects and the severing of consensual meanings from the domain of language all mean that his plots do not allow us to align causal plausibility to the characters' suffering in any straightforward way. The terms of our sympathy for Beckett's characters and our own potential for identification with them are seriously challenged, thus requiring us to rethink the Aristotelian relation between plot, pity, and fear. All definitions of suffering have to find a way of correlating two central vectors: Self as a category has to be defined as fully as possible and then correlated to the category of World. But often Self and World are not easily separable even for definitional purposes, since the boundaries of the one overlap with the other and the two are completely co-constitutive. While the Self may disintegrate in direct response to reversals of fortune, it may also, properly speaking, suffer a sense of biographical discontinuity simply at losing the capacity to produce a coherent account of the world to itself and to others. And how does one choose between courses of action when they are framed by belief systems that do not enjoy the individual's unconditional assent – as in the case of the Magistrate's reaction to the violence of Empire that we

---

[18] See especially Nussbaum's "The 'Morality of Pity': Sophocles's *Philoctetes*."

shall see in our discussion of J. M. Coetzee's *Waiting for the Barbarians* in Chapter 7? Or are the products of oppression – as in the case of Sethe and her response to slavery, as we shall see in picking up Toni Morrison's *Beloved* in Chapter 6? What amounts to a loss of hermeneutical coherence is what unites Achebe's Ezeulu, Soyinka's Professor, Coetzee's Magistrate, Morrison's Sethe, and links the unnamed narrator of Tayeb Salih's *Season of Migration to the North* to Shakespeare's Othello, Beckett's Estragon and Vladimir, and Fanon's persona in *Black Skin, White Masks*, even if from completely different universes of experience and genres of representation.

In the Akan culture from which I hail, there are certain infractions that are placed under the rubric of *musuo*, or "harms to the soul," that seem to me analogous to the category of impediments to ethical choice in Aristotle's formulation of impediments to *eudaimonia*. Kwame Gyekye has defined *musuo* in terms of "extraordinary moral evils" akin to social taboos and he lists under them "suicide, incest, having sexual intercourse in the bush, rape, murder, stealing things dedicated to the deities or ancestral spirits, etc."[19] All the transgressions Gyekye names fall squarely under the rubric of cultural taboos among the Akan, and his interests are in their socially oriented character rather than in the harmful effects they may have on the individual. Deep harms that impact directly on individuals must also fall under *musuo*, however, since it is an umbrella category in his description. When a trusted person sleeps with a friend's wife, the Akan say *wa di no awu*, which may be translated as "he has served/given him death," (i.e., "he has killed him"). Such grave acts of betrayal are also referred to as *wakum ne sunsum* ("he has killed his soul"). The killing of someone's *sunsum*, or what I am describing here as a harm to the soul, is thought by the Akan to deeply impact upon the victim's emotions and may cause the affected individual to suffer a loss of faith in society that may consequently also affect their capacity for making ethically informed choices. Such *musuo* are even thought to trigger suicidal thoughts, so extreme is the effect of such harms to the *sunsum*. Another instance of *musuo* is when a greedy *abusuapanin* (the head of a family) sells some valuable heirlooms (*agyapadeε*) or consecrated jewelry (especially gold ornaments), that have been passed down from generation to generation. In this case, it is said that *wakum wɔn sunsum* (he has killed their/the family's soul). Such offences lie under the class of major financial malfeasance that impacts upon the core of the family unit and destroys it from the inside.[20]

---

[19] Kwame Gyekye, *An Essay on African Philosophical Thought: The Akan Conceptual Scheme*, revised edition (Philadelphia: Temple University Press, 1995), 131–133.
[20] Many thanks to Kwesi Ampene at the University of Michigan for confirming these nuances for me. Personal communication, March 6, 2018.

Such *musuo* would also, I think, fall under the general Aristotelian rubric of causative reversals of fortune, not from the view of the alteration of material circumstances (the loss of a job, losing a house) but rather from the immeasurable impact these have on the exercise of ethically significant choices for the individual and the community at large. The effect of a *musuo* on interpersonal relations is to impair faith in the affected person's own sense of judgment in that they become afflicted by strong feelings of guilt, confusion, deep sorrow, and may seriously begin to doubt their own capacity for doing good or for living a meaningful life (and even opening up the possibility of suicide) as they move forward. For the rest of the community, on the other hand, the perceived poisoning of the sources of generally held beliefs causes an attenuation of the shared sense of collective values, that may then come to impact upon interpersonal relations within the community. ("One finger dipped in palm oil," say the Akan, "ends up soiling all the other fingers of the hand.") Like sacrilegious taboos (murder, for example, or appropriating sacrifices intended for the gods), the Akan also consider such harms to the soul as sometimes requiring acknowledgement and propitiation as a means of repairing the disrupted ties of *philia*, both familial and friendly. This is distinct from the categories of propitiation for the communally inflected *musuo* that Gyekye focuses on, which typically involves priests and persons with specifically designated ritual functions. The person suffering a harm to the soul has to not only undergo personal psychic adjustment, but the entire community of *philia* has also to undergo a form of ritual restoration. What I want to derive from the Akan category of *musuo* as the *strong emotional effects* of harms to the soul, seem to me to have implications for interpreting the mechanisms of *hamartia* and *anagnorisis* that we see in Greek tragedy. For the Akan might reinterpret Aristotle's categories as pertaining to the relationship between knowledge and community, since *anagnorisis*/tragic knowledge is not always the exclusive purview of the individual tragic protagonist but in certain instances is coproduced through the interaction of their guilt with the sense of contamination and anxiety of their wider community. In contrast to Aristotle's concepts, Akan *musuo* names actions (sleeping with another man's wife; stealing sacrifice intended for the gods) that are deeply personal in their implications for the continuing exercise of ethical choice, as well as being collective in recognizing the disruption to the well-being of the community at large. The duality I see encoded in the Akan concept also means that individual actions are always judged to have an automatic social or communal ramification and that while it is the individual that may experience the reversal of the capacity to act or to make ethically salient choices, the community is not entirely excluded from the existential malaise brought on by the *musuo*. This fusion of individual culpability with collective existential malaise appeals to me because it restores an idea of collective responsibility that is often foreclosed by the exclusive Western focus on individual agency. It is not merely the contrasts between the two categories of self and society that I want to illustrate, but rather the fluid and interacting contours of the two.

The Akan concept of *musuo* will help us evaluate various scenes in postcolonial tragedy with the specific purpose of harnessing Aristotle to a different kind of interpretation. The concept of *musuo* is applicable to a discussion of Okonkwo's killing of Ikemefuna and his own suicide in Chinua Achebe's *Things Fall Apart*; to Elesin's failure to undertake the ritual suicide in Wole Soyinka's *Death and the King's Horseman*; to Arundhati Roy's Rahel and Estha and their inadvertent role in the death of their cousin in *The God of Small Things*; as well as to Sethe's killing of her daughter in Morrison's *Beloved*. In each instance, what we might describe as *musuo* is split between the actions of an individual protagonist and the disruption of the hermeneutical framework by which witnesses to the *musuo* come to respond to it. And yet *musuo* is not as useful for exploring the deeply private crises that afflict Coetzee's Magistrate in *Waiting for the Barbarians*, Tayeb Salih's Mustafa Sa'eed in *Season of Migration to the North*, and Beckett's Murphy. The difference in the theoretical applicability of a concept such as the Akan *musuo* to the two sets of texts has to do with the different ways in which the two sets of characters harness guarantees from an imagined community on whose behalf they might be deemed to represent. This guarantee is highly elusive, as I shall elaborate in the Conclusion, and depends primarily on the degree to which the authors of the works themselves feel they are spokespersons for a community or sociopolitical entity that lies beyond them.

Given that every traditional society will likely have their own designation of harms to the soul, my use of the Akan concept of *musuo* here is not meant to offer yet another universalizing category, but to suggest how some of Aristotle's key concepts may be productively translated into different cultural idioms to help expand the ambit of his insights. If the plight of the tragic protagonist has the power to invoke our sympathies, it is not only because he or she experiences physical and emotional pain, important though these are for our initial identification. Rather, it is because tragedy demonstrates that the conditions for exercising meaningful ethical choices that have consequences for how a life is lived do not remain entirely within the grasp of the individual. It is the iconic condensation of this central

insight about suffering, and the fact that it is presented to us in a form that
encapsulates the relation between choice and unforeseen consequences,
that encourages us to return to tragedy again and again despite all the
conceptual discomfort that it may also give us.[21]

***

Frantz Fanon also provides us with another important dimension of what we
might define as postcolonial tragedy. Fanon is correctly taken in postcolonial
studies as an exemplary theoretician of colonial struggles. The key principles
that he put forward regarding colonial violence, the complicities of postcolonial elites, and the overall nature of colonized identities under erasure
remain pertinent to the field to this day.[22] He is also useful for thinking
about tragedy. At one point in his reflections in "The Fact of Blackness,"
Fanon proffers a peculiarly fertile self-reflexive insight that discloses something of his overall hermeneutic: "in one sense, if I were asked for a definition
of myself, I would say that I am one who waits; I investigate my surroundings, I interpret everything in terms of what I discover, I become sensitive."[23]
This statement is paradigmatic of the discursive maneuvers that underpin
Black Skin, White Masks in general. In this one statement, Fanon imputes the
role of an interlocutor for eliciting a definition of the self ("if I were asked");
the eternal vigilance that he brings to bear on that enterprise ("I am one who
waits . . . I become sensitive"); and, above all, the degree to which all that he
discovers depends ultimately on a fervent interpretation of his surroundings,
both historical and cultural.

As Sekyi-Otu correctly points out in *Fanon's Dialectic of Experience*,
Fanon's discourse is a mixture of propositions and almost immediate self-
revisions. He identifies Fanon's rehearsal of linguistic acts within which lie
many subtle and surrogate dramaturgical devices: "stage directions, signals of
imminent plot twists and complications, markers of incipient ironies and
reversals, choric commentaries and points of strategic complicity or critical
difference between protagonal utterance and authorial stance."[24] In contrast
to what we see in Aristotle, what I want to describe as Fanon's existential
poetics are coded in his writings primarily in terms of the fraught

[21] This question is the focus of A. D. Nuttall's *Why Does Tragedy Give Pleasure?* (Oxford: Oxford University Press, 2001).
[22] For a fine comparison of Fanon with other decolonization critics, see Anjali Prabhu, "Fanon, Memmi, Glissant and Postcolonial Writing," *The Cambridge History of Postcolonial Literature*, vol. 2, ed. Ato Quayson (Cambridge: Cambridge University Press, 2012), 1068–1099.
[23] Frantz Fanon, *Black Skin, White Masks*, trans. Charles Lam Markmann (New York: Grove, 1967), 120.
[24] Ato Sekyi-Otu, *Fanon's Dialectic of Experience* (Cambridge, MA: Harvard University Press, 1997), 8.

hermeneutics of identity that unfold within the racial economy of colonialism. Fanon's account throughout *Black Skin, White Masks* is depopulated of *philia* at a fundamental level, thus indicating the loss of worldly goods as an ontological condition of his existence within the colonial racial economy. What is conveyed in essays such as "The Fact of Blackness" is his sense of being surrounded by a proliferation of skeptical interlocutors, all of whom pose searing questions to his racial identity. Unlike Aristotle, whose descriptions of tragedy are predominantly formalist and institute a necessary distance from the object being described, the starting point of Fanon's existential poetics is a series of real and imagined scenarios in which his identity is experientially put under duress and continually forced to be revised and reinstated. Fanon typically stages his argument along three overlapping discursive axes: first, in the description of an anecdote or a cluster of anecdotes related to a personal experience; second, in the report of something overheard or told to him in a social encounter; and third, and most elusive, in his responses to something written on the condition of the black man. This third category of readings he considers social acts, on a par with things overheard or said to him directly. His responses in all three instances are expressed via the panoply of devices that Sekyi-Otu describes for us, but their "dramatic" nature also resides in the unfailing reiteration of two additional conceptual maneuvers. Fanon portrays every encounter as the simultaneous coalescence of experience and exegesis. That is to say, every experience is at one and the same time exegetical. He interprets, and shows himself interpreting, even as he experiences. But flowing out of this simultaneous collocation of experience and exegesis, is what Cornelius Castoriadis describes in another context as "systematic delirium."[25] Systematic delirium is a process of abstraction that is constructed according to incoherent principles, assimilating different and apparently incompatible categories of social existence into one another. The colonialized Other has been described in colonial discourse variously as black, dirty, lying, childlike, incapable of self-regulation, uncivilized, barbarian, effeminate, oversexed, etc.[26] This Other is primarily a location within a structure of denominations (i.e., a form of naming that is both structured and *structuring*). It is a structure of denominations because it provides the foundation for the *social currency* of particular cultural stereotypes that come to shape social relations. This structure writes itself in history through a series of cross-cultural encounters

---

[25] Cornelius Castoriadis, *The Imaginary institution of Society* (Cambridge: Polity, 1975), 57.
[26] For an extensive description of these colonial descriptions of blackness, see Patrick Brantlinger, "Victorians and Africans: The Genealogy of the Myth of the Dark Continent," *Critical Inquiry*, 12.1 (1985): 166–203.

in which Otherness is assigned a particular quality of impoverishment and evolutionary backwardness as its indelible signatures. No idle semiotic, the structure of denominations spawns both material and psycho-existential effects. Systematic delirium in this formulation is not akin to madness, ecstasy, or the loss of lucidity. Quite the opposite. Rather, the delirium emerges from the intensity of the perceived epistemological disjuncture, the existential sense that one is standing where one ought not to be and therefore, for Fanon, every experience must constantly be interrogated, redefined, and even allegorized.

A prime example of systematic delirium occurs in the episode where Fanon is pointed at by a frightened child whilst he is walking through a park. The child points at him and exclaims "Look, mama, a Negro." This is what we then see:

> "Look, a Negro!" The circle was drawing a bit tighter. I made no secret of my amusement.
>
> "Mama, see the Negro! I am frightened!" Frightened! Frightened! Now they were beginning to be afraid of me. I made up my mind to laugh myself to tears, but laughter had become impossible.
>
> I could no longer laugh, because I already knew that there were legends, stories, history, and above all *historicity*, which I had learned from Jaspers. Then, assailed at various points, the corporeal schema crumbled, its place taken by a racial epidermal schema. In the train it was no longer a question of being aware of my body in the third person but in a triple person. In the train I was given not one but two, three places. I had already stopped being amused. It was not that I was finding febrile coordinates in the world. I existed triply: I occupied space. I moved toward the other ... and the evanescent other, hostile but not opaque, transparent, not there, disappeared. Nausea ...
>
> ...
>
> My body was given back to me sprawled out, distorted, recolored, clad in mourning in that white winter day. The Negro is an animal, the Negro is bad, the Negro is mean, the Negro is ugly; look, a nigger, it's cold, the nigger is shivering, the nigger is shivering because he is cold, the little boy is trembling because he is afraid of the nigger, the nigger is shivering with cold, that cold that goes through your bones, the handsome little boy is trembling because he thinks that the nigger is quivering with rage, the little white boy throws himself into his mother's arms: Mama, the nigger is going to eat me up.
>
> All round me the white man, above the sky tears at its navel, the earth rasps under my feet, and there is a white song, a white song. All this whiteness that burns me . . . .[27]

---

[27] Fanon, *Black Skins*, 112, 113–14.

The specific context of this *unheimlich* moment is Fanon's extended discussion of the degree to which the black man is located within a set of social relations in which he is always-already known. This is because his identity is structured by the gaze of whiteness that shapes the black man's identity through the reiteration of negative stereotypes. The episode acts as a *mise en abyme*, a dramatic fragment within which is mirrored the entire structure of denominations. In it we see several defining features of Fanon's existential poetics. The sudden and uncomfortable experience of being gazed at is expressed from within the context of a quotidian encounter: a walk in the park. He is suddenly made self-conscious of his identity as a bogeyman. But he is also immediately conscious that the child is refracting a larger set of stereotypes. It is this that gives him the uncontrollable impulse of nervous laughter, which he barely manages to suppress. It has to be noted that the child's gesture is an interpellation not because he is fully conscious of the Law of the Colonial Gaze, but because the gesture gathers its force from the structure of an enunciative possibility. It is, in an apparently innocent context, a speech act thoroughly saturated with the full force of colonial relations and does not depend exclusively upon instruments of force or coercion. When the child hails him and Fanon turns in response, it is due to the internalized inflection of a social reflex and part of the structure of formal denominations that he has been at pains to deconstruct. In other words, knowing what he already knows, he already knows that the child thinks of him as a Negro, and it is the confirmation of this knowledge, yet again, that discombobulates him.

Fanon oscillates rapidly in his mind between this particular experience of being interpellated as a bogeyman and a different experience on a train, where, even though there is no specific person pointing at him, he feels himself being placed within the racial drama of stereotypes. This oscillation from an immediate and dramatically realized experience to another one of equal import but which he deliberately leaves vague and inchoate, is also part of his exegetical procedure. The effect of the oscillation is to situate each individual instance of experience as part of a larger drama that demarcates all aspects as interacting to produce the same effect, irrespective of the different dramatis personae within each encounter. In this conflation of experience and exegesis, terror also appears, in a way almost homologous to the affect of guilt that Judith Butler argues as marking the predisposition to turn in response to being hailed. Butler's argument that the instinct to turn on being hailed by the policeman is a predisposition produced by guilt pushes Althusser's notion of interpellation further than in Althusser's original thesis. This guilt comes from the superego, which, read via

Freud, derives from the familial relations that constitute the warped desires of the individual in the first place.[28] But counter to Butler's intervention, in Fanon's walk in the park, the terror cuts in multiple directions. Fanon is as terrified as the child, almost as if he harbours a morbid dread of fulfilling the child's worst fears. They both shiver, him with cold and isolation and the child with fear, but even though on the surface their bodily reactions to the encounter appear the same, they are products of entirely different experiential quotients. For the child is hailing him while Fanon is experiencing the interpellation. Furthermore, the child misinterprets him (the nigger) as perhaps shivering with rage (rather than terror), so that there is an extra layer of confusion imposed upon Fanon's visceral response. The multifarious sitings of terror then serve to illustrate what Fanon has already told us about being "tripled" on the train. The entire passage moves seamlessly between third- and first-person standpoints such that the "nigger" seems at one point to be Fanon himself, but at another to stand for the generality of all black people. This may be attributed to the existential representativeness of the colonized self, one which for Fanon is experienced not in a distantiated way as if at the theatre, but as an intensified vector of the personal and the quotidian. In this way he is split between the singular and the collective in the very immediacy of his everyday experiences.

There is one final detail we must attend to before moving away from this fertile passage. The affect of terror that we have just noted, in turn merges into the incredibly powerful image of dismemberment. Note here that Fanon says his body was "given back to [him]," but altered beyond recognition. This restoration is done under the auspices of a "white winter day" (elsewhere he refers to the blue sky). When Fanon invokes the trope of dismemberment, he immediately imports into the quotidian encounter the idea of the *pharmakos* or the ritual sacrificial carrier of Greek tragedy. The effect of this is to elevate the character of "Fanon" into the status of a tragic protagonist – heroically wading through stereotypes – within the existential denominations of a racialized discourse. We see hints here of tragic absoluteness and thus of representativeness, as if what he is describing has significance well beyond his own self (which it does). Later on, in the course of his reflections on the means of countering the negative stereotypes of blackness, Fanon decides to experimentally immerse himself in the positive images of Negritude. These images celebrate the organic relationship between bodily rhythm and the natural environment, and the

---

[28] Judith Butler, *The Psychic Life of Power: Theories in Subjection* (Stanford: Stanford University Press, 1997), 106–131.

opposition between African organicism and the implied emotional emptiness of an over-achieving but essentially sterile West. In these sections Fanon quotes extensively from the poetry of Senghor, Damas, Césaire, and others of the Negritude school, and appears to celebrate their insights as a counter to the disparagements of the black man. "Eyah," he exclaims at one point, "the tom-tom shatters out the cosmic message. Only the Negro has the capacity to convey it, to decipher its meaning, its import. Astride the world, my strong heels spurring into the flanks of the world, I stare into the shoulders of the world as the celebrant stares at the midpoint between the eyes of the sacrificial victim."[29] He is not to remain in this state of elation for long, as shortly after this he has to contend with Sartre's view that Negritude is only a stage in the dialectical movement of class consciousness. The important thing to note in his invocations of Negritude, however, is that in these sections Fanon is not the sacrificial victim we encountered earlier, but the apocalyptic Horseman, riding to judgment upon the world. The concept of the *pharmakos,* though not of the apocalyptic Horseman, is going to be directly pertinent to our discussions of the works of Chinua Achebe, Wole Soyinka, and Toni Morrison, in Chapters 3, 4, and 6 respectively.

While Sekyi-Otu correctly inserts Fanon into the dialectical heritage exemplified by Hegel and Sartre, both of whom Fanon is clearly indebted to, it is also possible to take the discursive dramaturgical structure in Fanon's writing as the elaboration of a poetics whose form of expression is the conversion of the self into a spectator-witness of others as well as of one's own self. Inspired by Sekyi-Otu, I would like to suggest that Fanon's writing defines a poetics of tragedy that conflates epistemology, aesthetics, and ethics in a unified idiom of experiential immediacy. While the term "poetics" is generally conceived of as a discourse on literary art and its formal features, social inflections, and modes of interpretation; my argument here is that at every stage of his writing, and particularly in *Black Skin, White Masks,* the devices that Fanon deploys coalesce into a veritable experiential poetics of the self. This posits the self within a psycho-existential theatre of spectatoriality: gazed at and self-perceiving but also located as the primary site for the critical evaluation of colonialism. The idea of psycho-existential spectatoriality will be useful for discussing several works in this book, including especially Tayeb Salih's *Season of Migration to the North* and Wole Soyinka's *Death and the King's Horseman.* For the consciousness of the characters in each of these works is shaped along an

---

[29] Fanon, *Black Skin,* 124.

axis of self-referentiality that is itself the product of psycho-existential conditions.

***

There are several points of contrast to be discerned between Fanon and Aristotle. As we have already noted, in Fanon the implied gap we find in Aristotle between the dramatic action and the spectator/interpreter is completely annulled. In Aristotle the emotional response of pity and fear is the product of the plot, the unfolding of the dramatic action that depends on a specific structure of sequentiality, and the tying of reversal to discovery and thus to causal plausibility. What in Aristotle's *Poetics* was essentially the distantiation effect of the aesthetic domain that allowed a judgement on the ethico-cognitive status of the tragic action/plot, is in Fanon completely collapsed into the immediacy of experience. For Fanon is at one and the same time the tragic protagonist suffering impediments to the articulation of *eudaimonia,* and also a spectator to his own unravelling. The two sides are intimately connected. The effect of this urgent unfolding of the self as simultaneously subject and object is then to force epistemology, aesthetics, and ethics together into what Román de la Campa has usefully termed "episthetics."[30] Episthetics enjoins an intellectual activism because the object of analysis is anomalous and calls to be rectified even in the process of analysis. In Fanon the so-called object is not separable from his own self. It *is* his self. The second difference from Aristotle lies in the assumed therapeutic effect of the tragic drama. For Fanon, the only therapy is justice. Whatever local catharsis is made possible is instantly rendered worthless because the process of catharsis is itself entrapped within conditions of injustice. Without freedom, then, man cannot enjoy the art of living. But perhaps the most significant difference between Fanon and Aristotle can be traced to the meaning of *hamartia* and how it might derive from the consciousness of the tragic protagonist. In Fanon, the pitfall of *hamartia* can be forestalled through a process of constant interpretative alertness to the negative possibilities inherent in the experience of living under the threat of erasure at all times. Hence, for him, *hamartia* would have to be related to the ever-ready impulse toward interpretation ("I interpret my surroundings"), rather than in the pause, suspension, or abeyance of ethical choice, as we find in, say, Aeschylus' *Agamemnon* (in the character of Agamemnon), Sophocles' *Philoctetes* (the character of Neoptolemus), or Euripides' *The Bacchae* (in both Pentheus and Agave).

---

[30] Román de la Campa, *Latin Americanism* (Minneapolis: Minnesota University Press, 1999).

Edginess and Precarity

If, as Fanon suggests, the black self in the context of colonial relations or other relations of oppression is produced at the point of interpellation, then because of the incessant reiterative character of this interpellation, it ought to be always-already anticipated by the black body in forms of sensitivity and alertness. An immediate implication of the racial economy as derived from Fanon's poetics, then, is that the (post)colonized self is constantly under threat of severance from the domain of worldly goods and thus of privacy and *oikos*, the zones designated in Greek tragedy as the primary space of *philia*, and of emotional safety. As Achille Mbembe points out in another context, colonialism sought to produce humans that were existentially ill:

> The ill human was the human with no family, no love, no human relations, and no communion with a community. It was the person deprived of the possibility of an authentic encounter with other humans, [and] others with whom there were a priori no shared bonds of descent or of origin. . . . To the contrary, it [colonialism] did everything to deaden people's capacity to suffer because the natives were suffering, everything to dull their capacity to be affected by this suffering . . . . By claiming to be acting on behalf of the interests of the natives, and thus in their stead, the colonial machinery sought not merely to block their desire to live. It aimed to affect and diminish their capacity to consider themselves moral agents.[31]

Even though Mbembe insists that he is inspired mainly by Fanon, it is impossible to miss echoes of Aristotle's *The Nicomachean Ethics* in what he says here. At any rate, the self that is adduced by Fanon in the context of colonial relations is one that is continually being generated *in the face of traumatic history* to the degree that the difference between both private and public is blurred and the colonial/postcolonial subject is set permanently on edge. The edge I have in mind here must be thought of in terms of the cliff edge of existence, as well as in the more colloquial sense of uncertainty, anxiety, and even terror. While we might disagree on where exactly this sense of edginess comes from, many of the images of catastrophe from the postcolonial world that proliferate in the media today (Syrian refugees streaming across Europe; Africans drowning in the Mediterranean whilst desperately attempting to escape the continent; the genocide of Rohingyas in Myanmar) instruct us that there is something salient in the idea of postcolonial edginess.

---

[31] Achille Mbembe, *Necropolitics*, (Durham: Duke University Press, 2019), 5, 6.

As I shall argue in Chapter 9 on Beckett, this edginess can also be seen in the everyday streets of today's postcolonial cities, where unemployed youth and street children trawl under the harsh sky to sell products from the West to countrymen and foreigners riding in fancy air-conditioned cars; or in the abjectly homeless children and their parents squatting in abandoned and derelict buildings in Accra, Lagos, Mumbai, Rio, and other places. The edginess I have in mind here is also to be found on the social peripheries of metropolitan cities in the West – in London's Brixton and Los Angeles's Compton, Brussels's Matonge, and the banlieues of Paris – where immigrants from the global South eke out a precarious and terrified existence. The aboriginal and native minorities of Australia, Canada, and the USA, as well as their counterparts, the descendants of enslaved and oppressed peoples, are also not exempt from the conditions of postcolonial edginess.

***

Colonialism may be argued as having engendered a series of historical contingencies that accentuate the contradictions inherent to the lifeworlds upon which it impacted. While colonialism has been amply studied in terms of its effects on religion, culture, belief systems, and on the discombobulation of what Fanon describes as the epidermal "bodily schema," what I want to highlight in *Tragedy and Postcolonial Literature* is the production of a sense of indeterminacy and precarity both within the colonial period and in its aftermath. This does not obviate or preclude the successful narratives of resistance to colonialism and its aftereffects. However, most such accounts in postcolonial studies adopt a hydraulic approach to the colonial encounter and ultimately imply a Romantic rather than a tragic view of the response of the oppressed to colonial conditions. The Romantic thread in postcolonial theory has been persuasively critiqued by David Scott (on whom more in subsequent chapters).[32] However, as we shall see, not all the tragedies we will be looking at disclose the same modalities of edginess and precarity. This is because the conditions that overdetermine the sense of edginess differ from context to context. Hence, I will be arguing in Chapter 4 that Wole Soyinka's Professor in *The Road* illustrates a sense of edginess through the amplifying delirium that he experiences from attempting to merge Yorùbá and Christian epistemologies in pursuit of the Word. In contrast, Achebe's Ezeulu in *Arrow of God* gives us a hypothetical counter to Fanon's terror of

[32] See David Scott, *Conscripts of Modernity: The Tragedy of Colonial Enlightenment* (Durham: Duke University Press, 2005).

interpellation while still illustrating a mode of edginess borne from his fruitless attempts at redefining his role as the chief priest of Ulu to a community in the throes of colonial modernity. Ezeulu explicitly denies the premise of colonial interpellation and yet is himself also on edge because of the dramatic changes that have taken place in his society; changes that he sees as undermining his capacity to act both as the unquestioned instigator of social transformation and the exclusive spokesperson of Ulu. He also senses that the presence of Christianity in Umuaro raises fundamental questions about history that he is keen to uncover but is unclear what the answer to his intuitions might be. His quest for meaning on both fronts thoroughly eludes him, until his madness at the end of the novel. In Chapter 7, on the other hand, we will find that the characters in J. M. Coetzee's novels are afflicted by second thoughts in a manner that brings to mind the structure of skeptical interlocution and the abolition of *philia* that we saw in Fanon. With the particular case of the Magistrate in *Waiting for the Barbarians*, this thought-affliction produces an edginess that is directly related to his unerring perception of the force of the Empire's ideology and to his sense of having been compromised for being their unwitting agent and executor. As the novel progresses, the Magistrate's edginess moves from being a feature of his internal interlocution to being defined by his material conditions: he is thrown in jail and tortured. It also impacts on the moral contradictions of his position – having to choose between allegiance to the Empire and care for the barbarian girl. And in Chapter 6 we will see that for Toni Morrison's Sethe, the edginess comes from the brutal conditions of slavery from which she has recently escaped, as well as from her own traumatic attempt at murdering her children so as to take them out of the brutal circuitry of enslavement. In Chapter 8, Arundhati Roy's *God of Small Things* shows us how the conditions of edginess and suffering emerge for Ammu, Rahel, and Estha from their entrapment in patriarchal codes that denominate them as bearers of ethical deficit for being husbandless and fatherless. The novel dramatizes the tragedy of their condition through the emergence of profound guilt in Rahel and Estha for their part in the deaths of their cousin, and and in that of Velutha, the god of small things of the title. In Beckett's *Murphy* in Chapter 9, on the other hand, we find that the eponymous character's quest for self-validation is an aspect of an autistic spectrum disorder and that it is his relentless attraction to patterns that draws him to Mr. Endon at the Magdalen Mental Mercyseat. Mr. Endon's refutation of any form of analogy over the game of chess they play is what spins Murphy out of himself and ultimately leads, in an absurd but also interconnected concatenation of small steps, to his death by way of a gas explosion in his garret. In contrast to all these works, Chapter 2 will take us through the dynamics of the interpellation of Othello's blackness in the cosmopolitan contexts of Shakespeare's play. But here the focus will also be on the effects of what I want to describe as Iago's modularity, that is to say, on his capacity to "make images" and then to use them as the means for eliciting strong emotional reactions from his interlocutors.

For some, a torturous form of reasoning would seem necessary to justify including Shakespeare in a book on postcolonial tragedy. And yet his place is guaranteed not because he is himself a postcolonial, especially as he wrote well before the phase of British empire and colonialism and their aftermath, but because his work has served to illuminate postcolonial conditions in different epochs and climes. One need only think of the impact *The Tempest* has had on arguments concerning territorial colonialism and the colonized's appropriation of the colonial language as a tool to fight back, or the impact of *Othello* and *The Merchant of Venice* in illuminating the processes of endemic racism, anti-Semitism, and othering to be found in many societies assumed to be cosmopolitan, or that of *Antony and Cleopatra* in illustrating the relationship between gender and empire to see that, even if he is not Nigerian, Indian, or Libyan, Shakespeare is amenable to many postcolonial applications.[33]

Disputatiousness and the Unruly Affective Economy

The history of tragedy is conventionally traced from the dramatic theatre of fifth-century Athens through its efflorescence on the Jacobean and Elizabethan stage and then through its shifts into different mediums and genres from the eighteenth century onward.[34] There are different elements of this standard history that are pertinent to an understanding of

---

[33] I am by no means the first to claim a postcolonial position for Shakespeare. Adaptations of his work abound in the field, with both tragedies and comedies offering ample payout in postcolonial studies. For just one example of such adaptations – in the context of India – see Ankhi Mukherjee's fine discussion in *What Is a Classic: Postcolonial Rewriting and Invention of the Canon* (Stanford: Stanford University Press, 2014), 182–213. There is also a long-standing half-joking reference to Muammar Gaddafi's claim that Shakespeare was a crypto-Arab called Sheik Zubayr bin William. The legend of the Arab provenance of Shakespeare popularized by Gaddafi is separately traced by M. M. Badawi and Ferial Ghazoul to Ahmad Faris Al-Shidyaq, a mid-nineteenth-century Lebanese journalist, satirical writer, and keen admirer of Shakespeare. See M. M. Badawi, "Shakespeare and the Arabs," *Cairo Studies in English* (1963/1966), 181–196 and Ferial Ghazoul, "The Arabization of Othello," *Comparative Literature*, 50.1 (1988): 1–31.

[34] See, for example, Jennifer Wallace, *The Cambridge Introduction to Tragedy* (Cambridge: Cambridge University Press, 2007).

postcolonial tragedy, and we might highlight the disputatiousness of Greek tragedy as a starting point. Whether in Sophocles' *Oedipus Rex, Philoctetes,* and *Antigone*; in Aeschylus' *Oresteia* trilogy and *Prometheus Bound;* or in Euripides' *Medea* and *The Bacchae*, the disputatiousness of Attic tragedy is everywhere in evidence. While Hegel is correct in turning to *Antigone* as part of his illustration of the dialectical clash between apparently irreconcilable ethical standpoints, it is Jean-Pierre Vernant who provides the most systematic account of this disputatiousness. Vernant sees Greek tragedy as the medium for detailing the transitions and entailments that took place between the domains of religion and law that were the central shapers of Greek life in the fifth century.[35] He unpacks concepts such as *dike* (justice), *nomos* (law and custom), and *ethos* (the fundamental character or spirit of a culture) via what emerges as a philological anthropology amply animated by functional structuralism; a set of theoretical and methodological dispositions that we also see put to great effect in the work of Claude Lévi-Strauss and Erich Auerbach, both of whom have also produced important insights on tragedy.[36] Furthermore, the disputatiousness of Greek tragedy is also tied to what Richard Halpern has described as the "general metabolic conditions of the city" (in the Greek sense of *polis* and not in our contemporary sense of urban dwelling).[37] Reading from Aeschylus' *Oresteia* and other Athenian tragedies, Halpern argues that the disputatiousness of Greek tragedy illustrates among other things, the conversion of male child into soldier and thus into the domain of death, and the assimilation of nurture into that of provision; symbolized respectively by the *oikos* and the military in Greek tragic drama. "Another way to put this," Halpern adds,

> is that Greek theater's metapolitical vocation, its capacity to reflect upon the boundaries between the political and non- (or sub-, or even anti-) political, is abetted by its own ambiguous location within the social order – a place that is neither that of the household nor that of the workshop nor that of the battlefield nor that of the courtroom, neither the place where tapestries are

[35] Jean-Pierre Vernant, "Tensions and Ambiguities in Greek Tragedy" in Jean-Pierre Vernant and Pierre Vidal-Naquet, eds., *Myth and Tragedy in Ancient Greece* (London: Zone Books, 1988), 29–48.

[36] See especially, Claude Lévi-Strauss's conjuration of tragic tropes and his discussion of Oedipus in *Tristes Tropiques* (Paris: Librairie Plon, 1955). Erich Auerbach's opening essay on "Odysseus' Scar" in *Mimesis: The Representation of Reality in Western Literature* (Princeton: Princeton University Press, 1953), in which he compares passages from *The Odyssey* and the Old Testament, also remains a source of great inspiration for many commentators on different modes of tragic sensibility in antiquity and the classical period.

[37] Richard Halpern, *Eclipse of Action: Tragedy and Political Economy* (Chicago: Chicago University Press, 2017), 106.

dyed nor that where infants are nursed nor that where empires are expanded nor that where justice is dispensed, but a place that nevertheless bears a strange and partial kinship to all of these.[38]

The fraught metabolic conditions of the city, or of community in my reading, is also pertinent to interpreting postcolonial tragedy. For when we speak of postcolonial tragedy (and not merely of postcolonial literature, a more general label) we find that the most expressive examples display strong forms of disputatiousness regarding the *polis* of their social imaginaries. Even as there are also transitions and transpositions between law and the sacred in some postcolonial tragedies, the cause of disputatiousness is tied mainly to the struggle against anachronistic or false universals, with colonial modernity, slavery, diaspora, and the predatory and violent postcolonial nation-state being exemplars of such universals.[39] History becomes a constriction rather than an opportunity. In the domain of characterization, this is represented through what I have already described as edginess, intense anger, and impatience that seem not to have any direct explanation at the foreground of diegetic events. The trope of disputatiousness as tied to historical constriction is to be seen in Wole Soyinka's *Death and the King's Horseman*, in Chinua Achebe's *Arrow of God*, Naguib Mahfouz's *Midaq Alley*, Jean Rhys's *Wide Sargasso Sea*, C. L. R. James's *The Black Jacobins*, and Gabriel García Márquez's *One Hundred Years of Solitude*, all of which we will encounter in various forms in this book.

While we do find degrees of disputatiousness in Jacobean and Elizabethan tragedy, it is Shakespeare that provides us with a second productive rubric for defining the condition of postcolonial tragedy. I am using disputatiousness here to refer not just to disputes between characters, but to the often violent processes of historical and social transition that engender such disputes in the first place. Disputatiousness in historical and social transitions has a correlative in the unruly affective economies that mark the characters' fractured sense of their place in society. The Shakespearean tragedies of an almost pure historical disputatiousness, such as *Julius Caesar*, *Coriolanus*, and *Titus Andronicus*, are not considered among his best, and for good reasons. For it is the addition of an unruly affective economy that places plays such as *Hamlet*, *Othello*, *King Lear*, *Macbeth*, and *Antony and Cleopatra* above those of a purely historical disputatiousness. Shakespeare's finest tragedies correlate an unruly affective economy to different modes of disputatiousness that emerge from

[38] Halpern, *Eclipse of Action*, 107.
[39] Judith Butler, *Giving an Account of Oneself* (New York: Fordham University Press, 2005).

changes in the represented historical worlds of the plays. These include transitions in the political realm, as in *Hamlet* and *Macbeth*; the unstable recodification of the relations between gender, local governance, imperial rule, and the claims of romantic love, as in *Othello* and *Antony and Cleopatra*; and the progressive shifts in the relationship between the king's body as a surrogate of the body-politic and the spheres of the natural order, as in *King Lear*. The dimension of an unruly affective economy amplifies the interiority of the characters on stage and renders them ciphers of the changing social and historical realities of which they are a part. We will look more closely at this question of disputatiousness with respect to *Othello* in Chapter 2, especially in relation to Othello's doomed quest for epistemological certainty and the violent emotions that he comes to express as an aspect of this.[40] I want to argue additionally that Shakespeare also provides correlatives of affective unruliness in his characters' fixations with an aesthetics of the self, seen predominantly in the rhetorical language of aesthetic self-conception that we find in several of his plays, but especially in *Hamlet*, *Othello,* and *Antony and Cleopatra*. The fixation with an aesthetics of the self can become an impediment to action, as is famously the case with Hamlet, or may lead to attempts at translating painful and uncomfortable events into a discourse that renders them more palatable as spectacles, as in Gertrude's reordering of Ophelia's suicide into an ekphrastic tableau of nature's conspiracy in act 4 scene 7 of the play. Gertrude's description has unsurprisingly inspired many paintings, as she elevates Ophelia's death into an iconic image even as she laments her sad demise.[41]

Even though there is no difficulty in claiming *Hamlet* as providing the fullest exemplification of the unruly affective economy, the Prince of Denmark is by no means the only tragic character that we might place under this rubric in Shakespeare's plays. Both Enobarbus and Antony in

---

[40] Studies of emotions in Shakespeare's plays were for a long time dominated by humoral theories, with the psycho-physiological implications of the humors furnishing a number of insights, including the dangers of the passions as potential threats to society. Even though some of this will be relevant to the discussion of Othello, my main interest is in pinpointing emotions and affects as problems that have to do with self-management, as well as their correlation to an overly aestheticized sense of the self. For recent collections providing overviews of the history of emotions as they pertain to Shakespeare, see Richard Meek and Erin Sullivan, eds., *The Renaissance of Emotion: Understanding Affect in Early Modern Literature and Culture* (Manchester: Manchester University Press, 2014) and R. S. White, Mark Houlahan, and Katrina O'Loughlin eds., *Shakespeare and Emotions: Inheritances, Enactments, and Legacies* (London: Palgrave, 2015).

[41] John Everett Millais's *Ophelia* (1852) is perhaps the most well-known. See also the painting by Alexandre Cabanel, an interpretation of the same scene (1883), and John William Waterhouse's rendition of the character (1889), which has Ophelia not lying in water but sitting on a willow bough aslant the brook with flowers in her lap.

Antony and Cleopatra and to different degrees Othello, Lear, Macbeth, and even Richard II present us with good examples. Othello's sudden epileptic fit and Lady Macbeth's somnambulant "Out, damned spot!" are both excellent places from which to unspool the unruly affective economies of Shakespeare's other characters. For the postcolonial tragedies in this book, the relationship between social and historical disputatiousness and unruly affective economies is amply illuminated in the work of J. M. Coetzee, Toni Morrison, Chinua Achebe, and Wole Soyinka, both as a variant of emotional turmoil but also as the yoking of affect to historical transition and to an aesthetics of the self. The question of an aesthetics of the self as inextricably linked to an unruly affective economy will be explored fully with respect to Mustafa Sa'eed in Tayeb Salih's *Season of Migration to the North* in Chapter 5.

The interior landscape of characters becomes most pertinent to the novel and the shift from the public place of the theatre to the private sphere of reading. This is also accompanied by a shift from the intensification of Time – and thus of the urgency of choice-making as depicted on stage – to the slow temporality of social relations as captured in the discourse of the novel. As Terry Eagleton notes in commenting on this shift: "In the topography of the novel there are fewer precipices and hairpin bends, fewer walls to be forced up against. The novel in this view is a matter of *chronos*, of the gradual passage of historical time, whereas tragedy is a question of *kairos*, of time charged, crisis-racked, pregnant with some momentous truth."[42] It is important to note that Eagleton here speaks simply of the novel and not the *tragic* novel, and indeed that he thinks of the novel form in general as somehow diluting the force of tragedy. This is not a view I share, and in my discussion of specific postcolonial tragic novels I shall be making precisely the opposite point. Significantly, however, by the nineteenth century disputatiousness and an unruly affective economy do not remain necessarily tied together within the novel in general and the link remains loose even in the tragic novel. In the historical novel as described by Georg Lukács, disputatiousness is linked to war and intrigue and thus to different registers of violence.[43] The most pertinent example of the historical novel for my purposes is not Tolstoy's much-lauded *War and Peace*, as in Lukács' account, but rather his *Hadji Murat*, which seems to me to bear all the hallmarks of a postcolonial sensibility.

---

[42] Terry Eagleton, *Sweet Violence: The Idea of the Tragic* (Malden, MA: Blackwell Publishing, 2003), 181.
[43] Georg Lukács, *The Historical Novel* (Nebraska: University of Nebraska Press, 1983; first published 1965).

But as we will see in the chapter on Achebe, in postcolonial variants, even if the force of disputatiousness and violence is present, it is blunted by its assimilation to an idiom of disenchantment. In both *Things Fall Apart* and *Arrow of God*, the violence of historical transition recedes from the sphere of direct representation and is instead relocated to the interactions between individuals. Violence in Achebe is registered not as a clash between armed antagonists, as we find in *Hadji Murat*, but as the negotiation of different and incompatible personal interpretations of history and the public sphere. And unlike what we find in, say, Marquez's *One Hundred Years of Solitude*, Isabel Allende's *House of Spirits*, or Rushdie's *Shame*, where there is an explicit mobilization of sentiment against the false universalism represented by hegemonic political ideologies, in Achebe such mobilization either does not take off, as in *Things Fall Apart*, or is not even formulated as a viable option, as in *Arrow of God*.[44]

Historical Transition, Ethical Choice, and the Problem of Narrating the Self

The argument of this book turns on two further questions. These relate to the impediments to the exercise of ethical choice under different social and political conditions and the question of giving an account of oneself when the instruments of such a self-accounting have been contaminated by history. Many tragic themes become relevant to these two questions: suffering, the relationship between ethical choice and contingency, the vagaries of reputation, and the ambiguation of attitudes to collective and individual pasts. My emphasis for the two questions will be on the representation of pathos and suffering, rather than on fate, necessity, and catastrophe. I take my cue for this emphasis on pathos and suffering primarily from Blair Hoxby, who argues that the poetics of tragedy until at least the period of Romantic philosophy, emphasized pathos as its one indispensable ingredient and that this earlier emphasis allowed for the discussion of a broader range of tragic materials. As he notes:

> Commentators concluded that, although Aristotle held complex plots in particularly high esteem because recognitions and reversals were effective

---

[44] On the postcolonial historical novel, see Hamish Dalley, "Postcolonialism and the Historical Novel: Epistemologies of Contemporary Realism," *The Cambridge Journal of Postcolonial Literary Inquiry*, 1.1 (2014): 51–68; also, Eleni Coundouriotis, *Claiming History: Colonialism, Ethnography, and the Novel* (New York: Columbia University Press, 1999); Margaret Atwood, "In Search of Alias Grace: On Writing Canadian Historical Fiction," *The American Historical Review*, 103.5 (1998): 1503–1516; and James M. Callahan, *Great Hatred, Little Room: The Irish Historical Novel* (Syracuse, NY: Syracuse University Press, 1983).

means of stimulating the passions, pure displays of pathos were tragic and were in themselves the primary goal and justification of tragedy .... In contrast to their Romantic philosophers, early modern critics prized Attic tragedies (*Philoctetes, Alcestis, The Trojan Women,* and *The Phoenician Women*) that consisted of little more than scenes of suffering and woe laced together.[45]

The emphasis on pathos was the dominant one until the decisive intervention of the Romantic philosophers who, by reinterpreting tragedy through a rereading of Kant's sublime, sought to rescue from it something of transcendental value with regards to the human encounter with the ineffable. According to Hoxby, this leads to a decisive shift in tragic theory away from the drama of pathos, as seen in *Philoctetes,* say, in favor of *Oedipus, Antigone, The Bacchae,* and *Medea,* in which the final and inevitable catastrophe is what determines our response to the tragedy. While some of the postcolonial works that I will be looking at in this book do end in catastrophe, it is the depiction of pain and an unrelieved emotional suffering that proves consequential for their tragic tenor. The intriguing opinions on tragedy expressed by Obi Okonkwo in Chinua Achebe's *No Longer at Ease* adds credence to this perspective:

> Real tragedy is never resolved. It goes on hopelessly forever. Conventional tragedy is too easy. The hero dies and we feel a purging of the emotions. A real tragedy takes place in a corner, in an untidy spot, to quote W. H. Auden. The rest of the world is unaware of it. Like that man in *A Handful of Dust* who reads Dickens to Mr. Todd. There is no release for him. When the story ends he is still reading. There is no purging of the emotions for us because *we are not there.*[46]

The trigger for Obi's views is the fate of Scobie, the central character of Graham Greene's *The Heart of the Matter,* who commits suicide at the end of that novel set in colonial Sierra Leone. To Obi, Scobie's suicide is a too-easy resolution to what seems to him like a straightforward Aristotelian tragedy. On closer inspection we find Obi's interpretation of what constitutes *catharsis,* and by implication the Aristotelian tragic formula that produces it, to be not entirely accurate. Aristotle's model does not depend on the hero's death at all, just on the reversal of fortunes and the atrophying

---

[45] Blair Hoxby, "What Was Tragedy? The World We Have Lost, 1550–1795," *Comparative Literature,* 64:1 (2012): 5, 6.
[46] Chinua Achebe, *No Longer at Ease* (London: Heinemann, 1964), 33; emphasis added.

of the capacity to undertake ethically salient choices. His prime example of tragedy is *Oedipus Rex*, and as we know, Oedipus does not die in the course of the play. Obi introduces the question of death as a way of demarcating a form of relief from the domain of pure suffering. In addition, he thinks that the spectator/observer is implicated in the suffering before them because they are incapable of doing anything to relieve it, and yet continue to watch. And so, Obi transfers the premise of tragedy away from the question of catharsis and onto that of responsibility. This actually brings him quite close to playwrights like Bertolt Brecht and Augosto Boal, for whom Aristotle's theory of catharsis might be said to have been something akin to bourgeois masturbation since it did not adequately address the imperatives of radically breaking the audience from the grips of political normality.[47]

When Obi references Evelyn Waugh's Tony endlessly reading Dickens to the demented Mr. Todd, he is also indirectly raising the question of the link between malaise and stasis, and of stasis as a form of imprisonment. Through his fictional mouthpiece Achebe has essentially given us two types of tragic closure that he considers not adequately tragic: the first pertains to suicide and the inception of a too-easy catharsis for the spectator, and the second to an endless stasis which also fails as a form of tragic closure because we are not necessarily physically there at its inception and unfold-ing. But what is this "there" before which we are presumed not to be present? Does this speak merely to the necessary ontological gap between the spectator/reader and the unfolding action on stage or in a novel, or is it referring to the problematic of empathy and identification, and thus of witnessing in general? And where does effective tragic closure inhere? Is it at the scene of unrelieved emotional suffering without end before which we bear witness, or, as we might also propose, at the moment of the *anagnorisis* of the protagonist that in its turn triggers a form of recognition for the reader and audience? While the protagonist's tragic recognition is not always made explicit to the audience at the moment of the reversal of fortune or even at the character's death (think of Henrik Ibsen's Hedda Gabler and Junot Díaz's Oscar Wao, where we have no way of knowing whether there was *anagnorisis* or not, in contrast to Shakespeare's Othello

---

[47] Brecht's responses to Aristotle's theory of tragedy have been variously commented upon. See, for example, Angela Curran's "Brecht's Criticisms of Aristotle's Aesthetics of Tragedy," *The Journal of Aesthetics and Art Criticism*, 59.2 (2001): 167–184. Augusto Boal for his part wrote a full-scale critique of Aristotle's theory (he labelled it as "oppressive") as a means of clarifying his own dramatic practices that were directly aimed at instigating revolutionary freedom for all oppressed people. See his *Theatre of the Oppressed* (New York: Theatre Communication Group, 1985).

and Chinua Achebe's Okonkwo, where the *anagnorisis* is clearly demarcated for us), the point is that tragic recognition goes in more than one
direction at once. What Achebe emphasizes through his mouthpiece Obi,
is that it is the fact of remaining alive in the face of catastrophe that
generates the real difficulty for the tragic protagonist and thus, concomitantly, for the reader or spectator. Death is a relief.

The fact that pathos and suffering dominate postcolonial tragedy should
not be entirely surprising since in every instance the emphasis is primarily
on the nobility of struggling against the odds irrespective of whether this is
ultimately successful or not. For much postcolonial tragedy, there is
nothing so grand as railing against the gods. It is living in the knowledge
of almost complete futility that is the real problem. As Beckett puts it in
The Unnameable: "What am I to do, what shall I do, what should I do, in
my situation, how proceed? By aporia pure and simple? Or by affirmations
and negations invalidated as uttered, or sooner or later?" and "where I am,
I don't know, I'll never know, in the silence you don't know, you must go
on, I can't go on, I'll go on."[48] This calls to mind again Enya's "Anywhere
Is," where "everywhere I turn to/ begins a new beginning/ and never finds
a finish." To go on in spite of all evidence to its futility is what is truly
tragic.

The question of giving an account of oneself turns on the norms and
instruments of self-accounting when these are either compromised or
otherwise rendered inadequate by history. Different interpretations of
this conundrum have been provided by thinkers as varied as Adriana
Cavarero, Jacques Lacan, Daniel Dennett, Kwame Gyekye, and others.[49]
In *Giving an Account of Oneself*, Judith Butler writes of the difficulties
that lie in the way of providing an account of one's actions that is both
coherent and adequately commensurate to the life lived. One of the key
problems she notes is that the process is often subject to degrees of
blindness, due to the genesis of the self being entangled with the selves
of others. Parts of the self are lodged and indeed lost in the unfolding
relationship between the self and its primary interlocutors. Something of
Lacan's propositions regarding the mirror stage is pertinent to Butler's
exploration, even though she does not refer to him directly in her own

---

[48] Samuel Beckett, *Three Novels: Molloy, Malone Dies, The Unnamable* (London: Grove Press, 1958),
291, 414.
[49] Butler, *Giving an Account*; Daniel Dennett, *The Intentional Stance* (Cambridge, MA: MIT Press,
1989); Adriana Cavarero, *Relating Narratives: Storytelling and Selfhood* (London: Routledge, 2000);
Jacques Lacan, *Écrits* trans. Bruce Fink (London: Routledge, 2007); and Kwame Gyekye,
Unexamined Life: Philosophy and the African Experience (Accra: Ghana Universities Press, 1988).

disquisition on the matter.[50] We will revisit Lacan's mirror stage in our discussion of Tayeb Salih's *Season of Migration to the North* in Chapter 5. While there are a number of objections that one might raise against Butler's views on self-accounting, what is of most significance for my own argument in this book, is her relative lack of interest in any narrative theory of the self, especially the self as internally fractured and interlocutory as opposed to just facing outward to an external point which elicits the self-accounting. As Stephen Greenblatt has argued, in the Renaissance the self was first and foremost a rhetorical construct that was projected specifically toward certain assumed expectations. But, as we shall see in Chapter 2 with respect to Shakespeare's *Othello*, these expectations were not exclusively to be seen as coming from particular characters. There was also the introjection of expectations that were themselves of a purely rhetorical kind and elusive in the extreme. Iago did deceive Othello, but in Othello's request for ocular proof of his wife's infidelity he was also asking for a form of epistemological certainty as a prop to action.

In the postcolonial texts that I shall be exploring in these pages, the instruments for narrating the self are shown to be either inadequate, or, more problematically, seriously contaminated by a history not of one's making or choice. Massive historical, social, economic, and cultural transformations can readily be identified as having taken place in the societies that came under European merchant rule, slavery, settler colonialism, empire, Christianity, and from the nightmarish residues they left behind. The most important effect of the many transformations, is however, not the material and sociocultural changes that might readily be illustrated, but rather in the degree to which such changes trigger an ambiguation of responses to individual and collective pasts.

Historical transition in the postcolonial world often proliferates epistemological aporia and generates problems of interpretation regarding the pastness of the past and its significance for the present. While there may be a general consensus that the past is past, there are often also strong disagreements on how distant the past really is and how the present might be constituted in relation to that past. As William Faulkner memorably quipped, "The past is never dead. It's not even past."[51] In Trump's America, as in Aung San Suu Kyi's Myanmar, the particular problem of inadequate pastness is seen in injunctions directed at equity-seeking groups

---

[50] See Jacques Lacan, "The Mirror Stage," in *Écrits*, 502–509.

[51] William Faulkner, *Requiem for a Nun* (New York: Vintage, 2011; first published 1951), 73.

to "get over it" because the world has changed and there is no use dwelling on a past of collective injury. This injunction of course plays into the hands of those who find the past uncomfortable to acknowledge and recompense. Hence it is that interpretations of the past become fraught with danger and produce an ambivalence that comes to bear upon the status of ethical choice and how this relates to action, whether of a heroic or quotidian kind. Whereas moral judgment may have appeared predictable and the heroic code secure in a previous epoch, the process of historical transition progressively puts these in doubt. From a specifically tragic perspective, the effect of collective or individual ambiguity with respect to the past is that it renders the underlying cultural codes either no longer entirely relevant or makes these codes seem subservient to inherently narrow or unrepresentative principles, what Judith Butler calls *anachronistic* or *false universals*.[52] A universal becomes anachronistic or false when it ceases to be grounded in an organic relation to existing social forces and is either imposed from the outside or represents an overly narrow interest that insists on its own continuing domination.

The key problem for the postcolonial world, then, is the status of ethical choice in phases of transition when the old order may be changing, but a new order has not yet taken its place. It is at this conjuncture of historical transition and problematic ethical choice that I want to situate my explorations of postcolonial tragedy. This is not because it is only the postcolonial world that gives us examples of historical transition and the ambiguation of ethical choice, but because whether we consider India, or Africa, or the Caribbean, or Latin America, or indeed the many racial minorities lodged firmly at the heart of the West itself, it is the postcolonial condition that discloses the most pressing questions of ethical choice as the products of continuing precarity and edginess. It is these conditions of precarity, now articulated in the form of endemic and blatant inequalities at both local and global levels that the postcolonial world illustrates, and which its literature gives voice to in ample measure.

Why Postcolonial Tragedy (and Not Just Tragedy)?

To answer this question, I have to make a detour through the work of George Steiner, Raymond Williams, and Terry Eagleton, three critics whose writings have had a particularly strong impact on how I think about tragedy. To start with, one cannot imagine two thinkers more

---

[52] Butler, *Giving an Account*, 4–7, emphasis added.

different in their conceptions of tragedy than George Steiner and Raymond Williams.[53] In *The Death of Tragedy*, first published in 1963, Steiner makes the controversial claim that the modern world is incapable of sustaining tragedy.[54] He repeatedly asserts that much of this impossibility derives from the collapse of the art-and-lifeworld compact that supported the tragic viewpoint up to the seventeenth century: "I shall often come back to the notion that certain essential elements of social and imaginative life, which had prevailed from Aeschylus to Racine, receded from western consciousness after the seventeenth century – that the seventeenth century is the 'great divide' in the history of tragedy."[55] The reason for his choice of the seventeenth century is only partly to do with the rise of Romanticism, which engendered a disposition for him poignantly encapsulated in the work of Rousseau that focused on the reformability of the self and thus of the ultimate amelioration of tragic circumstance and of catastrophe. Steiner asserts the contrary as a firm tenet of belief: "I emphasize this because I believe that any realistic notion of tragic drama must start from the fact of catastrophe. Tragedies end badly."[56] Reformability comes along with other ultimately anti-tragic cognates, such as the possibility of regret and thus of absolution and forgiveness. For him true tragedy completely abjures the possibility of either compromise or redress. The focus on catastrophe is thus also counter to any acknowledgment of the status of pathos and suffering as distinct and separable aspects of tragedy, contrary to what we gleaned from Hoxby. What Steiner sees as the imaginative withdrawal from the contemplation and presentation of uncompromising fate is cause for much regret:

> in the spirit of the modern age [is] a prevailing nervousness, a falling away of the imaginative. Something is lacking of the superb confidence needed of a man to create a major stage character, to endow some presence within himself with the carnal mystery of gesture and dramatic speech … .

---

[53] Their differences are regularly remarked upon by scholars of tragedy. For example, Richard Halpern, *Eclipse of Action*, and Miriam Leonard, *Tragic Modernities* (Cambridge, MA: Harvard University Press, 2015), both pay specific attention to the differences between Steiner and Williams in setting up their own arguments.

[54] George Steiner, *The Death of Tragedy* (New York: Alfred Knopf, 1963).   [55] Steiner, 113–114.

[56] Steiner, 8. The idea of tragedy requiring catastrophe is in fact central to the tradition, and is espoused variously by Bradley, Lukacs, Goldmann, and Ricoeur among others. See A. C. Bradley, *Oxford Lectures on Poetry* (Oxford: Oxford University Press, 1909); Georg Lukács, *Soul and Form* (Cambridge, MA: MIT Press, 1978); Lucien Goldmann, *Racine* (Cambridge: Rivers Press, 1972); and Paul Ricoeur, *The Symbolism of Evil* (New York: Harper and Row, 1967). And for a fine discussion of the impact of the Romantic critics' views on the later discussion of what constitutes tragedy, see Blair Hoxby, "What Was Tragedy? The World We Have Lost, 1550–1795," 1–31.

Manifestly, the Greek and the Elizabethan achievement seems to lie on the back of all later drama with a wearying weight of precedent.[57]

Furthermore, Steiner's assertion that mythology and ritual represent the crystallization of collective sentiment that was most forcefully expressed by the Greeks and in a later secular vein by Shakespeare and Racine, also means that his views on tragedy appeal to a sense of homogeneity and organicity that he takes to be definitive of the relationship between tragic playwright and audience. His view that "the Elizabethan playwrights were exceptionally fortunate, the audience for which they wrote being both representative of great variety and yet homogenous," discloses this nostalgia for a lost organicity, in this case projected backwards onto the Elizabethan world.[58]

The direct opposite of Steiner, Williams wrote his own book, *Modern Tragedy* (1966), in response to Steiner's work.[59] Although, like Steiner, Williams recognizes the same history of tragedy from its genesis in Athenian theatre and the course it took throughout European history, for his part he refuses to sever tragedy as art from tragedy as experienced in the violent disappointments of the lifeworlds of post-war Europe. Williams establishes the link between literary tragedy and lived life for specifically political reasons. As Pamela McCallum notes in her introduction to the Broadview edition of *Modern Tragedy*, he "restores an affective relationship with the past that has the potential to loosen blockages and release energies for future projects of social and political transformation."[60] For Williams, tragedy is relevant not in its ultimate outcome or denouement, contrary to Steiner, but in the recognition it provides of revolutionary process:

> The tragic action, in its deepest sense, is not the confirmation of disorder, but its experience, its comprehension and its resolution. In our own time, this action is general, and its common name is revolution. We have to see the evil and the suffering, in the factual disorder that makes revolution necessary, and in the disordered struggle against the disorder. We have to recognize this suffering in a close and immediate experience, and not cover it with names. But we follow the whole action: not only the evil, but the men who have fought against evil; not only the crisis, but the energy released by it, the spirit learned in it. We make the connections, because that is the action of tragedy, and what we learn in suffering is again revolution, because we acknowledge others as men and any such acknowledgement is the

---

[57] Steiner, 121.   [58] Steiner, 114.
[59] Raymond Williams, *Modern Tragedy*, ed. Paula McCallum (New York: Broadview Press, 2006).
[60] Pamela McCallum, "Introduction" to Williams, *Modern Tragedy*, 17.

beginning of struggle, as the continuing reality of our lives. Then to see revolution in this tragic perspective is the only way to maintain it.[61]

The separation of ideas of the tragic from tragic theatre and their redeployment for an understanding of historical processes had already been launched by the German idealists at the start of the nineteenth century. German philosophers, following the historic events of the French Revolution, reinterpreted the Kantian sublime so as to highlight the various means by which the sublime elicits human responses to its representational incommensurability and thus ultimately impacts upon the contemplation of ethical action. Thus Schelling, Schlegel, Hegel, Höderlin, Schopenhauer, and others inspired Nietzsche, Freud, Marx, Benjamin, Schimdt, and Arendt to collectively establish new idioms by which to think about the relationship between the individual, tragedy, history, and ethics.[62] The ready elision between tragic theatre and real-life scenarios of revolutionary struggle for Williams is then part of this longer tradition, with the difference being, that, unlike the German philosophers' abstractions of an idealist universalism, Williams's Marxism insists on illuminating the revolutionary potential of tragedy for the close understanding of the complicated historicity of his own time. His focus on the *disorder* that necessitates revolution and the *disordered* struggle that is pitched against it, speaks directly to the progressive force of tragic action. This is very different from what we find in Steiner, where the focus is securely on the literary history of tragedy, with society and social relations remaining indirect abstractions, as we saw in his remark about the organic relationship between playwrights and audiences during the Elizabethan period.

And yet despite the radical differences between Steiner and Williams, they are firmly unified by an almost complete disinterest in what takes place outside the borders of Euro-America in the period in which they are writing. Williams does mention Korea, Suez, the Congo, Cuba, and Vietnam, albeit in the same sentence, to assert the link between what happens outside Europe and what is taking place inside of its borders:

---

[61] Williams, *Modern Tragedy*, 108.
[62] See especially Joshua Billings, *Genealogy of the Tragic: Greek Tragedy and German Philosophy* (Princeton: Princeton University Press, 2014); Miriam Leonard, *Tragic Modernities*; Julian Young, *The Philosophy of Tragedy: From Plato to Žižek* (Cambridge: Cambridge University Press, 2013). Peter Szondi's *An Essay on the Tragic* (Stanford: Stanford University Press, 2002), provides a handy introduction to the central figures linking German philosophy and tragedy. See also, Hoxby.

What are still, obtusely, called 'local upheavals', or even 'brushfires', put all our lives in question again and again . . . . It is impossible to look at this real and still active history without a general sense of tragedy: not only because the disorder is so widespread and intolerable that in action and reaction it must work its way through our lives, wherever we may be; but also because, on any probable estimate, we understand the process so little that we continually contribute to the disorder.[63]

And yet these obtuse "local upheavals" are not the primary or even supplementary sources for his reflections on tragic lifeworlds in the post-World War II phase. It should be noted that in the specific case of Britain, the shedding of its worldwide empire was a fraught and painful process that had direct impact on its own social imaginary.

In his book *In 1926*, Hans Ulrich Gumbrecht provides us with a thick description of the historical period in which Heidegger's *Being and Time* was published in 1926, including the transitions in the European lifeworlds between the world wars that were of direct pertinence to Williams's own account.[64] This is not the place to attempt a thick description for *The Death of Tragedy* and *Modern Tragedy* of the kind that Gumbrecht offers so beautifully for Heidegger, but even a cursory look at BBC news headlines from the 1950s and early 1960s suggests that there were indeed several emergent nodal points for understanding world historical events that did not merely lie outside the horizon of Europe, but were integral to how it conducted its own affairs internally.[65] The news headlines on the BBC in the period are amply composed of items that pertain to Europe, the United Kingdom, and the colonial world at large. These events describe the arc of major world-historical transformations. Thus, we find reports on riots in Cairo as part of the long lead-up to the 1956 Suez crisis (on January 26, 1952); the Independence of Ghana (March 7, 1957) and Malaya (August 31, 1957) that were celebrated with chanting on the streets of both countries; and the escalating crisis between France and Algeria (covered by various news items between 1958 and 1961). All these demarcate historical changes in the colonial world that entangled Europe itself.[66] These news items are

---

[63] Williams, 105.

[64] Hans Ulrich Gumbrecht, *In 1926: Living at the Edge of Time* (Cambridge, MA: Harvard University Press, 1997).

[65] BBC On This Day, 1950–2005, http://news.bbc.co.uk/onthisday/hi/years/default.stm, last accessed Jan. 15, 2018.

[66] As Neil Lazarus notes in his introduction to *The Cambridge Companion to Postcolonial Literary Studies*, highlighting world-historical events from the perspective of the formerly colonized world means giving special place to acts of resistance and opposition to colonial and imperial rule that may not have necessarily had an impact beyond the places from which they were launched and yet were

amply intermixed with news stories pertaining specifically to the United Kingdom: drivers cheer the end of fuel rations (May 26, 1950), King George opens Festival of Britain (akin to the Great Exhibition of 1851 but on a more modest scale; May 3, 1951), dozens die at the Farnborough Air Show in Hampshire (September 6, 1952), housewives celebrate the end of rationing (July 4, 1952), and the British public gets "Asian flu" vaccine (October 6, 1967).

It is perfectly conceivable, though highly improbable, that both Steiner and Williams had little to no interest in news of events taking place outside of Europe (in the case of Williams, he clearly had at least some interest, as we just noted). Their general lack of detailed discussion of the relationship between Europe and the world beyond it should, however, be sharply distinguished from their lack of reference to literary works from the colonial and early post-Independence periods. At the time of the publication of their books on tragedy, the term "Commonwealth literature" was only at its inception, with the first courses on the subject having been introduced at Penn State University in 1961 and the University of Leeds in 1964 and focusing mainly on the literature of former settler colonies such as Australia and New Zealand. Steiner and Williams could not have been expected at the time to refer to works from these places.

The paucity of references to literature from Europe's former colonies is more difficult to explain in Terry Eagleton's *Sweet Violence*, which was published in 2005.[67] South African Athol Fugard toured the United Kingdom and Europe with *Sizwe Bansi is Dead*, *The Island*, and *Master Harold and the Boys* regularly from the early 1970s, and Chilean Ariel

---

very meaningful for the local actors. It also means providing a slightly different inflection to certain significant dates in world history. 1945 is a good example of this. This date immediately invokes the end of World War II but it is also a date where many significant changes were taking place in the formerly colonized world, and not all of which had a bearing on the war at all. In the same year, we find the following events:

-   Algeria: French repression of nationalists triggering major uprising; thousands killed.
-   Revolution in Vietnam brings Ho Chi Minh's Viet Minh to power; French forces attempt to recapture colonial power; war ensues.
-   Philippines liberated from Japanese occupation.
-   Syria and Lebanon gain independence.
-   Fifth Pan-African Congress, held in Manchester, England, proclaims "right of all colonial peoples to control their own destiny."

The shifts in relations between colonizer and colonized, the alteration of the global political economy, and the rise of different social agents all over the world is best discerned when the chronology is read in comparative terms. See *The Cambridge Companion to Postcolonial Literary Studies* (Cambridge: Cambridge University Press, 2004).

[67] Terry Eagleton, *Sweet Violence* (Oxford: Blackwell, 2005).

Dorfman's *Death and the Maiden* premiered to much acclaim at London's Royal Court Theatre in 1991. Gabriel García Márquez won the Nobel Prize for Literature in 1982, with Wole Soyinka following in 1986, Naguib Mahfouz in 1988, Nadine Gordimer in 1991, Derek Walcott in 1992, Toni Morrison in 1993, V. S. Naipaul in 2001, and J. M. Coetzee in 2003, all of whose works provide diverse examples of tragedy, meaning that by the time of *Sweet Violence,* postcolonial writing should have been impossible to ignore in any serious work on the subject. Eagleton discusses Conrad's *Heart of Darkness* but does not mention Achebe's well-known 1977 critique of Conrad, never mind the classic *Things Fall Apart,* which was first published in 1958.[68] What is even more surprising is that there is only one sentence each on V. S. Naipaul and J. M. Coetzee in Eagleton's entire book. The reference to Coetzee is the more baffling because it does not cite a specific work but mentions Coetzee in passing, only to suggest that the Greek notion of *pharmakos* is not confined to Greek antiquity but has resonances even at the time of the writing of *Sweet Violence.*[69] This comes after a lengthy excursus on the trope of the *pharmakos*/scapegoat, a subset of the theme Eagleton introduces at the beginning of *Sweet Violence* from the biblical story of Abraham's near-sacrifice of Isaac. In this excursus Eagleton illustrates the occurrence of the *pharmakos* trope in Nathaniel Hawthorne's *The Scarlet Letter,* Dostoevsky's *The Brothers Karamazov,* Henry James's *The Golden Bowl* and *The Ambassadors,* and Melville's *Moby-Dick,* along with several others before coming to the passing reference to Coetzee. As we shall see in our discussions of Achebe and Soyinka, Coetzee is not the only postcolonial writer in whose work the *pharmakos* plays a prominent role.[70] In his 1990 essay titled "Nationalism: Irony and Commitment" written for the volume on *Nationalism, Colonialism, and Literature,* the only concession Eagleton makes to the world outside of Europe in an otherwise fine essay on Ireland is an opening reference to "an African character in Raymond Williams's novel *Second Generation.*"[71] Many people will be forgiven for not recognizing either Raymond Williams's novel or the African character cited from it.

---

[68] Chinua Achebe, "An Image of Africa: Racism in Conrad's *Heart of Darkness,*" *Massachusetts Review,* 18.4 (1977): 782–794. The essay was reprinted in *Heart of Darkness: An Authoritative Text, Background Sources and Criticism,* 3rd edition, ed. Robert Kimbrough (London: W. W. Norton, 1988), and subsequently reprised in various anthologies and collections.

[69] Eagleton, 295.   [70] Eagleton, 277–296.

[71] Terry Eagleton, Fredric Jameson, Edward W. Said, *Nationalism, Colonialism, and Literature* (Minneapolis: Minnesota University Press, 1990), 23.

An accusation of eurocentrism might seem appropriate at this point, except that it seems to me too blunt an instrument and one that woefully misses the point.[72] For if eurocentrism is the exclusive focus on Euro-America as a way of placing all others in its shadow, then the accusation does have some traction. But the term also carries an implication of parochialism and narrow-mindedness that proves it false as a general accusation. No one who has had any sustained acquaintance with Steiner, Williams, and Eagleton on tragedy (or on other subject for that matter) can imagine even for a passing moment that these thinkers are narrow-minded by any stretch of the term. The opposite impression is in fact the case. Instead of a bland accusation of eurocentrism, we should attend to a completely different yet cognate question. The question can be simply stated thus: how enough is Europe for Europe? Or, to put it more cogently, are European history and culture enough to explain Europe to itself? The patent absurdity of these questions should not divert attention from the fact that Europe has regularly been described and indeed internally critiqued as a self-autonomous topos by some of its most influential thinkers in the twentieth and twenty-first centuries. Even though the trenchant critiques of Europe developed by Foucault, Habermas, Rancière, and Deleuze have had an instrumental impact on postcolonial thought (to name only those from whose work I have drawn inspiration for my own), it is also true that these were developed with an almost exclusive focus on Europe itself.

Writing as recently as 2011, the philosopher Simon Glendinning proposes Europe as providing a distinctive understanding of the world. "The heirs of this understanding," he notes, "have their being in this European world, whether they like it or not, and indeed whether they know it or not – and, moreover, whether, geographically speaking, they are 'in Europe' or not."[73] Glendinning's absolute insistence on an all-encompassing idea of Europe that is traceable to the boundaries of the continent denominated by that name and that does not broach disavowal or even conscious acknowledgment ("whether they like it or not"), does not take into account the fissures and constitutive contaminations that have and continue to define Europe. Glendinning's Europe is "a thing with one face, a thing," to borrow from Louis MacNeice's "Prayer Before Birth," something

[72] Indeed, Gayatri Spivak makes precisely this point with respect to Marxism. See her review of Derrida's *Spectres of Marx*, "Ghostwriting," *Diacritics*, 25. 2, Summer (1995): 64–84.
[73] Simon Glendinning, "Europe, for Example?," *LSE Europe in Question Discussion Paper Series* (LEQS), 31 (2011): 6.

which the poet prayed to be delivered from.[74] Glendinning's is a species of theory, in this case from the philosophical domain of metaphysics, that proposes universalism while being thoroughly derived from the perspective of methodological nationalism, magnified in this case to encompass and privilege the continent of Europe to itself and to the rest of the world.[75] As Achille Mbembe adroitly puts it:

> Theory has been not only the name of the West's attempt at domesticating contingency, but also the way in which the West has distinguished itself from the 'Rest' . . . . Whether it is possible to abide by the universalistic aspirations of social theory without replicating the metaphysical and normative implications of its Western origins is a question we can no longer postpone.[76]

There are many possible answers to the problem Mbembe proposes here, one of which is to revisit the question of Europe-as-self-autonomous topos not by resituating it within the context of its colonial history, an obvious maneuver common in postcolonial studies, but rather by highlighting the ways in which its self-constitution provides ample examples of the dialectical relationship between external and internal forms of colonialism that have shaped metropolitan Europe itself, as much as it has impacted upon its colonies.

As discussed earlier in this Introduction, significant to understanding postcolonialism are the varieties of colonial space-making that have shaped and continue to shape the world.[77] What we have to add to our earlier typology, however, is that colonial space-making was an aspect of both external colonialism – the conquest of territories – and internal colonialism – the management of heterogeneous populations in the name of the empty

---

[74] Louis MacNeice, "Prayer Before Birth," www.poemhunter.com/poem/prayer-before-birth/, last accessed July 6, 2020.

[75] The concept of methodological nationalism assumes the nation-state to be the primary horizon for understanding politics, culture, and society, such that even international relations are considered instantiations of individual national interests. The concept comes from the critique of the sociology of the state launched by scholars of migration and diaspora studies. For the original source of the term, see Andreas Wimmer and Nina Glick-Schiller, "Methodological Nationalism and Beyond: Nation Building, Migration, and the Social Sciences," *Global Networks*, 2.4 (2002), 301–334; and also Ato Quayson and Girish Daswani, "Introduction," *Companion to Diaspora and Transnationalism Studies* (New York: Blackwell, 2013), 1–26.

[76] Achille Mbembe, "The Planetary Library: Notes on Theory Today," in *Out of the Dark Night: Essays on Decolonization* (New York: Columbia University Press, 2020).

[77] See, Ato Quayson, "The Journal of Commonwealth Literature: the 1980s," 50th anniversary issue of the *Journal of Commonwealth Literature*, September (2015): 1–18; also "Introduction: Postcolonialism in a Changing Frame."

cipher of the nation both in Europe and elsewhere.[78] Colonial space-making does not merely designate the formation, constitution, and governance of a geographically demarcated area, though that is definitely also important, but is ultimately about the distribution of social and political goods along axes of power that are tied in various ways to race, ethnicity, and perceived cultural differences. Such space-making is the result of a series of interconnected and highly complex sets of procedures and instruments whether with respect to external or internal colonialisms. While the hegemonic relations of power and the ideas and assumptions undergirding them may be challenged, the platforms upon which the relations take shape are as much cultural and symbolic as they are political and spatial. The more starkly racially differentiated the social environment is, the more explicitly colonial are the relations of hierarchy and privilege in that society. In external colonialism, colonial space-making often altered – whether deliberately or incidentally – preexisting relations among well-constituted local groups (such as in India between the Mughals and the Hindus, or in Nigeria between the northern Muslims and the coastal Yorùbá and Igbo), or it reconfigured the hierarchies between indigenous and diasporic populations (such as in Southeast Asia or Latin America), or it established a pigmentocracy within settler/local relations (such as in the post-slavery societies of the Caribbean and South Africa).

In contrast, with respect to internal colonialism, population management principles often established distinctions between races of the same kind (the English and the Irish in Britain, or the English and the Boers in South Africa), while simultaneously magnifying distinctions among races and ethnicities of different kinds in the service of colonial regulation (the complicated stacking of the races that includes Europeans, Aborigines, and

---

[78] On internal colonialism, see Richard Koebner, *Empire* (Cambridge: Cambridge University Press, 1962), and Michael Hecter, *Internal Colonialism: The Celtic Fringe in Britain's National Development* 2nd edition (London: Routledge, 1998, first published in 1966). Internal colonialism has to do with the management of heterogeneous populations in the name of the empty signifier of the nation. The examples of internal colonialism are many and varied, and have had several historical articulations. British policies in Ireland stretching from at least Cromwell until the Good Friday Agreement of 1998 exemplify a long-term history of such colonialism. White Australia and Canada's policies toward their Aboriginal populations; China's response to the Muslim Uyghurs; Russia during the incorporation of various republics that came to form the Pale of Settlement in the nineteenth century (eastern and central Poland, Lithuania, Latvia, Byelorussia, and Ukraine) and also under Stalin; and Israel's continuing policies regarding the Palestinian question, all illustrate versions of intraverted colonialism. I wish to thank Richard Drayton for a very helpful conversation regarding these ideas and for suggesting a preliminary list of readings to fine-tune them. For a preliminary account of my thoughts on intraverted and extraverted colonialisms, see Ato Quayson, "Comparative Postcolonialisms: Storytelling and Community in Sholem Aleichem and Chinua Achebe," Special Issue on Jewish Studies and Postcolonialism, *The Cambridge Journal of Postcolonial Literary Inquiry*, 3,1 (2015): 287–296.

migrants from erstwhile colonies inside of the settler colonies of Canada, Australia, South Africa, and, some might add, the United States).[79] The various diasporas from the Global South that reside in various metropolises of the Global North serve to compound the picture for internal population management even further. Whether in its external or internal variants, colonial space-making ultimately involves the differential constitution of citizens and subjects.[80]

If we insist on seeing Europe itself as produced by both internal and external forms of colonialism, what does this do to our attempt to reread tragedy from a postcolonial perspective? Unlike what we find in general discussions of tragedy, and of which Steiner, Williams, and Eagleton offer significant examples, my primary aim is to establish a comparative framework for exploring tragedy from a simultaneously postcolonial *and* Western perspective.

I shall be elaborating on the following themes in *Tragedy and Postcolonial Literature*: suffering and ethical choice; *musuo* and *pharmakos*; historical disputatiousness and the giving an account of oneself; the elusiveness of self-authorship; split *anagnorisis* and the question of bearing witness; and the vagaries and pitfalls of cosmopolitanism, among others. In my view, all of these themes are best pursued in direct relation to the broad history of tragedy. This is because, in the practice of reading postcolonialism *through* tragedy and vice versa, nothing must be left out of account. The nature of our discussion will only be enriched if we draw from a broad range of literary traditions. This has implications for the pursuit of universal humanism, for today we can no longer propose a singular genealogy for tragedy without acknowledging its variant oscillations, its interdependencies, the different media and venues in which it has been expressed, and its worldliness in past, present, and possible futures. My theoretical model here does not disavow Europe but rather ingests it.

---

[79] For especially astute discussions on these relations of population management and control in Europe and in Africa, see Robert Young, *The Idea of English Ethnicity* (Oxford: Blackwell, 2008), and Mahmood Mamdani, *Define and Rule: Native as Political Identity* (Cambridge, MA: Harvard University Press, 2012).

[80] Mahmood Mamdani, *Citizen and Subject: Contemporary Africa and the Legacy of Late Colonialism* (Princeton: Princeton University Press, 1997), and Ann Laura Stoler, *Race and the Education of Desire: Foucault's History of Sexuality and the Colonial Order of Things* (Durham: Duke University Press, 1995).

CHAPTER 2

Ethical Cosmopolitanism and Shakespeare's Othello

Shakespeare is constantly reproduced in the general discourses of culture and is used to authorize practices as diverse as buying perfume, watching Masterpiece Theater, or dispatching troops to far-flung corners of the globe.

Jean E. Howard and Marion F. O'Connor, *Shakespeare Reproduced*[1]

Every major rethinking of literature and theory has a way of returning to particular texts, whatever the theoretical resistance to the very idea of a canon; and often to discover that what was canonical was not so much, or not just, the text in question but the received readings of it, its normalization as a cultural icon or familiar construct.

Patricia Parker and Geoffrey Hartman, *Shakespeare and the Question of Theory*[2]

In their introduction to *Post-Colonial Shakespeares*, Ania Loomba and Martin Orkin note that the energies for what have become postcolonial readings of Shakespeare were already in place in the revisionist studies of the new historicists and Marxist and feminist critics starting from the late 1980s.[3] These studies provide fresh insights into the relation between Shakespeare and shifting attitudes to race, class, and gender in the early modern period and also enable a consideration of the extent to which some of these attitudes persist in the West today. More importantly, the new critical readings suggest discursive corollaries between the worlds depicted in Shakespeare's texts and our own postcolonial worlds, in a comparative framing that, in another context, I refer to as *postcolonializing* Shakespeare. As the two epigraphs to this

---

[1] Jean Howard and Marion F. O'Connor, *Shakespeare Reproduced: The Text in History and Ideology* (London: Routledge, 1988), 15.

[2] Patricia Parker and Geoffrey Hartman, *Shakespeare and the Question of Theory* (London: Routledge, 1993), vii.

[3] Ania Loomba and Martin Orkin, eds. *Post-Colonial Shakespeares* (London: Routledge, 1998), 1–22.

chapter show, whether from a popular cultural or theoretical perspective, the return to Shakespeare is never only about the Elizabethan contexts in which his plays were first produced. It is also about the familiarity of Shakespeare in terms set by the worlds in which he is being reread. But what might it mean to turn to Shakespeare for some clues about cosmopolitanism? It is now perhaps not controversial to state that multiethnicity has been a central part of human experience since the historical inception of cities. But the concomitant observation that multiethnicity does not signify the social acceptance of strangers would also be completely in order. One only has to think of the writings of V. S. Naipaul, Toni Morrison, Anita Desai, Salman Rushdie, Chimamanda Ngozi Adichie, Zadie Smith, Taiye Selassie, Hanif Kureishi, Junot Diaz, and various others to get a broad sense of the terms in which the promises *and* the vagaries of cosmopolitanism have been understood in postcolonial literature. As an extension of this overall postcolonial interest in cosmopolitanism, it is hard to think of a Shakespeare play with more resonance for debates on the relationship between cosmopolitanism, multiculturalism, and postcolonialism in today's world than *Othello*. This means that while paying close attention to the details within the play itself, I shall be attempting to calibrate my reading for the illumination of cosmopolitan contradictions beyond the content reflected in the text itself or indeed in the period of its earliest performance. As I write when defining my key terms in the opening of *Calibrations: Reading for the Social*, while the etymology of the word "calibrations" may be traced to scientific texts of the nineteenth century where the focus was in its association with the perfection of instruments of measurement, what I sought to do as a literary critic was neither mechanistic nor vulgarly instrumentalist:

> In my view the social is coded as an articulated encapsulation of transformation, processes and contradictions analogous to what we find in the literary domain. Departing from the mechanistic implications of its scientific usage, I want to emphasize instead the action of gradually identifying patterns for comparison across apparently disparate and incommensurable domains through a process of identifying the multilayered and interactive dimensions of such domains. To this end, the repeated fine-tuning of literary analysis is to be seen only as a starting point. In my reading there is a concomitant fine-tuning of a perspective on the social involved in the reading of the literary. Furthermore, I use the term calibrations to point towards the activity of the calibrator, and the degree to which this fine-tuning procedure is dependent upon a particular interpretative and subjective perspective. In reading for

the social across the literary I do not intend to imply any simple notion of literature as a mirror.[4]

Following on these views, my suggestion then is that literature be seen as a variegated series of thresholds and levels all of which determine the production of "the social" as a structure both within the interaction of the constitutive thresholds of the literary and in the domain of social relations beyond the text itself. Thus, it is in the dedication to identifying how the relations among the variegated thresholds encapsulate or reflect upon the social that calibrations make sense as a mode of interpretation.

Given Shakespeare's significance for debates about identity politics, colonialism, gender relations, and various other things both in postcolonial studies and other areas, he provides a very good platform for thinking about how to calibrate from literature to the social and back again. As will become evident, the contradictions of cosmopolitanism I have in mind as we read *Othello* relate as much to the contexts of its first performance and publication in the seventeenth century as they do to our own urban social condition in the twenty-first century. I turn to *Othello* here also to explore the ways in which the play frames our possible identification or nonidentification with the plight of Othello in terms firmly linked to what I interpret as the play's contradictory cosmopolitanism. The only other Shakespeare play that allows us to explore similar questions of cosmopolitanism is *The Merchant of Venice*, which, like *Othello,* is also set in Venice but focuses on the negative attitudes of the Venetian Christians toward the Jewish Shylock within the expanding mercantile and financial world of the play. We shall have something to say on the contrast in the cosmopolitan vision of these two Shakespeare plays later on in the chapter.[5]

Ever since Thomas Rymer's 1693 *A Short View of Tragedy,* generations of critics and audiences have expressed shock at the interracial relationship captured in the play.[6] When Iago tells Brabantio that "you'll have your

[4] Ato Quayson, *Calibrations: Reading for the Social* (Minneapolis: Minnesota University Press, 2003), xvi.
[5] This chapter was first triggered by a conversation I had with Ankhi Mukherjee at the 2017 ACLA conference in Utrecht. We were talking about our current writing projects and, when I told her about what I was thinking for this book, she immediately said I must write a chapter on Othello because her daughter, Tiyash Banerjee, who happened to have then just been admitted to my old college at Cambridge, had in high school once read a chapter I had written on *The Merchant of Venice* that she had found thoroughly inspirational. I want to thank Ankhi for that pleasant anecdote and to dedicate this chapter specifically to Tiyash in the hope that, like me, her enjoyment of Shakespeare will never wane. For that earlier chapter, see my "Postcolonializing Shakespeare: Parables from the Canon," *Postcolonialism: Theory, Practice, or Process?* (Cambridge: Polity Press, 2000), 156–184.
[6] Thomas Rymer, *A Short View of Tragedy* (London: Scolar Press, 1970). First published 1693.

daughter covered with a Barbary horse; you'll have your nephews neigh to you. You'll have coursers for cousins and jennets for germans!" he is raising the prospect of miscegenation, which has been of particular concern in many multicultural societies the world over, and indeed in some not especially noted for their multiculturalism, such as China and Japan.[7] While *Othello* has been popular with audiences and critics throughout its performance history and is second only to *Hamlet* in the number of film adaptations, it was the 1987 theatrical production in apartheid South Africa where all of its Renaissance anxieties about interracial romance could be seen most sharply against a modern backdrop.[8] The production at Johannesburg's Market Theatre was directed by Janet Suzman and starred John Kani as Othello and Joanna Wienberg as Desdemona. Even though the Market Theatre had always drawn a mixed-race audience, the response to this production of *Othello* was substantially different, with the five-week run seeing an audience about 40 percent black thronging to see the show every night. Kani's performance attracted mixed reviews, but it was the general response of the audience on the first night that showed the strong feelings that had been aroused. A large section of the white audience stormed out when Othello and Desdemona embraced and had their first passionate kiss, with Suzman later receiving hate mail from theatregoers and even from some who had not seen the play. The play was being staged only two years after the annulment of the Immorality Act, which, with various amendments since 1927, had prohibited sexual relations between whites and nonwhites in South Africa.[9]

Kani recalls that when he was first offered the role, he took a very deep breath before agreeing. "Then," he continues, "my heart started thumping and I immediately knew how much trouble I was in for. But I looked on the light side and said, 'There goes the native causing more trouble, and this time he has Shakespeare to do it for him.'"[10] It wouldn't be Kani's first

---

[7] William Shakespeare, *Othello*, 2nd edition, Arden Shakespeare Third Series, with an introduction by Ayanna Thompson (London: Arden, 2016), 1.1.110–112. All references to the play will be from this edition.

[8] Andrew Hadfield counts six film adaptations of *Othello* to *Hamlet's* nine, but neglects to mention the version by Janet Suzman of 1988. See his *A Routledge Literary Sourcebook on William Shakespeare's Othello* (London: Routledge, 2003), 1.

[9] Notwithstanding the annulment of the Immorality Act, all the other repressive acts prescribing segregation and censorship, such as the Separate Amenities Act, the Group Areas Act, the Job Reservations Act, the Publications Act, and the Population Act were still firmly in place by the time of Janet Suzman's production. See Adele Seeff, "Othello at the Market Theatre," *Shakespeare Bulletin*, 27.3 (2009): 377–398.

[10] John D. Battersby, "The Drama of Staging *Othello* in Johannesburg," *New York Times*, Oct. 26, 1987; www.nytimes.com/1987/10/26/theater/the-drama-of-staging-othello-in-johannesburg.html, last accessed Aug. 6, 2018.

time causing trouble either. Just a few years earlier, the 1982 production of Strindberg's *Miss Julie* saw half the theatre walk out when Kani's character, John, kissed Sandra Prinsloo's Julie, and he received multiple death threats and even an assassination attempt. By the time Kani performed *Othello*, he was already internationally well-known for his role in Athol Fugard's *Sizwe Bansi is Dead*, for which he jointly won a Tony Award with Winston Nthsona in 1975, and also for his depiction of Vladimir in Samuel Beckett's *Waiting for Godot* at the Old Vic in 1981. Kani had always taken strong political positions against the apartheid regime and so he was no stranger to controversy.

If Shakespeare was useful for exploring the fear of miscegenation posed by the marriage of a black man to a white woman in the predominantly segregated society that was apartheid South Africa, then, in Suzman's view, the Elizabethan playwright had "examined the idea of apartheid four hundred years before the term was coined."[11] That this view is applicable to practically all multiracial societies from Elizabethan England through American Jim Crow to South Africa during a large part of the twentieth century is not easily contested. And yet it is not only on the question of race relations that the play finds resonance. While the issue of racial stereotyping is the most obvious aspect of the play's contradictory cosmopolitanism, what gives it special salience for thinking about postcolonial tragedy is how it dramatizes the constraints a racially marked member of society experiences in attempting to give an account of himself. These constraints on Othello are centered on what I want to describe as the play's modularity, which is itself focalized through Iago's chicanery and machinations. A cluster of seventeenth-century definitions of the word "module" bear the meanings of both true and false representations, as well as of repeatable typology and of governance. The argument of this chapter will then be that it is Iago's management of modularity (in the tripartite sense of true/false representations, typology, and governance) that disrupts the play's cosmopolitan potential, especially as expressed before the senate in Venice. The play returns us to a mode of cosmopolitanism only at the end of the action, when the ethico-cognitive structure of its inexorable tragic plot invites some sympathy for the gullible Othello. But this is no longer the cosmopolitanism of multiethnicity or multiculturalism but rather an invitation to contemplate an ethical humanism that transcends the internal racial and gender boundaries depicted in the play. The play's move from multicultural cosmopolitanism to ethical humanism is thus an enactment of sharp contradictions within cosmopolitanism itself,

---

[11] Janet Suzman, "*Othello* – A Belated Reply," *Shakespeare in South Africa*, 2 (1988): 90–96.

between the visible and often superficial demands of interracial mixture and cultural interactions and the more difficult challenge of empathy beyond all markers of difference. The interplay of variant understandings of cosmopolitanism in *Othello* suggests ways in which we might draw upon Shakespeare for debating similar questions in our own times.

Features of Cosmopolitanism

Exploring the contradictions of cosmopolitanism in the world of *Othello* requires some qualification. This is partly because of the complicated implications of the term itself. Since the proliferation of a wide range of books on the subject in the 1990s, cosmopolitanism has been taken to encapsulate a range of features that appear in various configurations in different political and social contexts. Pauline Kleingeld and Eric Brown open their entry on cosmopolitanism in the *Stanford Encyclopedia of Philosophy* in this way:

> The nebulous core shared by all cosmopolitan views is the idea that all human beings, regardless of their political affiliation, are (or can and should be) citizens in a single community. Different versions of cosmopolitanism envision this community in different ways, some focusing on political institutions, others on moral norms or relationships, and still others focusing on shared markets or forms of cultural expression. In most versions of cosmopolitanism, the universal community of world citizens functions as a positive ideal to be cultivated, but a few versions exist in which it serves primarily as a ground for denying the existence of special obligations to local forms of political organizations. Versions of cosmopolitanism also vary depending on the notion of citizenship they employ, including whether they use the notion of 'world citizenship' literally or metaphorically. The philosophical interest in cosmopolitanism lies in its challenge to commonly recognized attachments to fellow-citizens, the local state, parochially shared cultures, and the like.

Like Anthony Appiah, Pheng Cheah, Bruce Robbins, and others that have explored the meanings of the term, Kleingeld and Brown go on to trace its history to the Greeks and the Romans, and then through the major qualifications of the term in the Enlightenment philosophy of Kant, Montesquieu, Diderot, Addison, Hume, Jefferson, and others who bequeath to our own period the key understandings of cosmopolitanism.[12] As they note,

---

[12] Pauline Kleingeld and Eric Brown, "Cosmopolitanism," *Stanford Encyclopedia of Philosophy*; https://plato.stanford.edu/entries/cosmopolitanism/, last accessed Aug. 7, 2018. Broader discussions of the genealogy of the concept are to be found in Anthony K. Appiah, *Cosmopolitanism: Ethics in a World of Strangers* (New York: Norton, 2007); Pheng Cheah, *Inhuman Conditions: On Cosmopolitanism and Human Rights* (Cambridge, MA: Harvard University Press, 2006); and Rebecca L. Walkowitz, *Cosmopolitan Style: Modernism Beyond the Nation* (New York: Columbia University Press, 2006),

a common thread in all definitions of cosmopolitanism is the acceptance of the diversity of human culture as a central principle for the formation of political communities, whether these are national or much smaller in scale. The impediments to such an inclusive principle tend to come from the assertion of narrowly focused identities or interests.

The various uses of the term cosmopolitanism may be summarized as entailing four distinctive features that, while not being mutually exclusive, nevertheless do not always appear conjointly in the belief systems of individuals and societies. These beliefs may be listed as follows: 1) cosmopolitanism is a statement of style; 2) cosmopolitanism entails forms of multiculturalism and racial intermixing; 3) cosmopolitanism implies participation in connections and the consolidation of the venues where these connections take place; and 4) cosmopolitanism is a form of ethical universalism.[13] The last definition is the one emphasized by Kleingeld and Brown, but the others also bear indirectly on the world of *Othello* and directly on commonplace usages of the term in the present day. Cosmopolitanism of style is simply the sign of elite consumption patterns, not always democratic and evenly distributed. The availability of goods, as well as knowledge, from across the world found in many of today's large cities indicates above all else the degree to which the processes of globalization have become standardized. Ultimately, the cosmopolitanism of style is a function not of equity but of wherewithal. Many people who claim to be cosmopolitan have no real interest in the cultures whose goods they like to consume, but on the positive side of this they may also be able to make immediate friends with people from other parts of the world that share similar interests, on the basis of the cosmopolitanism of new knowledge economies. You will encounter young people in Lagos and Accra who can readily recite the team sheets for Manchester United's Champions League games since 1999, never mind the games in which Barcelona's Lionel Messi has scored a hat-trick.

Multiculturalism is also taken to be a necessary feature of cosmopolitanism but is a prickly concept in its own right. The lay view of multiculturalism implies a world in which different races, ethnicities, cultures, sexual dispositions, and religious affiliations intermingle and coexist peacefully within the same socio-political domain. This would provide the default mode for describing the cosmopolitan world of *Othello*, at least in the first act set in Venice. However, as Will Kymlicka has shown,

with the edited collection by Paulo Horta and Bruce Robbins providing various perspectives attempting to look at cosmopolitanism "from below." See their *Cosmopolitanisms* (New York: New York University Press, 2017).
[13] This typology is inspired by Craig Calhoun's discussion of the concept in his "A Cosmopolitanism of Connections," Horta and Robbins, 189–200.

multiculturalism, strictly speaking, describes system-wide accommodations that guarantee the rights of different categories of minorities within a given democratic dispensation. Using a general rule that he applies to a range of Western liberal democracies, he suggests that multiculturalism is a specific set of policies that target three different constituencies, namely, autochthonous groups (such as the Aborigines of Australia and Canada), sub-state actors (such as the Quebecois in Canada or the Basque separatists in Spain), and immigrants. The composite of all the targeted policies is what constitutes a multicultural environment and not just the intermingling of different ethnic and cultural groups. This also implies that there are different configurations of multiculturalism and that the accommodations and guarantees may be understood as applicable on a sliding scale within any given environment. Even though, like Kleingeld and Brown, most commentators would agree that monoculturalism is inimical to cosmopolitanism, the fact of multicultural accommodations does not necessarily imply there will be equality or even tolerance for cultural difference. Day-to-day social interactions between different races and cultural groups are often disturbed by the presence of racial stereotypes, even in highly multicultural places such as Canada, the USA, and the United Kingdom, the three countries that are cited by Kymlicka as being the best exemplars of multicultural accommodations. Racial stereotypes derive from the historical oppression of different ethnic groups, which coalesce over time into racial hierarchies that are then naturalized by those who see themselves as benefiting most from the process of naturalization. The idea of natural hierarchies, then, gives force as much to supremacist groups as it does to racial, religious, sexual, and gender microaggressions on an everyday basis. In extreme instances it can even lead to the hijacking of democratic institutions in multicultural and multiethnic societies by narrowly focused and exclusionist racial agendas. This is the lamentable case of Trump's America.[14]

For its part, the cosmopolitanism of connections assumes that the world is deeply interconnected through multiple enabling venues of cultural interaction and interconnectivity, such as theatres, universities, cinemas,

---

[14] For this now commonplace view, see Ta-Nehisi Coates, "The First White President," *The Atlantic*, Oct. 2017; www.theatlantic.com/magazine/archive/2017/10/the-first-white-president-ta-nehisi-coates/537909/, last accessed Aug. 17, 2018. But see also Spike Lee's film *The BlacKkKlansman* (2018), which tells the riveting story of the infiltration of the Ku Klux Klan in the 1970s by the first black policeman to work at the South Carolina Police Department and the worrying similarities between the racist and anti-Semitic discourses of the period and what is to be seen in America under Trump.

libraries, markets (broadly defined), and social media, and that these have to be celebrated and actively protected as the necessary conduits for the consolidation of cross-cultural understanding. The rise in the phenomenon of "fake news," bigotry, and intolerance of all kinds, and the fact that these are circulated predominantly through social media means that any cosmopolitanism centered on such platforms requires serious reconsideration. Given that the algorithms that run platforms such as Facebook and Twitter tend to class news feeds in relation to things shared by friends and family, they inadvertently (or is it deliberately?) consolidate enclaves that confirm already-held prejudices and actively shut out contrary opinions.

It is the cosmopolitanism of ethical humanism, however, that is the most demanding of all the definitions, for it implies a fundamental rethinking of the very basis of human society. Kant is most often credited with the tradition of understanding cosmopolitanism in universalist terms, and caring for people and aspects of the world that do not form part of one's own organic community remains the most radical implication of cosmopolitanism.[15] At its best, the cosmopolitanism of ethical humanism is supposed to encompass the human, as well as the animal and material worlds, in a single and holistic domain of interest. This variant of cosmopolitanism expands beyond caring about people from different racial and cultural communities to caring about the very planet on which such communities make their existence in the first place. One problem that is nestled within the cosmopolitanism of ethical humanism is what constitutes care for others and where the limits of that care lie. Tragedy may be said to play a part in this domain in that it invites attention toward the fate of others unlike us. This is a standard argument made about literature in general, but it can be reasoned that tragedy has a prime place in the forms of identification that literature provides because of its ethico-cognitive characteristics. When Aristotle writes in his *Poetics* that tragedy is a plot entailing devices of reversal and recognition and triggering pity and fear the better to purge them, this is partly what he means: that identification with the tragic protagonist depends on a particular form of urgency that can only be conveyed through the action of the tragic plot. While his remarks were focused mainly on the theatre, as we saw in the Introduction, the ethico-cognitive structures of tragedy have successfully been transferred into other literary, filmic, and operatic media that now actively bear the burden of conveying the tragic. The point to be made here, however, is that

---

[15] On this, see especially Pauline Kleingeld, *Kant and Cosmopolitanism: The Philosophical Idea of World Citizenship* (Cambridge: Cambridge University Press, 2012).

pity and fear toward the fate of others is also a means by which to minimally school us in the ethical identification with persons not like us, and thus is a critical part of an ethical cosmopolitanism.

Cosmopolitan Contradictions in *Othello*

Othello is believed to have been first performed in 1603 or 1604. The story from Giovanni Battista Giraldi's *Hecatommithi*, which Shakespeare drew upon for the play, only provided a set of stock characters that he then animated with more complex motivations and put in motion to form a tighter and more complicated plot. Several sources have been taken as providing the ambient ideas about blacks, Turks, and exotic Others that circulated in the Renaissance and Elizabethan period and which can safely be assumed to have influenced Shakespeare in his depiction of the cosmopolitan world of Venice in *Othello*. Richard Haklyut's *Principal Navigations, Traffics, Voyages, and Discoveries of the English Nation* (1589), John Pory's translation of Leo Africanus's *The History and Descriptions of Africa* (1600), Robert Greene's *Selimus, the Emperor of Turks* (1594), the character of Ithamore the Turk in Christopher Marlowe's *The Jew of Malta*, and Shakespeare's own Aaron in *Titus Andronicus* (1594), have all been identified as pretextual references for racial ideas that appear in *Othello*.[16] Selimus and Ithamore were both violent and tyrannical while Aaron is the expression of "vigorously energetic evil" and embraces his blackness in order to hurl it as a weapon against the white world.[17] These characters lacked any of the tortured complexity that Shakespeare invested in the character of Othello on the onset of his jealousy.

Ideas about Venice and the cosmopolitan sophistication of its peoples were also in general circulation in the period. Especially suggestive, as we shall see in a moment, were the impressions of Venice encapsulated in the travelogues of Thomas Coryat (1577–1617), but ideas pertaining to blackness and Turks were closer to the Elizabethan consciousness than were those relating to Venice's sophistication. Even though Coryat's travelogues were only published in 1611, and thus well after the first performances of *Othello*, they still provided a lively introduction to the social world of the play for contemporary audiences. To "turn Turk" denoted the danger of

---

[16] For a discussion of the close relation between the descriptions that Leo Africanus provides of himself and Shakespeare's descriptions of Othello's life and career, see Lois Whitney, "Did Shakespeare Know Leo Africanus?," *PMLA*, 37.3 (1922): 470–483.

[17] Stanley Wells and Gary Taylor, headnote to *Titus Andronicus* in *The Oxford Shakespeare: The Complete Works* (Oxford: Oxford University Press, 1988), 125.

reverting or converting from Christianity to Islam and spoke directly to perceptions in the period of the dangers posed by the Ottoman Empire, that was by turns a trading partner and a military adversary on various fronts.[18] Africans were an increasing presence in places like London and had begun to be perceived as posing problems for the populace by the end of the sixteenth century. African slaves started arriving in England from the 1570s and were used in three primary capacities: as household servants, as prostitutes or sexual conveniences for the well-to-do, and as court entertainers.[19] In 1596 Queen Elizabeth wrote to the Lord Mayor of London and his aldermen to have "ten blackamoors" sent out of the realm, "of which kind of people there are already here too many." A week later she dispatched an open warrant to the Lord Mayor and all vice-admirals, mayors, and other public officers informing them that eighty-nine English prisoners were going to be released from Spain and Portugal in exchange for an equivalent number of "blackamoors." If this piece of business was designed to expunge her realm of black people it signally failed, because in 1601 she felt obliged again to issue a proclamation in which she declared herself:

> highly discontented to understand the great numbers of negars and Blackamoores which are crept into this realm ... who are fostered and relieved [i.e. fed] here to the great annoyance of my own liege people, that want the relief [i.e. food], which those people consume, as also for that most of them are infidels, having no understanding of Christ or his Gospel.[20]

Even though our own modern-day notions of race and racism were to properly take shape only in the nineteenth century, the Elizabethan audience had their own lively sense of the differences among nations, races, and religions. And this is partially hinted at in the Queen's concerns. The world

---

[18] For a useful summary of these views on Turks and the scholarly debates around them, see Debra Johanyak, "'Turning Turk', Early Modern English Orientalism, and Shakespeare's *Othello*," in Debra Johanyak and Walter S. H. Lim, eds., *The English Renaissance, Orientalism, and the Idea of Asia* (London: Palgrave, 2009), 77–96. For his part, Jonathan Burton interprets Leo Africanus's *Historie* as a strategic form of "autoethnography" that attempts to invoke, but at the same time undermine, European conceptions of Moors, Africans, and various others. See his "'A Most Wily Bird': Leo Africanus, *Othello* and the Trafficking in Difference," Ania Loomba and Martin Orkin, eds., *Post-Colonial Shakespeares* (London: Routledge, 1998), 23–42.

[19] Peter Fryer, *Staying Power: The History of Black People in Britain* (London: Pluto Press, 1984), 4–10.

[20] Cited in Fryer, 11–1. But see also Julia Briggs, *This Stage-Play World: Texts and Contexts, 1580–1625*, revised edition (Oxford: Oxford University Press, 1997), 95–96. See also Eldred Jones, *Othello's Countrymen: Africans in English Renaissance Drama* (Oxford: Oxford University Press, 1965); Kim F. Hall, *Things of Darkness: Economies of Race and Gender in Early Modern England* (Ithaca: Cornell University Press, 1995); and Virginia Mason Vaughan, *Othello: A Contextual History* (Cambridge: Cambridge University Press, 1996).

then was considered vast and less uniform; differences in belief, taste, and the effects of geographical provenance were thought to be more fundamental to identity, to the degree that the word "infidel" carried both a religious and civilizational charge.[21] It is against such Elizabethan attitudes to blacks that Shakespeare sets up the image of the cosmopolitan yet racially charged dynamic of Venice and Cyprus in which Othello, a highly regarded military general, is a Moor, and Cassio, his ensign, is a Florentine, while the text suggests that Iago, Othello's servant, and Brabantio, his father-in-law, are of Spanish origin. The play thus presents a crucible for testing social ideas about race and difference that were popular in England itself.[22]

Thomas Coryat was an avid English traveler whose descriptions of his journeys through Italy, France, Germany, and other European countries provided lively impressions of the various places that he visited. As noted earlier, although this travelogue, *Coryat's Crudities,* was published at least eight years after the first performance of *Othello,* Coryat is a suggestive source on ideas about Venice in the late sixteenth and early seventeenth centuries. Apart from his descriptions of the courtesans of Venice, he also paints a portrait of a city alive with multicultural activity and describes in great detail the city's Grand Canal and the many palaces and fine buildings that line it on both sides. Coryat reserves his highest praise for the Piazza San Marco and for the famous cathedral that dominates it at the eastern end. It is here that he gets the most pronounced view of Venice's cosmopolitanism:

> Truley such is the stupendious (to use a strange Epitheton for so strange and rare a place as this) glory of it, that at my first entrance thereof it did even amaze me or rather ravish my senses. For here is the greatest magnificence of architecture to be seene, that any place under the sunne doth yeelde. Here you may both see all manner of fashions of attire, and heare all the languages of Christendom, besides those that are spoken by the barbarous Ethnickes; the frequencie of people being so great twice a day, betwixt six of the clocke

[21] For more on this, see Ania Loomba, *Shakespeare, Race, and Colonialism,* (Oxford: Oxford University Press, 2002).

[22] See Michael Neill, "Othello and Race," in Peter Ericson and Maurice Hunt, eds., *Approaches to Teaching Shakespeare's Othello* (New York: MLA Publications, 2005), 47. Neill suggests that Iago's name is the Iberian version of James, the patron saint of the Reconquista, Sant' Iago Matamoros (Saint James, the Moor Slayer) and that he is thus both a Spaniard and also ironically playing on English and European portrayals of wars with the Ottoman Empire. And Patricia Parker has written recently on how the name Brabantio recalls the geographical Brabant, and therefore suggests certain geopolitical concerns held by England regarding Spain's expansionist designs in Europe. See Patricia Parker, *Shakespearean Intersections: Language, Contexts, Critical Keywords* (Philadelphia: University of Pennsylvania Press, 2018), 210–272.

in the morning and eleven, and againe betwixt five in the afternoon and eight, that (as an elegant author saith of it) a man may very properly call it rather *Orbis* than *Urbis forum*, that is, a market place of the world, not of the citie. . . .. This part of the Piazza is worthy to be celebrated for that famous concourse and meeting of so many distinct and sundry nations twice a day. . . .. [Here] the Venetian long gowned Gentlemen doe meete together in great troupes. For you shall not see as much as one Venetian there of the Patrician ranke without his blacke gowne and tippet [hat]. There you may see many Polonians, Slavonians, Persians, Grecians, Turks, Jewes, Christians of all the famousest regions of Christendome, and each nation distinguished from another by their proper and peculiar habits. A singular shew, and by many degrees the worthiest of all the European Countries.[23]

Coryat's senses are ravished by the sight of multicultural intermixture that is laid out before him at the piazza. The OED gives one meaning of "ravish" that was commonly in use in the period as "to transport (a person, the mind, etc.) with the strength of some emotion; to fill with ecstasy, intense delight, or sensuous pleasure; to entrance, captivate, or enrapture." But the word also bore the sense of contemplation, so that the combination of the two meanings implies Coryat was both in rapture and in deep reflection. All the signals of cosmopolitan multiculturalism that engendered this ravishment for Coryat are expressed to him in the different styles of dress and language that are on display at the piazza. The languages of Christendom, including those of the "Barborous Ethnickes" he references, suggest the presence of different races, presumably including some black people. This is an impression corroborated by Vittore Carpaccio's *Miracle of the True Cross at the Rialto Bridge* (1494) a century earlier, along with other paintings of Renaissance Venice. Vittore's painting is set in front of Venice's Rialto (the city's stock exchange that also appears in *The Merchant of Venice*) and displays a bustling multicultural scene with nobles, clerks, and prelates, as well as Turkish traders (in white turbans) and an African gondolier at the foreground of the work.

The black gondolier in this and other Renaissance paintings was no imaginative figment.[24] As Kate Lowe has shown from a study of notarial records, wills, court cases, as well as the records of gondolier associations, there were several black gondoliers in Venice during the sixteenth and

[23] Thomas Coryat, *Coryat's Crudities reprinted from the edition of 1611. To which are now added his letters, from India. Together with his orations, character, death, &c. with copper plates*, vol. 1 (London: printed for W. Carter, Samuel Hayes, J. Wilkie, and E. Easton at Salisbury, 1776; first published 1611), 215, 220.

[24] Other well-known paintings include Vittore Carpaccio's *Hunting on the Lagoon* (1490), and Gentile Bellini's *Miracle of the True Cross at the Bridge of S. Lorenzo* (1500).

seventeenth centuries. Even though there is a vast gap between a black gondolier and the accomplished military general we see in Othello, it was not unknown for manumitted black servants and slaves to take on significant civic roles in Venetian society, with Cristoforo Moro being at least one black person to occupy the important office of doge (chief magistrate) from 1462 to 1471.[25] It is this aspect of Venice's multiculturalism, enshrined in Shakespeare's period in the institutions of trade and judicial practice, that prompts Coryat to enthuse that it is an "Urbis forum," or what we might translate as a universal *agora* in the sense of both marketplace and political assembly of all nations.

Notwithstanding the attractiveness of this multicultural description, Coryat's views formed only one half of an idealized image of Venice, and another conception that was also to have a resonant afterlife throughout the sixteenth and seventeenth centuries. The other half was composed of an image that was the direct opposite of Coryat's and turned on Venice as a place of composed and cohesive government regulated through strict cultural hierarchies. This was the view, for example, of Cornelio Frangipane (1508–1588), the nobleman, lawyer, and poet who hailed from Fruili, one of the most economically deprived and war-ravaged of Venice's colonies, and who stated that "In Venice, all are foreigners who are not Venetians," thus suggesting something of the lines of social exclusion that play a part in the world of *Othello*.[26] As Natalie Rothman notes about the differences between the two representations of Venice:

> Whereas Frangipane lumped all non-Venetians together, Coryat instead emphasized the diversity and multiplicity of clearly demarcated and highly organized 'nations' in the Venetian metropolis, each self-conscious of its difference from all the others. Coryat's depiction rendered Venice as a welcoming and receptive hub, where subjects hailing from far-flung places did not simply find their place but gave the city its unique character. Frangipane's Venice was a lightning rod for republican unity and civic virtue; Coryat's Venice was a beacon of tolerance in an internally segmented structure.[27]

---

[25] Kate Lowe, "Black Gondoliers and Other Black Africans in Renaissance Venice," *Renaissance Quarterly*, 66.2 (2013): 412–452. Other well-known paintings of the period depicting black gondoliers as part of the social landscape include Vittore Carpaccio's *Hunting on the Lagoon* (1490), and Gentile Bellini's *Miracle of the True Cross at the Bridge of S. Lorenzo* (1500). See also Robert Smith, "In Search of Carpaccio's African Gondolier," *Italian Studies*, 34 (1979), 45–59, and Peter Mark, "Africans in Venetian Renaissance Painting," *Renaissance 2. A Journal of Afro-American Studies*, 4 (1975): 7–11.

[26] Quoted in E. Natalie Rothman, *Brokering Empire: Trans-Imperial Subjects Between Venice and Istanbul* (Ithaca: Cornell University Press, 2012), 1.

[27] Rothman, 2.

Brabantio's patrician revulsion at the thought of Othello's marriage to his daughter in *Othello* act 1, scene 1 echoes something of Frangipane's sense of the city, as does Iago's cynical urbaneness. The role-playing that we find depicted in Iago's light-hearted banter with Desdemona about the different types of women in 2.1, and his later darker views on Venetian women which he uses to poison Othello's mind ("I know our country disposition well/ In Venice they do let God see the pranks/ They dare not show their husbands"), may be taken as a negative corollary of this same urbaneness. We cannot lose sight of the fact that Iago's apparent urbaneness in these and other interactions provides a very thin veneer over his chauvinism, which the audience sees directly through his various soliloquies. None of the Venetian men in the play are entirely exempt from this streak of chauvinism, as we shall see in a moment.

Rothman goes on to demonstrate how many colonial subjects sojourned in Venice from the 1550s to the 1700s and the ways in which their status was mediated by competing hierarchies of wealth, gender, age, and juridical standing. Rothman's *Brokering Empire* teems with cultural ethnicities and social functions similar to what we find in Coryat's description of the piazza: Jewish and Arab brokers, Armenian court translators, Ottoman ambassadors, and a plethora of Venetian commercial and political elites. And as she adroitly shows, the composite households of commercial brokers acted as switchboards of interchange between "locals" and "foreigners" that provided opportunities both for the ongoing recalibration of these two categories and for the insertion of various ethnicities into the complex multicultural cosmopolitan mix that was Venice. She suggests that it is best to think of Venice in the sixteenth and seventeenth centuries as a trans-imperial city that allowed people of different racial and cultural backgrounds to straddle and help broker "linguistic, religious, and geopolitical boundaries across Venetian and Ottoman imperial domains."[28] To see Othello as a trans-imperial subject is to recognize the degree to which his presence in the play signals a set of relations that, while centered on his race, also disclose the complex calibration of the dialectic between hierarchy and openness that has always informed cosmopolitan contexts to this day.

The world depicted in *Othello* illustrates only minimal aspects of cosmopolitan multiculturalism, mainly through the variety of backgrounds attributed to the central characters in the play. But we might also argue for a sense of cosmopolitan ethical humanism in the scene before

[28] Rothman, 11.

the Venetian senate, where Brabantio accuses Othello of witchcraft in winning his daughter and the claim is refuted through the judicial process rooted in the weighing up of stories. It is in this sense that we must take Desdemona's "I saw Othello's visage in his mind" and the Duke's "And, noble signior,/ If virtue no delighted beauty lack,/ Your son-in-law is far more fair than black."[29] The obvious racial coding of the two statements provides a hint of the coupling of evil with dark skin color that Iago, Roderigo, and Brabantio put in circulation early in the play, but which Desdemona and the Duke are here both trying to disavow. That the Duke's remark may be for purely pragmatic reasons (they do want their greatest military general to go and fight the Turks) must not becloud the fact that both statements are also meant by Shakespeare to highlight the perception of Othello's similarity to his interlocutors, at least in the sense that a person's worth cannot be judged merely from looking at the color of his or her skin. Given that the process of Othello's descent into barbarism is also designed to elicit pity and fear, what Shakespeare achieves for the Elizabethan audience is at once a confirmation of their most atavistic racist stereotypes (of black men and "turning Turk") and also an invitation to investigate the nature of these stereotypes and concomitantly of evil. Since Shakespeare transcribes evil onto the white character of Iago and since what might readily have been confirmation of Othello's barbarism is equally attributable to naivety and deception, the standard distribution of blame and censure along color lines (black equals evil, white equals good) is disrupted in the play, forcing a reexamination of the means by which the thoughtless judgment of others is arrived at. Even though in reflecting the world of sixteenth-century Venice *Othello* encapsulates some features of multiculturalism, it is in the contradictory status assigned to its vision of ethical humanism that the play suggests some salience for our own present-day debates on cosmopolitanism.

Othello and the "Fact of Blackness"

At the heart of the contradictions in the play's cosmopolitanism is the depiction of the Venetians' response to what Virginia Mason Vaughan has termed the "chromatic sign" of Othello's difference, namely, his blackness.[30] Every character in the play is obliged to respond to this inescapable social fact, including Othello himself. While in the opening scene it is behind his back that all mentions of blackness and its presumed

---

[29] Shakespeare, *Othello*, 1.3.253 and 1.3.289–291.   [30] Vaughan, *Othello: A Contextual History*, 51.

negative attributions are made, the sense of disdain that they carry ("thick-lips," "old black ram," "devil," "lascivious," "barbary horse," etc.) are carried over into the deliberations before the Senate in 1.3. These are set against the more positive views about him by the Duke and Desdemona, as we have already noted. However, what is surprising is Othello's almost studied lack of response to the interpellation of his blackness in either positive or negative terms throughout act 1. He already shows hints of this apparent non-response in 1.2 when Brabantio's search team finally finds him on that raucous opening night. Othello had earlier been met by another search team led by Cassio, one of the three dispatched from the signiory in their desperation to find him so they could give him his commission for Cyprus. The very first thing that Brabantio says when he claps eyes on Othello is "Down with him, thief," upon which both sides draw their swords.[31] Brabantio continues to cast even worse aspersions on Othello by accusing him of enchanting Desdemona and binding her in chains of magic. He asks how his daughter could have run to "the sooty [black] bosom/ Of such a thing as thou? To fear, not delight," further adding that Othello is "a practiser/ Of arts inhibited and out of warrant."[32] Since Othello has indeed married Brabantio's daughter without her father's knowledge, it is perhaps not surprising that he does not respond directly to these accusations or insults but rather tries to defuse Brabantio's anger and the obvious threat of violent conflict between the two search parties: "Keep up your bright swords, for the dew will rust them./ Good signior, you shall more command with years/ Than with your weapons."[33] If at the heart of Brabantio's accusations is the idea that Othello must have deployed magical means to engender irrational romantic choices in Desdemona against what he took to be her natural disposition, it is also evident that Othello does not react to this particular interpellation of him as a black man, but only responds with poise and self-restraint to what appears to the audience as a blatant racially charged provocation.

Brabantio's negative interpellation of Othello's blackness continues when they arrive before the Senate and, even though he does not directly use the epithet "black" in laying out his accusations before the Duke, its earlier association with supernatural activity ensures that the word hangs in the air:

> She is abused, stolen from me and corrupted
> By spells and medicines bought of mountebanks,

---

[31] Shakespeare, *Othello*, 1.2.59.   [32] Shakespeare, *Othello*, 1.2.70–71, 78–79.
[33] Shakespeare, *Othello*, 1.2.59–61.

For nature so preposterously to err
Being not deficient, blind, or lame of sense
Sans witchcraft could not.[34]

And yet again there is no direct response to this from Othello. In fact, the eloquent story he tells of how he won Desdemona's love is significant for appealing to everyone's natural disposition to sympathize with a tale of woe and tribulation. It scrupulously disconfirms any idea at all of blackness as attached to his adventures:

Her father loved me, oft invited me,
Still questioned me the story of my life
From year to year – the battles, sieges, fortunes
That I have passed.
I ran it through, even from my boyish days
To th'very moment that he bade me tell it,
Wherein I spake of most disastrous chances,
Of moving accidents by flood and field,
Of hair-breadth scapes i'th'imminent deadly
breach,
Of being taken by the insolent foe
And sold to slavery; of my redemption thence
And portance in my travailous history;
Wherein of antres vast and deserts idle,
Rough quarries, rocks and hills whose heads touch
heaven
It was my hint to speak – such was my process –
And of the cannibals that each other eat,
The Anthropophagi, and men whose heads
Do grow beneath their shoulders.[35]

Beyond the evidence of his extraordinary storytelling powers is the fact that Othello is here also divulging important information about his life course up to the point of this telling. And yet none of the events he describes are exclusively within the realm of experience of black men. The information about the landscapes he has traversed since childhood indicates not only a life of precarity and "travailous history", but also his passage through different topographies. Slavery, the "antres vast," (large caves) "deserts idle," cannibals, and Anthropophagi are added to "accidents by flood and field" and fierce deeds of battle to define various *counter-social* topographies, or spaces actively designed to destroy society and its social relations. The spaces that Othello has been obliged to traverse are certainly

---

[34] Shakespeare, *Othello*, 1.3.61–65.　　[35] Shakespeare, *Othello*, 1.3.129–146.

arduous but they do not necessarily prove his blackness. The life course he sets out coincides with the life cycle that Kate Lowe describes for black slaves that ended up in Venice, many of whom became mercenaries either in private militias or in those of the Venetian state. However, since slavery during the Renaissance period was not limited to black people but also encompassed white Europeans, Othello's story has a double edge to it; on the one hand, it signals a default understanding of the fate of blackness, but on the other it shows how that fate might happen to anyone, irrespective of their race. In 1554, for instance, as Robert C. Davies informs us in *Christian Slaves, Muslim Masters*, a raid of the southern Italian town of Vieste captured 6,000 white people who were then taken as slaves to North Africa. An Algerian raid of the Bay of Naples took another 7,000 in the same year, driving the price of slaves so low that it was said that a Christian could be swapped "for an onion." Entire Adriatic coastal regions were depopulated for fear of Turkish slave raids, making Othello's story equally applicable to white Europeans as well as black Africans in the period.[36]

The mention of the Anthropophagi also orients Othello's account toward exoticism rather than specifically to blackness. The Anthropophagi were first written about by Herodotus in The *Histories* and by Pliny the Elder in *The History of the Natural World*, where they are described as one of several tribes that live near Scythia. Scythia was not in Africa; in classical antiquity it was a region thought to encompass Central Asia and parts of Eastern Europe along the Black Sea. This would place the Anthropophagi anywhere in the general area of Bulgaria, Georgia, Moldova, and even Russia on today's maps. The legend of the Anthropophagi being from Scythia was repeated in 1550 in Richard Sherry's *Very Fruitful Exposition*: "They say there be people not farre from Scithia, whyche of eatynge mans flesh, be called Anthropophagi, that is devourers of men." John Marston also mentions them in his *The Metamorphosis of Pigmalions Image and Certain Satyres* of 1598. And a year before *Othello's* first performance in 1603 or 1604, the Anthropophagi had also been attributed to "Brasilea" (i.e., South America) in Robert Broughton's *First Part of the Resolution of Religion*.[37] It is Richard Hakluyt who first places the Anthropophagi in Africa in his *Principal*

---

[36] Lowe, 412–452. On white slavery during the period, see Robert C. Davis, *Christian Slaves, Muslim Masters: White Slavery in the Mediterranean, The Barbary Coast, and Italy, 1500–1800* (London: Palgrave Macmillan, 2003).

[37] All these examples are given in the OED in the entry under Anthropophagi. www.oed.com/view/Entry/8472?redirectedFrom=anthropophagi#eid; last accessed Oct. 30, 2019. For an account the depiction of Anthrophagi and other monsters in maps and atlases in Shakespeare's time, see J. Milton French, "Othello among the Anthropophagi," *PMLA*, 49.3 (1934): 807–809.

Navigations, a source considered to have been directly relevant to Shakespeare's portrait, but it is clear from the overall cultural genealogy of the term that they were considered of variant vintage and the placeholder for exotic and strange lands. The exoticizing impulse is often extended to South America as well. In his 1982 Nobel acceptance speech, Gabriel García Márquez wryly notes an example of European travellers' penchant for exoticizing strange lands during the period, which he claims to have been something he drew upon for his own genre of magical realism:

> Antonio Pigafetta, a Florentine navigator who went with Magellan on the first voyage around the world, wrote, upon his passage through our southern lands of America, a strictly accurate account that nonetheless resembles a venture into fantasy. In it he recorded that he had seen hogs with navels on their haunches, clawless birds whose hens laid eggs on the backs of their mates, and others still, resembling tongueless pelicans, with beaks like spoons. He wrote of having seen a misbegotten creature with the head and ears of a mule, a camel's body, the legs of a deer and the whinny of a horse. He described how the first native encountered in Patagonia was confronted with a mirror, whereupon that impassioned giant lost his senses at the terror of his own image.[38]

The deadpan inflection of the words "strictly accurate" in Márquez's account, coupled with his nonchalant listing of what are evidently fantastical elements from Pigafetta's journal are stylistic devices that will by now be familiar to vast numbers of readers of his novels. Pigafetta's *The First Voyage Around the World, 1519–1522* was widely popular when it was first published in 1534 and purported, like many travelers' stories of that period, to provide a true account of the places he had visited.[39] If, for Shakespeare's audience, such accounts were meant to titillate the imagination with their exotic descriptions of strange places, we must recall that even in the twenty-first century there are some that still think Africans live in trees, so the appeal to exoticism seems to persist in certain quarters to this day. And yet in his speech before the Senate, Othello is not playing the race card, at least not in any explicit and unambiguous way.

Conventionally, Othello's reference to his redemption from slavery is interpreted as a dual reference to his freedom and his conversion to Christianity, but there are good grounds to suspect that it may also have been referring to his entry into Venice as a soldier-recruit attached to

---

[38] Gabriel García Márquez, Nobel Lecture, 8 December, 1982, in *Nobel Lectures: Literature 1981–1990*, ed. Sture Allén (Singapore: World Scientific Publishing Company, 1993), 11–14.

[39] Antonio Pigafetta, *The First Voyage Around the World, 1519–1522: An Account of Magellan's Expedition,* ed. Theodore J. Cachey, Jnr. (Toronto: Toronto University Press, 2007).

a particular military household. This would have been entirely consistent with how slaves were inserted into Venetian society as either servants or slaves, then trained to take on the primary profession of their masters, with the boundary between servant and slave often being blurred in their professionalization.[40] Entailed in Othello's identity as he describes it to the Duke and the senators, then, is that he has no geographical or cultural anchor to his being, except for what he derives from his understanding of the mores of Venice. This is somewhat contradicted for us later in the account he gives of the fateful handkerchief to Desdemona in 3.4, where he states that it was given to his mother by an Egyptian and that it had magic in it to subdue his father. But in his speech before the Senate, he seems to be implying that he is black only in appearance, but not through his provenance, life course, or even cultural orientation. He declares that:

> Rude am I in my speech
> And little blest with the soft phrase of peace,
> For since these arms of mine had seven years' pith
> Till now some nine moons wasted, they have used
> Their dearest action in the tented field.[41]

He is not only humblebragging about his eloquence by pretending his speech could be considered "rude," but also, through the phrase "till now some nine moons wasted," hinting at the fact that whatever he has absorbed in civil demeanor has been through the cultured life of Venice. Crucially, Othello is unlike any other Shakespearean tragic hero in not having an organic relationship to a kingdom or an empire (as is the case for Hamlet, King Lear, Macbeth, and Antony) or to a political class through whose interests his identity acquires its agonistic dimensions (in the case of Coriolanus). Unlike many conventional accounts of cultural minorities, in this narrative Othello has no collective culture to (re)turn to. This lack might explain why, in later describing his parents to Desdemona and how he was bequeathed the charmed handkerchief, he produces a story that is so redolent of magic and strangeness. His tale confirms the worst stereotypes about his "people," but it might also be taken as simply invoking the deeply personal pedigree of that material object, all the more significant given the absence of a collective culture. In other words, even in the story of the handkerchief, Othello is telling a private rather than a collective cultural story. The upshot of the tale he tells about the wooing of Desdemona before the Duke and senators is thus a refutation of the central premise of

---

[40] Lowe, 419–423.   [41] Shakespeare, *Othello*, 1.3.82–86.

the accusation made against him by Brabantio, that is, that he is black and therefore nefarious, and given to irrational and evil practices. Othello's acquiescence to a negative form of blackness comes not in the face of Brabantio's insults and aspersions, as we have just seen, but rather during the temptation scene with Iago, when his blackness is entangled in his mind with a form of civilizational deficit that is also compounded by his sense of affronted masculinity.

Othello's first acquiescence to a negative idea of his blackness comes after Iago insinuates that there is something odd in Desdemona not choosing the "many proposed matches/ Of her own clime, complexion and degree,/ Whereto we see, in all things, nature tends."[42] When Iago exits at the end of that exchange, Othello begins to itemize his own defects in a soliloquy, and it is in this itemization that he explicitly concedes to a form of blackness:

> Haply for I am black
> And have not those soft parts of conversation
> That chamberers have, or for I am declined
> Into the vale of years – yet that not much –
> She's gone, I am abused, and my relief
> Must be to loathe her.[43]

While there is no logical connection between "I am black"; not having the suaveness of what the Venetian "chamberers" have; and being much older than his new bride, the upshot of all these characteristics is that Othello now feels strongly that his identity as a black person marks an essential deficit. Even though his immediate reaction in this soliloquy is to loathe Desdemona, the deficit he is describing here is not the same as the moral deficit that Brabantio attributes to him in act 1. Here the question seems to be more that of his comparative lack of cultural knowhow and savoir faire, something that he assumes Iago has in abundance. This sense of lack stands in odd contrast to the pride he draws from his military achievements and his service to the state in earlier scenes.

Less than 100 lines later, the confusion in Othello's mind about his feelings toward Desdemona is declared in what some commentators have noted as a clear species of self-loathing:

> By the world,
> I think my wife be honest, and think she is not,
> I think thou art just, and think thou art not.

---

[42] Shakespeare, *Othello*, 3.3.233–235.   [43] Shakespeare, *Othello*, 3.3.267–272.

> I'll have some proof. Her name, that was as fresh
> As Dian's visage, is now begrimed and black
> As my own face. If there be cords or knives,
> Poison, or fire, or suffocating streams,
> I'll not endure it. Would I were satisfied![44]

As we saw from our discussion of Fanon's "The Fact of Blackness" in the Introduction colonial racial ideology distorts the schema of the black body. The distortions are entailed in the saturation of the social sphere with negative stereotypes of blackness ("Look mama, a negro") as being synonymous with lying, excessive sexuality, violence, and overall backwardness. Othello's reference to his face being "begrimed and black" is a meta-theatrical reference to the tradition of blackface that white performers of his character used until well into the nineteenth century, but it also refers to a sense of the disruption of his bodily schema, as Fanon describes it.

There are, however, a number of significant differences between what Fanon describes and what we see in *Othello*. For as we have already seen, when the negative attributions of blackness are hurled in his face in act I he scrupulously refuses to respond to their central premise of barbarism and civilizational deficit. His sense of being remains whole and undisturbed. The problem emerges when he begins to compare himself to others, first to younger Venetian men and then to Desdemona herself. It is in the vise-like grip of these comparisons, which are first suggested by Iago but that Othello then takes upon himself, that he acquiesces to the interpellation of his blackness as a form of deficit. After this acquiescence, the admission of a cultural lack is progressively replaced by forms of irrational thinking and behavior that eventually confirm the original accusations of barbarism hurled by Brabantio to his face and whispered behind his back by Iago and Roderigo. Even if the admission of cultural lack is not the same as the admission of barbarism, the first is embraced as a firm self-generated belief while the second – though originally refuted through his story-telling – is enacted in the choices he makes when his masculinity is threatened. His surrender to an unruly affective economy eventually undoes all that he values and treasures, including his true wife and his good name.

Modularity and the Question of Value

> He [Iago] is an amateur of tragedy in real life; and instead of
> employing his invention on imaginary characters, or long-forgotten

---

[44] Shakespeare, *Othello*, 3.3.386–394.

incidents, he takes the bolder and more desperate course of getting up his plot at home, casts the principal parts among his nearest friends and connexions, and rehearses it in downright earnest, with steady nerves and unabated resolution.[45]

Ever since William Hazlitt made these remarks about Iago in 1817, it has become conventional to interpret him as a surrogate dramaturge, with a superb grasp of human nature and a meta-theatrical understanding of how to manipulate others. To "turn Othello Turk" and flip him from elegance and eloquence to barbarism and violence, Iago deploys a series of tightly interconnected devices of both a practical and rhetorical nature. From a formalist perspective, the devices Iago deploys may be defined in terms of a reiterated structure by which he converts all elements at his disposal to practical use in his scheming, including chance and happenstance as well as the psychological orientations of the other characters he interacts with. This modular reiteration serves to foreclose choice not just for Othello but also for Roderigo, Emilia, and Cassio. This is not to suggest that the other characters do not exercise choice, but that their exercise of choice is so seriously overdetermined by the modular structure within which they operate, that the choices are, in effect, contaminated in the very processes of making them. In stating this claim, I am aware that I run the risk of placing the exercise of choice in *Othello* too firmly in the vicinity of a brute determinism. However, as I hope to show, even if Iago's grip of the action does suggest the god-like manipulativeness of a spider, it is the dialectical interplay between the events he instigates and the psychological orientations of the other characters that intermesh to inflect the action toward tragedy. The interplay is not between determinism and free will, but between determinism and contingency. Contingent facts such as Emilia's attempt to finally impress her husband by stealing her mistress's handkerchief and giving it to him; Cassio's irascibility when drunk; Desdemona's determination in pursuing a suit of forgiveness for Cassio; and Roderigo's gullibility all play a part in solidifying circumstances that make things go one way rather than another. However, Othello does not recognize contingency as such from early on. Until the very end, he sees what are effectively contingent facts as purely monological and exclusively confirming what Iago insinuates they are. It is only Iago that seems to realize the polyvalent potential of contingent facts, and so he is able to manipulate everybody else accordingly. The foreclosure of ethical choice also marks the failure of *Othello's* overall vision of an incipient ethical

---

[45] William Hazlitt, *Characters of Shakespeare's Plays* (Boston: Wells and Lilly, 1818), 72.

humanism, since by the end it is clear that to be Venetian or non-Venetian entails essential differences that implicate both race and gender that cannot be attenuated either through interaction or circumstance. What ethical humanism we can find is instituted in the sharp reversal of fortunes and the blurring of the clear-cut distinctions between good and evil.

The word "module," from which the cognate forms "modular" and "modularity" are derived, has a number of definitions, four of which are directly pertinent to interpreting Iago's manipulations. As the OED tells us, the term "module" means among other things: a) "a mere image or counterfeit," that is to say, a false image or representation; b) a model of representation or perfect exemplar of something else; c) "a regularly formulated plan or scheme of government"; and d) "a physical representation or model (usually on a small scale), of a material object" or abstract idea. The first two items bear poetic or rhetorical implications and are often in dialectical relationship to each other, while the third relates to political theory. The fourth definition derives primarily from architecture and is synonymous with the concept of typology. Typology in itself implies the repetition of specific structural features that define recognizable aspects of a building and its component parts; a city block; or even an entire neighborhood.[46] Thus, in architecture, the module or typology of a bedroom is considered to be different from that of a kitchen, with a set of minimal features providing the means to distinguish the one from the other. Iago's modularity integrates features of all four definitions: it incorporates the repetition of a structure of actions and of government (in the sense of management and control), and is also about the rhetorical orchestration of false arguments that prop up deceptive images and representations. As Patricia Parker points out, there is a comparative paucity of interest in the criticism of *Othello* about "Shakespeare's extensive play on the terms of language and discourse, and on rhetoric as *a structure as well as trope*," that is to say, criticism rarely gets beyond what the characters say and the ways in which they say it.[47] Parker adroitly shows, for example,

---

[46] Colin Burrow pairs the word "model" (from module, as per the OED) to *exemplum* and *paradeigma*, tracking in them the central problem of *imitatio*, not between authors and things, but in the imitation between authors. The relation between model and authorship obviously has application to Shakespeare's Iago, even though in his case the authorship is not from one model to another, but rather from a conception of control that inhabits his own mind. His authorship is a species of pure fiction, since the imitative practice on which it depends has nothing to do with reality but is strictly the product of his fevered and hyper-inventive imagination. See Colin Burrow, *Imitating Authors: Plato to Futurity* (Oxford: Oxford University Press, 2019), especially pages 18–19, 61, and 311–334.
[47] Patricia Parker, *Literary Fat Ladies: Rhetoric, Gender, Property* (London: Routledge, 1988), 77; emphasis added.

that what appears in the Folio as "close dilations, working from the heart,/ that passion cannot rule" ramifies within *Othello* as an intricate relationship between its close echo of "delations." The two proximate homonyms imply amplification, accusation, and delay, and generate a "semantic crossroads or freighted term" that has an impact across several levels of the action.[48] The rhetorical semantic crossroads signaled by dilations/delations and the various other rhetorical devices Parker identifies are the dialectical half of Iago's modular orchestration of the advice and arguments that he claims are "probal to thinking." The other half is composed of invocations of false images and representations, the repetition of specific scene-setting procedures, and the generation of government, all of which we shall attend to presently.

Other instances of Shakespeare's use of module includes King John's declaration to the Bastard – "And then all this thou seest is but a clod/ And module of confounded royalty" – which illustrates Shakespeare's use of the word as false representation, while Bertram's invitation to the Second Lord Dumain in *All's Well That Ends Well* – "Come, bring forth this counterfeit module, he has deceived me like a double-meaning prophesier" – illustrates its usage as a stand-in for a double-meaning representation or image.[49] In *The Tempest*, the schemes that Prospero sets up to control Miranda and Ferdinand; the shipwrecked crew from Milan; Ariel; Caliban; and the island in general are modules of both self-governance and the governance of nature. The efficacy of Prospero's power is firmly entangled with his capacity for creating false images and dreamlike sequences in the minds of those whose behavior he attempts to regulate. Iago delivers nine soliloquies throughout the play. As Harry Berger notes, he seasons his first four soliloquies with: "a generous salting of explanations, progress reports, psychological profiles of his victims, plot projections, and even little demonstrations of hands-on plot cookery. And all the while he coaxes, cajoles, confides, confesses, gloats, and sneers."[50]

---

[48] Patricia Parker, "Shakespeare and Rhetoric: "dilation" and "delation" in *Othello*," Patricia Parker and Geoffrey Hartman, eds., (London: Routledge, 1993), 56. Parker has written extensively on the rhetorical devices in Shakespeare plays. See also her "Othello and Hamlet: Dilation, Spying, and the 'Secret Place' of Woman," *Representations*, 44 (1993): 60–95; "Dilation and Inflation: *All's Well That Ends Well, Troilus and Cressida*, and Shakespearean Increase," *Shakespeare from the Margins: Language, Culture, Context* (Chicago: Chicago University Press, 1996), and *Literary Fat Ladies: Rhetoric, Gender, Property* (London: Routledge, 1988). Joel Altman's *The Improbability of Othello: Rhetorical Anthropology and Shakespearean Selfhood* (Chicago: Chicago University Press, 2010) also has highly suggestive readings of the rhetorical devices in the play and provides parallels to Parker's work on the subject.

[49] Shakespeare, *King John*, 5.7.57–58 and *All's Well That Ends Well*, 4.3.99–103, respectively.

[50] Harry Berger, Jr., *A Fury in Words* (New York: Fordham University Press, 2013), 184.

The various dramaturgical devices that Berger lists here provide significant insights into the shaping of Iago's modularity. Throughout the play, or at least until the failed plot to assassinate Cassio in act 4, scene 2, Iago's plans unfold through systematically defined devices of scene-setting and interpretation. As a general rule, he always announces what he is going to do beforehand (the scene-setting) either directly to the audience or to a character onstage, then predicts what the outcomes of what he is going to do will be; and finally, in the most uncanny conflation of roles, he steps forward to interpret the scene he has so cleverly set up.

Iago's adroitness at scene-setting starts from the very first scene of the play. After swearing his hatred for Othello and persuading Roderigo that he will procure him Desdemona's favor, Iago turns to the business of rousing Brabantio to anger and triggering a cacophonous sequel. He does this with the first of many injunctions throughout the play to the gullible Roderigo:

> Call up her father,
> Rouse him, make after him, poison his delight,
> Proclaim him in the streets, incense her kinsmen,
> And, though he in a fertile climate dwell,
> Plague him with flies! Though that his joy be joy
> Yet throw such changes of vexation on't
> As it may lose some color.
> . . .
> Do, like timorous accent and dire yell
> As when by night and negligence the fire
> Is spied in populous cities.[51]

Poison, incensement, plague, changes of vexation, and the "timorous accent and dire yell" are all terms to escalate panic, items that he will repeat to greater success in Cyprus. At this early stage, the rousing of Brabantio does not appear to be part of an explicitly laid-out plan, or at least not one that Iago makes us aware of beforehand, although the play opens mid-conversation with Iago and Roderigo walking outside Brabantio's mansion, so presumably it was their destination all along. The note to 1.1 provided by E. A. J. Honingmann says, "Location: a street outside Brabantio's house in Venice. Shakespeare is vague about many details . . . we have to piece them together. Iago and Roderigo, it seems, have been arguing for some time. It is night."[52] When Iago tells Brabantio to "Arise, arise,/ Awake the snorting citizens with the bell" he does so by painting a picture of Othello "the black ram" lying on top of

---

[51] Shakespeare, *Othello*, 1.1.67–72, 74–76.   [52] E. A. J. Honingmann, Shakespeare, *Othello*, 119.

Desdemona, "tupping [Brabantio's] white ewe" and warns him that the devil might make him a grandsire; his design is clearly to alarm the older man and immediately set him to a particular course of action.[53]

While these modules of false images have the desired effect of arousing the parental anxiety Brabantio has for his daughter, this is quickly coupled to the terror of miscegenation that the pornographic and animalistic image of a black ram on a white ewe vividly evokes both in Brabantio's mind and in that of the audience. Once Brabantio orders the bells struck loudly, Iago has effectively ceded the labor of sowing panic and escalating chaos to Brabantio himself. He then proceeds to tactfully disentangle himself from the foreground of events. Bidding farewell to Roderigo on the grounds that it is not wise for him to be shown explicitly against Othello, he rapidly makes his exit. This first instalment of scene-setting proves to be only the first stage of a larger modular sequence, for at the start of the next scene, Iago delivers what is the second manipulative instalment, this time by reporting to Othello the aspersions that Roderigo has cast on Othello's name as well as Brabantio's designs on Othello's reputation:

> Nay, but he prated
> And spoke such scurvy and provoking terms
> Against your honour,
> That the little godliness I have
> I did full hard forbear him. But I pray, sir,
> Are you fast married? Be assured of this,
> That the magnifico is much beloved
> And hath in effect a voice potential
> As double as the duke's: he will divorce you
> Or put upon you what restraint or grievance
> The law, with all his might to enforce it on,
> Will give him cable.[54]

Iago deploys various techniques of fearmongering here that for now are unsuccessful, but will later have more effectiveness when he repeats them in Cyprus. He tells Othello of dark aspersions being cast on his good name, insinuates his love for him in his claim of restraint at the provocation that he felt on hearing Roderigo's insults, and then switches suddenly to the threat to Othello's happiness posed by Brabantio's determination to dissolve the secretly contracted marriage between Othello and Desdemona. The switch from reporting Roderigo's aspersions to insinuating Brabantio's threats is itself a form of discursive escalation, since it moves from the

---

[53] Shakespeare, *Othello*, 1.1.87, 88.   [54] Shakespeare, *Othello*, 1.2.7–17.

insults of an ordinary soldier to threats from a magnifico. But the fact that Iago insinuates the secrecy of Othello's marriage with a rhetorical question ("But I pray, sir,/ Are you fast married?") also means that he is subtly trying to instigate fear or at least anxiety in Othello about the security of his marriage. The reference to Brabantio's standing in society ("a voice potential/ As double as the duke's") compounds this by hinting that his reputation might not be enough to withstand the accusations of such a high-ranking member of Venetian society. Othello's response, "Let him do his spite;/ My services, which I have done the signiory,/ Shall out-tongue his complaints," proves adequate for the time being, yet also reveals him to be not fully cognizant of the terror of miscegenation that his marriage to Desdemona has aroused in other members of the society, emblematized in a species of superb dramatic irony, of course, by Iago, who stands right before him.

We already see at play in these early stages the essential features of Iago's modularity. These involve setting a scene and managing its possible outcomes by inciting the predictable psychological motivations of his interlocutors. It also involves the production of false but potent images that, coupled with the other elements of a scene, demarcate certain moral boundaries and thus elicit identification with one side or other of what such an image implies. Iago's eliciting of identification through the deployment of particular images is key to his modularity, and comes to ramify strongly on how he gets Othello to finally switch from suave speechifier to incoherent barbarian. After sowing the scene of chaos and confusion in front of Brabantio's mansion, Iago exits the stage for purely pragmatic reasons, but, in later modules, he will only withdraw to a different part of the stage, so as to be able to play the deadly observer of others' interactions. The element of stepping forward to interpret the scene that he has set in the scene with Brabantio is also only embryonic in act 1, but takes its full form after Cassio's drunken quarrel in Cyprus. If, in these early stages, the elements of Iago's method are not fully worked out, they are going to develop to devastating effect in later instalments of his modularity.

After act 1, the play moves to Cyprus where Othello is to hold his commission. The orchestration of the drunken brawl scene in Cyprus that takes place on the Venetians' first night in Cyprus is the second instalment of Iago's modularity and much more complex in its set-up. Iago provides the audience with a prologue to what he proposes to do at the end of 1.3 but at this point whatever plans he has are laid out only in general terms:

> Cassio's a proper man: let me see now,
> To get his place, and to plume up my will

In double knavery. How? How? Let's see:
After some time to abuse Othello's ear
That he is too familiar with his wife.
He hath a person and a smooth dispose
To be suspected, framed to make women false.
The Moor is of a free and open nature
That thinks men honest that but seem to be so,
And will as tenderly be led by th' nose
As asses are.
I have't, it is engendered! Hell and night
Must bring this monstrous birth to the world's light.[55]

The progression from "let me see now" and "How? How? Let's see" to
"I have't, it is engendered" is not just the process of making up his
mind, but the means by which he attempts to elicit the audience as
interlocutory coconspirators. The elicitation of the audience into particular interlocutory positions through soliloquy is a meta-theatrical
device common in Shakespeare and ranges from an invitation to sympathize with the speaker's anguished soul (as with Hamlet, Pericles,
Enobarbus, Lear, and Richard II); to identifying the constraints placed
upon the expression of the character's deepest aspirations (female characters in disguise in all the romantic comedies for example); to the
spitting out of vivid diatribes against the social order (Shylock, Aaron,
and Edmund).

On news of the "certain perdition of the Turkish fleet," Othello declares
a night of celebration in commemoration of both their destruction and his
nuptials. Ominously, as it later turns out, each man is encouraged to
participate in "what sport and revels his addictions lead him." Cassio's
weakness is alcohol, and this inspires Iago to plan his demise in greater
detail:

If I can fasten but one cup upon him,
With that which he hath drunk tonight already
He'll be as full of quarrel and offence
As my young mistress' dog. Now my sick fool, Roderigo,
Whom love had turned almost the wrong side out,
To Desdemona hath tonight caroused
Potations pottle-deep, and he's to watch.
Three else of Cyprus, noble swelling spirits
That hold their honours in a wary distance,

---

[55] Shakespeare, *Othello*, 1.3.393–403.

The very elements of this warlike isle,
Have I tonight flustered with flowing cups,
And the watch too. Now 'mongst this flock of drunkards
Am I to put our Cassio in some action
That may offend the isle.[56]

The orchestration of Cassio's drunkenness requires Iago to consider the interplay of various characters and contingent factors, including that of "sick fool, Roderigo," who has attempted to drown his unrequited love for Desdemona in drink, and the three noblemen of Cyprus, whom Iago has already "flustered with flowing cups." Among this "flock of drunkards" he then proposes to release Cassio, who will by then be inebriated enough to be easily provoked by Roderigo. However, finally achieving the objective of abusing Othello's ear and depreciating Cassio's stock in Othello's eyes requires corralling the unwitting Emilia, his wife and Desdemona's servant, to persuade Desdemona to listen to Cassio's suit when it comes, and, by further orchestration, to arouse Othello's suspicions regarding that suit once it eventually reaches him through Desdemona.

After the drunken brawl that engulfs not only Cassio and Roderigo but also Montano and the other lords from Venice, Iago instigates the loud ringing of the bells, which then rouse Othello to the battlements. Othello's anger is palpable at this disturbance of his and the public's peace:

Why, how now, ho? From whence ariseth this?
Are we turned Turks? And to ourselves do that
Which heaven hath forbid the Ottomites?
For Christian shame, put by this barbarous brawl;
He that stirs next, to carve for his own rage,
Holds his soul light: he dies upon his motion.[57]

This provides the cue for Iago to step forward to provide an interpretation of the scene he had announced he was going to set up and which he has adroitly brought to fruition through the manipulation of contingent details of revelry, drink, and the disputatiousness of affronted masculinity. He begins his interpretation to Othello first by hedging, "I do not know, friends all, but now, even now," but then moves progressively, via various forms of coy circumlocution, to pin the blame for the commotion firmly on Cassio:

Touch me not so near.
I had rather have this tongue cut from my mouth

---

[56] Shakespeare, *Othello*, 2.3.45–58.   [57] Shakespeare, *Othello*, 2.3.165–170.

Than it should do offence to Michael Cassio,
Yet I persuade myself to speak the truth
Shall nothing wrong him.[58]

The movement from scene-setting to interpretation in this modular sequence allows Iago to conflate two aspects of his dramaturgy that had, up to this point, remained separate; this time, unlike in the previous instance of modularity, he practically closes the circuit of playwright, actor, audience/observer, and critic/interpreter, and fully insinuates his power over the unfolding of future events.

The scene in 4.1 where Iago sets Othello up to eavesdrop on his conversation with Cassio as he purports to extract an admission about the handkerchief, is a miniaturized version of the modularity we have seen thus far. The lead-up to what amounts to a play-within-a-play orchestrated by Iago, is slow and laborious, but crucially involves the planting in Othello's mind not only that Desdemona must be more attracted to the darlings of her own nation, but that she has gone ahead and had her way with Cassio, with the handkerchief only providing the final confirmation. Othello is by this time completely apoplectic and falls into a fit. Coincidentally, Cassio walks onstage at this point and tries to revive him but is prevented by Iago on the excuse that The lethargy must have his quiet course, If not, he foams at the mouth, and by and by Breaks out to savage madness.[59]

As Othello stirs, Iago shoos Cassio away and delivers the instructions that will convert Othello from eavesdropper and observer to assumed interpreter/critic:

Stand you a while apart,
Confine yourself but in a patient list.
Whilst you were here o'erwhelmed with your grief
– A passion most unsuiting such a man –
Cassio came hither. I shifted him away
And laid good 'scuse upon your ecstasy,
Bade him anon return and here speak with me,
The which he promised. Do but encave yourself
And mark the fleers, the gibes and notable scorns
That dwell in every region of his face;
For I will make him tell the tale anew
Where, how, how oft, how long ago, and when
He hath and is again to cope your wife.

---

[58] Shakespeare, *Othello*, 2.3.217–221. [59] Shakespeare, *Othello*, 4.1.53–55.

> I say, but mark his gesture; marry, patience,
> Or I shall say you're all in all in spleen
> And nothing of a man.[60]

There are several aspects to this instruction. Since Othello is not going to be privy to the words that Iago and Cassio will exchange, he is being instructed to note the fleers (sneers), gibes (insults and taunts), and scornful looks that will flit across Cassio's face. It is a mark of Othello's naivety that it does not occur to him to wonder how he might additionally interpret the gestures and features on Iago's face. But Iago's instruction to Othello involves a number of assumptions. It requires Othello to have some certainty, not only to recognize the expressions on Cassio's face, but also to automatically correlate them to specific meanings (scorn, confession, etc.). This species of mind-reading from the gestures on another's face discursively inverts Desdemona's claim, before the Duke and senators, of seeing Othello's visage in his mind; in her case, it is his eloquent stories which corroborate the contents of that mind and disconfirm stereotypes of blackness before her eyes. But it also calls to mind King Duncan's wry warning in *Macbeth* that "There's no art/ To find the mind's construction in the face."[61] The irony in Duncan's case is, of course, that he failed to see that Macbeth was plotting on his very life when he agreed to spend a night at his castle.

Because he has already successfully convinced Othello that his wife slept with Cassio, Othello's mind is made-up and all that he requires further is ocular proof of the handkerchief supposedly passed from Desdemona to Cassio as a token of their adulterous love. Bianca is a courtesan who has a strong amorous interest in Cassio. Even though Cassio is not particularly inclined, he goes along with her ministrations as a way of stroking his own masculine ego. In their conversation, Iago gets Cassio to speculate on how much more successful his suit to Othello might have been had Bianca been pleading on his behalf. This draws laughter and "locker-room talk" from the hapless Cassio, all of which is observed by the watching Othello as providing confirmation of all his suspicions. Toward the end of the conversation between Iago and Cassio, Bianca walks onstage waving the accursed handkerchief and asks why Cassio wants its strawberry embroidery "taken out," or copied. This is the final straw for Othello.

Iago accomplishes several things with this adroit scene-setting and manipulation. First, he provides Othello with the ocular proof he had so

---

[60] Shakespeare, *Othello*, 4.1.75–89.   [61] Shakespeare, *Macbeth*, 1.4.13–14.

forcefully demanded ("Villain, be sure thou prove my love a whore,/ Be sure of it, give me ocular proof/Or by the worth of man's eternal soul/Thou hadst been better have been born a dog/Than answer my waked wrath!").[62] In the made-up story Iago tells earlier of Cassio's dream confessions, in which he purports the two of them to have lain together one night, Iago produces a carefully managed false module (image) that seems to Othello to confirm Cassio's innermost thoughts, so that, by the time of the eavesdropping scene, Othello believes that he already "knows" what Cassio must be thinking with regards to Desdemona.[63] It is this that gives him the misconception that he is able to read Cassio's deepest thoughts through his gestures and facial expressions. Iago has effectively activated the roles of playwright scene-setter, audience/observer, and critic/ interpreter, but this time has ceded the latter two roles to Othello. This discursively enframes what Othello hears and sees so as to create a mind-picture module that serves to confirm his suspicions of his wife. The framing also incorporates an interpellation of his blackness that Iago merely insinuates but Othello gives full expression to. As we will recall, this takes Othello in the opposite direction from his previous response to Brabantio's interpellation of his blackness, where he refused to answer to the obviously negative premises of the attributions. What Iago delivers is not a module in the first sense of a true image or representation, but in the second sense of falsehood, suggested in Bertram's remark in *All's Well That Ends Well*. By enframing the conversation he has with Cassio to Othello beforehand, Iago creates an indelible mind-picture that invites a form of moral judgment from Othello. This then allows Othello to persuade himself that Desdemona has comprehensively denigrated herself and deserves to die in order to prevent her leading other men to their destruction. This species of warped logic is the direct outcome of Iago's modularity in this scene.

By the end of the play, Othello struggles to put on display a different module of himself that he hopes will rectify what the Venetian senators see laid out before them. When he pleads to them, saying, "I pray you, in your letters,/When you shall these unlucky deeds relate/Speak of me as I am/ Nothing extenuate" he is effectively inviting them to ignore the evidence of their senses, that is, of the sordid facts that are amply in evidence of him having just strangled his wife.[64] In effect, he is asking them to disavow the evidence of epistemological certainty that had been the central aspect of his

---

[62] Shakespeare, *Othello*, 3.3.362–366   [63] Shakespeare, *Othello*, 3.3.416–428.
[64] Shakespeare, *Othello*, 5.2.338–340.

insistence on ocular proof. And so he proceeds, in what turns out to be futile desperation, to remind them of his service to the Venetian state and says that "in Aleppo once" when he encountered "a turbaned Turk" who "traduced the state," he grabbed the infidel and struck him thus, enacting in his own suicide the final conflation of the duality of civilized barbarian by which he has been defined in the play. What is effectively the failed attempt to replace a false module with a true one begs the question of what is a false image and what is a true one, given that the entire play has been devoted to demonstrating the ways in which false images are made to seem real by both characters. But what the last scene of the play illustrates, and what has already been amplified and modulated in various directions throughout the action of the play, is that cosmopolitanism is not just about images that pertain to otherness and strangers, but is also about the means by which modules or stereotypes produce forms of agreement both by those deploying them and, even more worryingly, by those against whom the stereotypes are deployed.

Conclusion: Social Identification and the Ethics of Cosmopolitanism

One fine Saturday afternoon in 2018, Ving Rhames was catching up on the sports news on ESPN in his home in Santa Monica, when he heard a sharp knock on the door. He opened it to find a couple of policemen with a police dog. A red dot was pointing at the center of his forehead. The police had been called by a neighbor from across the street who said she had seen a "big, black man" pacing about inside Rhames's house. The neighbor, a white woman, suspected that the man pacing might be a burglar. The policemen lowered their weapons when one of them recognized Rhames as a parent whose son played basketball against his own son's school. It was quickly established that they had made a mistake and, after apologizing profusely, the policemen went with Rhames to confront the neighbor. She completely denied lodging the complaint. Rhames, it must be noted, is a well-known actor whose credits include critically acclaimed performances in Quentin Tarantino's *Pulp Fiction* and Christopher McQuarrie's *Mission Impossible – Fallout,* among various others.[65]

---

[65] The case was widely reported in the media. See, for example, Travis M. Andrews, "Police held 'Mission Impossible' actor Ving Rhames at gunpoint for entering his own home," *Washington Post,* July 29 2018; www.washingtonpost.com/news/arts-and-entertainment/wp/2018/07/29/police-held-mission-impossible-actor-ving-rhames-at-gunpoint-for-entering-his-own-home/?noredirect=o n&utm_term=.baed6144a29e, last accessed Sept. 7, 2018.

The case of renowned Harvard Professor Henry Louis Gates, Jr. garnered even more publicity when it occurred. Gates had come back to his home in a highly salubrious part of Cambridge, Massachusetts to find to his frustration that the lock to his front door was jammed. He went to the back of the house instead and tried to find a way inside. Eventually, upon managing to enter, he was startled by a loud knock on the front door. He opened it to find a young police officer who demanded his identification papers. After handing in his Harvard card and driver's license, he was irritated by the policeman's request for him to provide actual proof that he owned the house in which he was standing. Gates lost his temper and exchanged some sharp words with the policeman, who promptly put him in handcuffs and marched him to the police station. It has to be noted that when this event occurred in 2009, "Skip" Gates was already sixty-six years old, graying, and after a number of hip surgeries, walked with a cane at all times.[66] It is almost inconceivable that this would have happened to him had he not been black.

Stories such as these can be multiplied many times and do not occur only in the United States or indeed to black people as highly placed as Rhames and Gates, but routinely to blacks of all classes and backgrounds in some of the most cosmopolitan places in the Western world. Sometimes a black person's encounter with the police leads to tragic death, something that has become the subject of many social media discussions and the focus of the Black Lives Matter movement. One only has to recall the terrible image of a white policeman with his knee on the neck of the dying George Floyd on May 25 2020, in Minneapolis, to get a garish replication of the terrible effects of anti-black violence at the hands of law enforcement agencies in America.[67] The civil demonstrations in response to that terrible image which exploded in America and across the world testify to the visceral shock that many people felt toward the event. But what is it that allows people such as Ving Rhames and Skip Gates to be simultaneously some of the most recognizable black personages in academic and popular culture and yet, at the same time, mistaken for criminals, and sometimes accused by their own neighbors? The default answer to this question

---

[66] For a broad account of Gates's arrest and what happened in its aftermath, see https://en .wikipedia.org/wiki/Henry_Louis_Gates_arrest_controversy, last accessed Sept. 7, 2018.

[67] For a list of names of black people that have died as a consequence of police brutality in the USA alone, dating back to 2014, see https://interactive.aljazeera.com/aje/2020/know-their-names/index .html; last accessed June 26, 2020. The list would be much more extensive if it was to include names of such victims in the United Kingdom, France, Italy, China, and elsewhere where anti-black racism at the hands of the police is commonplace.

("these are racist societies, duh") is the least satisfactory, mainly because it completely sidesteps a number of complications pertaining to the fact that some of the people making these racist accusations are surrounded by diversity and would most likely even identify as cosmopolitan. This contradiction, however, is at the heart of cosmopolitanism itself. It is not that these neighbors of Ving Rhames or Skip Gates retained some racial prejudice toward them *despite* their cosmopolitanism; rather, insofar as cosmopolitanism is based upon the simultaneous proximity to and distance from the racial Other, their prejudice may be largely *because* of their cosmopolitanism. There exists the sheet-wearing, cross-burning segment of the American population, which may very well fuel its supremacist regime of intolerance through limited or no experience with black people, but for those living in racially diverse locations, the prejudices that they carry are more often subconscious, and thrive through good intentions and the illusion of proximity to or familiarity with people of all races.

In the cases of both Rhames and Gates, their presence in the media serves to illustrate the point perfectly: being often on movie and television screens allows the larger society a controlled outlet through which to safely identify with blackness without the added trouble of actually interacting with real black people and having to know them in any social proximity. There are many examples of this outside of film and academia. Cosmopolitans worldwide enjoy musical genres such as hip hop, salsa, and zumba, and in fact may participate in the production, language, sartorial aesthetic, and dance forms of these now global genres, without having to make any serious attempt at socializing, on a day-to-day basis, with the communities that originated them. With the rise of identity politics, and indeed identity capitalism, the adoption of black and minority styles can also lend nonracial bodies an air of "wokeness" or social currency, alleviating some of the guilt which is now increasingly associated with whiteness in certain circles. Wokeness is also often accomplished through expressions of ethical humanism, such as making charitable donations to various causes, a phenomenon especially evident around Christmas, when there are many appeals to adopt an unfortunate child in some poorer part of the world, or donate to the cure of river blindness, or even simply to give up old clothes for the use of less fortunate people elsewhere in the world. These surges of charitable impulses must not be underestimated in their production of fellow-feeling; however, a charitable impulse does not cancel out the possibility of harboring harmful misconceptions about racial minorities. In the often segregated environments of many global cities, where racial minority neighborhoods are among the poorest and worst resourced, these forms of pity-charity can actually fortify the divide between benevolent patrons and their anonymous beneficiaries by effacing the agency, complexity, and heterogeneity of the latter. To put the matter somewhat formulaically then: the racial discourse of cosmopolitanism affirms the attractions of interracial equality and even racial mixing but also, at the same time, short-circuits the humanity of the racialized body and reduces it to a permanent state of being always-already known, of being interpellated as bearing a constitutive lack. This is the dynamic of the racial stereotype, as Fanon pointed out in *Black Skin, White Masks*.

In *Othello*, Brabantio, Roderigo, and Iago's pitching of negative epithets of blackness at Othello behind his back is only one dimension of the play, and perhaps the least interesting one, since it simply affirms the daily racial aggressions that take place in all cosmopolitan multicultural societies. What is of greater interest is that throughout the play Shakespeare sets the blatant discourse of racial repugnance alongside the audience's identification with the humanity of the black character, through the ways in which the repugnance of the white characters comes to atrophy the black character's own capacity for making ethical choices, and in Othello's case, of affirming his love for his wife and protecting the norms of marriage. If Othello is in part an intemperate, gullible, fool (why didn't he just ask his wife about the handkerchief nicely and much earlier? And why did he spend so much time with Iago instead of with his wife in the first place?), the means by which he descends into a form of apoplectic anger and masochistic self-regard is also comprehensible as a probable outcome of his social interpellation. This descent is the flipside of the process of racial stereotyping. The true force of the interpellation in the play derives not just from the negative connotations that being black holds in the Renaissance period, but also from Othello's internalizing of this negativity which generates self-loathing and an unruly affective economy within himself. This illustrative crucible of interpellation ⇒ projection ⇒ introjection ⇒ self-loathing is the process by which the black self is atrophied into precisely the brute voraciousness of the stereotype that is initially called up to define him or her. But we can also assert that no one is immune from the inter-subjective inscriptions that the social world places upon the self, for the self is first and foremost the product of social relations. This counts for both the perpetrators of false images as much as for the victims of such images.

In Italo Calvino's *Invisible Cities*, after Marco Polo has invoked the empire through various charades and images to the Khan, the Khan enquires earnestly of his adroit interlocutor and master image-maker: "On the day when I know all the emblems," he asked Marco, "shall I be able to possess my empire, at last?" to which the Venetian answers: "Sire, do not believe it. On that day you will be an emblem among emblems."[68] The mighty Khan seeks to place his knowledge of the empire in the service of power, but Marco Polo reminds him that in doing so the Khan will himself be reduced to the level of an image, in other words, to the level of the same inventory of images by which he seeks to encompass and control the world. If we want to extrapolate from *Othello* in order to understand the effects of stereotyping in our own multicultural and cosmopolitan worlds, we are obliged to place Iago's explicit modular designs in parenthesis and to speculate that in real-world encounters, the process of stereotyping reduces the humanity of the one doing it as much as it does that of the object of the stereotyping itself. If Shakespeare incites pity and fear for his hero, he does not do this merely as a purgation of the emotions as per Aristotle's formulation, but as a means of educating and elevating our sense of what it is to be thus and not thus, cosmopolitan and not ethnicist, humanist and not parochial, but harboring all these opposites and contradictions in ourselves all at once. This is the tragic cosmopolitan lesson of *Othello* for our times.

[68] Italo Calvino, *Invisible Cities* (New York: Harcourt, 1974), 22–23.

CHAPTER 3

History and the Conscription to Colonial Modernity in Chinua Achebe's Rural Novels

Chinua Achebe is justifiably famous for peppering his dialogue with memorable Igbo proverbs, starting from his first novel, *Things Fall Apart*, and subsequently throughout his writing career.[1] The following are a few that I have myself put to good use since being introduced to his work as a fifteen-year-old:

> "A toad does not run in the day time for nothing; when you see it you must know that something is after its life."
>
> "Eneke the bird was asked why he was always on the wing and he replied: 'Men have learnt to shoot without missing their mark and I have learnt to fly without perching on a twig.'"
>
> "The earth is like a mask dancing. If you want to see it well you do not stand in one place."
>
> "The lizard that fell from the tall iroko tree nodded, saying 'If no one will praise me, I will praise myself.'"
>
> "A man does not challenge his *chi* to a wrestling match."
>
> "The eye is not harmed by sleep."
>
> "A man who lives on the banks of the Niger should not wash his hands in spittle."
>
> "Let the kite perch and let the eagle perch too – if one says no to the other, let his wing break."
>
> "If a man returns from a long journey and no one says *nno* (welcome) to him, he feels like one who has not arrived."

The first three of the proverbs listed here hint specifically at practical and epistemological responses to historical transition. But many of Achebe's proverbs convey, in one way or another, the sense of transition between

---

[1] All references will be to Chinua Achebe, *Things Fall Apart* (London: Heinemann, 1958) and *Arrow of God* (London: Penguin, 2016; first published 1964).

tradition and modernity. Even though the representation of the transition between the two is well encapsulated in Achebe's sophisticated incorporation of the cadences and sensibilities of the Igbo gnomic tradition into the structure and grammar of English, it is his representation of historical transition as the product of the contradictions of colonial modernity from which I suggest we interpret his tragic vision. When Okonkwo beheads the district commissioner's messenger at the end of *Things Fall Apart*, he thinks he is defending the norms and traditions of his own people. He raises his arm against what he understands to be the corruption of his people's will in their encounter with the new forces of colonialism. But in the flash of his machete's descent, his people respond with bewilderment rather than with action. Okonkwo knows from hearing the tumult and confusion in their voices that he is completely isolated and that they will not go to war with the white man as he had hoped. In contrast to Okonkwo, Ezeulu's response in *Arrow of God* to both Christianity and the colonial administration is a mixture of curiosity, some disdain, but also astounding indifference. Unlike Okonkwo, Ezeulu expresses in his character a qualified sense of being a "conscript of modernity," as defined by David Scott in his book of the same title. Simon Gikandi has noted that what is often at stake in Achebe's writing is the attempt to recover the integrity of African culture, to negotiate the forces that block this process and to assert through narrative the capacity of his people for change and transformation by "return[ing] history to them."[2] This aspect of Achebe's returning history to his people is what interests me in this chapter. For, as we shall see, what we might describe as an epistemological restoration project is elaborated in his rural narratives with respect to the conditions of colonial modernity, the continuing attraction to traditional values, and the complicated tragic responses to both. His proverbs offer a lively backdrop to this discussion.

Colonial Modernity and Historical Lifeworlds

Modernity in Europe had both material and ideational prerequisites. As Stephen K. White notes in commenting on Jürgen Habermas's work, lifeworlds in modernity are marked by the fact that

---

[2] Simon Gikandi, *Reading Chinua Achebe: Language and Ideology in Fiction* (London: James Currey, 1991), 10. I consider Gikandi's reading of Achebe to be the most compelling amongst the many things that have been written on him, and his work has been fundamental to how I myself think of Achebe at all levels of implication.

an increasing number of spheres of social interaction are removed from guidance by unquestioned tradition and opened to coordination through consciously achieved agreement. Simultaneously with this advance in communicative rationalization, there also occurs an advance in the rationality of society as measured from a functionalist or systems perspective. This latter sort of rationalization means that there is an expansion of social subsystems that coordinate action through the media of money (capitalist economy) and administrative power (modern centralized states).[3]

Colonial modernity for its part shared with its European counterpart several features, including the privileging of Reason as the ultimate seat of judgment, which in the colonies was installed as an aspect of the bureaucratic administrative apparatus; the concentration on the infrastructure of roads, railways, and sea travel as the primary motors of social transformation; and finally, in the emergence of new aspirational matrices aimed at displacing those that had been extant prior to colonialism. Tied to these three core beliefs in the colonial era was the concomitant role of the nuclear (read Christian) family as the building block of modern society, and the notion that wealth accumulation was to be a function of personal effort and the entrepreneurial profit motive rather than of inheritance. As important as the shared elements of European and colonial modernity were, even more significant were the socio-structural contradictions unleashed with the introduction of formal colonialism, with its differential race and class relations, its privileging of sedentarism over nomadism, and the overall incoherence of the steady cooptation of local traditional elites from the 1850s onward.[4] Abiola Irele puts the matter succinctly in his comments on French colonialism in West Africa, but his remarks are also perfectly suited to the British colonial example in the region, something that we see amply illustrated especially in *Arrow of God*:

> the French concentrated their efforts on creating new loyalties by dethroning previous rulers and replacing them with selected individuals, who would be beholden to the colonial authorities. An essential plank of this French policy was the systematic devaluation of traditional beliefs and forms of cultural expression, and the active promotion of what can only be called a French ideology, of which an ideal image of France as a benevolent agent of African promotion was the central reference. It did not matter that this

---

[3] Stephen K. White, "Introduction," *The Cambridge Companion to Habermas*, ed. (Cambridge: Cambridge University Press, 1995), 8.

[4] For the features and contradictions of colonial modernity, see Mahmood Mamdani, *Divide and Rule; Citizen and Subject: Contemporary Africa and the Legacy of Late Colonialism* (Princeton: Princeton University Press, 1996); and Fred Cooper, *Colonialism in Question: Theory, Knowledge, History* (Berkeley: California University Press, 2005).

ideology was contradicted by the reality of French colonial policy and practice. The civil service which was rapidly put in place, often administered by former officers of the French army, was essentially an instrument of economic exploitation; while in the circumstances it had to assume a formal character based upon an elaborate system of procedures and regulations, its essential function was furthered through the more brutal form of forced labor, with devastating effects upon whole communities throughout the expanse of the territories under French rule in West Africa.[5]

In Chinua Achebe's *Things Fall Apart* and *Arrow of God,* the representation of the schism between subsystems of consensus-making and the dictates of tradition is by no means straightforward. The expansion of social subsystems unfolds against a background of different historical rhythms, not all of which are explicitly foregrounded within the novels. For the history of the colonial encounter is synchronous with other types of historical processes that subtend colonial history but also provide significant nodes of interruption to it. In Achebe's novels, these other, barely visible histories generate a number of rhetorical sedimentations to the representation of both historical processes and the Igbo ethno-text (ethnographic details), that also illustrate the subtle and not-so-subtle disruptions of colonial modernity.[6] To grasp the nature of the multi-synchronous historical character of these texts, we are obliged to read both historical and ethnographic details as discursive thresholds rather than as particularities. As I have written elsewhere about the relationship between particularities and thresholds in postcolonial writing, my view is that the salience of historical and ethnographic details comes not from what they may divulge about non-Western cultural knowledge systems, important though this is, but rather from the fact that they act as focalizations through which the interplay of various levels of the text configure into a fertile conundrum.[7] All such literature, read as literature and not simply as ethnographic, political, or other non-literary discourse, is ultimately about the orchestration of questions and problems, the answers to which must never be taken as straightforward, but only as generative of further questions. Particular

[5] Abiola Irele, "Preface," *The Fortunes of Wangrin,* by Hamadou Ampate Ba (Bloomington: Indiana University Press, 1999), x.

[6] Achebe's novels have conventionally been read as providing both ethnographic and historical details. This tendency is so strong as to convert his texts into cultural testimonials, rather than literary artifacts in their own right. For a critique of this tendency in the criticism of African literature, see Ato Quayson, "Criticism, Realism and the Disguises of Both: an Analysis of Chinua Achebe's *Things Fall Apart* with an Evaluation of the Criticism Relating to it," *Research in African Literatures,* 25.4 (1994): 117–136.

[7] See *Calibrations: Reading for the Social* and "Ethnographies of African Literature: A Note," in *Contemporary African Fiction,* Bayreuth African Studies, 42, (1997), 157–66.

cultural details within such texts are thus only chimerically particular; their "real" particularity must be seen as a function of the ways in which they intermesh with other elements within an overlapping and interacting literary structure that proffers details of difference, and yet, at the same time, undermines them as stable reference points for distinguishing the text-as-different. The particular cultural detail is only interesting insofar as it reveals the discursive oscillations within the form of the representation. The relationship between particularity and threshold may also be seen as that between figure and background, or between window and vista, or between vector and totality, each of which can be explored in smaller or greater detail depending on the scalar orientation of the interpretation at work. But whichever way the relationship of particularity and threshold is interpreted, its meaning must be conceived as a process, that is to say, in terms of a series of textual transactions whereby a seemingly innocent and self-evident cultural detail progressively changes its status as it is read alongside other details and dimensions of the text in question.[8]

Within Achebe's rural novels, historical and cultural particularities are embedded into the overall discursive workings of the texts such that their salience lies not merely in their value for providing historical or cultural verification of a traditional African lifeworld before and during colonialism, but in how they instigate insights into the discursive contexture (or textured context) of the literary representation as such. The way that historical details operate within *Things Fall Apart* and *Arrow of God* is by means of what I want to describe as a volatile proximity between overlapping historical epochs. This is encapsulated as a series of movements between differently situated foregrounds and backgrounds; the meanings attributed to key cultural concepts such as the *chi*, the *osu*, the white man as a cipher of strangeness but also of power; and the discursive attributions of the place name Abame/Abam across the two novels.

Some details in the novels are pertinent to understanding the historical background of lifeworlds under colonial modernity in Igboland. In *Things Fall Apart,* the killing of the white man on the bicycle at Abame corresponds to something that took place in historical reality: the death of a Dr. Stewart in Ahiara in 1905. That incident occurred during the British military campaigns to subdue Igboland from 1901–1916, the largest expedition of which was launched against the Arochukwu Confederacy in 1901–1902.[9] There also existed at the time a real town called Abam (not Abame),

---

[8] See Quayson, *Calibrations*, xx–xxii, xxviii–xxxi.
[9] See Elizabeth Isichei's *History of the Igbo People* (London: Macmillan, 1976), 123–134.

that was part of the Arochukwu and was much feared as a source of slave raiders. After the smashing of Abame in *Things Fall Apart*, a missionary's translator points out that the British have a queen and not a king. And at the end of the novel the district commissioner also refers to the queen. But Queen Victoria ascended to the throne in 1837 and died in 1901. It would thus seem that the novel ends around 1900, making the reference to the 1905 campaign at Abame an anachronism. We can, however, safely assert the following from other contextual clues: by the time we meet Okonkwo as an adult, some twenty years have passed since he defeated Amalinze the cat in a wrestling match. This would put him at around thirty-eight years old. In the opening of chapter 21, we are given a passing reference to the trading store for selling palm-oil and kernel at "great price", which would itself put the novel's events sometime between the 1880s to 1900s, when the change in the local economy from slavery to what historians call legitimate trade, had led to the rise of palm oil as a major export. However, Achebe introduces a number of anachronisms to increase the dramatic character of the colonial encounter. As we shall see in a moment, the historical period from the 1880s was particularly tumultuous in all of West Africa but especially in the area around the Bight of Biafra, the historical setting of the novel.

The events in *Arrow of God* on the other hand are more precisely datable. On the first page of chapter 3 of the novel we are told that it was "mid-February." Contextual clues suggest that this is 1919, a few months after World War I, which ended in November 1918. The first time he is introduced in the novel, we are told that Mr. Winterbottom had seen active service in the Cameroon campaign of 1916 and that it was his illustrious career in World War I that saw him admitted into the colonial service in Nigeria. The posting at Okperi is his first as district commissioner. Clarke, the assistant district commissioner, receives "the weekly Reuter's telegram sent as an ordinary letter from the nearest telegraphic office fifty miles away. It carried the news that Russian peasants in revolt against the new régime had refused to grow crops."[10] This is interpreted correctly by Nicholas Brown as a useful instance of dating in the novel, except that his assertion that the telegram "fixes the date of the novel at 1921" has to be set against other anachronisms within the text.[11] What Clarke opens next after the Reuters telegram is a report by the "Secretary for Native Affairs on Indirect Rule in Eastern Nigeria." The report

[10] Achebe, *Arrow of God*, 180.
[11] Nicholas Brown, *Utopian Generations: The Political Horizon of Twentieth-Century Literature* (Princeton: Princeton University Press, 2005), 122.

is a new instalment in the long-running debate in the colonial administration about the introduction of warrant chiefs for acephalous societies such as the Igbos. As A. E. Afigbo shows, the Warrant Chief policy was initiated in the 1880s with different evolving components that included the constitution of Native Courts, revenue collection, and the adjudication of conflicts under customary law. But it was Lord Lugard, following his earlier success at introducing Indirect Rule in Northern Nigeria, who gave the policy of Indirect Rule and Warrant Chiefs its coherent ideological rationale from 1914 onward. Within a year of Lugard's departure from Nigeria in 1919, the policy was exposed to serious debate among colonial officials, with strong reservations leading to the setting up of a commission to propose recommendations for its fine-tuning. The Tomlinson Report on The Eastern Provinces of 1923 set out a number of recommendations, but various points leading up to it had been subjects of intense debate among colonial officials since the commission was first established some three years earlier (i.e., in 1920).[12] It is one of the pre-Tomlinson Report recommendations that Clarke is shown looking at in the novel. As we shall come to see later, it is the debate on Warrant Chief policy and the contradictory positions adopted by the colonial administration at their district headquarters at Enugu, that are focalized in Winterbottom's irate insistence on the prerogatives of experience over those of the chattering commissions of enquiry.

At the opening of chapter 4 of the novel, Ezeulu thinks to himself that five years have already passed since he agreed to send one of his children to the church school. This would be five years following the quarrel between Umuaro and Okperi that triggered the intervention of Winterbottom and the "breaking of the guns," which must have taken place either late in 1919 or some time in 1920. Thus, the narrated events in the novel can be taken to have spanned the period roughly between 1919 and 1925. However, anachronisms appear here too. And as we have already noted, Clarke is shown reading one of the recommendations of the pre-Tomlinson Reports, likely from 1920, but Achebe lifts the lieutenant-governor's memorandum that Winterbottom reads from in chapter 5 from Sir Donald Cameron's 1934 *The Principles of Native Administration and Their Application.*[13]

---

[12] A. E. Afigbo, *The Warrant Chiefs: Indirect Rule in Southeastern Nigeria, 1891–1929* (London: Longman, 1972); for a contrasting view that reinterprets the dynamics of gender relations implicit in the policy of warrant chiefs, see also Nwandwo Achebe, *The Female King of Colonial Nigeria: Ahebi Ugbabe* (Bloomington: Indiana University Press, 2011), and Ifi Amadiume, *Male Daughters, Female Husbands: Gender and Sex in an African Society* (London: Zed Books, 1989).

[13] Cameron's memorandum is detailed in Anthony Kirk-Greene's *Principles of Native Administration in Nigeria: Selected Documents, 1900–1947* (Oxford: Oxford University Press, 1965). The name for Achebe's Winterbottom was inspired by a historical figure, a Dr. Thomas Winterbottom, whose "An

Furthermore, the well-established colonial headquarters at Okperi with its strict social hierarchies, its hospital run by white nurses, and the various road construction schemes described in the novel, all suggest the ethos of a more firmly established colonialism, something hinted at in the passage in which Winterbottom reads from Cameron's *Principles*.

Even though *Things Fall Apart* and *Arrow of God* are populated with dateable historical details, they are not historical novels in the sense laid out by Lukács. Lukács's description of the key elements of the historical novel include, among other things, the depiction of the space-time of the nation-state, the juxtaposition of historical and fictional characters, and the mingling of both exemplary and middling characters that might serve to encapsulate the Hegelian articulation of ethical standpoints. Furthermore, as Perry Anderson adroitly notes, the classical historical novel draws from a "pre-constituted repertoire of scenes or stories of that history, still overwhelmingly written from the standpoint of battles, conspiracies, intrigues, treacheries, seductions, infamies, heroic deeds and deathless sacrifices – everything that was not prosaic daily life in the 19th century."[14] If Walter Scott's *Waverley* and *Ivanhoe* and Leo Tolstoy's *War and Peace* offer the conventional keys for illustrating Lukács propositions, then from a postcolonial perspective it is Tolstoy's *Hadji Murat* that comes closest to capturing the historical transition from autonomous traditional order to one under colonialism and which finds a counterpart in Achebe's rural novels. And yet even a casual comparison of *Hadji Murat* with *Things Fall Apart* and *Arrow of God* shows that Achebe's novels lack some of the core ingredients of the classical historical novel. In Achebe, there are none of the legendary military exploits of various historical characters or the highly intricate orchestration of conflicting political interests amongst local leaders and between local leaders and the imperialists (Chechnyans on one side and Russians on the other in *Hadji Murat*). Even though we see the reaction of autonomous traditional societies to the impositions of colonial rule in Achebe's novels,

Account of the Native Africans in the Neighbourhood of Sierra Leone" was written at the end of the eighteenth century. For this and other clues dating Achebe's rural novels, see Neil ten Kortenaar, *Postcolonial Literature and the Impact of Writing* (Cambridge: Cambridge University Press, 2011), 32–33, 42–43; and Nicholas Brown's fine chapter on *Arrow of God* in *Utopian Generations* already cited. I want to say very special thanks to ten Kortenaar for reading an early draft of this chapter and for giving me generous and very useful comments.

[14] Perry Anderson, "From Progress to Catastrophe" *The London Review of Books*, 33.15 (2011): 24–28. From a postcolonial perspective, see also Hamish Dalley, "Postcolonialism and the Historical Novel: Epistemologies of Contemporary Realism," *Cambridge Journal of Postcolonial Literary Inquiry*, 1.1 (2014): 51–68.

in each case there is also the marked and signal failure to mobilize sentiment against the invaders.[15] This is quite different from *Hadji Murat*. And yet at the same time, Achebe's novels reflect a deeply historical sensibility. They define a certain multi-synchronicity that entails a number of overlapping and incomplete transitions between different historical epochs. Multi-synchronicity is what Fredric Jameson defines in *The Political Unconscious* as "The coexistence of various synchronic systems or modes of production, each with its own dynamic, or time scheme."[16] It is the aspect of different temporal time-schemes in this definition that most pertains to Achebe's rural novels. In them, we find that incomplete transitions are expressed in terms of the contradictory impulses underpinning character choices as an interpretation of historical opportunities. The grasping of the opportunities provided by Christianity and the new colonial administration for personal advancement is set against the proliferation of epistemological aporia that breed incomprehension and a sense of malaise for middling characters, as we find with Nwoye, Obierika, and Edogo. Aporia and epistemological uncertainty are not in the purview of *Hadji Murat*, for Tolstoy's novel centers mainly on the external dynamics of the historical transition, with war and political maneuvering used to register the external material manifestations of that transition.

In contrast, while both of Achebe's novels reflect upon the ethical choices made in pursuit of what it is to be heroic, the fact that the historical transitions have produced disagreement about what might constitute the appropriate parameters for action means that when his tragic heroes assert their ultimate decisions, their choices are met either by complete incomprehension, as in the case of Okonkwo, or utter disdain and bewildered disapproval, as in that of Ezeulu. In *Arrow of God* more than in *Things Fall Apart* the primacy of immediate sense perception and thus of personal choice is set against the disputatiousness of diverse positions within the communities, thus rendering the possibility of a totalizing historical retrospective practically impossible to achieve unless we focus exclusively on the individual tragic characters to the exclusion of all else. This is not unusual in most discussions of Achebe. However, this is not the interpretative route I intend to take.

---

[15] Nicholas Brown, *Utopian Generations*, 122.
[16] Fredric Jameson, *The Political Unconscious: Narrative as a Socially Symbolic Act* (Ithaca: Cornell University Press, 2011), 97

I find that the "widening gyre" that Achebe invokes for *Things Fall Apart* by deriving it from Yeats's "The Second Coming" hints at the volatile proximity between epochs. Changing social realities are partly sedimented in the novel, as we shall see, in cultural subsystems such as the *osu*, and partly as an unstable historical signifier encapsulated in the place name of Abame. And contrary to Yeats's view that in such a historical transition, "The best lack all conviction, while the worst/ Are full of passionate intensity,"[17] Achebe's tragic heroes are full of both conviction and passionate intensity. This is because, like the great tragic heroes and heroines born of disputatious environments before them, Okonkwo and Ezeulu express, first and foremost, an absolutism of values rather than of compromise. This is the mold in which we encounter Clytemnestra, Medea, Oedipus, Antigone, Coriolanus, King Lear, and Othello, among various others. In the case of Okonwko his absolutism leads to a solitary suicide, but for Ezeulu, his refusal to eat the last of the ritual yams triggers consequences that are not commensurate with the decision itself in that it delivers his entire community into the arms of a waiting Christianity. The yams that the people of Umuaro surrender to the Christians activate the ritual switch from charged sacred objects engendered from within the community's own symbolic system, to new objects of abjection and devotion implied in the Christian call for conversion. Their yams are performative of the materiality of nourishment and symbolic sacrifice, but as objects in the realm of Christianity, become both tithe and sacrament and so come to bespeak a radical new order of things.

History as Volatile Proximity: The Case of Abame/Abam

An important point for grasping the multi-synchronicity and volatile proximity of different historical epochs in the lifeworlds of Achebe's rural novels is the status assigned to the name Abame/Abam within them. Abame/Abam is the metonymic placeholder for the activities of the historical Arochukwu Constituency (Aro), and, simultaneously, of the catastrophe that is colonialism. The Arochukwu were historically extremely powerful and well-organized as the dominant trading conglomerate of states in the Bight of Benin, which is where the two novels are set. The Aro were also highly influential in the slave trade. They dominated the trade by harnessing their already-existing control of inland trade routes

[17] Yeats, W. B. "Second Coming"; www.poetryfoundation.org/poems/43290/the-second-coming, last accessed July 6, 2020.

that they had dominated since their incorporation as a confederacy of trade diasporas from their founding in the 1680s.

Arochukwu's activities in the capture, export, and domestic use of slaves continued well into the nineteenth century and brought them to clash with the colonial administration toward the end of the century. While the Igbo societies depicted in Achebe's novels operated a form of village republicanism based on gerontocracy, the Aro were known to run a centralized state confederacy system over a large area that depended heavily on trade, the extraction of tribute, and slavery. And even though the termination of slavery is conventionally associated with the slave trade's abolition in 1807, the process for the freeing of slaves in West Africa did not properly begin until the Slave Emancipation Act of 1833, when the British signed an agreement with the Dutch, the Danes, and the Portuguese to put a collective stop to the trans-Atlantic trade and to free all slave captives. But the British zeal to end the trans-Atlantic trade did not align with their efforts to deal with internal domestic slavery, which was coextensive with the trans-Atlantic version but had distinct features, as Kirstin Mann, Paul Lovejoy, and other scholars of slavery in West Africa have shown.[18] In West Africa, the conversion of local societies from previously exporting slave economies into those of trade and wage labor was not completed until roughly the 1920s. But the conversion from exporting slave economies into economies of legitimate trade was also heavily dependent on domestic slavery. The rise in Atlantic slavery had had the effect of intertwining slave export to the Americas with the dynamics of domestic slavery such that, even after the end of the export trade, the Aro continued to retain local trade in people as the basis of wealth and power.[19] By the 1880s, the Aro had also turned to foodstuff production for domestic and market consumption, yet also continued to dominate what was left of the slave traffic until persistent conflicts with the colonialists led to the British Aro Expedition of 1901–1902 that finally destroyed Aro authority. Two things to note with respect to Achebe's *Things Fall Apart* and *Arrow of God* is that in the historical period in which they are set, the threat of slave raids from the powerful Aro was a real and continuing danger, and secondly, that the place name of Abame/Abam registers this reality.

---

[18] Kristin Mann, *Slavery and the Birth of an African City: Lagos, 1760–1900*, (Bloomington: Indiana University Press, 2007). See also Paul E. Lovejoy, *Transformations in Slavery: A History of Slavery in Africa*, 3rd edition (Cambridge: Cambridge University Press, 2012).

[19] For more on this see G. Ugo Nwokeji, *Slave Trade and Culture in the Bight of Biafra: an African Society in the Atlantic World* (Cambridge: Cambridge University Press, 2010), 116–132, and also Elizabeth Isichei, *A History of the Igbo People*.

Abame is mentioned several times in the two novels, but to quite different discursive effects. It is first mentioned in *Things Fall Apart* by Obierika in conversation with the family and friends that gather to support him host his daughter's marriage suitor. The conversation in which Abame first gets mentioned takes place amongst the gathered menfolk, who share stories about the stark differences in cultural practices that they have noticed among various neighboring clans. Predictably, the conversation starts with stories of the doings of titled figures:

> "It was only this morning," said Obierika, "that Okonkwo and I were talking about Abame and Aninta, where titled men climb trees and pound foo-foo for their wives."
>
> "All their customs are upside-down. They do not decide bride-price as we do, with sticks. They haggle and bargain as if they were buying a goat or a cow in the market."
>
> "That is very bad," said Obierika's eldest brother. "But what is good in one place is bad in another place. In Umunso they do not bargain at all, not even with broomsticks. The suitor just goes on bringing bags of cowries until his in-laws tell him to stop. It is a bad custom because it always leads to a quarrel."
>
> "The world is large," said Okonkwo. "I have even heard that in some tribes a man's children belong to his wife and her family."
>
> "That cannot be," said Machi. "You might as well say that the woman lies on top of the man when they are making the children."
>
> "It is like the story of white men who, they say, are white like this piece of chalk," said Obierika. He held up a piece of chalk, which every man kept in his obi and with which his guests drew lines on the floor before they ate kola nuts. "And these white men, they say, have no toes."
>
> "And have you never seen them?" asked Machi.
>
> "Have you?" asked Obierika.
>
> "One of them passes here frequently," said Machi. "His name is Amadi."
>
> Those who knew Amadi laughed. He was a leper, and the polite name for leprosy was "the white skin."[20]

It is not clear why in the midst of the discussion of different cultural practices, Obierika inserts the story of the white man who is thought to be white like a piece of chalk. Why this analogy? Is it to suggest that the world is full of strange stories, some of which are of cultural differences while others are purely fantastical? While the analogy with the piece of chalk and the leper are supposed to simultaneously domesticate (chalk being an instrument of Igbo hospitality) and alienate (lepers often lived in

---

[20] Achebe, *Things Fall Apart*, 51–52.

settlements separated from the rest of the clan), the effect is to discursively insert the white man into narrative orbit as part of the signifying matrix centered on Abame, who are in this conversation considered to be the site of strange customs, and thus, like the white man-as-leper, subjects of laughter and derision.

The second mention of Abame in the novel is again by Obierika, but this time in much less happy circumstances. He has come to visit his friend Okonkwo in exile at Mbanta, where Okonkwo has been banished for seven years following his inadvertent shooting of a young man at his warrior father's funeral in Umuofia. Obierika introduces Abame ominously enough and this time he is talking only to Okonkwo and Uchendu, Okonkwo's elderly uncle:

> "Have you heard," asked Obierika, "that Abame is no more?"
> "How is that?" asked Uchendu and Okonkwo together.
> "Abame has been wiped out," said Obierika. "It is a strange and terrible story. If I had not seen the few survivors with my own eyes and heard their story with my own ears, I would not have believed. Was it not on an Eke day that they fled into Umuofia?" he asked his two companions, and they nodded their heads.
> . . .
> "During the last planting season a white man had appeared in their clan."
> "An albino," suggested Okonkwo.
> "He was not an albino. He was quite different . . . And he was riding an iron horse. The first people who saw him ran away, but he stood beckoning them . . . The elders consulted their Oracle and it told them that the strange man would break their clan and spread destruction among them . . . And so they killed the white man and tied his iron horse to their sacred tree because it looked as if it would run away to call the man's friends. I forgot to tell you another thing the Oracle said. It said that other white men were on their way. They were like locusts, it said, and that first man was their harbinger sent to explore the terrain. And so they killed him."
> . . .
> "Their clan is now completely empty. Even the sacred fish in their mysterious lake have fled and the lake has turned the color of blood. A great evil has come upon their land as the Oracle had warned."[21]

As we saw earlier, Obierika's account coincides with the historical events that took place after the killing of Dr. Stewart at Ahiara and the latching of his bicycle to a tree. Peculiarly, in this passage the straying white man is no

[21] Achebe, *Things Fall Apart*, 97–98.

longer a leper but an albino, a shift in the terms of analogy away from what we saw in the earlier passage, thus drawing him closer to the domain of acceptability. Even though albinism was considered as much of a disability as leprosy, in the novel it carries less stigma than the latter. Uchendu mentions toward the end of their conversation, that, despite the wondrousness of the stories of the white man, there is no story that is not true, for the albinos they have amongst them at Mbanta may have come to their clan by mistake, having "strayed from their way to a land where everybody is like them."[22] The shift of the cipher of whiteness between the two domains of disability will subsequently be fused with the strange peculiarities of the Christian missionaries and even later with the communal catastrophe that is engendered in the contact with colonialism. The use of disability from source of wonder to signal of historical catastrophe may also be taken to illustrate the concept of aesthetic nervousness I write about elsewhere. For disability often marks the point where the already-existing protocols of representation are either usurped or resignified.[23] We shall see a fuller example of aesthetic nervousness in Chapter 9 on Samuel Beckett's *Murphy.* In *Things Fall Apart,* the decimation of Abame acts as a warning about the power of the white man that is coded as a cultural anomaly through the idiom of disability, and thus rendered as at first an object of derision and laughter but then resignified as one of imminent historical danger. Given the brutal decimation of Abame, however, the overall effect of its various mentions is ultimately to graft Abame to the power of white authority, such that any time the town is mentioned across the two novels it immediately invokes a warning rather than merely a place name or the site of peculiar cultural differences.

In *Arrow of God* on the other hand, Abame acts exclusively as a warning coextensive with the usage we found in the latter part of *Things Fall Apart.* As Moses Unachukwu notes in his address to the age group convened to discuss a response to Obika's whipping by Mr. Wright, the white road overseer: "When Suffering knocks at your door and you say there is no seat left for him, he tells you not to worry because he has brought his own stool. The white man is like that. Before any of you here was old enough to tie a cloth between the legs I saw with my own eyes what the white man did to Abame. Then I knew there was no escape. Daylight chases away darkness so will the white man drive away all our customs."[24] As a Christian convert,

[22] Achebe, *Things Fall Apart,* 99.
[23] See my *Aesthetic Nervousness: Disability and the Crisis of Representation,* 15–19, 24–28.
[24] Achebe, *Arrow of God,* 84.

Moses Unachukwu is keen to use the devastation of Abame as a sign of the inexorable advance of Christianity. However, even if signifying the power of the white man, the name Abame repeats the dimension of local existential threat that echoes *Things Fall Apart*. But this reference is also shifted in *Arrow of God* onto references to the historical Abam, which, given the closeness of this variant spelling to Abame, serves to fuse historical and fictional referents in the mind of the reader. Thus, in the second chapter of the novel, Ezeulu reminds the clan elders:

> In the very distant past, when lizards were still few and far between, the six villages – Umuachala, Umunneora, Umuagu, Umuezeani, Umuogwugwu and Umuisiuzo – lived as different peoples, and each worshipped its own deity. Then the hired soldiers of Abam used to strike in the dead of night, set fire to the houses and carry men, women and children into slavery. Things were so bad for the six villages that their leaders came together to save themselves. They hired a strong team of medicine-men to install a common deity for them. This deity which the fathers of the six villages made was called Ulu. Half of the medicine was buried at a place which became Nkwo market and the other half thrown into the stream which became known as Mili Ulu. The six villages then took the name Umuaro, and the priest of Ulu became their Chief Priest. From that day they were never beaten by an enemy.[25]

It was the threat of slave raids from Abam that acted as the trigger for the founding of Umuaro in the first place. In *Arrow of God*, the Abame/Abam pair acts as the metonymic displacement of two distinctive historical epochs. These appear in the text at two closely related levels. Given that Abam is the metonymic stand-in for the Arochukwu, the reference bears a historical overload pointing to an entire process of transition from the slave trade, through legitimate trade, to the economy of colonial modernity dominated by the white man as depicted in the novel. But these phases of transition are also situated in different relations of proximity and distance from the foreground of narrated events. The historical threat of slavery posed by Abam and thus of the Arochukwu is limned out and inserted into the domain of the distant foundational narratives of Umuaro, while colonial modernity is located in the text as an aspect of living memory, registered as we have seen by Moses Unachukwu as he bears witness to the rout of the fictional Abame. The Abame/Abam pair thus marks the movement of historical necessity that divulges itself as the threat of devastation against traditional autonomy, first as the traditional world moves

---

[25] Achebe, *Arrow of God*, 14–15.

from slavery and then through colonialism. In both *Things Fall Apart* and *Arrow of God*, then, the invocation of Abame/Abam marks the volatile proximity between different historical and epochal processes, and it is against these transitions that we have to evaluate the tragedy that befalls the central characters of Okonwko and Ezeulu and their communities. As we shall see shortly, in *Things Fall Apart*, the volatile proximity between epochs is also visible in the confrontation of traditional village life with the subsystem of the *osu* cult in their conversion to Christianity, while for *Arrow of God*, the volatile proximity is personified in the different socio-political dispositions of Ezeulu, the Chief Priest of Ulu, and Nwaka, the wealthiest member of the clan who speaks for a new social subsystem of power and affirmation.

The Discursive Particularity of *osu*

In contrast to Abame/Abam, the *osu* provide us with a more explicit example of the dynamic relationship between particularity and threshold we noted earlier. The *osu* are represented in *Things Fall Apart* primarily as a peripheral social category that nonetheless come to have a decisive impact on the tragic turn of events. Historians of the Igbo generally agree that the *osu* cult was originally a priestly caste that was progressively transformed into a collection of persons dedicated specifically to the service and care of a deity and that the cult shared a number of features across Igboland. This included their sacred status, which was expressed in strict rules separating their settlements from those of the freeborn and in the interdiction of inter-marriage between the two categories of persons. They were also distinguished from the freeborn by never cutting their hair (much like the Nazirites of the Old Testament or modern-day Rastafarians), and their status was passed on to their children in perpetuity. Significant too in the character of the *osu* cult is that they were typically either immigrant outsiders or people whose social status had somehow been degraded, such as ex-slaves or persons who had committed some abominable act and been surrendered to the deity for cleansing.[26] All these features are hinted at in *Things Fall Apart*. However, perhaps the most telling aspect of the *osu* system that is not directly referenced in *Things Fall Apart*, but is

---

[26] See, S. N. Ezeanya, The Osu (Cult-Slave) System in Igbo Land," *Journal of Religion in Africa*, 1.1 (1967): 35–45 and Romeo I. Okeke, *The "Osu" Caste System Concept in Igboland* (Enugu: Access Publishing, 1986); Augustine S. O. Okwu, *Igbo Culture and the Christian Missions, 1857–1957: Conversion in Theory and Practice* (Lanham: University Press of America, 2009); and G. Ugo Nwokeji, *The Slave Trade and Culture in the Bight of Biafra*, 198–200.

pertinent to interpreting it, is that, historically, the *osu* cult system was the source of human sacrifice whenever such sacrifice was called for by the larger community. As T. O. Elias, S. N. Nwabara, and C. O. Akpangbo pointedly assert in their description of the law to prohibit the cult that was being debated in Eastern Nigeria after Independence,

> an Osu is more or less like the untouchables of India and probably in worse position. Osu was regarded as a degraded human being not fit for the companionship and association of decent and reputable men and women in the society, an outcast fit only to be sacrificed to the idol for the propitiation of the gods. An Osu initially was as it were a non-person sacrificed to a local deity or idol.[27]

And in the words of Jude Mgbobukwa, "he is made to be the absorber of the iniquities, weaknesses, and problems of the people. He is also made to take on himself the death of the freeborn."[28] Their status as *pharmakoi* historically had both literal and metaphorical dimensions, as various scholars have shown.[29] Because the original function of human sacrifice was not entirely abrogated even when the practice was outlawed by the colonial administration in the 1870s, the *osu's* life was technically forfeit if the deity so demanded. Thus, the cult system provided a reservoir of *homo sacer,* in Giorgio Agamben's memorable formulation.[30] While such human sacrifice became increasingly rare by the late nineteenth century, the point is that the sacred status assigned to the *osu* was at once a mark of their privilege and of their damnation.

The character of the cult underwent dramatic cultural changes through-out the nineteenth century in direct response to the long phase of social transformations from slave economies to legitimate trade we have already alluded to. Of the many social changes that took place in this period, the most pertinent to *Things Fall Apart* is that, by the 1880s, the *osu* cult had been converted into a safe haven for escapee slaves. On arrival at a shrine

---

[27] T. O. Elias, S. N. Nwabara, and C. O. Akpamgbo, Abolition of Osu System Law, Eastern Regional House of Assembly, 1963 (1956), caption 1.

[28] Jude Alusi Mgbobukwa, *Osu and Ohu in Igbo Religion and Social Life* (Nsukka: Fulludu Publishing Company, 1996), 39.

[29] For a detailed and helpful discussion of the many inflections of the term "human sacrifice" in West Africa, see Robin Law, "Human Sacrifice in Pre-Colonial West Africa," *African Affairs,* 84.344 (1985): 53–87; and with a specific focus on the Igbo, Elizabeth Isichei, "The Quest for Social Reform in the Context of Traditional Religion: A Neglected Theme in African History," *African Affairs,* 77.309 (1978): 463–478; and Victor C. Uchendu, "Slaves and Slavery in Igboland, Nigeria," in Suzanne Miers and Igor Kopytoff, eds., *Slavery in Africa: Historical and Anthropological Perspectives* (Madison: University of Wisconsin Press, 1977), 121–132.

[30] Gorgio Agamben, *Homo Sacer: Sovereign Power and Bare Life* (Stanford: Stanford University Press, 1998).

and the enunciation of a special formula, the escapee slave became an *osu*, and could not be captured and sold back into slavery. He or she enjoyed the full benefits of the status, duties, and obligations of cult membership.[31] In *Things Fall Apart* the *osu*'s cultural particularity is not as significant as the fact that they act as the fulcrum for the layering of different dimensions of Achebe's tragic vision, including the empathetic identification we come to have with Ikemefuna, who is discursively an *osu* figure, as we shall see presently, and also in their contribution to the dialectical spatial morphology of purity and danger that unfolds within the text.

As readers of *Things Fall Apart* will recall, Ikemefuna is a young boy who is surrendered by Mbaino to Umuofia as recompense for the inadvertent killing of a young Umuofian girl on her way to the market at Mbaino. The then fifteen-year-old Ikemefuna is surrendered to Umuofia along with a young virgin to avert the threat of war and imminent destruction, given the known ferociousness of Umuofia's warriors. We are told nothing further about the girl except that she was given to the man whose wife had been killed. But we learn a great deal about Ikemefuna: "As for the boy, he belonged to the clan as a whole, and there was no hurry to decide his fate. Okonkwo was, therefore, asked on behalf of the clan to look after him in the interim. And so, for three years Ikemefuna lived in Okonkwo's household."[32] "Belonging to the clan as a whole" turns out to be an ominous formulation, but we are not to find its full implications until much later in the narrative. Ikemefuna settles into the household and quickly becomes highly popular and much-loved, especially by the thirteen-year-old Nwoye, Okonkwo's eldest son. One day, three years later, and completely disrupting the rhythms of normalcy that have now been attached to Ikemefuna, the oracle declares that he must be killed. This is a shock to everyone in Okonkwo's household, but it does not prevent Okonkwo from joining other men of Umuofia in taking Ikemefuna into the forest to kill him. Despite the fact that he had been warned privately against this by Ogbuefi Ezeudu, a formidable and highly respected elderly warrior ("That

---

[31] "If the Atlantic slave trade changed the character of the institution [of *osus*] in other parts of Igboland, it was the ending of the trade that generated these changes in Arondizuogo. Flight from oppression that hallmarked the tensive transition of the late nineteenth century was the immediate cause of the institution in Arondizuogu . . . . At the destination, the refugee would say the ritual: "Arusi, mbaa!" (Shrine, I submit myself to your protection) . . . . The idea of seeking refuge in shrines as an escape from oppression emanated from the beliefs, social constructions, fears and myths of immigrants from other parts of Igboland, particularly from Nri-Awka," G. Ugo Nwokeji, *The Slave Trade and Culture in the Bight of Biafra*, 199, 200. For more on the features of the *osu* cult, see also S. N. Ezeanya, 35–45.

[32] Achebe, *Things Fall Apart*, 9.

boy calls you father, do not bear a hand in his death"), Okonkwo goes along and even delivers the cowardly final blow that kills Ikemefuna as he runs in blind terror toward him.

This quite astonishing moment of cowardice ushers both Okonkwo and us readers into an emotionally tumultuous place, for Ikemefuna's killing provides a major pivot for the interplay of pity and fear within the novel. This is focused primarily on the reaction of Nwoye, for whom "something seemed to give way inside him, like the snapping of a tightened bow."[33] And yet our all-too-natural horror and fixation on the event and the novel's reversion to Okonkwo's brief period of melancholy that follows, detracts from the fact that Ikemefuna's killing contravenes a number of principles pertaining to human sacrifice among the Igbo and other ethnic groups in West Africa. Historically and as a general rule, an oracle would not have asked for the sacrifice of a human being unless this was required to avert an epic existential threat to the clan, as in say, the imminence of war or a disease epidemic, or as part of funeral immolations, commonly either to send people to accompany a king or some other person of great standing. Human sacrifice was also practiced, as Robin Law points out, in the hope of restoring to health a terminally sick person.[34] The trope of human sacrifice is itself quite commonplace in literature, from Homer to the present day, so that Ikemefuna has good company in world literature.[35] However, because of the apparently capricious nature of the oracular demand in *Things Fall Apart* and its disconnection from averting any personal or collective crisis, Ikemefuna's death has nothing of the sacrificial resonance of Iphigenia's in Aeschylus' *Agamemnon*, for example, where the Greek military leader is tasked with the sacrifice of his daughter to propitiate the goddess Artemis, so that the winds are stilled for the Greek army to be able to attack Troy. (We will revisit Aeschylus' play in our discussion of moral contradiction in Chapter 7 on J. M. Coetzee.) It also has none of the bloody poignancy of the propitiatory beheading of Pentheus by his deranged mother Agave in Euripides' *Bacchae*. Nor does it have the same significance as Abraham's near-sacrifice of Isaac that inaugurates the covenant between Yahweh and Abraham and cements the foundational relationship with the biblical Israel.[36] Ikemefuna's sacrifice is literally out of the blue.

---

[33] Achebe, *Things Fall Apart*, 43.   [34] Robin Law, "Human Sacrifice," 57–58.
[35] For a comprehensive overview of literary representations of human sacrifice, see Derek Hughes, *Culture and Sacrifice: Ritual Death in Literature and Opera* (Cambridge: Cambridge University Press, 2007).
[36] For the tragic implications of this biblical episode, see Terry Eagleton's *Sweet Violence*.

Second, as we noted earlier, among the Igbo, in dire cases where human sacrifice was required, the person to be sacrificed would have been drawn from the cult of *osu* and not from among the freeborn. So why does Achebe orchestrate to have Ikemefuna sacrificed in place of an *osu*? Given that Ikemefuna was surrendered as recompense for the life of an Umuofian, he automatically occupied a degraded social status and should technically have been placed in the care of the cult of *osu* that we find peripherally represented in the novel. By placing Ikemefuna instead in the lively hub of Okonkwo's household and thus within the foreground of the narrative events, we are induced to identify with him, our identification being mediated by Nwoye, who completely adores the lad, but also by Okonkwo himself, who keeps lauding the positive impact he is having on the boys in his household. A silent contrast is, however, implied between the representation of Ikemefuna and that of the girl who was brought to Umuofia along with him. Because she is never named or described for us, the girl completely fades out of the text. This is exactly what would have happened to Ikemefuna had he been consigned to the cult of *osu*. Thus, Ikemefuna does double duty within the narrative of *Things Fall Apart*. He provides a way for us to judge Okonkwo's cowardice whilst also showing us what it might entail to be an ordinary *osu* whose life is always-already forfeit. Achebe deals head-on with the emotionally charged question of *osu* status in Independence Nigeria in his second novel *No Longer at Ease*, where the crisis turns on the doomed post-colonial romance between the Western-educated and highly sophisticated Obi, who is himself a direct descendant of Okonkwo through Nwoye, and Clara, Obi's *osu* girlfriend.[37] But it is clear that in his first novel, Achebe is tinkering with the enigmatic question of the *osu* cult system and putting it into narrative play as a means of indicating the volatile proximity between different understandings of insider/outsider status, and beyond that, of the historical transition between sacred and profane.

Okonkwo's machete descends twice in the novel, first in the killing of Ikemefuna, and second in the decapitation of the *kotma* (court messenger) toward the end of the novel. There is a signal invocation of elemental qualities that converts each scene into an image of foundational ethical choice. This subtends the overall status of the *osu* as an aspect of the dialectic between sacred and profane in the novel, a dialectic that also implicates the spatio-morphological relations between the *ilo* and market

---

[37] See Taiwo Adetunji Osinubi, "Abolition, Law, and the Osu Marriage Novel." *The Cambridge Journal of Postcolonial Literary Inquiry*, 2 (2015): 53–71.

place on the one hand and the Evil Forest on the other. On Ikemefuna's journey into the forest with the Umofians about to kill him, this is what we are shown:

> The sun rose slowly to the center of the sky, and the dry, sandy footway began to throw up the heat that lay buried in it. Some birds chirruped in the forests around. The men trod dry leaves on the sand. All else was silent. Then from the distance came the faint beating of the *ekwe*. It rose and faded with the wind – a peaceful dance from a distant clan.
>
> . . .
>
> The footway had now become a narrow line in the heart of the forest. The short trees and sparse undergrowth which surrounded the men's village began to give way to giant trees and climbers which perhaps had stood from the beginning of things, untouched by the ax and the bush-fire. The sun breaking through their leaves and branches threw a pattern of light and shade on the sandy footway.[38]

Everything in this passage appeals to the perspectival sensorium, from the heat released from the footway, the sounds of chirruping birds and the distant sound of the *ekwe* drum that accentuates the almost eerie silence, to the dappled pattern of light and shadow thrown on the ground by the sun streaming through leaves and branches. This appeal to the sensorium is also a means of registering how primeval the forest is, untouched by human effort and perhaps standing thus from the beginning of time and history. It is within the invocation of primeval timelessness that Achebe stages the infanticide, something that is itself a guarantor of the strongest sentiments in tragedy, as Aristotle adroitly notes in the *Poetics*: "But when the sufferings involve those who are near and dear to one another, when for example brother kills brother, son father, mother son, or son mother, or if such deed is contemplated, or something else of the kind is actually done, then we have a situation of the kind to be aimed at."[39]

The second descent of Okonkwo's machete recalls this earlier sense of primeval elemental qualities, but from an entirely different purview, since this time the tragic act is witnessed by his entire community, who function much like the classical choruses of Greek tragedy. The scene in question takes place at the marketplace, where Okonkwo's tribesmen and women have been called to discuss what response might be appropriate to the egregious insult visited upon Umuofia's elders by the white district commissioner. On the pretense of inviting them to join him for a palaver, the district commissioner has them suddenly disarmed and quickly handcuffed

---

[38] Achebe, *Things Fall Apart*, 41.   [39] Aristotle, *Poetics*, 50.

by the court messengers just when their delegation leader is about to speak. He then instructs that Umuofia be asked to deliver a fine of two hundred bags of cowrie shells in exchange for the freedom of their leaders, but when he leaves the scene, the elders are set upon by the court staff and beaten badly. The elders even suffer the added humiliation of having their heads shaved clean with a blunt razor. They are finally released upon the payment of two hundred and fifty bags of cowrie shells, the figure inflated by the court messengers for their own profit. Thus, when Umuofia gathers to talk at the market-place the mood is far from lighthearted. There is a sense of ominous expectancy in the air. Okonkwo is sitting at the edge of the gathered crowd; this is what we see:

> At this point there was a stir in the crowd and every eye was turned in one direction. There was a sharp bend in the road that led from the market-place to the white man's court, and to the stream beyond it. And so no one had seen the approach of the five court messengers until they had come round the bend, a few paces from the edge of the crowd. Okonkwo was sitting at the edge.
>
> He sprang to his feet as soon as he saw who it was. He confronted the head messenger, trembling with hate, unable to utter a word. The man was fearless and stood his ground, his four men lined up behind him.
>
> In that brief moment the world seemed to stand still, waiting. There was utter silence. The men of Umuofia were merged into the mute backcloth of trees and giant creepers, waiting.
>
> The spell was broken by the head messenger. "Let me pass!" he ordered.
>
> "What do you want here?"
>
> "The white man whose power you know too well has ordered this meeting to stop."
>
> In a flash Okonkwo drew his machete. The messenger crouched to avoid the blow. It was useless. Okonkwo's machete descended twice and the man's head lay beside his uniformed body.
>
> The waiting backcloth jumped into tumultuous life and the meeting stopped. Okonkwo stood looking at the dead man. He knew that Umuofia would not go to war. He knew because they had let the other messengers escape. They had broken into tumult instead of action. He discerned fright in the tumult. He heard voices asking: "Why did he do it?"

It is not entirely insignificant that Achebe's *Things Fall Apart* was written partly as a riposte to Conrad's unflattering representation of Africa. His essay on Conrad's racism is justifiably famous, but his critique of the earlier writer did not preclude some degree of admiration for Conrad's craftsmanship.[40]

---

[40] Chinua Achebe, "An Image of Africa: Racism in Conrad's *Heart of Darkness*."

In *Heart of Darkness* the jungle and its invocation as a primeval place means that Marlow and the white pilgrims traveling down the Congo river come face-to-face with the "beginning of things" and their journey is filled with a sense of suppressed anticipation mixed with dread.

While the scene in *Things Fall Apart* also invokes a sense of suppressed anticipation, in its precise details the encounter between Okonkwo and the court messenger is reconfigured into a dramatic moment in which the people of Umuofia are suddenly merged with primeval nature. They lose their individuality completely, and the murder is ultimately witnessed by a "backcloth of trees and giant creepers." It is a momentous archetype that is distinct from Conrad's in part because of the different historical contexts represented in the two novels, but also because the conflict in *Things Fall Apart* is ultimately that of the epic clash between native autonomy and colonial invasion that potentially implicates the destiny of an entire people. It is also distinct from the scene of Ikemefuna's murder: while there the primevalness of the scene was reported through the narrator's description, it was not quite clear to what extent the elements of that primevalness were being registered as an aspect of Ikemefuna's own anxious viewpoint as he was walked into the heart of the forest. The Umuofian men must have perceived the somber peculiarity of the setting to some extent themselves, since they commented on and attempted to provide an interpretation of the significance of the *ekwe* drum that they heard beating from a distance. Ikemefuna's death scene has none of the features of collective witnessing that we see in the scene in which Okonkwo beheads the *kotma*. Here the tableau of suppressed anticipation, as we shall see in Chapter 7, anticipates the perception of the Magistrate in Coetzee's *Waiting for the Barbarians*, "that for the duration of this frozen moment the stars are locked in a configuration in which events are not themselves but stand for other things."[41]

But the archetypal potential of this moment in *Things Fall Apart* collapses almost as soon as it flashes forth, for Okonkwo's act produces not the mobilization of sentiment against the colonizer that he had hoped for but rather a major epistemological impasse for his people. The overt clue to this epistemological impasse is the querulous question that he hears from the clan folk: "Why did he do that?" This question indicates the degree to which his action eludes the possibility of interpretation from within the hermeneutical codes that exist within the clan itself. In earlier times, his action would have been read straightforwardly as an

---

[41] J. M. Coetzee, *Waiting for the Barbarians* (New York: Penguin, 1980), 40.

unambiguous call to arms against the disrespectful colonial administration. For despite coming from very humble beginnings, Okonkwo has consistently been rewarded by Umuofia for espousing a robust form of military ethic. But when his machete falls for a final time his gesture is both the strong assertion of this ethic and also his final severance from the clan. To retrace the source of this epistemological impasse we must go not only through the many revelations of Okonkwo's fiery character, but also to the subtle alterations in the relationship between the sacred and the nonsacred within Umuofia. These are linked primarily to the spatial reconfiguration to the sacred semiotic within the clan, but also to the place of the *osu* as the focal point of the dialectical relationship between purity and danger.

Apart from Okonkwo's household, which acts as an organizing hub for the percolation of all the major events in the novel, there are two other key chronotopes that demarcate the spaces of Igbo social organization as represented in the novel. These are the Evil Forest and its counterpoint and opposite, the *ilo* and marketplace.[42] In *Things Fall Apart*, the *ilo* and marketplace play the role of the Greek agora in the sense that they combine at once the space of commerce and exchange with those of debate and deliberation. It is at the *ilo* that the masked *egwugwu* and much-feared representatives of ancestral spirits emerge out of the bowels of the earth to sit in judgment over civil and criminal cases. The *ilo* is also the space where the annual wrestling match is staged. The Evil Forest, on the other hand, is where humans considered to be either congenitally anomalous or afflicted by terminal diseases are cast out. These include baby twins and people suffering from unnameable and thus incomprehensible diseases. In *Things Fall Apart* the *ilo* and the marketplace thus jointly represent the space of cultural and juridical values while the Evil Forest represents the space of anomaly and sacred danger. This begins to change imperceptibly when the Christians arrive in Igboland. When they first arrive singing their strange songs and preaching the new religion, they are received by the people with a mixture of scepticism and bewilderment. The Christians initially represent a peculiar problem for the villagers since they do not come either as harbingers of war or purveyors of trade. When they ask for a place to build their new home they are given a chunk of the Evil Forest, with the idea that if their God and his son Jesu Kristi are really that powerful they should soon have the opportunity to prove it against Amadiora of the thunder and

---

[42] For a careful and superbly argued discussion on the status of the Evil Forest as a space of exception and its relation to the ideal of *civitas* in Achebe's novel, see Ainehi Edoro-Giles's "Achebe's Evil Forest: Space, Violence, and Order in *Things Fall Apart*," *The Cambridge Journal of Postcolonial Literary Inquiry*, 5.2 (1918): 176–192.

other fearsome gods of Umuofia. Several weeks pass and nothing happens to the Christians. And so, we are told: "Everyone was puzzled. And then it became known that the white man's fetish had unbelievable power. It was said that he wore glasses on his eyes so that he could see and talk to evil spirits. Not long after, he won his first three converts."[43] Early converts to the church include the *osu*, men without title, and women who had lost twin children.

Several significant transitions are triggered by the arrival of the Christians. At one level we find that they introduce a new meritocracy to displace what has undergirded the tribe before their arrival. For when the Christians preach that all men are equal before their God, it strikes a special chord in those such as the *osu*, who have experienced degraded personhood within the clan. It is not entirely insignificant that it is Enoch, himself a converted *osu*, who triggers the final showdown between Umuofia and the Christian church. Enoch tears the mask off an *egwugwu* on an important feast day and by this is said to have "killed" an ancestral spirit. This brings immediate and violent reprisals: the elders of the clan ask the church to be evacuated and they burn it to the ground. This in turn leads to the elders being reported to the white district commissioner, their arrest and humili-ation, and eventually Okonkwo's killing of the district commissioner's messenger, as we have already noted. Okonkwo's killing of the court messenger immediately recalls the killing of Ikemefuna, but the conun-drum concealed in the character of the young boy is now made manifest as an epistemological crisis for the entire clan. The point to note, however, is that whereas we see through the character of Ikemefuna the discursive interplay between foreground and implicit background of *osu* (sacred) and household (nonsacred), the interplay of sacred and nonsacred in the novel is also discursively conducted around the additional spatial vectors of Evil Forest and *ilo*/marketplace. But the shift in the relative statuses of the Evil Forest and the *ilo*/marketplace have to be understood as the product of the historical transition that has been marked by the arrival of the Christians.

For, in gaining a foothold in Umuofia, the early Christians do not merely attract converts from among the socially marginalized; they also fundamentally alter the terms of the sacred/profane semiotic that defines different spaces within the clan community. When Okonkwo's machete descends for the second and final time and he confronts his people with an epistemological crisis, this crisis is produced by the fact that even though the *ilo*/marketplace is physically located where it has always been, its status

---

[43] Achebe, *Things Fall Apart*, 106.

within the sacred symbolic nexus has subtly shifted away from being the site of the collective expression of unanimity among the clan. This has happened because the status of the Evil Forest has itself undergone a dramatic change by being successfully occupied by the Christians. Their occupation effectively moves the Evil Forest from the periphery of the cultural imaginary to its center, thus symbolically also shifting the *ilo/* marketplace away from its presumed centrality as the site of unanimity. Things fall apart not just because the center cannot hold, but because the nexus of symbolic cultural affirmation has moved from where it was presumed to be. This is part of the inexorable tragedy of the novel.

Character, Context, and the Conditions for the Exercise of Ethical Choice

Sample student essays on *Things Fall Apart*, which are liberally available on the Internet, often have seductive yet facile comparisons between Okonkwo and Oedipus, usually posed through the lens of the concept of tragic flaw.[44] While the two characters do share certain similarities, such as being faced with an ultimate tragic choice; unlike Oedipus, Okonkwo does not lend himself to steady deliberation or even to countenancing the opinions of others. Throughout the novel, Okonkwo's character throws up problems of interpretation for his community, given that he tends to act impulsively and against the norms of acceptable behavior dominant within his culture. Whether it is with the beating of his wife during the Week of Peace, something that he fully knows to be anathema to his community; his participation in the killing of Ikemefuna, against which he is warned beforehand; or his inadvertent killing of the son of Ogbuefi Ezeudu at the warrior's funeral; at each stage Okonkwo's actions present enigmas for those around him. Only the shooting of Ogbuefi's son at his father's funeral is not a conscious act, and yet the event is prepared for through reference to the same rusty gun with which he almost shoots one of his wives in an earlier scene. All the enigmas around Okonkwo, as we have seen, coalesce into an epistemological crisis on his killing of the *kotma* in his last act in the novel. This raises an important question: what is tragic about

---

[44] These are too many to list, but for representative samples, see the ones on Barteby.com, articlemyriad.com, bestessayhelp.com, fourlibrary.com, and several others like them. The general principle underlining these comparisons is a somewhat simplistic definition of tragic flaw and of fate, along with the corralling of Oedipus to illuminate Okonkwo. Okonkwo shares something with Oedipus but only in respect to his ultimate, tragic choice of suicide.

Okonkwo, and how do we evaluate the status of ethical choice in relation to his actions?

Okonkwo is the product of a number of contradictions, both of character and of the material conditions in which he is required to make ethical choices. In the first place he strives hard to distance himself from the failures of his father. The profile of the flute-playing, dissolute, and heavily indebted Unoka is not one that Okonkwo wants to identify with, and all his considerable energies are geared toward silencing the echoes of his father's failure from his mind. This is what makes Okonkwo desperate to suppress any signs of weakness or compassion within him, as well as any and all signs of compromise.

Alongside Okonkwo's conscious fear of being thought weak is another weakness that does not necessarily make it to the forefront of his mind. As we are told in the novel, "Proverbs are the palm-wine with which words are eaten" among his community. The idea that proverbs are a choice rhetorical medium for communication is amply illustrated as much in the wide range of proverbs that appear in the novel as in the reverence that is given to people such as Obguefi Ezeugo, frequently invited to address the gathered clan when major decisions are collectively deliberated upon. Okonkwo has a bad stammer, so bad that whenever he cannot get his words out he reverts to using his fists. He does this repeatedly throughout the novel. In a culture that prizes so highly the art of rhetoric, Okonkwo's speech impairment would have been experienced as a painful disability. This is subsumed under the mark of his extraordinary prowess for work and for war that allows him to rise to become one of the most highly regarded lords of the clan and a member of the terrifying council of *egwugwu*. And yet the true debilitative force of Okonkwo's impairment shows itself starkly in the final scene when set against the background of the clan assembly and in his confrontation with the court messengers. So filled with rage, he is fatally lost for words. One can only imagine how the scene would have played out if it was his more eloquent friend Obierika whom the messengers had encountered at the edge of the gathering. Even though his stammer is rarely referenced in the novel, all the instances in the novel when Okonkwo acts precipitously point to it.

Okonkwo's attempt to assert for the final time the claims of the ethic of honor for which he has been much rewarded throughout the novel must also be understood against the subtle changes that have taken place within the clan, especially during the seven-year hiatus when he was in exile in his mother's homeland. We are told, for instance that "There were many men and women in Umuofia who did not feel as strongly as Okonkwo about the new dispensation. The white man had indeed brought a lunatic religion, but he had also built a trading store and for the first time palm-oil and kernel became things of great price, and much money flowed into Umuofia."[45] The reference to the trading store provides two clues about the material transformation of productive cycles in the period in which the novel is set. The first is that it highlights the shift from subsistence farming to cash crop agriculture that was part of the wider transformation from slave economies to legitimate trade in the long nineteenth century that we noted earlier. Palm oil and palm kernel products were crucial lubricants for the Industrial Revolution in Europe and led to the development of a robust and wealthy indigenous class in Igboland and elsewhere in West Africa during the period. This class was to progressively define a different social subsystem overlapping and yet ultimately distinct from established traditional norms and values, and avidly embracing Christianity and Western-style education. It was not untypical for this Christianized class to send their children to the best schools in Europe, such that by the end of the nineteenth century they formed the emerging professional class of doctors, lawyers, and cultural commentators that also came to profess strong forms of proto-nationalism in organizations such as the National Congress of British West Africa (the NCBWA).[46]

The rise in the significance of palm oil as a source of wealth also meant a progressive diminution in the relative value of yams, the men's crop whose planting we get detailed descriptions of earlier in the novel. Okonkwo's final stance is thus simultaneously also against what are effectively the social, political, and economic transformations being wrought by colonial modernity, registered blatantly in the new colonial administration, but also more subtly in the new opportunities for wealth creation encapsulated in the booming trade of cash crops. This is not to speak of the effects of Christianity, which, as we have noted, subtly alter the relations between sacred and profane in Umuofia to the point of confounding the differences between friend and foe. When Okonkwo finally attempts to push the moment to its crisis, he does so in a manner that is comprehensible only in the terms of an older claim that is no longer particularly relevant to the present historical conditions of his community. We are not privy to the thinking behind his act of suicide at the very end, but given that he knew

---

[45] Achebe, *Things Fall Apart*, 126.
[46] On the complex nature of this process in Nigeria and elsewhere in West Africa, see especially P. F. de Moares Farias and Karin Barber, eds., *Self-Assertion and Brokerage: Early Cultural Nationalism in West Africa* (Birmingham: Centre for West African Studies, 1990), and David Kimble, *A Political History of Ghana: The Rise of Gold Coast Nationalism, 1850–1928* (Oxford: Clarendon Press, 1963).

his abominable death would have him cast without ceremony into the Evil Forest, never to be invoked as a tribal ancestor, the decision must have come from a deep sense of existential alienation.

Or it may have been the ultimate gesture of freedom that Schelling praises in *Oedipus Rex*:

> It was by *allowing* its hero to *fight* against the superior power of fate that Greek tragedy honored human freedom. In order not to exceed the limits of art, Greek tragedy was obliged to have the hero *succumb*; but in order to compensate for this humiliation of human freedom imposed by art, it also had to allow him to *atone* and *make amends* – even for a crime committed through *fate* . . . It was a great thought: to willingly endure punishment even for an *unavoidable* crime, so as to prove one's freedom precisely through the loss of this freedom and perish with a declaration of a free will.[47]

At the heart of Schelling's remarks on Greek tragedy is a major conundrum, namely, how to combine the recognition of fate and necessity with an acknowledgment of human freedom. He attempts to reconcile these through a dialectical reading whose central tenets also prove productive for interpreting Okonkwo's choice. In Sophocles' *Oedipus,* the hero's fate in killing his father and marrying his mother is already fulfilled by the time the play opens. The crime, already predicted by the oracle, takes on the status of necessity. However, it is a crime that also automatically entails a necessary punishment on its coming to light. For Oedipus' actions imply two separate yet profound infractions, one against the family (parricide and incest) and the other against the king (regicide). There are thus two outcomes that properly relate to the discovery of the infractions, the first is exile from Thebes and the second is to have to live with unrelieved guilt. Both outcomes intimately touch Oedipus as son and as king. The world of Sophocles' play heightens the time lag between crime and punishment that already exists in the myth from which it derives, and converts it into the compressed timeline of the heightened process of discovery that shapes the plot of the play. At the same time, the play populates and intensifies the hiatus between ignorance and knowledge with the bewildering pollution that afflicts the Thebans and their crops, and incites a quest motif; the

---

[47] F. W. J. Schelling, *Philosophical Letters on Dogmatism and Criticism*, in *The Unconditional in Human Knowledge: Four Early Essays, 1794–1796*, translated by Fritz Marti (Lewisburg, Pa: Bucknell University Press, 1980), 192–193; emphasis in original. For a handy discussion of Schelling's views on tragedy, see Peter Szondi, *An Essay on the Tragic*, translated by Paul Fleming (Stanford: Stanford University Press, 2002), 7–10; also Miriam Leonard, *Tragic Modernities* (Cambridge, MA: Harvard University Press, 2015), 52–56; and Joshua Billings, *Genealogy of the Tragic: Greek Tragedy and German Philosophy* (Princeton: Princeton University Press, 2014), 84–88.

enigmatic oracle of the blind hermaphrodite prophet Tiresias; and finally Oedipus' almost dervish-like quest to find out who killed King Laius. This quest is progressively conflated in the dramatic action with the quest to know himself, such that the shift in motivational focus progressively produces its own internal drive beyond what appears initially as a law-and-order question for him and the Thebans. What Schelling points to in his appraisal of tragic action is the supreme significance invoked in Oedipus taking on the punishment for his crimes as a self-imposed choice *before* he comes to be formally punished. This to Schelling is the ultimate declaration of human freedom in the face of necessity.

In *Things Fall Apart,* necessity and fate are not expressed as clearly as in *Oedipus* but are articulated in the novel through the Igbo concept of *chi.* But the *chi* is an elusive medium of interpretation. It is defined as one's personal god, and we are told many times that when a man says yes strongly, his *chi* also says yes. The problem, however, is that the *chi* may also say no when the man is saying yes, as is evident in the events that follow Okonkwo's inadvertent shooting of the young man at the funeral. Okonkwo's entire homestead is burned to the ground and he is sent into exile and has to rebuild himself and his family painfully and slowly in the land of sojourn. He suffers an immediate reversal of fortune, and as we might recall from Aristotle's discussion in *The Nicomachean Ethics,* suffers the fundamental loss of the comforts of his original community. Okonkwo's *chi* has proven unreliable as a barometer of his fate. Rather, what the *chi* concept seems to be pointing to, is the dialectical relationship between determinism and contingency, and not between necessity and free will as in Sophocles' play, which illustrates a completely different dialectical relationship. It is free will that invokes the strong yes to which a person's *chi* is held to respond, but the fate signaled by this yes can only be actualized through a series of contingent events, only some of which lead to the fulfillment of strongly expressed desires. It is the interaction of character orientation with contingent events that repeatedly produces unpredictable patterns denominated by the *chi.* Okonkwo has no idea that his rusty musket is going to go off in the middle of the funeral and kill the young man. This accident leads to his exile and thus to his formal separation from the historical material processes that alter the clan, so that on his return the clan is no longer what he thought it was before he left. And once the *kotma* confronts him at the end there is only one possible outcome, which is again the product of a long line of contingent events and processes, as we have seen. And Okonkwo knows that after that epic act of defiance, to be caught and tried by the white man means abject humiliation and certain death. There is just no doubt about it. Unlike Oedipus, Okonkwo's abominable act of committing suicide has not been fated from the beginning. There are no oracular predictions of his life beforehand but only the grind of self-crafting in a world that originally gives the assurance of predictability (say yes strongly and your *chi* will say yes with you) yet is also amply infused with the vagaries of historical transformation and thus also of contingency.

And at a personal level, his suppression of any signs of compromise or weakness also means that Okonkwo surrenders himself too readily to expressions of violence. In none of the examples of communal or ethical trespass we have noted (the killing of Ikemefuna, etc.) does he plan what he does beforehand. Rather, it is because he is impulsive in his violence that he ends up being over-exposed to accident and contingency and thus to processes that will come to reverse his most cherished goals and ambitions. Accident and contingency are firmly in the territory of tragedy, but quite different from the case of Oedipus Rex for whom the violent disposition only serves to fulfil a catastrophic choice (patricide, incest) that had already been foretold by the oracle. Like Oedipus (who takes out his eyes), Okonkwo decides to take his own life as the ultimate and uncompromising assertion of his own freedom, elevating a simple act performed amongst "the Primitive Tribes of the Lower Niger" into one of ultimate, universal tragic significance.

The Malaise of Colonial Modernity: The Mind of Ezeulu

Achebe's shift from the world of *Things Fall Apart* to that of *Arrow of God* marks a move from the pressures placed on traditional autonomy in the precolonial phase to that of a full-blown colonial modernity. In *Arrow of God*, Achebe eschews the somewhat naive ethical antithesis of colonizer versus colonized that governed parts of the earlier novel and which is superbly focused through Okonkwo himself. In contrast to the first novel, colonial modernity here becomes the backdrop for a display of major societal malaise that was completely absent from the world of *Things Fall Apart*. Philosopher Charles Taylor defines modernity as the "historically unprecedented amalgam of new practices and institutional forms (science, technology, industrial production, urbanization), of new ways of living (individualism, secularization, instrumental rationality), and of new forms of malaise (alienation, meaninglessness, a sense of impending social dissolution)."[48] Unlike White's definition of modernity that we

---

[48] Charles Taylor, "Modern Social Imaginaries," *Public Culture*, 14.1 (2002): 91–124.

alluded to earlier, Taylor's definition has the distinct advantage of placing equal emphasis on the malaises of the self, as well as the structural features of modernity. This provides a productive way of framing colonial modernity in Achebe's novel, starting with the degree to which attitudes to the past are ambiguated both for the central character Ezeulu, and for the different social subsystems within Umuaro.

Like Okonkwo, Ezeulu is intensely averse to any form of opposition. And yet he expresses a certain curiosity about the Christianity that has arrived amidst his people that is in direct contrast to Okonkwo's attitude to the same phenomenon. The contradictions to Ezeulu's character – of resolute traditionalism coupled with an abiding curiosity about world-historical processes – are akin to the conditions for the conscription to modernity that David Scott so eloquently writes about in his *Conscripts of Modernity*. As Scott notes in rereading C. L. R. James's *The Black Jacobins*, Toussaint Louverture is that anti-colonial figure that is utterly dispassionate in his pursuit of Enlightenment ideals of progress, and yet by the same token, is resistant to the pluralism of opinion that might contradict his pursuit of such ideals in the first place. Toussaint's descent into despotism is born precisely out of this contradiction. To Toussaint we might add Ezeulu as providing a fine fictional study in the conscription to modernity, but in his case, the appeal to Enlightenment ideals is replaced with an abiding curiosity about the meaning of the new religion for his people. The counterpoint to Ezeulu's curiosity regarding the Christians, is, however, an almost equal lack of interest in the significance of the colonial administration to the lifeworld of Umuaro. This duality toward world-historical processes also places him in direct contrast to Okonkwo.

Early on in the novel, Ezeulu expresses a pragmatic reaction to Christianity that illustrates an important dimension of his conscription to colonial modernity. He is trying to persuade his son Oduche to attend the church school:

> It was five years since Ezeulu promised the white man that he would send one of his sons to church. But it was only two years ago that he fulfilled the promise. He wanted to satisfy himself that the white man had not come for a short visit but to build a house and live.
>
> At first Oduche did not want to go to church. But Ezeulu called him to his obi and spoke to him as a man would speak to his best friend and the boy went forth with pride in his heart. He had never heard his father speak to anyone as an equal.
>
> "The world is changing," he had told him. "I do not like it. But I am like the bird Eneke-nti-oba. When his friends asked him why he was always on

the wing he replied: 'Men of today have learnt to shoot without missing and so I have learnt to fly without perching.' I want one of my sons to join these people and be my eye there. If there is nothing in it you will come back. But if there is something there you will bring home my share. The world is like a Mask dancing. If you want to see it well you do not stand in one place. My spirit tells me that those who do not befriend the white man today will be saying *had we known* tomorrow."

And when Ezeulu's wife protests against this decision, he rounds on her furiously:

"How does it concern you what I do with my sons? You say you do not want Oduche to follow strange ways. Do you not know that in a great man's household there must be people who follow all kinds of strange ways? There must be good people and bad people, honest workers and thieves, peace-makers and destroyers; that is the mark of a great obi. In such a place, whatever music you beat on your drum there is somebody who can dance to it."[49]

Ezeulu is an extremely proud and arrogant man and as priest of Ulu has very little patience for anyone who disagrees with him. But here we find him reasoning with his son almost as a friend and sharing his sense that the white man has built a house and come to stay and so needs to be fully understood. As the priest of Ulu, he himself has no desire to attend the white man's church but wants to embed his son in the church on what amounts to a long-term intelligence-gathering mission. The contrast with Okonkwo's response to the Christians is instructive. Ezeulu justifies this pragmatic approach with reference to two proverbs, as if to insert the new Christianity into the modalities of his tribe's traditional hermeneutic. Eneke-the-bird's permanent flight celebrates well-known instincts of survival culled from the natural world, but the reference to the mask dancing is at once socio-spiritual and aesthetic. For it refers to a beautiful annual spectacle among the Igbo that invokes the dreaded masked *egwugwu* ancestral spirits we encountered in *Things Fall Apart*.

But does this not also mean that Ezeulu sees the arrival of the white man as perhaps an iteration of the symbolic authority normally associated with his own ancestors? The answer at this point appears to be yes, but this will be sharply qualified later in the novel when he stands face-to-face with the deputy district commissioner. This apparent dialectical assimilation of opposites within *the mind of the central character*, as we shall see in our next chapter, also appears in Wole Soyinka's *Death and the King's*

---

[49] Achebe, *Arrow of God*, 45–46, emphasis in original.

Horseman, where Elesin Oba commits the blasphemy of mistaking the rude intrusion of the white district commissioner into his attempt at ritual suicide as somehow the intervention of his own gods. Elesin hesitates for one moment only, but this is enough for him to fail to make the crossing and to trigger a major existential crisis for his people. In the case of Ezeulu, the crisis is more immediately registered in the bewildered reaction of the people in his household and of others in the clan at large. And yet, in his irritable response to Oduche's mother's protestations, he suggests that sending his son to the church is actually a form of cosmopolitan worldliness, for whatever music might be played, there will be someone in his homestead able to interpret the music and dance to it.

Partly because of the changes in the historical role of the priesthood of Ulu and partly because of his own ambition to become an agent of social transformation, Ezeulu seems to be seriously irritated by the implied limitations of his role. Very early in the novel we see him contemplating his power:

> Whenever Ezeulu considered the immensity of his power over the year and the crops and, therefore, over the people he wondered if it was real. It was true he named the day for the feast of the Pumpkin Leaves and for the New Yam feast; but he did not choose it. He was merely a watchman. His power was no more than the power of a child over a goat that was said to be his. As long as the goat was alive it could be his; he would find it food and take care of it. But the day it was slaughtered he would know soon enough who the real owner was. No! the Chief Priest of Ulu was more than that, must be more than that. If he should refuse to name the day there would be no festival – no planting and no reaping. But could he refuse? No Chief Priest had ever refused. So it could not be done. He would not dare.
>
> Ezeulu was stung to anger by this as though his enemy had spoken it.
>
> "Take away that word dare," he replied to this enemy. "Yes I say take it away. No man in all Umuaro can stand up and say that I dare not. The woman who will bear the man who will say it has not been born yet."
>
> But this rebuke brought only momentary satisfaction. His mind never content with shallow satisfactions crept again to the brink of knowing. What kind of power was it if it would never be used? Better to say that it was not there, that it was no more than the power in the anus of the proud dog who sought to put out a furnace with his puny fart . . . He turned the yam with a stick.[50]

The sting of anger is returned to elsewhere in the novel, where Ezeulu's contrary thoughts are described as though he has been stung by a "black

---

50 Achebe, *Arrow of God*, 3.

ant." This metaphor conveys a sense of viscerality to his thought processes, something that we later realize is part of an unstable mental disposition. Throughout the novel, Ezeulu's mind is marked by the structure of skeptical interlocution, of which we shall see an even fuller expression in the characters of Coetzee's novels in Chapter 7. We recall Taylor's remarks about the new malaises of alienation, meaninglessness, and the sense of impending social dissolution that mark modernity, except that Ezeulu's malaise does not lead directly to a sense of lethargy but rather to a surfeit of disquiet and anger, unlike the many other modernist characters whom we might compare him to in Conrad, Eliot, Woolf, Joyce, Beckett, and others.[51]

While what we find in *Arrow of God* as the structure of skeptical interlocution is fundamental to the characterization of Ezeulu's conscious-ness, the texture of disputatiousness that we see inside his mind also happens to be the central organizing principle of the novel in general.[52] In *Arrow of God*, the dynamics of historical transition are registered not only within the interlocutory structure of Ezeulu's consciousness or in the argumentative nature of Umuaran society, but more fundamentally at the elusive level of the discursive interface of epistemology, storytelling, and history that we see displayed throughout the novel. Rumors, gossip, and foundational narratives are all shown to hold different epistemological implications for action. Crucial foundational narratives, such as how the clan managed to own the land on which they are now settled, the history of the synthetic god Ulu as the response to the existential threat of the slave raiders of Abam, and the status of the sacred python that is counterpoised to the Ulu cult, are all subject to contradictory interpretations at different points in the novel. The overall unanimity that we saw in *Things Fall Apart*, is here replaced by radical disagreement, expressed most strongly in a proverb repeated more than once in the novel: "Wisdom is like a goatskin bag; every man carries his own." Such a proverb would have been unthink-able in the world of Umuofia. In contrast to the unstable assent given to foundational narratives in the novel, gossip and rumor elicit more ready agreement than the foundational narratives of the clan. This hints at the fact that the transition produced by colonial modernity has also succeeded in reconfiguring epistemological categories of knowledge. We see then that

---

[51] Prufrock, Marlow, Leopold Bloom, Mrs. Dalloway, and Murphy, are all potential literary cousins of Ezeulu, the difference being that, unlike them, he retains an insuperable desire for action.

[52] For a fuller account of the disputatiousness inherent to the world of *Arrow of God*, see my "Self-Writing and Existential Alienation in African Literature: Chinua Achebe's *Arrow of God*," *Research in African Literatures*, 42.2 (March 2011): 30–45.

Achebe is giving free play to both dominant and residual cultural categories by suggesting a discursive inversion of the role of *grand récit* and *petit récit* (i.e., that the dominant foundational tales appear dubious while rumors and gossip retain believability) and yet also simultaneously affirming the order of things (i.e., that it is the foundational tales that are the subject of deliberative exchange for the *polis*, while gossip and rumor retain their salience largely at the level of the *oikos*). The simultaneity of inversion and affirmation then encapsulates the ambiguity of transition located at the intersection of both content and form. As Gikandi has adroitly noted, "for the community in *Arrow of God* – and thus too, the narrator and the reader – the necessity of art and the meaning of reality have changed; there is neither certainty about the direction of cultural process under colonialism, nor any sense of conviction about the final outcome of the history initiated by the colonizer."[53]

On Colonial Interpellation

A significant aspect of the ethos of colonial modernity that distinguishes *Arrow of God* from *Things Fall Apart* is the degree to which colonial interpellation is rendered as an explicit theme. This derives substantially from the implications of seeing and being seen, which in turn depend on the information economies that define the relation between colonial knowledge-making and the elusiveness of the native populations to such knowledge systems. There are many examples of the links between information-gathering and interpellation, seen especially in the sections that feature discussions among the white colonial officials. As the colonial official "on the ground," Winterbottom is proud of his knowledge of the natives. But in various instances, this knowledge is based on faulty information-gathering techniques and indeed on hearsay and gossip. He hears many stories about the high-handedness of Chief Ikedi, the warrant chief that had been appointed for Okperi after much deliberation. Chief Ikedi is said to be extorting monies from his subjects with the promise of preserving their homesteads in the surveys he carries out for the newly commissioned road. After much investigation, Ikedi is suspended but later reinstated by the Senior Resident "who had just come back from leave and had no first-hand knowledge of the matter."[54] Ikedi is a wily customer, and having returned to his position is very careful to cover his tracks; it is quite impossible to incriminate him in any subsequent scandal. This native

[53] Gikandi, *Reading Chinua Achebe*, 52.   [54] Achebe, *Arrow of God*, 57.

elusiveness does not deter Winterbottom from jumping to conclusions about the native mind based on his own shallow understanding. In telling Tony Clarke about the causes of the quarrel between Umuaro and Okperi into which he intervened, Winterbottom reports motives and a sequence of events that are completely different from the ones that Achebe shows us in the relevant sections of the narrative. The complex causes behind the quarrel that are related to us over the course of fifteen pages (from pages 14–28) are simply reduced by Winterbottom to being the product of prodigious alcohol consumption:

> This war started because a man from Umuaro went to visit a friend in Okperi one fine morning and after he'd had one or two gallons of palm wine – it's quite incredible how much of that dreadful stuff they can tuck away – anyhow, this man from Umuaro having drunk his friend's palm wine reached for his ikenga and split it in two ... This was of course the greatest sacrilege. The outraged host reached for his gun and blew the other fellow's head off. And so a regular war developed between the two villages, until I stepped in.[55]

Even though almost every detail of this account of the feud is wrong, the point is not its accuracy or inaccuracy, but that it forms the basis for the colonial knowledge economy about the native. We might recall the district commissioner's anthropological musings at the end of *Things Fall Apart* as to what portion of his planned book he ought to dedicate to the strange case of the dead Okonkwo, whose corpse his clansmen refused to take down from the tree where he hanged himself. Like the district commissioner in the earlier novel, Winterbottom is completely self-assured about the reliability of his knowledge, and thus the ultimate justness of the civilizing mission of which he is the proud agent "on the ground."

Late in the novel, an encounter takes place between Ezeulu and the assistant district commissioner, Tony Clarke, that forcefully foregrounds the problematic relationship between colonial knowledge and colonial interpellation. When Ezeulu is invited by the assistant district commissioner to be informed of the administration's decision to make him political head of his people under the auspices of the Warrant Chief system, his response is astounding in its simplicity:

> The expression on the priest's face did not change when the news was broken to him. He remained silent. Clarke knew it would take a little time for the proposal to strike him with its full weight.

[55] Achebe, *Arrow of God*, 37–38.

"Well, are you accepting the offer or not?" Clarke glowed with the I-know-this-will-knock-you-over feeling of a benefactor.

"Tell the white man that Ezeulu will not be anybody's chief, except Ulu."

"What!" shouted Clarke. "Is the fellow mad?"

"I tink so sah," said the interpreter.

"In that case he goes back to prison." Clarke was now really angry. What cheek! A witch-doctor making a fool of the British Administration in public!"[56]

As Nicholas Brown notes in his fine chapter on Achebe,

if we keep in mind the original meaning of . . . the negation of the field of human possibilities by an essentializing gaze that collapses these possibilities into a single, reified actuality – we can understand this return of the gaze as a change in polarity from . . . *shame* to *pride*. The returned gaze is not so much a genuine realignment of terms as a challenge that marks the prideful assumption of a position – or, if one likes, an identity or 'object-state' – which had been given in advance as shame.[57]

Brown here is speaking of an oscillation between poles, for the colonial gaze seeks both to denominate the native as knowable and also to generate in him or her a sense of obsequiousness (shame) that might be conducive to subjugation. The shift we see in the encounter between Ezeulu and Clarke is not, however, from shame to pride, since shame is alien to Ezeulu's character, but from a philanthropic interpellation based on faulty knowledge on Clarke's part to a prideful assertion of absolute difference in the case of Ezeulu. This pride completely unsettles the colonial gaze, as we see in Clarke's spluttering anger. Setting aside the assistant district commissioner's profane incredulity, what the extraordinary episode from *Arrow of God* illustrates is Ezeulu's absolute refusal to be interpellated as a functionary of colonialism. And yet his refusal is no simple disavowal or indeed gesture of mockery, as Clarke mistakenly assumes. It is that Ezeulu refuses to acknowledge the very premise of the interpellation in the first place. He is first and last the priest of Ulu. This obliterates the grounds upon which he might understand service to any other authority, spiritual, colonial, or otherwise. There is something to be said for Ezeulu's ego here too. While it is true that his commitment to being priest of Ulu takes precedence over any desire to serve another authority, as we saw in earlier quotes in this chapter, he is also someone who is dissatisfied with the limitations of his power and invents thought-experiments to test out those limits ("If he

[56] Achebe, *Arrow of God*, 174–175.
[57] Nicholas Brown, *Utopian Generations*, 118, emphasis in original.

should refuse to name the day there would be no festival – no planting and no reaping. But could he refuse? No Chief Priest had ever refused.") It is worthwhile not framing Ezeulu's refusal to accept Clark's offer as *entirely* motivated by ethical/religious integrity, but also by pride and ego, thus showing how the personal is indeed political or at least leads to political consequences.

The point of the failed interpellation of Ezeulu by Tony Clarke is not just to show the former's cultural pride, but to illustrate that the two of them occupy completely different realms of signification. For Ezeulu, Ulu signifies everything, for Tony Clarke, nothing. When Ezeulu goes mad at the end of the novel, it is not because he feels any pressure from the impact of colonialism, but because he seeks and fails to convert himself into an instrument of Ulu for the punishment of his own people. Ezeulu's mind has been converted into a theatre for the transposition of two distinctive struggles: the first struggle is between the synthetic god Ulu, of which he is the chief priest, and the older autochthonous Edimili, represented by the sacred python but also by the contrarian characters of Nwaka and Ezidimili, the python cult's priest; and the second struggle is between Christianity and the domain of native customs. Apart from the point where Ezeulu decides to send his son to join the Christians, at no point in the novel does he express any sense of curiosity about what the colonialists might be up to.

This lack of curiosity is in marked contrast to his attitude to Christianity, for whereas he has a pragmatic curiosity about it, he seems to have absolutely no interest either in being a part of the colonial administrative apparatus or indeed in finding out anything more about it. Once he dispenses with Clarke's vulgar incredulity on the question of power, he puts the workings of the colonial apparatus completely out of his mind. Just before he is ushered in to see Tony Clarke, Ezeulu spots the assistant district commissioner writing in a book with his left hand, and the first thought that comes to his mind is to "wonder whether any black man could ever achieve the same mastery over book as to write it with the left hand."[58] And yet Ezeulu's sense of curiosity about the technology of writing does not extend to an enquiry about the rest of the colonial bureaucratic apparatus that he sees amply laid out before him at Okperi. The one opportunity for the negative effects of colonialism to break into his mind occurs earlier when his son Obika is whipped by the white overseer, but this possibility is completely set aside when Ezeulu refuses

---

[58] Achebe, *Arrow of God*, 173.

to hear Obika's account of events and thus misses the opportunity to see the full character and scale of the colonializer's intrusion into his world. And here is one key source of his error of judgment. For he fails to see that the struggle that he wages against the rest of the clan in his refusal to eat the remaining ritual yams is ultimately the introduction of a dire existential crisis that will be resolved via his people's complete capitulation to the Christians, and thus, by implication, to colonialism itself. Ezeulu inadvertently delivers his people into the embrace of the Christians, who in the novel, as in history, are the harbingers of formal colonialism and its primary vanguard.

Conclusion

I have often wondered what it would be like to hypothetically bring Ezeulu and the Fanon of "The Fact of Blackness" into a conversation about colonial interpellation.[59] As we saw in the Introduction, in "The Fact of Blackness" Fanon describes how his bodily schema is discombobulated through the very process of his movements in space because for the colonial subject, quotidian space is never innocent of stereotypes that tincture the native and reconstitute him or her. I suspect that Ezeulu's advice to Fanon would simply be that there is no obligation to acquiesce in the act of being hailed and thus interpellated.[60] *Just say no!* might be Ezeulu's uncompromising suggestion. To which Fanon might retort that the hailing of the black body within the colonial regime of race relations is governed by modalities that transcend the site of hailing in the first place. The site of hailing, he might add, derives from the very foundational process for articulating individual self-identity as such. In other words, hailing and self-identification are aspects of the same and singular structure of denominations. For the colonial racial economy generates a hermeneutic of simultaneity, where assimilation and splitting are aspects of the same process. Let's recall the self-reflexive insight that Fanon proffers in his essay: "in one sense, if I were asked for a definition of myself, I would say that I am one who waits; I investigate my surroundings, I interpret everything in terms of what I discover, I become sensitive."[61] As we saw in the Introduction, this statement is paradigmatic of the degree to which all

---

[59] Frantz Fanon, "The Fact of Blackness."

[60] The entire apparatus of interpellation is famously introduced by Louis Althusser in "Ideology and Ideological State Apparatuses: Notes Toward an Investigation," *Lenin and Philosophy and Other Essays* (London: Verso, 1971), 85–125. Judith Butler critiques Althusser's formulation and extends it to cover the area of gender interpellation. See her *The Psychic Life of Power*.

[61] Fanon, "The Fact of Blackness," 120.

that he discovers depends insistently on a fervent interpretation of his surroundings, both historical and cultural. The differences between Fanon and Ezeulu must ultimately be attributed to differences in their material and historical contexts. For Fanon is writing about his own visceral responses to being situated within the pigmentocracy that structured race relations in Martinique, the Caribbean and the colonial world more generally. This pigmentocracy was central to the colonial project in many parts of the world, including India, Angola, South Africa, and in many parts of the United States. Ezeulu has no such pigmentocracy to contend with in the racially homogenous world of Umuaro.

And yet Ezeulu's hypothetical response to Fanon would have to be set against that of Okonkwo, for whom the only correct response to colonialism is to be culled from Fanon's invocation of the necessity of colonized violence against the colonizer for the purgation of the abased status to which colonialism has sought to reduce the native. This is what Fanon famously argues in *Wretched of the Earth*, whose final chapter is made up of a series of case studies of the Algerians and *pied noires* that came to him for psychiatric treatment. What emerges there is the complicated nature of the psychic wounding and the concomitant ambiguation of the colonized's attitudes to his or her own self-regard. So, if Ezeulu abjures Fanon, Okonkwo embraces him. And it is Achebe's superb illustration of the difficulties of arriving at any straightforward ethically salient choices of action that mark his two rural novels as wonderful illustrations of the tragic condition from the perspective of the Igbo world in transition under the long impress of colonialism. The resonances of *Things Fall Apart* and *Arrow of God* for understanding postcolonial tragedy in Africa and beyond are many, and for very good reasons.

CHAPTER 4

Ritual Dramaturgy and the Social Imaginary in Wole Soyinka's Tragic Theatre

Annemarie Heywood is right in pointing out that whether in his novels, poetry or plays, Wole Soyinka's essentially dramatic gifts are geared more toward anti-mimeticism than toward any form of naturalistic representation. This does not mean that he doesn't produce naturalistic works. The *Jero* plays, *The Swamp Dwellers, The Strong Breed,* and even to a degree, *The Lion and the Jewel* are good examples of mimetic and naturalistic writing that center on predictable character psychology and motivation and proceed through a linear mode. The same disposition is evident in his "factional" works such as *Aké, Isara,* and *Ibadan,* all of which are auto/biographical but with a heavy inflection of creative inventiveness. When staging character and setting in his anti-mimetic plays, however, Soyinka elects a dramatic medium that allows their largely aesthetic-political messages to be communicated through cryptic and often elusive ritual meanings. As Heywood goes on to note, Soyinka's anti-mimetic strand is marked by contrastive characterization and the tendency to frustrate any resolution to the conflicts set up within the dramatic action. The unfolding of the dramatic action is supposed to compound the conflicts at various levels and to intensify the structural implications of misunderstandings between characters as a feature of larger discrepancies within their political and historical contexts. Thus, many of Soyinka's plays, along with his novels *The Interpreters* and *Season of Anomie,* end on an "intolerable open paradox" with, at best, a dialectical balancing of the multifariously contending forces that have been exposed in the course of the action but never with any clear resolution.[1] His is the tragedy of caprice, and when this is confronted and appears to be somehow contained, then it is the tragedy of unpredictability.

---

[1] Annemarie Heywood, "The Fox's Dance: The Staging of Wole Soyinka's Plays," in Biodun Jeyifo, ed., *Perspectives on Wole Soyinka: Freedom and Complexity* (Jackson: University of Mississippi Press, 2001), 130–138.

The two plays that best illustrate Soyinka's aesthetics of tragedy are the well-known *Death and the King's Horseman*, and the lesser known *The Road*, both of which will be examined in this chapter.[2] *Death and the King's Horseman* presents a minute interpretation of the moving parts involved in an error of judgment, reversal of fortune, and *anagnorisis* that would have been much appreciated by Aristotle. It also has a number of other elements that are reminiscent of the Greeks, such as a strong degree of disputatiousness, a carefully choreographed chorus-function, and an idea of the *pharmakos* that aligns sacrifice directly with the welfare of the *polis*. What prevents us from asserting a simple line of Greek influence to Soyinka's dramaturgy is his explicitly acknowledged debts to Yorùbá cosmogony, especially with respect to the stories of Ógún and Esu, both of whom provide explicit ideational templates for several of his plays. *Death and the King's Horseman* draws inspiration from a real historical event that occurred during the colonial period, and which Soyinka adroitly manipulates to generate what he terms, in his Preface to the text, to be the "threnodic" essence of the play. The emotional crux of the play centers on the failed ritual suicide of Elesin Oba, the king's horseman of the title, who by tradition is supposed to extinguish himself some forty days after the death of the King. The play stages a confrontation between the colonial administration, represented by the fumbling, yet dangerously myopic Simon Pilkings, and a colorful cast of Yorùbá characters that include Elesin Oba, Iyaloja (head of the market women), Praise-Singer, and several others.

If the tragedy at the heart of *Death and the King's Horseman* is temporally bound to the crisis of signification triggered by the colonial encounter and its introduction of multiple meaning-systems, *The Road* is a kind of indirect sequel to it. Set after the British have left, when poverty and a lack of opportunities has produced a nihilistic, lackadaisical generation of Nigerian youth, this play utilizes aporetic, Beckettian voices that spring directly from postcolonial ennui. The tragic vision of *The Road* turns on the protagonist Professor's quest for the Word, the reality of which is much obscured in a mass of quotidian words that he scavenges from various sources, as if in a transposition of a quasi-Christian quest. But to complicate matters, the world of *The Road* is also infused with a Yorùbá sense of cyclical time, such that Professor's Word-quest, with all its implications of Christian teleology, has to be navigated through a traditional belief system that is diametrically opposed to any straightforward temporality.

---

[2] All references will be to Wole Soyinka, *The Road, Collected Plays*, vol. 1 (Oxford: Oxford University Press, 1973), 147–232, and *Death and the King's Horseman* (London: Metheun, 1975).

Professor's quest is pursued amongst unemployed motor-park workers in an unnamed Nigerian urban setting riddled with sundry threats of violence. The result is the focalization of hermeneutical delirium through the central character, a series of sudden stops and starts to the dramatic action, and twists and turns of increasingly heightened intensity that end in an explosive denouement when Professor is stabbed by one of his followers. In this final moment he is automatically converted into a *pharmakos*, the purgation of which induces a brief respite from the drudgery of the daily grind that is the lot of his followers, the unemployed men of the transport industry. Between these two plays are strung a number of key tragic concepts including the following: the status of sacrifice and its relation to the public sphere; the rhythms of contrasting epistemologies and the implications of epistemological impasse; and the relationship between historical transition and ethical choice in light of all these.

Soyinka's Theory of Tragedy

Soyinka provides us with an elaborate account of his own idea of tragedy in *Myth, Literature, and the African World*.[3] This draws on a number of different sources, including his own interpretation of tales from Yorùbá mythology and of Nietszche's *The Birth of Tragedy*. In exploring Soyinka's tragic theory, it is helpful to recall Lévi-Strauss on the continual processes of transformation that take place in all mythic systems:

> a mythic system can only be grasped as a *process of becoming*; not as something inert and stable but in a process of perpetual transformation. This would mean that there are always several kinds of myths simultaneously present in the system, some of them primary (in respect of the moment at which the observation is made), and some of them derivative. And while some kinds are present in their entirety at certain points, elsewhere they can be detected only in fragmentary form. Where evolution has gone furthest, the elements set free by the decomposition of the old myths have already been incorporated into new combinations.[4]

In the case of the Yorùbá, the process that Lévi-Strauss describes here seems to be less that old myths are continuously recombined with new ones, than

---

[3] Wole Soyinka, *Myth, Literature, and the African World* (Cambridge: Cambridge University Press, 1975). My discussion of Soyinka's tragic theory here draws on what I wrote on the question in *Strategic Transformations in Nigerian Writing* (Oxford and Bloomington: James Currey and Indiana University Press, 1997), 67–78.

[4] Claude Lévi-Strauss, *From Honey to Ashes*, trans. John and Doreen Weightman (London: Jonathan Cape, 1973; first published 1966), 354, emphasis added.

that there is a continual interchange of elements between individual myths, between myths, folktales and proverbs, and between praise names and epithets. As Karin Barber points out in relation to the Yorùbá *orísa* (mythical stories of the gods), there is a perceivable "inconsistency, fragmentation, and merging" of the qualities of individual *orísa*. The *oríkí* (praise-names and epithets) on the other hand, recover something of this state of flux by processes of naming that depend on an eclectic conglomeration of references.[5] Soyinka focuses attention on the Ógún myth so as to define the essence of his culture's sensibilities and of his own drama, and in doing this reaps a large payout of sign, symbol, and agency that allows him to graft the myth onto various characters and modes of expression.

A defining structural feature of Soyinka's meditations on Yorùbá mythology in *Myth, Literature, and the African World* is a process of relational differentiation. Soyinka isolates each element in his schema by simultaneously relating it to and differentiating it from other elements both internal to the Yorùbá worldview and refracted from outside of it. The important first step of seizing on a particular *orísa* to elaborate the belief system of his culture involves the continual differentiation of Ógún's qualities, not just from those of other *orísas* in the Yorùbá pantheon, but also from a Western paradigm represented for him in Nietzsche's meditations on tragedy, from which he draws an eclectic range of references. Nietzsche's move in *The Birth of Tragedy* to extrapolate from Greek ritual to an outline of what he takes to be the metaphysical relations between Apollonian and Dionysian characteristics and their implications for tragic form inflects the steps that Soyinka adopts in his own theorizing.[6] For Soyinka, Ógún's epic energy for destruction is in sharp contrast to Obatala's serenity and it is their synthesis that he perceives to be worked out in traditional Yorùbá votive drama. Nietzsche's postulation of the Greek need for the Olympian gods as a means of negotiating the terrors of existence finds a corollary in Soyinka's account of a Yorùbá yearning to bridge the gap between the people and their *orísas*. However, Soyinka also perceives fundamental differences between the Yorùbá pantheon and that of the Greeks. Though he suggests that in his love of palm-wine and his expression of violent anger and passion Ógún signals something of Dionysian and even Promethean virtues, the rituals of Ógúnian Mysteries are seen to be distinctive in a

[5] Karin Barber, "*Oríkí*, Women and the Proliferation and Merging of *Orísa*," *Africa*, 60.3 (1990): 313–336. See also her *I Could Speak Until Tomorrow: Oriki, Women, and the Past in a Yorùbá Town* (Edinburgh: Edinburgh University Press, 1991).

[6] Friedrich Nietzsche, *The Birth of Tragedy and the Genealogy of Morals*, trans. by Francis Goffling (New York: Doubleday, 1956), 19, 30–31, 50, 56.

number of crucial respects. Unlike the rituals surrounding Greek gods, Ógún's mysteries are based on a cultural appreciation of the absolute reality of both supernal and chthonic realms.[7] Furthermore, he sees an important difference in the ethical and moral basis of the two pantheons. Like the Greek pantheon, Yorùbá gods are often given to capriciousness and various excesses. However, in the Greek example, the "morality of reparation" seems entirely alien to the scheme of things. Punishments typically occur when the offence involves an encroachment on the earthly territory of another god. In contrast to this, Soyinka notes that for the Yorùbá, human society may itself exact penalties from their gods for both real and symbolic injuries, thus establishing a different relationship for thinking about both guilt and reparation.[8]

These provide important indices of the differences in the ethical and moral bases of the two pantheons. Whether Soyinka is correct in his assessment is less important than the fact that he labors to simultaneously establish affinities as well as differences between the two mythologies in order to carve a specific tragic template for his own use. In many respects, the process by which Soyinka attempts to differentiate his theory from that of Nietzsche's involves earthing the philosopher's abstractionism in a pragmatic traditional cultural context. By the time Nietzsche was writing *The Birth of Tragedy*, the Greek gods were mainly the subjects of artistic representations and philosophical disquisitions; they were not living belief systems in the way that, for the Yorùbá, their gods had and still have living expression in cults, the Ifá system of divination, and in personal names and epithets. Soyinka is at pains to capture all this, while struggling to adduce a specifically tragic sensibility from the Yorùbá myths.

Soyinka interweaves three distinct Yorùbá myths in mapping Ógún's singular career. First is the myth of Orísa-nla and the emergence of all the deities when Orísa-nla is smashed by a boulder into a thousand fragments.[9] The second, which centers specifically on Ógún, takes pride of place in Soyinka's theory and involves Ógún carving a pathway for the gods in their descent to earth.[10] Soyinka frequently refers to various dimensions of this story throughout his writings. In addition to this, there is also the story of Ógún's brief reign on earth at Ire and his act of precipitate violence in killing his own people when in a drunken stupor from too much palm-wine.[11] In traditional contexts among the Yorùbá, the story of Orísa-nla's

[7] Soyinka, *Myth, Literature*, 142   [8] Soyinka, *Myth, Literature*, 13–15.
[9] Soyinka, *Myth, Literature*, 27; see also Bolaji Idowu, *Olodumare: God in Yorùbá Belief* (London: Longman, 1962), 59–60.
[10] Idowu, 85–87.   [11] Soyinka, *Myth, Literature*, 29; Idowu, 86–87.

fragmentation is told to account for the emergence of the numerous deities and does not pertain to the qualities of any one *orísa* as such. But for Soyinka, Ógún bridges the pathway between gods and earth, thus becoming a culture hero and revolutionary. His actions map out the parameters of creativity as well as of hubris and excess. Also central to this formulation, is Ógún's role as *pharmakos* and the fact that he sacrifices himself to affirm the community's sense of corporate identity in the crossing from the supernal realm. All these elements of Ógún realities – the sacrificial role, his epic heroism, his creativity, and his excess – become central to how Soyinka comes to depict his own fictional characters and the social conditions in which different dimensions of the god's character are articulated through them.

Soyinka's theory of Ógún is grounded in a number of critical temporal and spatial presuppositions, many of which reside as much at the level of implication within the myths as in his explicit statements. By far the most important is that, for the Yorùbá, time is not an abstract linear concept but the crucible for the encounter between the three worlds of the living, the dead, and the yet unborn. As Soyinka firmly asserts, "life, present life, contains within it the manifestations of the ancestors, the living, and the unborn."[12] The juxtaposition of the three worlds also means that there is often a degree of leakage between them and that the world depicted in his plays always subtends those of the other realms. This subtension is not allowed to convert the domain of represented dramatic action into that of magical realism, something that we find in other writers that have drawn on a similar reservoir of Yorùbá mythopoeic resources such as Amos Tutuola and Ben Okri.[13] Rather, there is always an inescapable degree of pregnant suggestiveness, as if the domain of representation is offering one mode of interpretation dependent on what meets the eye, while also suggesting that this domain of what can be seen is also the large-scale metonymic displacement of the domain of elusive spiritual significations. As we shall see in *The Road*, sometimes this sense of metonymic displacement is focalized as a specific form of hermeneutical delirium expressed in the speech and actions of the characters. At other times in Soyinka's work, as in *Madmen and Specialists*, the spiritual realms that impinge upon the dramatic action elude easy access or indeed clear specification, and are only divulged through a series of mysterious prognostications that we glimpse

---

[12] Soyinka, *Myth, Literature*, 144.
[13] For a fuller account of this as a modality for understanding Yorùbá literary history, see Quayson, *Strategic Transformations*.

either in the words of the three disabled mendicants, or in the peculiar declamations of The Old Man.

Soyinka couples this first presupposition with an echo from Nietzsche that helps him further define Ógún's heroic vocation: there is a gap, an abyss between these three realms that requires continuous bridging by ritual and sacrifice. Even though the myth of Oríṣa-nla's fragmentation suggests that the Yorùbá *oríṣa* are supernal, Soyinka's invocation of the term "abyss" also suggests that there is a chthonic dimension to the relationship between the ancestors, the yet-unborn, and the dead. This difference remains unresolved in his theory. Nevertheless, among the Yorùbá the transitional abyss bridged by Ógún finds a correlative in the psyche of the individual dramatic actor, for a dimension of the abyss is invoked within the votary's psyche when he participates in the ritual of Ógún. Thus, tragic heroes such as Elesin Oba are positioned as Ógúnian votaries within the dramatic action in which they find themselves.

There are two specific areas of the votary's experience of the abyss that Soyinka goes on to translate for the tragic actor. The first is in preparation for the experience of catharsis, when the votary is possessed by the god and becomes his mouthpiece, uttering "visions symbolic of the transitional gulf, [and] interpreting the dread power within whose essence he is immersed as agent of the choric will."[14] The tragic actor is for him similarly positioned as a mouthpiece. A second aspect of abyss significant for understanding the individual actor's psyche is when he or she fulfils the requirement to establish ritual empathy with the gods "beyond the realm of nothingness (or spiritual chaos) which is potentially destructive of human awareness, through areas of terror and blind energies."[15] Whereas in the first instance, the actor seems to be a passive agent of Ógún's will, in the second she is a conscious activator of the processes by which her psyche conquers the transitional abyss that has been internalized through the tragic action. While in *Kongi's Harvest,* the male Daodu and the female Segi directly satisfy the template of successful Ógúnian action, both *Death and the King's Horseman* and *The Road* illustrate the signal failure of this process of transition and thus of the translation from myth to tragedy. The failure is partly because in both of the latter plays the problematic of choice in the face of crisis is never met exclusively in the domain of ritual and thus of traditional values. Rather, the material historical circumstances in which the ritual dispositions are set frustrate the articulation of straightforward Ógúnian tragic choice. As we shall see especially in *Death and the King's*

[14] Soyinka, *Myth, Literature*, 143.   [15] Soyinka, *Myth, Literature*, 146.

Horseman, Elesin's failure derives from historical factors as well as from the features of a defective personality, suggesting that the transition from Yorùbá mythology to tragic action that Soyinka extrapolates in his tragic theory fails to find secure foundation within his own theatrical practice. In other words, the plays institute different character dynamics and inter-actions that, while invoking the Ógúnian template, also qualify and displace it. "The play's the thing," as Hamlet puts it.

Sound, Space, and Failed Ritual in *Death and the King's Horseman*

Tejumola Olaniyan has argued for seeing theatrical forms in Africa as stretching on a continuum from festival theatre to art theatre. For him, European art theatre conventionally severs the stage action from the music, dancing, mime, and call-and-response routines that are endemic to festival theatre but which African playwrights such as Femi Osofisan, Wole Soyinka, Mohamed Ben Abdallah, and others reunite in their dramaturgy.[16] Soyinka incorporates several of the features Olaniyan describes for festival theatre into his dramatic compositions to invoke a traditional Yorùbá worldview, while simultaneously placing this worldview into a dialectical relationship with more secular and even diametrically opposed orientations. Unlike the partially operatic quality of plays such as *The Lion and the Jewel, Kongi's Harvest, Madmen and Specialists,* and *The Bacchae of Euripides,* where the drumming, singing, and dancing are used as highly stylized choreographic interludes to provide relief and internal commentary to the surrounding action, in *Death and the King's Horseman* the drumming and dancing are organically integrated into the action to establish a form of continual sonic modulation to the themes that unfold before us. Apart from short phases, such as when we are introduced to the Pilkings in their living room at the opening of scene 2 and also during the fancy-dress masque at the Residency in scene 3, the play is dominated from beginning to end by the different tempos of Yorùbá drumming, either directly in the foreground or overhead from a distance. In that respect, *Death and the King's Horseman* is by far the most musical play in all of African theatre. When the drumming is not taking place directly onstage but is only heard from afar, it elicits futile attempts at interpretation from the colonial characters at the foreground of

---

[16] Tejumola Olaniyan, "Festivals, Rituals, and Drama in Africa," in *The Cambridge History of African and Caribbean Literature,* vol. 1, eds., Abiola Irele and Simon Gikandi, (Cambridge: Cambridge University Press, 2004), 35–48.

the stage action, as if to suggest that the drumming presents problems for the colonial knowledge economy. The colonial misinterpretations of native customs that we see more amply encapsulated in Mr. Winterbottom in Achebe's *Arrow of God* are also very much in evidence in *Death and the King's Horseman*, but to much more devastating effect, for in Soyinka's play the misinterpretations instigate specific interventions into the world of the colonized that trigger the tragic crisis.

The opening stage directions of *Death and the King's Horseman* establish the role of drumming and dancing as instructive for delineating the Yorùbá cultural nexus:

> *A passage through a market in its closing stages. The stalls are being emptied, mats folded. A few women pass though on their way home, loaded with baskets. On a cloth-stand, bolts of cloth are taken down, display pieces folded and piled on a tray. ELESIN OBA enters along a passage before the market, pursued by his drummers and praise singers. He is a man of enormous vitality, speaks, dances and sings with that infectious enjoyment of life which accompanies all his actions.*[17]

Both the drumming, which sonically inaugurates the play and continues for its entire duration, and the visual liveliness of the marketplace, with its rich, colorful spectrum of traditional cloths, help locate the world of the play within a specifically Yorùbá cultural environment. The bolts of cloth are visual cues of the rich materiality of the culture, and also focus our attention on the status of Iyaloja, the chief of the market women, who later comes to perform important functions of cultural mediation and inter-pretation in the play. The marketplace itself is also transcendentally significant. Among the Yorùbá, the saying *Ayé lojà; òrun nilé* ("the earth is a marketplace and heaven is home") points to the conjunctural nature of the marketplace as the meeting site of the living, the dead, and the yet-to-be-born, suggesting the investment of all these worlds in the successful performance of the ritual suicide that is at the center of the tragedy.[18] The temporal setting at dusk also introduces an aspect of liminality and in-betweenness that is crucial for registering the potential for both fertile possibility and imminent danger in this night of nights for the Yorùbá.

---

[17] Soyinka, *Death and the King's Horseman*, 9.
[18] Special thanks to Adeleke Adeeko for providing me the Yorùbá language translation of the proverb at very short notice. Adeeko also pointed out in personal communication that there is a Yorùbá proverbial etiquette that enjoins principal actors in a spectacle to be singularly mindful of their task and not turn themselves into spectators, with "ẹni à ńwò kii wòran" being the formulaic expression. This is to say that the well-being of the spectacle should be the actor's only preoccupation. In this play, Soyinka's interpretation of rituals, Greek or Yorùbá, entails the mindful and forceful exercise of will. Anything less is tragic.

A contrast is also established between the joyful drumming, movement, and dancing of scene 1 and the mixed sonic ambience we find at the start of scene 2, where we are introduced to the cognitively dissonant image of Mr. and Mrs. Pilkings dancing to sounds of tango music being cranked out from an old gramophone while wearing *egungun* costumes. As in Achebe's *Things Fall Apart*, the *egungun* (or *egwugwu*, as it is spelled among the Igbo) represent the masked spirits of the ancestors. A further sonic layering is later added to the scene when Pilkings hears sounds of far-away drumming and is desperate to have them interpreted for him. He is told by his servant Joseph that the drumming sounds simultaneously like drums for a wedding or for a funeral. This irritates Pilkings, as the elusiveness of the drumming heard offstage poses a challenge to his predictive capacities for anticipating what the natives might be up to. We note by this stage the different kinds of modulation that the soundscape introduces into the play, both at the level of characterization and also in altering the thematic emphases of the tragic action as it unfolds.

One aspect of the drama as laid out in scene 1 that is liable to be drowned out in the mass of drums, dancing, and resplendent colors is the subtle dialectic that is established between a chorus-function encapsulated partly in the market women and, in a more condensed fashion, in Praise-Singer. The entry of the energetic Elesin Oba – "a man of great vitality" – pursued by drummers and Praise-Singer immediately converts the marketplace into a lively festival theatre setting, with the market women acting as primary choric observers to the ritual interactions that unfold between the central characters. Schlegel's well-known suggestion that the chorus of Greek tragedy stands as a surrogate of the ideal spectator implies a series of relations between chorality, unfolding action, and audience that is partially relevant to Soyinka's play. The chorus, Schlegel writes:

> In order not to interfere with the appearance of reality which the whole ought to possess, must adjust itself to the ever-varying requisitions of the exhibited stories. Whatever it might be and do in each particular piece, it represented in general, first the common mind of the nation, and then the general sympathy of all mankind. In a word, the Chorus is the ideal spectator. It mitigates the impression of a heart-rending or moving story, while it conveys to the actual spectator a lyrical and musical expression of his own emotions, and elevates him to the region of contemplation.[19]

[19] August Wilhelm Schlegel, *Lectures on Dramatic Art in Literature*, trans. by John Black (Aeterna Publishing, 2011. First published 1815), 42.

Given that the play was first produced not in Soyinka's native Nigeria but in London while he was a fellow at Churchill College in Cambridge, "the common mind of the nation" Schlegel points to, which we might interpret as the choric stand-in for a homogenously constituted cultural audience, can only be extrapolated by implication. What is more important, however, is that in *Death and the King's Horseman*, Praise-Singer and the market women perform the roles of simultaneously bearing witness and preparing Elesin Oba to fulfil votive roles, roles that would tie in with Soyinka's statements on the translational transactions between Yorùbá myths and his own theatre. And yet the witness/preparation function breaks down more than once in scene 1, suggesting that the dynamic relationship between collective (chorus) and individual (Elesin Oba) is also that of the contrast between cultural witnessing and mere spectatoriality. There is a subtle tension between the two roles. Whereas in the classical Greek context, the chorus witnesses but rarely affects or interferes with the action of the play, here, the women are part of the decision-making process that moves the play forward and yet are also from time-to-time rendered helpless in this role. They are real characters in the dramatized world and feel divided within themselves, but they ultimately *choose* to give up a girl who is already betrothed to another because they feel they cannot refuse Elesin one of his very last wishes. As we shall see in a moment, this turns out to be a mistake born from the misvaluation of contradictory ethical choices. The market women's chorus-function disintegrates, only to be reconstituted into a form of helpless spectatoriality, thus also suggesting the alteration of the relationship between Elesin and the community of cultural witnesses, who at the start seemed to be the exclusive guarantors of ritual affirmations.

Praise-Singer begins to chant Elesin's *oríkì* as a means of eliciting his ritual self and ascertaining his preparedness for the ritual crossing that is to take place later that night. The elicitation of Elesin's ritual self takes place through a careful process of call-and-response, where Praise-Singer chants aspects of their shared communal history in a dense proverbial idiom and Elesin responds accordingly, with a matching proverbial flourish:

PRAISE-SINGER: In their time the world was never tilted from its groove, it shall not be in yours.

ELESIN: The gods have said No.

PRAISE-SINGER: In their time the great wars came and went, the little wars came and went; the white slavers came and went, they took away the heart of our race, they bore away the mind and muscle of our race. The city fell and was

rebuilt; the city fell and our people trudged through mountain and forest to
found a new home but – Elesin Oba do you hear me?

ELESIN: I hear your voice Olohun-iyo.[20]

This ritual process of steady elicitation is, however, interrupted at three
different moments in quick succession, and in each instance the interruption is by Elesin himself. The first is when he stops the procedures to
declaim the lengthy story of the Not-I Bird, a source of great bafflement for
both Praise-Singer and the market women. This is what we see:

PRAISE-SINGER: There is only one home to the life of a river-mussel; there is only
one home to the life of a tortoise; there is only one shell to the soul of man:
there is only one world to the spirit of our race. If that world leaves its course
and smashes on boulders of the great void, whose world will give us shelter?

ELESIN: It did not in the time of my forebears, it shall not in mine.

PRAISE-SINGER: The cockerel must not be seen without his feathers.

ELESIN: Nor will the Not-I bird be much longer without his nest.

PRAISE-SINGER (*stopped in his lyric stride*): The Not-I bird, Elesin?

ELESIN: I said, the Not-I bird.

PRAISE-SINGER: All respect to our elders, but is there really such a bird?

ELESIN: What! Could it be that he failed to knock on your door?

PRAISE-SINGER (*smiling*): Elesin's riddles are not merely the nut in the kernel that
breaks human teeth; he also buries the kernel in hot embers and dares a
man's fingers to draw it out.[21]

Praise-Singer's "all respect to our elders" barely conceals the fact that he is
utterly confused by the story just told by Elesin. It turns out that the Not-I bird
is an entirely made-up mythical character that Elesin has created on the spur of
the moment so as to invoke his own tale of fearlessness and courage in the face
of Death. It is the first moment in the play where self-interest masquerades as
cultural knowledge and is severed momentarily from the communal repertoire.
The ritual call-and-response between them resumes after the lengthy digression
of the story of the Not-I bird but Elesin stops them again a few lines later to
complain that something has offended him bitterly. This throws everyone
onstage into shock and horror, but especially the market women, who think
they must have unknowingly infracted an unstated ritual code of great import.
It turns out that Elesin is pretending to be offended to get the women to feel
guilty for not draping him in the resplendent cloths they were packing up when
he first entered the marketplace. The women oblige him in great relief, and the

---

[20] Soyinka, *Death and the King's Horseman*, 10. On the significance of the dense proverbial language in
the play, see David Richards, "*Òwe l'esín òró*: Proverbs Like Horses in Wole Soyinka's *Death and the
King's Horseman*," *Journal of Commonwealth Literature*, 13.1 (1984): 89–99.

[21] Soyinka, *Death and the King's Horseman*, 11.

imminent crisis of his possible disapproval on the day of the culturally sanctioned liminal crossing is mercifully averted. The ritual call-and-response resumes but now explicitly incorporates the dancing and praise-singing of the market women in an explicit choric role as Elesin swirls round and round in the colorful cloths they have draped him in. The communal envelope of collective affirmation is complete at this stage and everyone's cultural role appears secure. But then all of a sudden comes the third and final interruption from Elesin:

PRAISE-SINGER: Elesin-Oba why do your eyes roll like a bush-rat who sees his fate like his father's spirit, mirrored in the eye of a snake? And all these questions![22]

This time Elesin has interrupted the ritual elicitation to call attention to a beautiful young girl that has just come through the passageway into the market. What appears to be a momentary distraction turns out to have major consequences for the tragic action. For Elesin now insists that he absolutely must have the young girl on this monumental night of nights. By this request he inadvertently presents his culture with a large and hitherto unanticipated ethical conundrum. For it turns out that the young girl is already betrothed to Iyaloja's own son. Iyaloja's initial hesitation (along with the shocked voices of the other women around her) is overcome, however, by her assertion that since Elesin is standing astride the space between the living and the dead, his every wish must be obeyed to smoothen the way of the crossing:

IYALOJA: Oh you who fill the home from hearth to threshold with the voices of children, you who now bestride the hidden gulf and pause to draw the right foot across and into the resting-home of the great forebears, it is good that your loins be drained into the earth we know, that your last strength be ploughed back into the womb that gave you being.[23]

What this rationalization really means is that Iyaloja is prepared to suspend the foundational ethics of familial relationships in favor of the equally substantial claim of communal security and cultural survival. The pitting of two contrasting ethical claims that we see here expressed in the form of an internal cultural contradiction is going to find its corollary in the contrasting interpretations of the relationship between duty and sacrifice from Yorùbá and colonial perspectives. Iyaloja is not to know this at this early stage, but her concession turns out to be a major error of judgment.

Each of the three interruptions in scene 1 share one key element: they are moments in which the other characters onstage are converted from communal chorus into the spectators of Elesin Oba specifically. We might note a

[22] Soyinka, *Death and the King's Horseman*, 18.   [23] Soyinka, *Death and the King's Horseman*, 22.

contrast in the oscillation between chorality and spectatoriality here, and what we find in Aeschylus' *Prometheus Bound*, perhaps the purest expression of chorality in Greek tragedy. In Aeschylus' play the central character is literally shackled to one spot and the chorus of Oceanids take on the simultaneous role of witness-spectator to the injustice that has been done to him by Zeus as well as being interlocutors to Prometheus' revelations. This witness-spectator role is broken in different ways by Hermes and Io, each of whom introduces dynamics of antagonism and supplication respectively, thus serving to qualify the role assigned to the chorus proper. In *Death and the King's Horseman*, what the conversion from one role to the other entails is the conscription of the other characters into a dramatic spectacle/ scene in which Elesin alone knows the script and can control its preferred interpretative outcome. This emerges particularly strongly in the interregnum of the Not-I bird story but is replicated in each of the other interruptions. In each instance Elesin proffers himself as the object of total attention and enacts a script that subverts the discursive codes of communal comprehensibility. The market women and Praise-Singer are transformed into momentary spectators, as though watching the dramatic action from a distance, and Elesin becomes the only actor in the one-man scene that unfolds before them. The fact that these one-man scenes arise without explicit demarcation except for Elesin's sudden turns of language also suggests that these interruptions are ultimately tools of temporization, as if he is attempting to defer the processual elicitation of his ritual self for as long as he can get away with. Read another way, the dramaturgical structure of interruptions and the fact that they are instigated by Elesin himself reveals his subliminal reluctance to take on the role of *pharmakos* for his community. At this point his identity is not that of communal *pharmakos* but of a private hedonist. His unpreparedness for the ritual crossing is amply illustrated in his shocking request to have the young girl married to him on the very day he is supposed to be undertaking ritual suicide. And yet so intently focused is his community in their collective ritual project that they completely ignore this dimension to his character. The shifting focus of the dramaturgy of scene 1 (from chorality to spectatoriality; communal to private, etc.) then prepares us for a fuller evaluation of the contradictions in the play when Elesin fails to make the crossing. The reasons he gives for his failure then remind us of the various discursive shifts of scene 1.

One of the peculiar features of Elesin Oba's character is that despite the many praise-names that are showered upon him at the start of the play, not one pertains to military prowess. This is decidedly odd for someone whose title as guardian of the king's stable implies the powerful position of commander of the king's army. In place of praise for his military exploits we find him called instead a "cockerel" and a "snake-on-the-loose in dark passages of the market." Elesin proudly says of himself that "when caught with his bride's own sister he protested – but I was only prostrating myself to her as becomes a grateful in-law."[24] If not even a single *oríkì* is invoked to highlight his skills as a military commander, might this not be interpreted as Soyinka's subtle critique of the Yorùbá culture's fixation on the ultimately flawed human vessel that is their chosen conduit for salvation? All they seem to have is the hedonistic, womanizing, and arrogant Elesin Oba. Thus, Iyaloja's erroneous decision to deliver her son's betrothed marks the larger failure of a cultural praxis whose terms may already have been thoroughly compromised in their choice of *pharmakos*. This larger cultural choice is masked as the urgent and implacable choice between salvation and collective ruination which then obscures the flawed character of the human vessel that the community settles its hopes upon. The compromise we see in Iyaloja's decision illustrates the degree to which ethical thinking is hijacked by the idiom of hierarchical power in a process of vulgar reversibility. Thus, Elesin as the *pharmakos* on this night of nights is allowed to be master of all he surveys, including the very terms by which his people derive ethically salient choices. As he is given the unquestioned capacity to set the ethical terms of action for his community, he comes to invert what should have been the proper hierarchy of social values.

The process of reversibility is later also encapsulated in scene 4 in the Pilkings' appropriation of the *egugun* masks to make an impression at the Residency gala, arranged to welcome the visiting Prince from England. That which is most sacred can be used, indeed *is* used, for entertainment purposes; in competition, and in frivolous jest. Similarly, the magnified status that Elesin Oba enjoys is also reversed by the same logic of aggrandizement that already operates within the culture through the mechanisms of reversed *oríkì*. He too can be profaned and relegated to animal status after having all through his life enjoyed the sanctified title and benefits of a king's horseman. When Iyaloja comes to speak to him while he is in detention, everything she spits out at him is a series of *oríkì* reversals:

IYALOJA: You have betrayed us. We fed you sweetmeats such as we hoped awaited you on the other side. But you said, No, I must eat the world's left-overs. We said you were the hunter who brought the quarry down; to you belonged the vital parts of the game. No, you said, I am the hunter's dog and I shall eat the entrails of the game and the faeces of the hunter. We said you were the hunter

---

[24] Soyinka, *Death and the King's Horseman*, 19.

returning home in triumph, a slain buffalo pressing down on his neck; you said wait, I first must turn up this cricket hole with my toes. We said yours was the doorway at which we first spy the tapper when he comes down from the tree, yours was the blessing of the twilight wine, the purl that brings night spirits out of doors to steal their portion before the light of day. We said yours was the body of wine whose burden shakes the tapper like a sudden gust on his perch. You said, No, I am content to lick the dregs from each calabash when the drinkers are done. We said, the dew on earth's surface was for you to wash your feet along the slopes of honour. You said, No, I shall step in the vomit of cats and the droppings of mice; I shall fight them for the left-overs of the world.[25]

The force of these accusations derives largely from the fact that each of them is a play on aspects of Ógún. For Ógún is traditionally also the tutelary deity of hunters, with palm-wine as his dedicated drink. Iyaloja's reverse-*oríkí* declamations retract the ritual elicitation that had first been established by Praise-Singer. She denudes Elesin of any semblance of cultural representationality. His failure at ritual suicide is a *musuo* that threatens the existential security of the entire community. Thus, Iyaloja's words instigates a damaging deflation that takes place within a material and spatial domain that is distinctly different from what we saw in the marketplace at the start of the play. To the resplendent materiality of the open-air marketplace is contrasted the bare mustiness of the former slave dungeon in which Elesin is held. And the cultural expressiveness of Praise-Singer and the market women is contrasted with the confrontation between a cultural spokesperson and an erstwhile culture hero who has suddenly lost all rights of recognition.

What has now been firmly established in the discourse of reversibility is taken in a different and more tragic direction in the reasons Elesin gives for his failure in response to Iyaloja's obvious disdain:

IYALOJA: I wish I could pity you.
ELESIN: I need neither your pity nor the pity of the world. I need understanding. Even I need to understand. You were present at my defeat. You were part of the beginnings. You brought about the renewal of my tie to earth, you helped in the binding of the cord.
IYALOJA: I gave you warning. The river which fills up before our eyes does not sweep us away in its flood.
ELESIN: What were warnings beside the moist contact of living earth between my fingers? What were warnings beside the renewal of famished embers lodged eternally in the heart of man? But even that, even if it overwhelmed one with a thousandfold temptations to linger a little while, a man could overcome it.

[25] Soyinka, *Death and the King's Horseman*, 68.

It is when the alien hand pollutes the source of will, when a stranger force of violence shatters the mind's calm resolution, this is when a man is made to commit the awful treachery of relief, commit in his thought the unspeakable blasphemy of seeing the hand of the gods in this alien rupture of his world. I know it was this thought that killed me, sapped my powers and turned me into an infant in the hands of unnameable strangers. I made to utter my spells anew but my tongue merely rattled in my mouth. I fingered hidden charms and the contact was damp; there was no spark left to sever the life-strings that should stretch from every finger-tip. My will was squelched in the spittle of an alien race, and all because I had committed this blasphemy of thought -- that there might be the hand of the gods in a stranger's intervention.[26]

Note the nature of Elesin's admission of failure here: the real blasphemy and thus the ultimate cause of his failure was in the concession, for one elusive moment, that there might be the hand of his own gods in the white man's intervention. In other words, in the liminal status of the crossing, the categories that had organized his world are warped such that he mistakes the white man for one of his own gods and vice versa. Or is his mistake that he believes it possible that his own gods could recognize the white man – and use him? It seems that this is his crucial mistake: a conflation of worlds. Elesin weakens enough to hope that his own selfish desire for life could be fulfilled by the white man, who is simultaneously a threat to his entire community. He does not make a god out of the white man so much as he inserts the white man into a symbolic spiritual paradigm that has no place for him. He is willing to interpret the white man as a personal savior to him, despite the fact that doing so sacrifices or betrays the tribe's ancient tradition. In his mind, Elesin introduces an innovation that had never been introduced before because he saw an opportunity that had never been introduced before him – to escape the ritual suicide. That he also admits to succumbing to the renewed embers lodged deep in the heart of man and thus of his essentially pleasure-seeking impulses must not becloud the nature of what he describes as his blasphemy.

Elesin Oba's hedonism, selfishness, and frivolousness are all character traits that seem to exist independently of British interference. Similarly, the errors of judgment made by the marketplace women seem possible without the British. This then raises the question: to what extent was Elesin's failure to commit suicide enabled by the excuse of the British interruption, and to what extent was Soyinka giving us reason to believe Elesin might have – in the absence of the British – latched on to any other local equivalent of an

---

[26] Soyinka, *Death and the King's Horseman*, 69.

excuse? The question, however, ignores the fact that the spiritually saturated context of the ritual crossing and the British colonial intervention jointly served to exacerbate whatever character flaws may have been present for Elesin. It is this state of emergency; the product of the conflation of ritual and material contingent factors, that makes his natural hedonistic dispositions the raw materials for cultural catastrophe. For Iyaloja, the matter is straightforward. She spits out that she wishes she could pity him; his reply is that he wishes to be understood, and not pitied. But his action in failing the ritual crossing is of such immense consequence that it represents for his culture no mere failure, but the sign of an epistemological and existential impasse. Hence, he cannot receive understanding within the terms provided within his own culture.

The terms of Elesin's reversal of fortune also illustrate the difficulty of giving an account of oneself when the cultural instruments by which such an account might be given have been contaminated by the modes of reversibility inherent to it. While the crisis is exacerbated by the colonist's intervention, it is clear that the essential terms of the crisis are already present within Yorùbá culture itself. The fact that the play ends on a note of hope with Olunde's ritual suicide in place of his father must not disguise the fact that the discourse of reversibility within the culture remains unchanged. And if the king's horseman, whose entire life from birth has been one long preparation for this night of nights, has failed in this momentous task and is to be replaced by a son who had been smuggled out to England to become a doctor, what does this say about the culture itself? Olunde chooses to take the place of his father without any prior cultural preparation, unlike his father. He has come back from England on the same ship that brought the Prince and only because he knows that as Elesin's eldest son, he is the one to perform the funeral rites over his father's body. The shock of finding his father not only still alive but attempting to flee his guards in scene 3 is almost enough to blind the young man. When he decides to take on the role of *pharmakos* it is in spite of everything that his life choices have given him. Thus, far from being a celebration of continuity for the Yorùbá culture (the way they see his sacrifice as a form of relief), it is a subtle indictment of their desire for cultural heroes in the first place.

If we consider Elesin a tragic figure, it is only partly because the colonial conditions under which he attempts heroic action enjoined by the mores of his culture combine with his personal dispositions to undermine his capacity for that particular form of heroic action. He is tragic also because, in the course of just one night, he has shifted from being a representational figure, the lord of all he surveys, including the very basis by which his culture determines what is right and what is wrong, to being a private citizen completely bereft of any of the traditional adulation accorded to a person of his significance. The arc of his fall defines the diminution and contraction from the colossal Ógún asked to bridge the gap between the living and the dead, to that of a marginalized figure whose suicide signifies nothing at all in the eyes of his community. His personal anguish is thoroughly privatized in the sense that it is his and his alone to bear. *Death and the King's Horseman* illustrates the loss of Ógúnian epic scale even when it is against that same scale that the entire tragedy for the community is to be judged. And the alteration in scale is at once the product of colonial intervention and the effect of a flawed cultural vessel. The two parts cannot be understood independently from each other.

Kóbóló Poetics and the Burdens of Free Time

The shift from the colonial clashes of *Death and the King's Horseman* to the vagaries of postcolonial urban existence in *The Road* is also a shift from the domain of explicit heroic action to that of existential malaise and the navigation of free time. As a general rule, the African informal economy and urban free time – one of its direct corollaries – have been tied by commentators securely to the different economic rhythms and cycles of employment, under-employment, and unemployment.[27] Workers in the informal economy include the likes of tailors, hairdressers, shoe-repairers, vulcanisers, lorry drivers and their touts, head porters, hawkers of various goods, sellers in markets and at road-side stalls, artisans, and many others. Their ranks are also joined by the confidence trickster who makes his living by preying upon the misplaced aspirations of urban dwellers for the get-rich-quick scheme, or for the chance to be introduced to a "big man," who might help them expand their opportunities. In recent decades, this group

[27] See Keith Hart, "Informal Income Opportunities and Urban Employment in Ghana," *The Journal of Modern African Studies*, 11, no. 1 (1973): 61–89, and "Bureaucratic Form and the Informal Economy," Basudeb Guha-Khasnobis, Ravi Kanbur, and Elinor Ostrom, eds., *Linking the Formal and Informal Economy: Concepts and Policies* (Oxford: Oxford University Press, 2006), 19–23; also Franklin Obeng-Odoom "The Informal Sector in Ghana under Siege," *Journal of Developing Societies*, 27 (2009): 355–392. Obeng-Odoom also notes the relevance of wage-labor that falls below the minimum wage, thus further expanding the purview of the informal sector. The precariousness of the informal sector and the ways in which people are trying to negotiate this in Accra and other parts of urban Africa is now the subject of large private-sector funded projects such as The Informal City Dialogues, which provides a forum for blogs, research papers, and ongoing interviews with slum dwellers. See http://nextcity.org/informalcity, last accessed Feb. 8, 2018.

has been joined by the visa contractor, who feeds hopes of escape while firmly benefiting from the gullibility of his clients. The current crop of evangelical pastors that have sprung up all over cities in Nigeria and elsewhere in Africa might also be added. Soyinka anticipates the ubiquitous evangelical pastor in his Brother Jero plays, the center of which is occupied by the inimitable Jeroboam Jero, of smooth tongue and grandiloquent gestures. As Carolyn Nordstrom has shown, the informal sector, as distinct from the private sector, is an essential part of all economies worldwide, even in the advanced economies of the West. But for African economies, the distinction between formal and informal derives from the relatively large size of the informal economy and the degree of shading between that and the formal sector.[28] The forever-expanding phase of "waiting for a job" has thus gradually been filled by new social forms as well as endlessly inventive modes for negotiating the economic lacunae of such a condition.

And yet it is not out of place to consider free time as directly related to the socio-spatial dynamics of the African city. It is in view of this that I proposed a formula in *Oxford Street, Accra: City Life and the Itineraries of Transnationalism*, through which we might unthread the general implications of urban free time. The formula is simply this: the poor have time while the rich have leisure.[29] This may also be viewed through a gender dimension, for if the poor have time and the rich have leisure, then women have neither time nor leisure.[30] But free time is not the same as freedom; it is experienced as a burden. For Africa's urban poor are desperate to exchange their free time for labor time, that is to say, to undertake forms of labor that might provide a regular income as well as predictable rhythms to everyday life. On these terms, the concept of free time also allows us to take a fresh look at the representation of class relations in African literature, but from a perspective different from that provided by the Marxist viewpoints of say, Sembene Ousmane's *God's Bits of Wood,* or Ngũgĩ wa Thiong'o's *Petals of Blood,* where the focus is predominantly on peasant and proletarian class consciousness and the various forms of heroic collective action that they undertake. In contrast to such heroic plots, the

[28] Carolyn Nordstrom, *Global Outlaws: Crime, Money, and Power in the Contemporary World* (Berkeley: University of California Press, 2007).

[29] *Oxford Street, Accra: City Life and the Itineraries of Transnationalism* (Durham: Duke University Press, 2014), 239–251.

[30] I am grateful to Alissa Trotz, at the University of Toronto, for bringing up this point in personal communication and subsequently in a review of the book. See her "Looking Well to See Well: Lessons from Oxford Street, Accra," *PMLA*, 131.2 (2016): 524–527.

representation of the burden of free time in Soyinka's *The Road* is encapsulated in the plot of inertia, which, though far less popular during the decolonial and early postcolonial periods, is highly suggestive for what it divulges about the affective nature of boredom that was central to the socio-cultural and political transformations of those periods. By the first decade following independence we find the plot of inertia giving formal representational shape to the relationship between the informal economy, urban free time, and boredom. This is what we find in Cameron Duodu's *The Gab Boys* (1967), Ayi Kwei Armah's *The Beautyful Ones Are Not Yet Born* (1968), Soyinka's *The Interpreters* (1965), and Dambudzo Marechera's *The House of Hunger* (1978) among various others. An exemplary instance of such plots of inertia is also to be seen in an Egyptian novel, Albert Cossary's *Laziness in the Fertile Valley*, which was published in 1945 (twenty-three years after Egypt gained partial independence from Britain and just seven years before full independence). Cossary's novel centers on a family afflicted with extreme lethargy that keeps them sleeping almost all their lives. The central characters are three brothers, their uncle, and their father, all of whom wake up only once a day to eat before going straight back to sleep. They almost never venture outside their apartment, and the father himself does not even leave his room. Unlike the other African novels that I have mentioned where the action is mainly located on the streets, *Laziness in the Fertile Valley* is distinctive for locating the malaise firmly within the domain of a family and thus of the domestic sphere. The novel is allegedly based on Cossery's own family, for whom unemployment and indolence were sources of pride, even resistance in the face of the new capitalist demands for modernization.

In South Africa too, the plot of inertia was an important aspect of the varied response to political crisis. Athol Fugard's *Sizwe Bansi Is Dead* (1972) and J. M. Coetzee's *Life and Times of Michael K* (1981) provide us with good examples, but this time further complicated by the nature of the responses to the enforced limitation of choices in apartheid South Africa. But post-apartheid South Africa has also gone through its phases of high hope followed by abject despair, so that over twenty-five years after the fall of apartheid, we now also encounter a novel such as Masade Ntshanga's *The Reactive* (2016). In the novel, the burdensome and prosaic organization of the everyday life of a person living with HIV is shaped around the what-if decision making reminiscent of novels with plots of inertia from other parts of the continent. Ntshanga's *The Reactive*, Phaswane Mpe's *Welcome to our Hillbrow* (2001), and novels like theirs mark a different response to the post-apartheid milieu than that registered by the often anguished and confessional truth-and-reconciliation literature of, say, Gillian Slovo's *Red Dust* (2000) and Antjie Krog's *Country of My Skull* (1998), a journalistic account of the work of the Truth and Reconciliation Commission, among various others.[31] These largely realist works were marked by a cluster of features that served to distinguish them from the more heroic traditions of Achebe, Ngũgĩ, Ama Ata Aidoo, and Assia Djebar, among others. Features of the literary plot of inertia may be taken to include the following: terminal idleness and inaction as a form of subversive refusal of the system; the slowing down of narrative or dramatic propulsion coupled with the punctuation of events and incidents without a definition of progression; more and more talk and less and less decisive action; a surfeit of self-consciousness (as in Ben Okri's Lagos-based short stories in *Stars of the New Curfew* and in Kojo Laing's *Search, Sweet Country*); and the struggle to signify a formal identity within differently inherited frames (as in *The House of Hunger*). The plot of inertia in African literature is not entirely devoid of comedy and laughter, as we find in Alain Mabanckou's *Broken Glass* and Fiston Mwanza Mujila's *Tram 83*, where the pointlessness of nothing to do is relieved by the most absurd scenarios, such as hilarious pissing competitions and collective life lived almost exclusively in a jazz bar in the two novels respectively. In all these works many events take place, but nothing happens.

The plot of inertia in the texts I list here is also tied to the depiction of a specific social type that is quite different from what we find in the literature of heroic exertion. Having written about this social type in *Oxford Street, Accra*, I would like to designate this character type with the concept of *kòbòlò*.[32] *Kòbòlò* (or *kòbòlòi*, the plural form) is a Ga word that has resonances for the description of street life in much of West Africa and indeed well beyond. It invokes the habits and lifestyle of the good-for-nothing street lounger, but, as a social category, also encapsulates a transitional state of urban existence that manifests itself at the intersecting vectors of space, time, and desire. While there are female *kòbòlòi*, the term normally designates a masculine sphere of urban crisis. If popular parlance, and indeed economists, perceive the *kòbòlò* in terms tied predominantly to the informal economy, it should also be noted that the term ultimately transcends inert economic categorizations. Like the Lagosian area boy and the

---

[31] As a quick aside, we should note that the plot of inertia seems to be more prevalent in contemporary post-apartheid South African writing than in that of the rest of Africa. The reasons for this will have to be explored on another occasion.

[32] For an elaboration of the social category of the *kòbòlò*, see Ato Quayson, *Oxford Street, Accra: City Life and the Itineraries of Transnationalism*, 199–203, 244–245.

Dakarois *fakhman*, the *kòbòlò* combines the meanings of a good-for-nothing rascal or mischief-maker (a propensity for petty criminality is implied) with that of a "street watcher," a designation that is especially pertinent to affluent South African urban districts where people worry about the safety of their parked vehicles. The *kòbòlò* in Johannesburg and Cape Town provides a form of informal security (for a price) that contributes to these cities' distinctive feel and to their urban myths and legends.[33] The *kòbòlò* is at once all and none of these and must be defined via a number of specific socio-cultural features that are tied to economic categories and yet break away from them to expose a peculiar form of urban lifestyle. The *kòbòlò's* existence is marked by a certain edginess, simultaneously derived from living on the margins and also from adopting a lifestyle that raises a middle finger to society in general. This is displayed first and foremost by their specific attachment to what appears on the surface to be indolence and laziness and their preferred speech forms, typically a variant of standard speech that is heavily larded with local-language borrowings, a form of pidgin or creolized street language.

Cheeky swagger and personal fearlessness mark *kòbòlòi's* standard demeanor and it is not unusual for them to also be adept at adopting various urban guises (not just job tasks). In literary form, these characteristics thus invoke trickster folk figures such as Anansi the Spider, Ijapa the Tortoise, and in Soyinka's work, Esu, the ultimate god of mischief in Yorùbá mythology.[34] It is also not unusual for the *kòbòlò* to be between short-term, low paying jobs in the informal economy, the defining condition being not the jobs themselves but the existential condition of impermanence that they encapsulate. The most important vector of the *kòbòlò's*

---

[33] As Kevin Lynch has noted in *Image of the City* (Boston: MIT Press, 1966), every city has an image of itself, produced by its architectural and planned environment, the connectivity of its roads and highways, and the distribution of its parks and gardens. His focus is on the three cities of Boston, Jersey City, and Los Angeles. In addition to the image of the city, however, it is important to add that every city has stories and urban myths that define it. Nowhere else in Africa do you find more "parking stories" than in Johannesburg and Cape Town. These are stories of finding parking and, more importantly, of returning to find your car where you left it. Central to this are the street valets (the *kòbòlò* of my designation) that offer to take care of your vehicle while you go and pursue your interests. Depending on who is telling these stories, they may be meant to illustrate the failure of municipal authorities, the rise in crime, or the heightened communal feeling that makes rich and poor "take care" of one another. Accra, Lagos, Nairobi, and other African cities have completely distinctive stories of urban knowhow and entrepreneurship. On South African urban myths, see Arthur Goldstuck, *The Ink in the Porridge* (London: Penguin, 1994).

[34] Henry Louis Gates has argued that the genealogy of the signifying monkey of African American folklore may be traced to the Yorùbá's Esu and that ideas about him persisted across the Atlantic and into the new world. See his *Signifying Monkey: A Theory of African-American Literary Criticism* (Oxford: Oxford University Press, 1988).

identity is street life, for the young adult *kòbòlò* does not become so by choice; he is always on a quest to escape the vagaries of such existence. The period of transition for the *kòbòlò* may be short or long, but the crucial detail is that the *kòbòlò* has only attenuated social and familial obligations during this phase of his life; the exit from this lifestyle is immediately marked by the taking seriously of such obligations if they exist, or by adopting them if they don't. Settling down to marriage, children, a steady job are all signs of moving out of the *kòbòlò* phase. All these features of *kòbòlò* existence are pertinent to interpreting *The Road*.

Social Periphery, Unemployment, and Hermeneutical Delirium

In adopting the plot of inertia in *The Road*, Soyinka combines the essential features of *kòbòlò* existence as found among a group of unemployed motor-park touts in an unnamed Nigerian urban context with a sense of hermeneutical delirium encapsulated in the figure of Professor. Professor is simultaneously their gang leader and the conductor of an invisible and ultimately fatal symphony that draws upon contradictory ciphers from Yorùbá and Christian epistemologies. This is how we first encounter him:

> *Professor is a tall figure in Victorian outfit – tails, top-hat, etc., all thread-bare and shiny at the lapels from much ironing. He carries four enormous bundles of newspaper and a fifth of paper odds and ends impaled on a metal rod stuck in a wooden rest. A chair-stick hangs from one elbow, and the other arm clutches a road sign bearing a squiggle and the one word, 'BEND'.*

> PROF: [*he enters in a high state of excitement, muttering to himself*]: Almost a miracle ... dawn provides the greatest miracles but this ... in this dawn has exceeded its promise. In the strangest of places ... God God God but there is a mystery in everything. A new discovery every hour – I am used to that, but that I should be led to where this was hidden, sprouted in secret for heaven knows how long ... for there was no doubt about it, this word was growing, it was growing from earth until I plucked it ... [35]

Professor's extravagant, motley Victorian outfit is a marker of the previous middle-class affiliation from which he has obviously been severed by the start of the play. The whiff of historical anachronism suggested by his peculiar sartorial style is not entirely misplaced, since his domineering character is also meant to recall a cross between a demented visionary

---

[35] Soyinka, *The Road*, 157.

and Fagin, the familiar lord of the underworld in Charles Dickens's *Oliver Twist*. Professor is engaged in a vigorous quest for what he calls the Word, the essence of which he strives to achieve by assembling a range of quotidian scripts (bundles of newspapers, paper odds and ends, road signs), along with the deployment of a hybrid hermeneutical orientation that combines Yorùbá semiotics with a quasi-Christian sensibility. He claims to have a pact with risks, dangers, and death but also guides the jobless lorry park touts and other *kòbòlòi* in the play to eke out a precarious living from petty document forgery; the provision of "protection" for politicians; and epic daydreaming. A sense of mystery lies upon the surface of Professor's speech acts while also being projected as tantalizingly concealed inside of the everyday scripts that he assembles. This enigmatic interaction between surface and depth ends up thoroughly baffling his hapless interlocutors. The enigmatic oscillation between surface and depth in a play set amongst the desperate unemployed *kòbòlòi* utterly dissipates any potential for revolution, since it is not designed to mobilize this class fraction's consciousness against the explicit conditions of their urban dispossession but rather to tether them to a form of bewildered servitude. Professor's aporetic speech breeds anxiety rather than enlightenment and becomes an instrument of control and power for his own use.

For Soyinka, the value of the aporia and hermeneutical delirium of Professor's speeches lies precisely in this: it is a mnemonic of disaster couched in modes of deferral, since the meaning(s) that might be adduced in what he says always lie elsewhere. In this respect, Soyinka's dramaturgy in *The Road* recalls Samuel Beckett's, where the meaning deferrals in *Waiting for Godot, Endgame, Krapp's Last Tape,* and other plays rivets our attention securely on the absurd semiotic of language itself as it tries and fails to represent the conditions under which his characters labor to make sense. We shall have more to say on this feature of Beckett's writing in Chapter 9 but Camus's searching words on the absurd in *The Myth of Sisyphus* is of particular resonance for the work of both playwrights:

> A world that can be explained by reasoning, however faulty, is a familiar world. But in a universe that is suddenly deprived of illusions and of light, man feels a stranger. His is an irremediable exile, because he is deprived of memories of a lost homeland as much as he lacks the hope of a promised land to come. This divorce between man and his life, the actor and his setting, truly constitutes the feeling of Absurdity.[36]

---

[36] Albert Camus, *The Myth of Sisyphus* (Paris: Gallimard, 1942), 18.

Martin Esslin glosses this passage in his influential study of the Absurd as signifying a sense of "metaphysical anguish," also suggesting that it is the loss of the signifiers of religious and transcendental roots that are responsible for the sense of existential loss.[37] Unlike what we find in Beckett's plays, it is rather an *over-saturation* of religious, metaphysical, and transcendental signifiers that marks *The Road's* overall discursive ambience. The conditions of existential confusion, shared in the setting of the drama in worlds on the peripheries of social existence and marked by the depiction of sparse material landscapes, unite the two playwrights. And in plays such as *The Road, Madmen and Specialists*, and *Kongi's Harvest*, the purpose of the deferrals is also to invoke laughter as a way of suggesting the laugh-to-avoid-crying realities of postcolonial Nigeria. This is similar to the tragicomic ambience of Beckett's plays, but of course in an entirely different, postcolonial context.

The Metaphysics of Bafflement

The Yorùbá metaphysical dimensions of *The Road* are invoked immediately in its title, since for the Yorùbá, roads are considered to lie under the tutelary protection of Ógún, the god of both war and roads. But in addition to his role as bridger of the chasm between gods and men that Soyinka elaborates in *Myth, Literature, and the African World*, Ógún is not a particularly kindly god and is thought to exact sacrifice by way of the many accidents that take place on roads across Nigeria.[38] As Kotonu, a character in *The Road*, notes: "The road and the spider lie gloating, then the fly buzzes along like a happy fool."[39] The spider's web, which is a prop that the characters frequently address onstage, acts then as an objective correlative of Ógún's hunger for roadkill. For Samson, Kotonu's assistant, this calls for explicit acts of propitiation:

SAMSON [*despondently*]: Kill us a dog Kotonu, kill us a dog. Kill us a dog before the
          hungry god lies in wait and makes a substitute of me. That was a thin shave.

---

[37] Martin Esslin's *The Theatre of the Absurd* (New York: Anchor Books, 1961), 5. For broader statements on the usefulness and applicability of perspectives from the absurdist tradition for understanding Soyinka, see Clive T. Probyn, "Waiting for the Word: Samuel Beckett and Wole Soyinka," *Ariel*, 12.3 (1981): 35–48, and John Nkegasong Nkemngong, "Samuel Beckett, Wole Soyinka, and the Theatre of Desolate Reality," *Journal of African Literature and Culture* (2006): 153–175.

[38] This aspect of the Ógún belief system is the inspiration for the title of Ben Okri's *The Famished Road*, which centers on the road as a key portal between the real and the esoteric worlds. On the links between the real world and that of spirits in Okri's *The Famished Road* and his other writings, see Ato Quayson, *Strategic Transformation in Nigerian Writing* (Oxford and Bloomington: James Currey and Indiana University Press, 1997), 101–156.

[39] Soyinka, *The Road*, 178.

A sensible man would see it as a timely warning, but him? I doubt it. Not for all the wealth of a traffic policeman. Dog's intestines look messy to me he says – who asked him to like it? Ógún likes it that's all that matters. It's his special meat. Just run over the damned dog and leave it there, I don't ask you to stop and scoop it up for your next dinner. Serve Ógún his tit-bit so the road won't look at us one day and say ho ho you two boys you look juicy to me. But what's the use? The one who won't give Ógún willingly will yield heavier meat by Ógún's designing.[40]

The lorry driver Kotonu and his long-term assistant Samson are recalling a horrible accident they witnessed over a broken bridge some days earlier. A lorry half packed with salted stockfish and half with human passengers speeds past them as they approach the wobbly bridge only to plunge into the ravine below. The shock of seeing the "beheaded fish" mixed with the bloodied bodies and screams of the still-dying that have been "belched from the bowels of some gluttonous god" sends Kotonu into hysterical shock; Samson for his part maintains a cool head and tries to interpret what the accident means in relation to Ógún. This scene of mayhem occurs offstage, but is the focus of a lengthy dialogue sequence in which Kotonu, Samson, and Professor adduce different meanings for the event. For Professor, it is another opportunity to probe the two men for signs of something that he thinks lies just beneath the surface of the catastrophe and that might point to the meaning of the relationship between death and Logos that he is so desperate to uncover. For Kotonu, the accident is a portent of future catastrophe that he suspects has direct pertinence to his continuing role as a lorry driver, while for Samson, it is a call for abjection and propitiation in the face of the might and capriciousness of Ógún. None of them attends directly to the fact that the accident is caused by the parlous state of the road itself, and that the bridge was in dire need of repair before the accident occurred. Rather, their various interpretations elevate the accident beyond the normal and lodge it within the domain of esoteric signification. The road as chronotope is returned to several times during the play, but always as a stand-in for something else and never in relation to its material dimensions. The transcendental character attributed to the road as a surrogate of Ógún's hunger also means that the social violence of the *kòbòlòi's* peripheral existence is concealed through the language of elusive ritual.

In what must be considered the most astute analysis of *The Road* thus far, Biodun Jeyifo argues that the play's motifs and metaphorical

---

[40] Soyinka, *The Road*, 198–199.

structures "seem to reflect a basic world of psychic, metaphysical colli-sion" that is overdetermined by the context of precarious existence inherent to life in the world of motor parks.[41] For him this is Soyinka's means of sublating the class war that pits the lumpenproletariat of Nigeria's urban poor against the invisible hegemony of insensitive state institutions, examples of which we find in *The Road,* represented in the characters of Chief-in-Town the politician, and Particulars Joe the policeman. When Jeyifo goes on to describe the unemployed drivers, touts, layabouts, and thugs as constituting both chorus and dramatis personae, he pinpoints an important aspect of Soyinka's dramaturgy that we already saw in *Death and the King's Horseman.* But Jeyifo insists that in *The Road,* the unemployed transport workers become merely instruments of "collective self-celebration" and "sub-cultural narcissism."[42] The nar-cissism cuts in every direction, as both Professor and the men that he lords over are ruled by the same impulses of self-inflation. This is the means by which they variously attempt to relieve their sense of entrap-ment within a precarious existence. However, the specific chorality within the play is often marked by sporadic interventions of singing and dancing that subtend the dialogue but are not necessarily integrated into the unfolding action, except in its explicitly ritual moments. This dynamic is also to be found in earlier plays by Soyinka such as *The Lion and the Jewel* and *Kongi's Harvest.* As we shall see, the peculiar rhythmic oscillation between potential violence, ritual collectivism, and the domain of agential action gets resolved only in the explosive tragic denouement at the very end.

A specific focus on the tragic dimensions of *The Road* obliges us to pay attention to the ritual aspects of the drama while also disentangling the bases of what might constitute ethical choice. The historical conditions we see in the play are quite different from what was laid out in *Death and the King's Horseman.* Unlike in that play, where the action unfolds across four different locations (marketplace, colonial parlor, residency, and dungeon), here the stage directions locate the entire play in front of a broken-down lorry, the metonymic fragment of a lorry park and thus of material condi-tions that demarcate the Nigerian urban periphery:

> *Dawn is barely breaking on a road-side shack, a ragged fence and a corner of a church with a closed stained-glass window. Above this a cross-surmounted steeple*

---

[41] Biodun Jeyifo, "The Hidden Class War in *The Road,*" *The Truthful Lie: Essays in a Sociology of African Drama* (London: New Beacon, 1985), 12.

[42] Jeifyo, 17.

tapers out of sight. Thrusting downstage from a corner of the shack is the back of a "bolekaja" (mammy wagon), lop-sided and minus its wheels. It bears the inscription – AKSIDENT STORE – ALL PART AVAILEBUL.[43]

"Aksident Store" is a witty name for a place that sells spare parts, its pidgin English suggesting something of the inventive automobile dismemberment and reassemblage that take place in such places to service broken down vehicles of all makes and sizes. While lorry parks are central to the social life of urban areas in Nigeria and indeed much of Africa, it is what they reveal about urban unemployment and homelessness, and the precarious existence of the *kòbòlòi* that constitute their dominant sociological relevance in *The Road*.[44] Jeyifo centers his reading mainly on a Marxist analysis of class relations, but what is of equal relevance is that the conditions seem to produce a series of patron/client and hierarchical relations that are undergirded by different degrees of potential violence. In the play this is articulated at different levels, first in the ever-present threat of conceptual violence perpetrated by the near-demented Professor, the threats of physical violence enacted in the name of political thuggery (protection for politicians), and finally, in the ever-present metaphysical reality of Ógún's hunger, as we have already noted.

There is an irruption of subterranean violence onto the surface of the play that finally collapses the façade of strained normalcy that has thus far governed the action. Much of this irruption centers around the transformation of Murano, a young man we are told earlier has been salvaged from an accident by Professor, and who in bringing in the daily evening's gourd of palm-wine for him and the unemployed transport workers, performs the function of Ógún votary and the potential pathway to the god's reality. Murano walks with a slight limp, which additionally invokes Esu, the limping Yorùbá god of trickery. That he is also a mute adds to his quality of liminality, mediating as he does between the worlds of the now and the afterworld, and between the realities of the Yorùbá gods of war and trickery. Professor declares:

> Murano could not reveal much, returning instinctively to his old trade, tapping wine from trees; beyond that, he had retained no further link to

---

[43] Soyinka, *The Road*, 151.

[44] On African lorry parks, see Michael Stasik's highly insightful essay, "Roadside Involution, Or How Many People Do You Need to Run a Lorry Park," in Kurt Beck, Gabriel Klaeger and Michael Stasik, eds., *The Making of the African Road* (Leiden: Brill, 2017), 24–57. For a riveting study of passenger vehicles as nodal points for the study of African urban social relations, see Matteo Rizzo, *Taken for a Ride: Neoliberalism, Precarious Labour, and Public Transport in an African Metropolis* (Oxford: Oxford University Press, 2017).

what he was or where he had been. That, that especially where he had been. And waiting, waiting till his tongue be release, [*desperately*] in patience and in confidence, for he is not like you others whose faces are equally blank but share no purpose with the Word. So, surely Murano, crawling out of the darkness, from the last suck of the throat of death, and Murano with the spirit of a god in him, for it came to the same thing, that I held a god captive, that his hands held out the day's communion! And I should not hope, with him, to cheat, to anticipate the final confrontation, learning its nature baring its skulking face, why may I not understand ... [*He stops, looks around him.*] So, why don't you ask him to try it on, see if it fits.[45]

Professor takes Murano into the store and when he reemerges a few moments later, he has donned full *egungun* costume. All eyes are riveted on the "apparition" and the instruments that the men had been playing as they drank the palm-wine suddenly fall silent. Professor shouts for the men to continue playing, and they resume, but this time a slow music of *agemo* emerges from the bowels of the earth. The *agemo* cult is a death-cult of dissolution and rebirth among the Yorùbá, so its musical invocation here suggests that Murano is at the crossroads of the living and the dead. Apart from Professor, everybody else onstage senses that they are bearing witness to an act of blasphemy and sacrilege. Say Tokyo Kid, a character who styles himself on the model of American westerns, tries to stop the sacrilege. He and Professor wrestle each other "with no sound but hissed breaths ... in tense elastic control."[46] Salubi finds an opportune moment to pass Say Tokyo Kid a knife that he promptly plunges into Professor's back. Afflicted by a moment of panic, Say Tokyo Kid attempts to pull out the knife. As if on cue, the masked Murano, who has stood completely still throughout this interlude suddenly comes to life to lift Say Tokyo Kid above his head and smashes him savagely on a bench. Say Tokyo Kid is unable to rise but only clutches at the train of Murano's mask. Rising gradually, a driver's funerary dirge begins as the mask spins and spins, sinking lower as Professor rises in an involuntary movement to gather his papers. He raises his hand in apparent benediction over the scene and intones a garbled blessing. As the mask continues spinning more and more slowly until it is "nothing beyond a heap of clot and raffia," Professor's head falls forward while the dirge wells to close the play. We will have noticed from the opening stage directions that a cross-surmounted steeple and the corner of a church's stained-glass window can be seen behind the Aksident Store. The church is referenced in conversation several times to provide

---

[45] Soyinka, *The Road*, 223–224.   [46] Soyinka, *The Road*, 228.

background to Professor's congregation and how he fell out with them because of his peculiar behavior and pronouncements. Just before the last violent segment of the play the sounds of organ music emanate from the direction of the church to suffuse the stage before Professor asks his men to drown it out with sounds of their own instruments. In displaying various musical traditions (Christian, call-and-response, *agemo* cult drumming, funerary dirge), different costumes (Particulars Joe's police uniform, Murano's masquerade), and language registers (the motor-park *kòbòlòi's* pidgin English spattered with Yorùbá and Professor's high-blown but aporetic speech forms), Soyinka coalesces the starkly different registers of signification that have been distributed throughout the play into one final multifaceted flourish. The effect is to yoke ritual firmly back into the domain of social confusion and to generate the effect of incomprehensibility as a residual problem rather than a solution to what has been represented in the play. As already noted, Jeyifo understands the central question to be the relations of class antagonism as represented by the lumpenproletariat of the motor-park industry on the one hand and the insensitive political order on the other, with Professor being representative of totalitarian hegemonic impulses as well as of the oppressed.

A question, however, remains: is *The Road* a tragic play or merely the interpretation of a set of socio-metaphysical contradictions? The central difficulty in answering this question lies in the fact that Professor is far from an admirable character. He is clearly a bully and a calculating manipulator of the unemployed motor-park workers around him. Furthermore, there is a sense of morbid cold-heartedness in his gloating over the interpretative possibilities at the site of terrible road accidents. This, coupled to his penchant for bafflingly elusive aporetic speech, ensures that it is very difficult to approve his status as a tragic character. And yet his hermeneutical delirium and his pact with danger are strangely attractive as mediums by which to negotiate an understanding of the Faustian quest for knowledge that has instigated the transgression of boundaries from Marlowe's Doctor Faustus through Goethe's *Faust*, to Stephen Spielberg's *Jurassic Park*, among others. For ultimately what makes Professor a point of tragic interest is that he attempts to transcend all limitations – Christian and Yorùbá – to gain access to forbidden territories of knowing. This is a hubristic ambition that must ultimately end in death. Supreme irony lies in the fact that the extent to which the Professor pursues his quest on a social periphery of want and penury produces the essential features of a corrupt worldliness even as a higher order of understanding is aimed at. In that sense his quest is over-determined by contradictory forces within the metaphysical as well as in the conditions of marginal social existence that produce confused modes of self-apprehension. The violence that we see at the end among the *kòbòlòi* has a long genealogy in the dire social conditions that frame them. The extraction of metaphysical value from these conditions is always compromised by the impossibility of transcending this genealogy.

Death and the King's Horseman and *The Road* demonstrate completely different contexts for thinking about the relationship between history, social conditions, and ethical choice. And both of them are so deeply immersed in Yorùbá metaphysics and rituals that it is impossible to disentangle their tragic visions from their overall Yorùbá sensibilities. But if the first play gives us a window into the interruption of the integrity of the known traditional world under colonialism, the second shows us that the interruptions continue into the postcolony as aspects of the impossibility of self-realization that are generated from the dastardly conditions of the urban periphery. In both instances, Yorùbá culture provides the background ideational matrix against which a foreground of tragic choice unfolds. But the fact that foreground and background collapse into each other at key moments also suggests that we cannot pose the question of tragic choice outside of the dialectical relation between one and the other. What Soyinka gives us then, are templates of ethical choice that resonate in several directions at once. For Elesin Oba's failure in undertaking the ritual suicide is due as much to his own hedonistic dispositions as it is to the interruption of the white man, an entity that he momentarily inserts into his own traditional modes of meaning-making. In this regard, Elesin Oba sets himself, for one tragic moment, outside of his own cultural modes of understanding even while he imagines his every action to be deeply from within it. In the case of Professor, his quest for certainty about death-in-life and life-in-death is undertaken from the dual perspective of debased Christianity and Yorùbá metaphysics, thus suggesting that he too tries to fuse incompatible metaphysical standpoints together in pursuit of a consoling epistemology. In each, the world goes awry, and what appears as ethical choice is hedged round by the possibility of its inversion from several directions at once. The frustration of resolution may be the preferred mode of Soyinka's anti-mimeticism, but the fact that these formal devices reveal something about the very question of ethical choice-making for Elesin Oba and Professor means this preferred mode is in tune with the problem of tragedy in the (post)colony, that is to say, both before and after colonization and at the intersection of a Yorùbá worldview with that of a more disenchanted and perhaps even secular viewpoint.

CHAPTER 5

Archetypes, Self-Authorship, and Melancholia
Tayeb Salih's Seasons of Migration to the North

To arrive at Tayeb Salih's *Season of Migration to the North* after Achebe and Soyinka's works is to shift from the predominantly colonial settings of those earlier texts to the dialectically intersecting contexts of colony and colonial metropole. On first reading, the novel's dual settings seem to have little in common with each other except as mediated through the character of Mustafa Sa'eed. Sa'eed migrates from Khartoum as a twelve-year-old to study in Cairo, then proceeds to Oxford and London, and then, after seven years in prison for murdering his English wife, he settles in a Sudanese village, Wad Hamid. The narrative is staged as Mustafa Sa'eed's retelling of the story of his life to an unnamed narrator, who has similarly returned to Wad Hamid after seven years studying poetry in England. The narrator is a native of the village, rather than an outsider like Mustafa Sa'eed. The two men's shared affinity for English poetry is what originally brings them together, but by the end of the novel, we find that the narrator's unexamined attitudes to his village have been deeply shaken by the story he has heard. Mustafa Sa'eed's life story is sometimes conveyed to us in the form of a straightforward dialogue between the two men and at other times as a fragmented interpolation in the mind of the narrator in other situations, as he interacts with other characters. The flashbacks and fragmentary disclosures of the story gradually generate an unmotivated fixation on Mustafa Sa'eed in the narrator's mind so that he becomes both an enigma and an obsession for the narrator. By the end of the novel, the narrator begins to see himself as a mirror image of Sa'eed. This mirroring effect recalls for us the Lacanian theory of the self's dependence on elusive refractions of the ego-ideal that start in the mirror phase of childhood but extend throughout the process of the individual's self-formation. In the context of the relationship between the unnamed narrator and Mustafa Sa'eed, however, we are required to augment Lacan's argument in his essay on "The Mirror Stage as Formative of the Function of the I" with reference to the shifting relationship between both negative and positive affects in the self's evolving relationship to the elusive ego-ideal.[1] For, after the mysterious death of Mustafa Sa'eed, what becomes evident are the narrator's self-loathing and his melancholic feelings of both introjection and disavowal, which are accompanied by feelings of intense resentment and anger toward Sa'eed. This serves to illustrate the fragmentation of the libidinal economy that was originally guaranteed by the lost object of attachment that was Mustafa Sa'eed, but that the narrator now experiences as a complicated mix of feelings and revulsions.

The novel is characterized by subtle intertextual arrangements and literary echoes, and these are part of a larger symphony of mirrorings that form a recurrent principle ramifying at different levels of the text. References from *Othello, Heart of Darkness, A Thousand and One Nights,* T. S. Eliot's "The Love Song of J. Alfred Prufrock," and many texts of the Arab Nahda (renaissance) are widely interspersed throughout *Season of Migration to the North,* and the novel's relationship to the Nahda is as important as its invocation of the Western literary canon. The Arab discourse of Nahda was dominated from the late nineteenth century by calls for structural reforms, modernization, and, as Wail Hassan puts it, the "selective synthesis and accommodation of technology and modern institutions to essentially traditional societies, belief systems, and social structures."[2] Muhsin Al-Musawi has also highlighted the issue of translation in discourses of the Nahda and the degree to which translation not only raised serious problems regarding the transfer of meanings between different languages, but also implicated significant questions about the very translatability of Arab tropes and concepts into European idioms and vice versa.[3] The question of the translatability of tropes and concepts is inarguably at the core of the intertextuality we find in *Season of Migration to the North.* Unlike other highly intertextual texts of African and Arab tragic literature such as Dambudzo Marechera's *The House of Hunger,* Kofi Awoonor's *This Earth, My Brother,* Assia Djebar's *Fantasia: A Cavalcade,* and Kamel Daoud's *The Meursault Investigation,* the intertextuality of *Season of Migration to the North* invites but also frustrates any simple comparison with the texts of the Western and Arab traditions from

---

[1] Jacques Lacan, "The Mirror Stage as Formative of the Function of the I," *Écrits: A Selection,* trans. Alan Sheridan (London: Tavistock, 1977), 1–7.

[2] Wail Hassan, *Tayeb Salih: Ideology and the Craft of Fiction* (Syracuse: Syracuse University Press, 2003), 6.

[3] Hassan, 6. For a more extensive evaluation of the *Nahda,* see Muhsin Al-Musawi, "The Republic of Letters: Arab Modernity? Part I," *Cambridge Journal of Postcolonial Literary Inquiry,* 1.2 (2014): 265–280, and "The Republic of Letters: Arab Modernity? Part II," *Cambridge Journal of Postcolonial Literary Inquiry,* 2.1 (2015): 115–130.

which it draws. The ebbing and flowing of intertextual signifiers reflect the highly elusive status of the central character Mustafa Sa'eed, around whom the inherent allusiveness of the novel is primarily constructed.

At the heart of Sa'eed's motivation in life is the drive toward self-authorship, that is to say, the ability to fashion his own identity autonomously and in complete control both of its contingent processes and of their final product. The problem of self-authorship is entangled with the process by which he becomes a highly successful intellectual in cosmopolitan London, as well as with the precarities of intimacy between him, as an Arab-African, and the many English women whom he lures into his bed. That Sa'eed marries and kills his wife Jean Morris in an extraordinarily sensual ritual murder on their marriage bed immediately invites comparison with Shakespeare's *Othello*. As we shall come to see later, Salih's novel replicates the essential tragic morphology of *Othello* through the handkerchief that he uses to focus the all-consuming and passionate hatred between Sa'eed and his English wife. And even though at his trial Mustafa Sa'eed is at pains to disavow Othello ("I am no Othello! Othello was a lie"), everything he does up to the court scene has been in direct invocation of his literary predecessor. As an added tier of the difference between Salih's novel and the texts we looked at in previous chapters, the interpellation of the colonial subject described by Fanon is in *Season of Migration to the North* replaced by a form of co-constitutive orientalism that situates colonizer and colonized in a relay of archetypes, with sexual desire warping the process of interpellation at various points. I use the term "archetypes" in preference to the more conventional "stereotypes" to indicate the ways in which the former draw upon the collective unconscious and thus raise intimations of cross-cultural transcendence. I am indebted here to Muhammad Siddiq's fine Jungian reading of the complicated process of Mustafa Sa'eed's psychological individuation. As Siddiq persuasively argues, Mustafa Sa'eed is regularly invested with epiphanic and transcendental force throughout the novel, whether amongst the Sudanese or amongst the many English women he consorts with. This suggests that there are deeply felt impulses that come to be focalized through Mustafa Sa'eed for both groups on different sides of the colonial divide.[4]

At the same time, Sa'eed's character is extraordinarily elusive and the cause of great bewilderment to everyone who interacts with him. He stirs in the English women deeply held feelings that go beyond their individual consciousness, and for the Sudanese characters, a sense that they are being transported beyond their immediate material conditions into a domain of

---

[4] Muhammed Siddiq, "The Process of Individuation in Al-Tayyeb Salih's Novel *Season of Migration to the North*," *Journal of Arabic Literature*, 9 (1978): 67–104.

transcendental significance. However, whereas Isabella Seymour, Sheila Greenwood, and Ann Hammond all subscribe to the relay of oriental archetypes by which he lures them into his bed, his wife Jean Morris strips him of the orientalist props to his identity and attempts to elicit from him instead a different kind of archetype, namely that of Othello. To become Othello, however, requires enacting a tragic action that involves both killing his English wife and killing himself, something that Mustafa Sa'eed implicitly acquiesces to but fails to completely accomplish in its second aspect. It is this failure that reveals to him the limits of his self-authorship and for which he lives the rest of his life in deep sorrow and regret. The complex co-constitution of oriental archetypes between English and colonized desiring subjects then revises the proposals regarding the colonial racial economy in Fanon's "The Fact of Blackness," which as we saw in the Introduction requires a form of critical and existential awareness for forestalling or assuaging the discombobulation of the black person's bodily schema as it is interpellated within the colonial racial economy. Instead Saleh illustrates the terms by which the colonial racial economy is reappropriated by Sa'eed, not for any simple affirmation of subaltern identity, but for the disavowal of the primary terms of colonialist and orientalist interpellation in the first place.

Race relations in Salih's novel are distinguished in significant ways from Shakespeare's play, where, as we saw in Chapter 2, the central problem is essentially that of a contradictory cosmopolitanism and not necessarily of colonialism as such. The tragic reversal that afflicts Sa'eed is distinguished from Othello's by being staged against the lively backdrop of the colonial realities of both Sudan and London in the early twentieth century. We are given insight into the colonial setting of Sudan through fragments of debates about neocolonialism and the country's compromised political elites that take place between the narrator and his farmer friend Mahmood in Wad Hamid, as well as between him and others he meets in Khartoum where he works in the Ministry of Education. Meanwhile, the realities of racism and race relations in metropolitan England are located firmly within the domain of intimacy between the Arab-African and the English women with whom he consorts. There is a clear historical context to this second vector of race relations within the novel, as we shall see.

In an open letter to the late Tayeb Salih, Somali author Sofia Samatar writes:

> I want to say how I felt when I read that you were inspired by the story of Mahmood Hussein Mattan, the last person to be hanged in Cardiff. He was

a Somali merchant seaman married to a Welsh woman. He was accused of slitting another white woman's throat. It was 1952. Police officers told him he would die for the woman's murder "whether he did it or not." In court, he was described as a "semi-civilized savage." He refused the offer of an interpreter, as Mustafa Saeed, your character and Mahmood Mattan's shadow, refused to defend himself in an English court. But unlike Mustafa Saeed, who really did murder his wife, Mahmood Hussein Mattan was innocent. His wife Laura fought ceaselessly to have his name cleared and his body humanely buried. She won her case in 1998.

His gravestone reads: KILLED BY INJUSTICE.[5]

Not only does Samatar find uncanny echoes of the Somali Mattan's story in that of the Sudanese Mustafa Sa'eed, she also notes "a fearful affinity" in the way in which in Salih's novel, "the characters look for themselves in the eyes of others and find themselves and are appalled."[6] Samatar's formulation of the dynamic of self-discovery and dismay as reflections in the eyes of racialized Others has direct bearing not only on the central character's relationship to women but also on the overall narrative structure of the novel, as we shall see presently. But to identify the inspiration of Mattan's story as the source for Sa'eed's character is also to be reminded that the class distinctions that Salih invests in him as a successful colonial Arab-African in metropolitan Britain (educated at Oxford, a lecturer in economics in London) distinguishes him from the larger demographic of working-class Arab-Africans who had come to settle in the country over several decades and for whom, similarly, intimate relations with white women were hemmed in by racial ideas.[7] Mattan's story must be read not merely as the source for Mustafa Sa'eed's character but as an insinuation of the social relations of race that Sa'eed sought to systematically upend by constructing eroticized and orientalist versions of the Arab-African for consumption by white women.

Alongside the fictional Sa'eed is the historical presence in various British port cities of Sudanese, Somali, and Sierra Leonean sailors who were conscripted to work on merchant ships from the introduction of the steam engine in the early nineteenth century. The first iron steamship

---

[5] Sofia Samatar, "Open Letter to a Late Author: Dear Tayeb Salih," *ArabLit Quarterly* (Fall 2018): 26.

[6] Samatar, 25.

[7] Mattan's story is very well documented. See, for example, Bellis Kettie, "The Last Innocent Person to be Hanged in Wales," www.walesonline.co.uk/news/wales-news/last-innocent-person-hanged-wales-14860984, last accessed Dec. 4, 2018; and "Mahmood Hussein Mattan: A Man Wrongly Accused of Murder in 1952," *African Stories in York and East Yorkshire* (blog), www.africansinyorkshireproject.com/mahmood-hussein-mattan.html; last accessed Dec. 4, 2018.

sailed across the Atlantic in 1827, but by the mid-nineteenth century, steam engines had become standard for all merchant ships. Given that maritime regulations dictated substantially higher rates of remuneration for sailors conscripted in British ports, it was not unusual for African sailors to jump ship at such ports to await better commissions. During World War I more African sailors were hired to make up for the shortfall in British seamen, after many of the latter were conscripted into the army. The multicultural ferment of port cities such as Cardiff, Liverpool, and Bristol led to nasty anti-black riots in 1919 that were driven primarily by two complaints; the first being labor related and the second, and by far the most vociferous, that African and Arab seamen were too-freely sleeping with white women. As Carina Ray points out, "the 'sex problem,' as one newspaper dubbed it, became a primary explanatory framework for understanding, and in many cases, rationalizing, the impetus behind the riots."[8] Even though the false accusation against Mattan comes some three decades later, in the context of Cardiff, it makes complete sense in relation to residual perceptions of blacks as sexually dangerous. It also makes sense in the continuing recurrence of discourses of law and order in the period, which required the police to pin crimes of passion on black men as a means of demarcating between purity and danger. Even though Salih does not expressly reference these interracial tensions or indeed the materialist conditions of race relations in Britain in *Season of Migration to the North*, his transposition of racial stereotypes onto the charged interpersonal relationships between Mustafa Sa'eed and the English women he sleeps with, invokes the danger that Africans represented to the English (and British) social imagination. Unlike the real-life Mahmood Mattan, Mustafa Sa'eed is not the victim of anybody's racism. Everything he does is an aspect of his larger quest for self-authorship, and thus the judgment we make of him has to take account of the contradictions in that process.

The Limits of Self-Authorship

The conversation that takes place early in the novel between Mustafa Sa'eed and his mother serves to highlight the theme of self-authorship not as promise but as enigma. Sa'eed recalls his mother in this way: "When I think back, I see her clearly with her thin lips resolutely closed, with

---

[8] Carina Ray, *Crossing the Color Line: Race, Sex, and the Contested Politics of Colonialism in Ghana* (Athens, OH: Ohio University Press, 2015), 165. For race relations in late nineteenth and early twentieth century Liverpool, see Jacqueline Nassy Brown, *Dropping Anchor, Setting Sail: Geographies of Race in Black Liverpool* (Princeton: Princeton University Press, 2005).

something on her face like a mask, I don't know – a thick mask, as though her face were the surface of the sea. Do you understand? It possessed not a single colour but a multitude, appearing and disappearing and intermingling."[9] The recollection of his mother's mask-like features that nevertheless hint at changing internal depths is the first clue of tragic inscrutability we find in the novel, which though here tied specifically to his mother, we will later discover to be a key aspect of the maternal archetype that governs his relationships with other women. The young Sa'eed is discovered by an English man who comes riding into their village from Khartoum on a horse to recruit boys for the new school that is set in "a nice stone building in the middle of a large garden on the banks of the Nile."[10] Sa'eed goes to the school and performs so well that in less than three years, arrangements are made for him to leave his village to go to Cairo from where he subsequently ends up in England. This is the conversation that takes place between mother and son on the eve of his departure:

> When the headmaster informed me that everything had been arranged for my departure to Cairo, I went to talk to my mother. Once again she gave me that strange look. Her lips parted momentarily as though she wanted to smile, then she shut them and her face reverted to its usual state: a thick mask, or rather a series of masks. Then she disappeared for a while and brought back her purse, which she placed in my hand.
> "Had your father lived," she said to me, "he would not have chosen for you differently from what you have chosen for yourself. Do as you wish, depart or stay, it's up to you. It's your life and you're free to do with it as you will. In this purse is some money which will come in useful." That was our farewell: no tears, no kisses, no fuss. Two human beings had walked along a part of the road together, then each had gone his way. This was in fact the last thing she said to me, for I did not see her again.[11]

His mother's "It's your life and you're free to do with it as you will" invites the twelve-year-old boy to contemplate the possibility of complete self-mastery in authoring himself, while the invocation of his dead father's blessing further secures for him the assurance of male approval, and even frames his journey as the fulfillment of an ancestral prophecy or genetic predestination. Mustafa Sa'eed subsequently interprets his mother's invitation to self-authorship through two modes of action that seem on the surface to be not only contradictory, but also mutually negating. He expresses the

[9] Tayeb Salih, *Season of Migration to the North* (London: Heinemann Educational, 1969), 19.
[10] Salih, 20.   [11] Salih, 23.

first mode through immersion in a purely libidinal sexual economy; while in England he sleeps with as many white women as he can. As he disingenuously puts it, his purpose is to "liberate Africa with my penis."[12] With this statement he asserts a causal link between his distorted relationships with white women and the economic, cultural, and psychological violence perpetrated by British colonial rule. At face value, his words suggest a form of colonial revenge drama, and yet the tone is facetious and sardonic.

The claim to a vengeful subaltern consciousness is also undermined by the fact that the decolonializing agenda he lays claim to takes as its privileged performative site not the public sphere of debate and political organization but that of private intimacy, where the stakes are those only of sexual pleasure and control. The irony of the degradation of any putative decolonial political agenda is especially heightened when set against the fact that Mustafa Sa'eed's entire life is framed by epochal political events in Sudan. Given that he is so highly educated and self-conscious, these epochal events will not have been lost upon him. As Wail Hassan points out in summarizing the political events in the novel:

> Mustafa's life coincides with the era of British colonization of Sudan: he is born on August 16, 1898, a date historically framed by the battles of Atbara and Omdurman (June and September of that year, respectively), in which Kitchener's army crushed the Mahdi's forces and completed the conquest of Sudan. His mother was a slave from southern Sudan, and his father belonged to a tribe that collaborated with Kitchener – a mixed Arab-African lineage marked both by social stigma and by treason . . . . In 1916, while he is studying in England, Britain and France signed the Sykes-Picot Agreement, which divided the Arab world into spheres of British and French influence; this, despite Britain's promise to Arab nationalist leaders of independence if they revolted against the Ottoman Empire (a promise that led to the Arab Revolt of 1917, orchestrated by Lawrence of Arabia). As a further betrayal, Britain issued the Balfour Declaration in 1917, which promised the establishment of a Jewish state on Arab land; and in 1922 the League of Nations formally recognized the British and French mandates to rule the area. In the same year, Mustafa is appointed lecturer at London University and begins a sexual crusade against Britain. Back in Sudan, Mustafa disappears from Wad Hamid in 1953, just before the end of the colonial period, the year of the formulation of a parliamentary system that would proclaim the country's independence in 1956. Major events of Mustafa's life coincide with milestones in the history of European imperialism in the Arab world; thus, he is metaphorically and psychologically a product of empire.[13]

---

[12] Salih, 120.   [13] Hassan, 91–92.

Even though Mustafa Sa'eed takes up the mantle of president of the Struggle for African Freedom during his time in England, and indeed writes books whose titles suggest trenchant critiques of Empire (*The Economics of Colonialism, Colonialism and Monopoly, The Cross and Gunpowder*, and, most tellingly, *The Rape of Africa*) the irony is that in expressing his crusade against the colonizer in wholly sexual terms, any interpretation of his actions as the unproblematic expression of a specifically decolonial political impulse is thoroughly compromised. In stating my views in this way, I am breaking fundamentally with the conventional explanation of his sexual exploits as an aspect of a decolonial revenge drama. For example, despite his otherwise fine reading of the novel, Wail Hassan is able to state that: "The figure of the English woman evokes hostile anxiety for him [Mustafa Sa'eed] because, notwithstanding the misogyny of colonial discourse, the British Empire expanded under the rule of a mighty woman, Queen Victoria, the eponym of the Age of Empire whose name denotes 'victory' over those she subdues."[14] The implication of a reading such as Hassan's is that the women Mustafa Sa'eed sleeps with are to be taken as an expressive fragment of a larger totality of which they are both symptom and instantiation. Apart from the signal historical inaccuracy of merging the 1920s and 1930s (the period in which Mustafa Sa'eed was sexually active in England) with the Victorian era (1837–1901), this reading grounds itself in a series of metonymic displacements. And so: Queen Victoria ⇒ matriarch of the British Empire ⇒ process of (misogynistic) colonial domination ⇒ everyday English women ⇒ contaminated by a form of similitude to Queen Victoria ⇒ thus English women are complicitous in the project of Empire ⇒ therefore to sleep with them and then abandon them is a form of resistance to Empire.

This logic seems to me to be deeply unsatisfactory for a number of reasons. It requires the simultaneous metonymization of individual English women and their conflation with an idea of Empire that obscures the distinctions between them and yet holds them both individually and severally responsible for political processes that were in actuality primarily shaped by men during the entire period of colonialism and Empire – something Mustafa Sa'eed, with his expansive knowledge of the history of colonialism, as evidenced by his library, would have been aware of. Moreover, this concept of enacting decolonial revenge through the seduction of white women implies that Sa'eed registers *personally* the offence of colonialism and internalizes a level of rage that we simply do not find

[14] Hassan, 93.

evidence for in the novel. He does not bear signs of an inferiority complex with regards to the Europeans he consorts with on a regular basis, for example, nor any desire to humiliate or injure the women he sleeps with as a way of reversing larger interracial power dynamics. If he preys upon white women, his motivations appear to be carnal before political, motivated by the pleasure of the chase and the sensuality of sex, rather than triumph over an opponent. Although he eventually succeeds in killing Jean, it is only after she repeatedly begs and goads and taunts him into it. It is clear that the violence of murder is unnatural to him, at odds with his philosophy toward white women in a way that the decolonial revenge motivation does not sufficiently account for. Furthermore, each of the women Mustafa Sa'eed sleeps with is uniquely characterized in the novel and is treated independently rather than as a general category by him. Sheila Greenwood is a country girl from the outskirts of Hull who works as a waitress and pursues night studies at the Polytechnic, while Isabella Seymour is twelve years his senior, "round of face and inclined to plumpness" and married to a surgeon with whom she has two daughters and a son. Meeting Mustafa Sa'eed aroused a hunger and desire in both women that they did not know existed. Only Ann Hammond appears discursively assimilable to the idea of a colonialist, but even this requires us to ignore the degree to which she and Mustafa Sa'eed mutually interpellate each other as colonizer and colonized in a simultaneous interplay of oriental archetypes and their reversals. We shall return to this last point more fully in a moment.

What is effectively Sa'eed's specious rhetorical ploy for rationalizing his sexual exploits is then adopted by critics as the expression of a subaltern political consciousness. Such a reading also ignores the fact that at no time does Mustafa Sa'eed himself make any explicit critique of Empire to the narrator during the entire course of telling him his story. Apart from the quip about the revolutionary potential of his penis, which is reported to the narrator by someone who worked in London with Sa'eed when he was president of the Society for the Struggle for the Freedom for African Freedom, everything he tells the narrator is of a deeply personal and troubled nature. Whatever political disposition Mustafa Sa'eed has is left for us to surmise from the title of the books he has published, which the narrator finds on entering his study toward the end of the novel. In other words, even though a critique of Empire and decolonial elites is central to debates on nation-building in the Sudan sections of the novel, such a critique remains entirely in the nebulous background of Mustafa Sa'eed's exploits in London and is never brought to the foreground of his conversations with the narrator in any specific way. With respect to the laboring Arab-Africans in British ports that we noted earlier, a similar process of implication also applies to the question of race-relations. From the story of Mattan's hanging and those of the many victims of violent race riots, it is clear these Arab-Africans did face a virulent racism. Mustafa Sa'eed is immune at least to that kind of racism, even if we cannot discount the likely microaggressions he must have faced as a cocky and upwardly mobile colonial subject in the intense environment of metropolitan Britain. And the microaggressions were also counterbalanced by the support he received from English liberals, some of whom stepped forward to defend him at his trial.

Mustafa Sa'eed's second mode of self-authorship derives from the total affirmation of his intellect as autonomous from the domain of ethics. Early in his studies in Cairo, he realizes that his mind is capable of grasping incredibly complex mathematical problems with the utmost ease. He learned to write in just two weeks, after which he "surged forward" with nothing to stop him. The dominant images by which he describes his mind are invariably of coldness and sharpness: "my mind was like a sharp knife, cutting with cold effectiveness," "my brain continued on, biting and cutting like the teeth of a plough," "my sole weapon being that sharp knife inside my skull, while within my breast was a hard, cold feeling – as if it had been cast in rock." Mrs. Robinson, the adoptive English mother whom he first meets in Cairo with her husband when he arrives there to study, tells him: "Mr. Sa'eed, you're a person quite devoid of a sense of fun ... Can't you ever forget your intellect?" Even though he does not answer her question directly, his continuing fascination with his intellect is couched in terms that suggest the degree to which he is completely enamored of it, almost as if his mind was a technical tool independent of him: "I was busy with this wonderful machine with which I had been endowed. I was cold as a field of ice, nothing in the world could shake me."[15] He goes on to become a star student at Oxford University, a lecturer at the University of London, a popular speaker on the lecture circuit, a writer of hefty academic books, as well as a painter, photographer, and poet. If we discern here echoes of Conrad's Kurtz and the suggestion that, like Kurtz, all of European civilization went into making Mustafa Sa'eed, we are not entirely mistaken, for as we shall see presently, the interlocutory relationship between Sa'eed and the unnamed narrator is similar to that between the deeply enigmatic Kurtz and the restless and intrepid Marlow.

The image of a knife that is used repeatedly as a metaphor for his cold intellect is later manifested as a real knife in his murder of Jean Morris. In

---

[15] Salih, 22, 26.

the sexually ritualized scene of his wife's murder, the knife becomes a phallic object of inexpressible desire. He places the knife on his wife's chest and presses down on it in imitation of love making. Later in the novel, a knife is used in the bloody murder-suicide scene of Bint Mahmoud and Wad Rayyes in the Sudanese village. This murder-suicide itself becomes a central turning point for the radical unsettling of the narrator's unexamined attitudes to his village lifeworld. Each mention of the knife in the novel thus establishes a connection with Mustafa Sa'eed either directly or by implication. The cumulative insistence on the knife, first as metaphor of mental capacities, then as phallic symbol, and finally as the instrument of castration, serves to situate it as one of the most suggestive incrementally repeated symbols in the novel.[16] More importantly, the knife also establishes the inextricable coupling of knowledge with desire and death, which are expressively bifurcated in both the metropolitan and colonial settings of the novel.

What I described earlier as the domain of libidinal sexual economy is, however, not completely devoid of epistemological orientation, for its activation requires the co-constitution of oriental archetypes that are drawn from Europe's long interactions with the Middle East and Africa. To the women that encounter him, Mustafa Sa'eed is the Arab-African of mystery and enigma. They invariably perceive him as the embodiment of some supernatural force and extension of nature. He is alternatively described as a pagan god, the devil, a symbol of Africa, the Nile, and of tropic climates. His color is said to be the color of darkness and magic, and his character is taken to invoke untamed wildness, danger, unbridled energy, and tantalizing promise. That the women consume him as an oriental archetype does not foreclose the fact that he himself actively induces the process of his own interpellation through a series of material and discursive invocations that point in the same direction. The process of oriental invocations is superbly encapsulated in his relationship with Ann Hammond, a student of Oriental languages at Oxford whom he meets after delivering a speech at the university:

> And so, it was with us: she, moved by poetry and drink, feeding me with sweet lies, while I wove for her intricate and terrifying threads of fantasy. She would tell me that in my eyes she saw the shimmer of mirages in hot deserts,

---

[16] Others include the mask, the sea, the sun, the palm tree, the Nile river, and other symbols of nature and the natural cycle, as well as the many references to the extensive typology of figures and gestures from both Western and Arab literature. For more on this, see Muhammad Siddiq, "The Process of Individuation in Al-Tayyeb Salih's Novel *Season of Migration to the North*."

that in my voice she heard the screams of ferocious beasts in the jungles. And I would tell her that in the blueness of her eyes I saw the faraway shoreless seas of the North. In London I took her to my house, the den of lethal lies that I had deliberately built up, lie upon lie: the sandalwood and incense; the ostrich feathers and ivory and ebony figurines; the paintings and drawings of forests of palm trees along the shores of the Nile, boats with sails like doves' wings, suns setting over the mountains of the Red Sea, camel caravans wending their way along sand dunes on the borders of the Yemen, baobab trees in Kordofan, naked girls from the tribes of the Zandi, the Nuer and the Shuluk, fields of banana and coffee on the Equator, old temples in the district of Nubia; Arabic books with decorated covers written in ornate Kufic script; Persian carpets, pink curtains, large mirrors on the walls, and coloured lights in the corners.[17]

To the saturated and intoxicating appeals to the senses that include those of smell (sandalwood and incense), sight (the diverse paintings), the hint of victuals (fields of banana and coffee), along with a titillating nod to the intellect (Arabic books with covers written in ornate Kufic strips), Ann Hammond replies: "You are Mustafa, my master and my lord, and I am Sausan, your slave girl." It is not clear what classical female character from Arab literature she is referring to here, but the Arabic word *jāria* translated here as "slave girl" is more technically an "odalisque" (i.e., one of the many sex slaves in the sultan's harem). This would lend significantly more power to the "master" and also has a specifically orientalist element of drama and spectacle coming from the mouth of Ann Hammond.[18] As we might recall in our discussion of Fanon from the Introduction, for him the various negative interpellations of the colonial racial economy have the effect of frustrating or blocking the "bodily schema" of the black self, thus engendering fear and self-loathing that require eternal vigilance as a coping mechanism.[19] The model of interlocution implicit in *Black Skin, White Masks* has the inherent structure of a call-and-response sequence (first the hailing/interpellation, then the response/resistance; and repeat). In contrast, in *Wretched of the Earth*, which is more directly attuned to the problem of collective self-making in the crucible of decolonization, Fanon calls for a righteous violence that is designed to fill the colonized with a sense of being and purpose. The co-constitutive orientalism we see in *Season of Migration to the North* means that, unlike Fanon, Mustafa Sa'eed's response to the European stereotyping of his Otherness is not

---

[17] Salih, 146.

[18] I want to thank Noor Naga for suggesting this fascinating translation and reading of this section of the novel. Personal communication.

[19] Fanon, *Black Skin, White Masks*, 120

through a process of incessant refutations but rather through the activation of oriental archetypes for his own pleasure and benefit. Sa'eed does not refute the oriental archetypes but actively encourages them as part of the process by which knowledge, sex, and control come to be inextricably intertwined in his own process of self-authorship.

Ironically, the tragic reversal and the concomitant *anagnorisis* that attends it are firmly brought together in his wife Jean, who encapsulates the high point of the co-constitution of oriental archetypes between the English women and Mustafa Sa'eed. She flips the power dynamic between herself and Sa'eed in ways that he could not quite have anticipated. Her game requires the employment of archetypes that serve to convert the usual patterns of sexual pursuit normally under his complete control into an instrument of his own hounding by her – and vice versa. For with Jean Morris, Mustafa Sa'eed is both hunter and quarry, an oscillation that distorts his carefully managed process of self-authorship. Their relationship is defined very early on as a form of predation that is starkly different from what had existed between him and the other English women. From first encounter, Jean seems to stalk him, "as though she made a point of being where I was in order to humiliate me."[20] She teases him while also repaying any acts of violence from him with even greater violence of her own: "When I slapped her cheek, she kicked me and bit into my arm with teeth like those of a lioness."[21] She was also a glib liar, a "mendicant Scheherazade" who would tell fibs about anything and everything. If we compare Jean Morris to Ann Hammond as both are placed in the role of the odalisque, we find that if Ann Hammond is a passive, submissive, do-what-you-want-to kind of slave girl, Jean Morris is a Shahrazad, spinning stories, intelligent, creative, and manipulative: a trickster who will outwit her master into giving her what she wants (in Shahrazad's case, what she wants is life, and in Jean Morris's case, what she wants is death).[22] Also, Jean's ferocity – her kicking and biting like a lioness – reverses the expectations of "civility" and "poise" associated with the British, and brings her closer to the stereotypical "barbarian" African/Arab.

It is on an unannounced visit to his house one day that the discursive terms of their relationship are set for good. Ann Hammond is with Mustafa Sa'eed at the time, but she quickly departs in tears. Jean then strips naked to stand imperiously before him:

---

[20] Salih, 155. [21] Salih, 155. [22] This idea is explored in more detail in Hassan, 105–110.

All the fires of hell blazed within my breast. Those fires had to be extinguished in that mountain of ice that stood in my path. As I advanced towards her, my limbs trembling, she pointed to an expensive Wedgwood vase on the mantelpiece. "Give this to me and you can have me," she said. If she had asked at that moment for my life as a price I would have paid it. I nodded my head in agreement. Taking up the vase, she smashed it on the ground and began trampling on the pieces underfoot. She pointed to a rare Arabic manuscript on the table. "Give me this too," she said. My throat grew dry with a thirst that almost killed me. I must quench it with a drink of icy water. I nodded my head in agreement. Taking up the old, rare manuscript she tore it to bits, filling her mouth with pieces of paper which she chewed and spat out. It was as though she had chewed my very liver. And yet I didn't care. She pointed to a silken Isphahan prayer-rug . . . It was the most valuable thing I owned, the thing I most treasured. "Give me this too and then you can have me," she said. Hesitating for a moment, I glanced at her as she stood before me, erect and lithe, her eyes agleam with a dangerous bitterness, her lips like a forbidden fruit that must be eaten. I nodded my head in agreement. Taking up the prayer-rug, she threw it on to the fire and stood watching gloatingly as it was consumed, the flames reflected on her face. The woman is my quarry and I shall follow her to Hell.[23]

When he walks up close to kiss her, he feels a violent jab from her knee between his thighs. He passes out and when he wakes up, she is gone. Several tropes emerge in this encounter. That Mustafa Sa'eed styles himself as the heat that needs to be cooled in Jean Morris's cold ice immediately pitches the metaphorical heat of the desert against the coldness of Europe, not only reflecting an aspect of the season of migration to the north of the novel's title, but also expressing a binary opposition in archetypal environmental terms. Jean triggers specific feelings of intense vehemence ("hell blazed within my breast") and physical reaction (thirst, trembling) as if he is being infantilized and is desperately losing control of his bodily functions. Most important in this encounter, however, is that Jean systematically shatters all the orientalist and class props through which he had hitherto expressed his identity and lured other women into his bed. The expensive Wedgwood vase, the Arabic manuscript, and the prized Isphahan rug – given to him by no other than his mentor Mrs. Robinson – have all been items with which he has incited an interpellation of his oriental exoticism. In contrast to Ann and the other women for whom these were the triggers for the co-constitution of oriental archetypes, Jean claims these key symbols of his identity only to destroy them. They are to her, inoperable as signifiers of his conveniently assumed

[23] Salih, 156–157.

identity. Rather, she designs to interpellate him completely anew even against his will. She activates the Othello archetype through the most universally recognizable device of Shakespeare's play, the handkerchief:

> Once I found a man's handkerchief which wasn't mine. "It's yours," she said when I asked her. "This handkerchief isn't mine," I told her. "Assuming it's not your handkerchief," she said, "what are you going to do about it?" On another occasion, I found a cigarette case, then a pen. "You're being unfaithful to me," I said to her. "Suppose I am being unfaithful to you," she said. "I swear I'll kill you," I shouted at her. "You only say that," she said with a jeering smile. "What's stopping you from killing me? What are you waiting for? Perhaps you're waiting till you find a man lying on top of me, and even then I don't think you'd do anything. You'd sit on the edge of the bed and cry."[24]

This is a deeply Shakespearean provocation indeed. Jean Morris's design is to invoke Mustafa Sa'eed as Othello, not merely in a process of orientalist interpellation, but in order to elicit from him a different form of aesthetic self-expression. It is almost as if she is saying to him: "I know you have laid on a false performance of your identity all your life and that you have fooled many women with it. But now I challenge you to be the real thing. Be as passionate and as great as Othello, you ridiculous and pathetic fake!" In Shakespeare's play, Othello had what amounted to an all-consuming passion for his wife and a sense of absolute duty regarding his commitments to Venice. But for Mustafa Sa'eed to become Othello, and Jean Morris his Desdemona, is also to articulate their relationship through a specifically tragic structural morphology that must issue in both their deaths. It requires not only that Sa'eed kill his wife as the surrogate of Desdemona with the skin of "monumental alabaster" but that he kill himself in place of the "turbaned Turk" that is Othello. This also implies that Jean has an inherent death-wish through which she might invest her life and her death with a special meaning via the idiom of tragedy. However, as she intuits correctly, Sa'eed is incapable of playing the tragic role she assigns him. He just does not have the guts to go the full length of it.

The process of Jean Morris's interpellation of Mustafa Sa'eed as Othello, however, requires some qualification to the original Shakespearean schema in light of the mixture of love and loathing that she consistently expresses toward him from their very first encounter. Desdemona never stops loving Othello; even when Emilia

---

[24] Salih, 162.

expresses doubts about his mood in act 4, scene 3, she is quick to jump to her husband's defense. In terms of the affective response to Mustafa Sa'eed that she articulates, Jean Morris's loathing marks her off not just as a potential Desdemona but also simultaneously as a cynical Iago. For it is Iago who perceives in Othello the mixture of military prowess, blind love, and abject barbarism that he then designs to bring to the surface. Like Iago, Jean Morris wants to purge Mustafa Sa'eed of what she sees as his inherent falseness but in such a way as to also convert him into the exemplar of focused tragic action. She sees in him none of the nobility inherent in Othello but only his innate potential for passion and destruction. Significantly, however, Sa'eed for his part also wants to unleash the full force of the contradictions he perceives in her character. He sees Jean as both madonna and whore, and it is the oscillation between the two that makes her simultaneously so strangely attractive and unbearably repulsive to him – an enigma that haunts him to his grave. In an angry scene when he first contemplates killing her, Sa'eed is suddenly overwhelmed by the memory of his mother and their parting:

> Suddenly I remembered my mother. I saw her face clearly in my mind's eye and heard her saying to me "It's your life and you're free to do with it as you will." I remembered that the news of my mother's death had reached me nine months ago and had found me drunk and in the arms of a woman. I don't recollect now which woman it was; I do, though, recollect that I felt no sadness – it was as though the matter was of absolutely no concern to me. I remembered this and wept from deep within my heart. I wept so much I thought I would never stop.[25]

It is not insignificant that he hears news of his mother's death nine months prior to his killing of Jean Morris when he was in the arms of another woman. But what is most telling is that he feels no sadness on originally receiving the news yet weeps uncontrollably on recalling her as he contemplates the murder of his wife. It is as if he has gestated the news of his mother's death in the form of a repressed memory that now gushes out uncontrollably when he is contemplating the killing of Jean Morris. He now weeps partly for the image of his mother, the madonna in his thoughts and a contrast to all the women he has slept with, and also for himself. And he weeps for his inability to hold human attachments and to feel emotions, for his coldness and complete indifference to women. The conflation of madonna and whore that has driven all his exploits with women is focalized

---

[25] Salih, 159.

here in Jean but in a manner that elicits from him a mixture of anger, desire, and also deep sadness. The oscillatory structure of attraction and revulsion with which Jean perceives him is mirrored exactly in the madonna/whore dialectic that defines her for him. When he weeps he also weeps for what he has lost and found in her, which he also knows he will have to destroy in order to achieve total self-completion. As it turns out, destroying the contradictory archetype that is Jean Morris does not spell freedom for Mustafa Sa'eed at all but rather marks the complete demise of the self-authorship that had been enjoined by his mother in the first place. What I have described here as the Othello-Desdemona archetype that Mustafa Sa'eed and Jean Morris evoke is not the only one at play in their relationship. Essential to the play of archetypes between them are others, all of which are defined by the essential terms of a primal opposition. And so, in addition to the Othello/Desdemona pairing we also have: Othello/Iago; hunter/quarry; master/slave; colonizer/colonized; Shahrazad /Shahryar; oriental /occidental; fire/ice; North/South. The significant feature of these primal archetypes, however, is that they are at once imposed and inverted, thus rendering all the binary oppositions inherently unstable.

It is precisely when Jean activates the Othello archetype that Sa'eed's process of self-authorship is undone. For what she desires is that they extinguish themselves together in a murder-suicide that would elevate them both into a tragic morphology that lies beyond banal judgement. Sa'eed himself experiences the moment of ritualized murder as a form of potential completion. As he tells the narrator, "Everything which happened before my meeting her was a premonition; everything I did after I killed her was an apology, not for killing her, but for the lie that was my life."[26] There are two potential meanings to the lie that he claims to have been his life. First is that it acknowledges the extent to which his life has been a manufactured fiction, entirely the product of his fertile imagination. But the lie also comes in not seizing the moment of invitation to complete the tragic morphology of Othello. At another point Mustafa Sa'eed phrases his regret to the narrator in a subtle echo of Eliot's Prufrock: "I hesitated that night when Jean sobbed into my ear, 'Come with me. Come with me.' My life achieved completion that night and there was no justification for staying on. But I hesitated and at the critical moment I was afraid."[27] Compare his

---

[26] Salih, 29.   [27] Salih, 68, 92.

conundrum to that of Prufrock's in Eliot's "The Love Song of J. Alfred Prufrock":

> And the afternoon, the evening, sleeps so peacefully!
> Smoothed by long fingers,
> Asleep . . . tired . . . or it malingers,
> Stretched on the floor, here beside you and me.
> Should I, after tea and cakes and ices,
> Have the strength to force the moment to its crisis?
> But though I have wept and fasted, wept and prayed,
> Though I have seen my head (grown slightly bald) brought in upon a platter,
> I am no prophet – and here's no great matter;
> I have seen the moment of my greatness flicker,
> And I have seen the eternal Footman hold my coat, and snicker,
> And in short, I was afraid.[28]

Throughout the poem, Prufrock is paralyzed by excessive anxiety and the fear of simply getting things wrong. His will to act is compromised due to his sense of complicity in the petit bourgeois lifestyle that he nonetheless feels compelled to critique. He wants to "bring the moment to its crisis" and yet is paralyzed by the contemplation of the very possibility of doing something that might make him transcend his quotidian circumstances. "No! I am not Prince Hamlet, nor was meant to be" he declares toward the end of the poem, and by this declaration immediately registers his lack of decisive capacity for tragic action, and by implication, of any form of greatness. But Prufrock's dilemma may also be interpreted as the product of an aesthetic capture of the will. He is the victim of an overly aestheticized sensibility. At every stage of the poem, Prufrock is afflicted by variant references from the literary and aesthetic tradition ranging from Homer, the Bible, Shakespeare, Dante, Michelangelo, Hesiod, Andrew Marvell, and many others. Much of what enervates Prufrock has to do with his expansive immersion in literary history and the fact that his every mundane experience seems to echo for him tropes from the literary and aesthetic domains. But these domains are marked predominantly by the deferral of ethical judgment rather than a call to action, their central objective being the contemplation of the pure and the beautiful. When Mustafa Sa'eed hesitates, he does so partly because of a loss of nerve, but also because to kill himself is to undo precisely the painstaking work of self-authorship that has turned on

---

[28] T. S. Eliot, "The Love Song of J. Alfred Prufrock," *The Wasteland and Other Poems* (London: Faber, 2001), 6.

well-crafted aesthetic values as much as on the suspension of moral judgment.

Lacan's Mirror Stage and the Interlocutor's Melancholia

The unnamed narrator is also a tragic character but in ways quite different from Mustafa Sa'eed. In his case he is guilty of a fundamental failure of ethical judgment that derives from his overly romantic understanding of village life and the formal grounds on which its belief systems have historically been grounded. It is this false understanding that first prevents him from actively opposing the proposed arranged marriage between Wad Rayyes and Hosna Bint Mahmoud. The murder-suicide is a *musuo* that shatters the collective peace of the community and triggers a complete crisis of consciousness for him. But unlike the case of Mustafa Sa'eed, the form of the narrator's crisis precedes its content. It is a form of crisis that is shaped by the nature of the interlocutory relationship between him as listener and Mustafa Sa'eed as enigmatic storyteller, so that the narrator yearns for completion in the biographical mirror that Mustafa Sa'eed holds up to him; it is, however, a mirror riddled with illusions and evasions. From their very first encounter, Sa'eed offers the narrator a mirror for the chimerical actualization of an ego-ideal, that in fact, lies beyond the narrator's reach precisely because of his self-satisfied return to the village of his birth. For even though the narrator has just returned to his village like a hero from studying abroad, Mustafa Sa'eed is where he himself would like to be: not only educated and cosmopolitan and with the superb capacity to affect the course of people's lives, but also a highly useful member of the village's agrarian community. Sa'eed is the ego-ideal which the narrator strives and fails to achieve. Sa'eed is in every way smarter, more accomplished, more cosmopolitan, and more useful in the village community, so that the narrator looks like a pale copy in comparison, and suffers from an inferiority complex, or perhaps even an imposter syndrome, because of this. He wants to *be* Sa'eed. As we shall see, he is even attracted to Sa'eed's wife. The irony of course is that in his cosmopolitan sojourn, Sa'eed himself has gazed at the heart of darkness and is trying to reverse the trajectory of his existential alienation by immersing himself in a village life that is diametrically opposed to the one he led in London. The hidden contradiction in this process of attempted reversal is one that the narrator is not to know until after Sa'eed drowns in the Nile in what looks suspiciously like a suicide.

The narrator represents a Marlow-complex that we might understand through a Lacanian model of ego identification as life-long quest. To summarize Lacan's argument in "The Mirror Stage": when a child is between six and eighteen months, they enter a curious phase in which they begin to recognize themselves in a mirror and start a long-term process of subjectivity that continues throughout life. The salient points of this mirror stage may be stated schematically as follows: 1) the baby learns to recognize its image and gestures in the mirror; 2) the baby discovers that the image in the mirror has its own properties and, furthermore, that it is whole (pun intended in both instances); 3) the baby develops an attachment to this specular image, which, though reflecting a unified object back to it, is actually deluding the baby with a sense of wholeness. The mirror phase is attended by signs of triumphant jubilation and playful discovery.[29] As Malcolm Bowie glosses it: "At the mirror moment something glimmers in the world for the first time ... . The mirror image is a minimal paraphrase of the nascent ego."[30] But the baby's sense of identification is delusional; even as it requires parental support or of some artificial contraption, it has begun to imagine itself whole and powerful. For Lacan, the ego is formed on the basis of an *imaginary* relationship of the subject with this specular image. Because this stage is actually not a phase but a stadium (*stade*), the mirror stage rehearses a life-long process by which the ego, as Maud Ellmann succinctly puts it, "constantly identifies itself with new personae in the effort to evade division, distance, difference, deferral, death."[31] The result, she continues, is "a wilderness of mirrors in which self and object oscillate perpetually, each eclipsed under the shadow of the other."[32] Ellmann's notion of perpetual oscillation is an interesting one which we will return to later.

Though not exactly a work of art, it is evident as we have already noted that Mustafa Sa'eed couches his autobiographical narrative in aesthetic terms that invite identification, horror, and also envy and lust on the part of the narrator. In London, the details of his life elicit longing and desire in the white women he consorts with, but in Wad Hamid, the details of his

---

[29] Revising this section, it suddenly strikes me that the deictic shifts in this sentence between the "he," "they," and "themselves," all of which are meant to denote "the child" in Lacan's formulation, inadvertently capture in the convolutions of grammatical usage the deep-seated divisions within the ego itself. For the child's ego at this stage, and subsequently in stretching through his or her entire life, is always an assemblage of images of the self, some of which are contradictory and that require constant negotiation in the flux of existence. I have deliberately left the contradictory oscillations in the personal pronouns in this sentence as they are to mark, in a subliminal way, this tension.

[30] Malcolm Bowie, *Lacan* (Cambridge, MA: Harvard University Press, 1993), 22.

[31] Maud Ellman, ed. *Psychoanalytic Criticism* (London: Routledge, 1994), 18.   [32] Ellmann, 18.

life story present a sense of enigma for the narrator. Both implicate forms of artistic craftsmanship, even if their impact in the two contexts are dramatically different. For the narrator, identification predominates over horror, until, that is, he begins to uncannily identify himself with the deceased Sa'eed while also revolting against this identification. More significantly, Mustafa Sa'eed's story generates anxiety for the narrator that it will produce *something else* that is not just the refraction of the ego-ideal, as in the child's mirror-identification, but its opposite and negation. The something else is an excess, a distortion, a dangerous supplement, and ultimately the complete overthrow of how the narrator experiences the mundane reality of village life.

The heart of the mirroring relationship between the narrator and Mustafa Sa'eed may also be understood in terms of melancholia. This adds the dimension of affect to Lacan's *stade* and reminds us that the process of ego-identification is not devoid of strong and contradictory emotions. Extrapolating from Freud's elaboration in "Mourning and Melancholia," we may note that melancholia makes itself manifest in three interrelated stages.[33] First comes the loss of the (loved) object. The reasons Freud assigns for this loss vary, but in melancholia the consequence of the loss is not the substitution of the lost object by another object of attention, but rather a form of recalcitrant non-substitution. Unlike in mourning, where after a requisite temporal lapse, the lost object is substituted by another object, in melancholia the libidinal charge of affects and drives released from the loved object is assimilated into the ego. The libidinal charge is introjected and comes to reshape the ego. But this assimilation does not produce mere nostalgia; it also triggers in various degrees resentment and anger and also threatens the partial distortion of the ego. Even though resentment and anger are properly targeted at the lost object for no longer being accessible to the self, because it has now been assimilated into the melancholic's ego it also triggers contradictory feelings that then become core aspects of the ego itself. The third phase is not really Freud's but an interpolation I am introducing inspired by a question that Anne Cheng poses in her book *The Melancholy of Race*.[34] Cheng asks an intriguing question, namely, when and under what conditions does grief become grievance? And what are the psychic mechanisms of this transposition? For the narrator of *Season of Migration to the North*, Mustafa Sa'eed

---

[33] Sigmund Freud, "Mourning and Melancholia," *The Standard Edition of the Complete Works of Sigmund Freud*, vol. XIV, trans. James Strachey (London: Hogarth Press, 2014), 243–258.
[34] Anne Cheng, *The Melancholy of Race: Psychoanalysis, Assimilation, and Hidden Grief* (Oxford: Oxford University Press, 2001).

represents Lacan's elusive ego-ideal only up to a point. His almost total lack
of recoil from the stories that Mustafa Sa'eed tells him means that for the
narrator there is a large degree of admiration if not complete identification
with him. This persists unacknowledged until after Sa'eed's death, when
the introjection of what amounts to the lost object comes to alter his
relationship to the ego-ideal that was Mustafa Sa'eed. It is the strongly
mixed feelings that the narrator experiences on Sa'eed's death that produce
a sense of grievance. This process of grief-to-grievance is compounded by
the fact that the narrator harbors strong yet ill-defined feelings toward
Hosna Bint Mahmood, Mustafa Sa'eed's wife in Wad Hamid, and that
these strong feelings are carefully repressed until they explode onto the
surface of his consciousness after the murder-suicide.

When he goes to visit Hosna to find out the contents of Mustafa Sa'eed's
will, the narrator is steeped in a sensorial overload from her perfume and
the enveloping qualities of the night:

> I said something that made her laugh and my heart throbbed at the sweetness
> of her laughter. The blood of the setting sun suddenly spilled out on the
> western horizon like that of millions of people who have died in some violent
> war that has broken out between Earth and Heaven. Suddenly the war ended
> in defeat and a complete and all-embracing darkness descended and pervaded
> all four corners of the globe, wiping out the sadness and shyness that was in
> her eyes. Nothing remained but the voice warmed by affection, and the faint
> perfume which was like a spring that might dry up at any moment.
> "Did you love Mustafa Sa'eed?" I suddenly asked her.
> She did not answer. Though I waited a while she still did not answer.
> Then I realized that the darkness and the perfume were all but causing me to
> lose control and that mine was not a question to be asked at such a time and
> place.[35]

The frankly ludicrous question he asks her as to whether she loved her
husband masks the narrator's growing sexual attraction to Hosna, the
effects of which he misattributes to what he sees as the elemental night
that "pervaded all corners of the globe" and to the almost overpowering
effect of her perfume. Later on, the narrator confesses that Hosna was "the
only woman he loved," and this in spite of the fact that he is already
married. Despite these subliminal feelings of attraction, the narrator persists in his quiescent affirmation of tradition and simply repeats the
marriage proposal he has been sent to deliver on behalf of Wad Rayyes.
Hosna's uncompromising declaration that if forced to marry Wad Rayyes

[35] Salih, 89–90.

she would kill him and kill herself does not get the narrator to veer off his quiescent traditionalism. Thus, the implication of his own growing attraction to Hosna is repressed in the service of tradition, and he leaves her only with the promise of acting as guardian to her sons, as requested in Mustafa Sa'eed's will. We have already seen the thematic of ethical judgment rendered subsidiary to the norms of tradition both in Okonkwo's killing of Ikemefuna and Iyaloja's agreeing to surrender her son's betrothed to Elesin Oba. The narrator of *Season of Migration to the North* joins them in a choice of tradition that paves the way for a tragic reversal of fortunes at personal and communal levels.

The narrator's repression of his feelings toward Hosna at this stage seems to be a disavowal of his ego-identification with Mustafa Sa'eed. But what appears as the disavowal of identification with Sa'eed is not a real disavowal but only a suspension. For it is restored with magnified force after the murder-suicide when the narrator is finally forced to confront his complicity in what was the patriarchal and repressive nature of his community's traditions. The process of identification with and then introjection of the lost object has for the narrator also been routed through an inter-psychic pathway colored by strong yet repressed sexual longings that are released in a concentrated form by the emotional vortex that the murder-suicide comes to represent. The anger he expresses after the terrible event is obviously an outcome of the guilt he feels for not having married Hosna. But because the anger is vehemently directed at Mustafa Sa'eed, it also betrays the character of melancholic transposition. The mirror ideal has produced a dangerous supplement that, once rendered conscious to the mind of the narrator, becomes the justification for an almost violent disavowal of the ego-ideal. This process is not so straightforward.

When the narrator vengefully enters Mustafa Sa'eed's study, all the mirroring motifs that we have seen playing out in the relationship between him and Sa'eed coalesce into a concentrated chronotope. The contents of the study echo the structuring motifs that have shaped the relationship between different vectors of representation, including that between the two men in their responses to the colonial library, since both of them have been highly educated in England. Sa'eed's study thus becomes a *mis-en-scène* of the structural logic that has been used to organize the entire text, and brings to mind the motif of the elusive garden of forking paths that Jorge Luis Borges makes famous in the story of the same title.[36] In an unusual piece of

---

[36] Jorge Luis Borges, "The Garden of Forking Paths," in *Labyrinths*, trans. Andrew Hurley (New York: Penguin, 1998), 119–128.

deep self-understanding as he walks to the study, the narrator declares: "The world has turned suddenly upside down. Love? Love does not do this. This is hatred. I feel hatred and seek revenge; my adversary is within and I needs must confront him. Even then, there is still in my mind a modicum of sense that is aware of the irony of the situation."[37] But whose love is he referring to here? The immediate context seems to be that of the tragic murder-suicide that he has just learned about, but the narrator moves immediately to declaring his hatred for Mustafa Sa'eed, suggesting then that the love he is referring to is his own love for Sa'eed. But this is, strictly speaking, a cathexis of two different loves, the one he subliminally feels for Hosna and the ego-identification he experiences for Mustafa Sa'eed. His love for Sa'eed precedes and causes his love for Hosna. They are not two parallel loves; rather he loves her and is attracted to her because she was Mustafa Sa'eed's wife. To desire what he desired is a way of mirroring Mustafa Sa'eed. The recognition that his adversary lies within himself illustrates the melancholic introjection we noted from Freud, and the sharply contrasting feelings of love and revenge he experiences point to the fact that the affects and emotions that were hitherto guaranteed by the libidinal economy attaching to the loved (and now lost) object have now been assimilated into his own ego. Who he loves and hates are simultaneously Mustafa Sa'eed, for abandoning him, and himself, for standing in the place of his alter ego and yet failing to behave decisively like him: "I begin from where Mustafa Sa'eed left off. Yet he at least made a choice, while I have chosen nothing."[38]

The entry into the study itself is across an evocative threshold of sensorial triggers; for he was "met by dampness and an odour like that of an old memory."[39] But there was also the smell of sandalwood and incense, a hint that perhaps this is where Mustafa Sa'eed came to say his prayers. The sensorial triggers of dampness, sandalwood, and incense then serve to register the space as a cavern of fleeting feelings and impressions, as if the narrator has ushered himself into a womb of space that is at once secular and sacred. It is night when he enters so he strikes a match whose light explodes into his eyes. He sees an image on the wall and walks toward it with hate in his heart. He thinks it is an image of his adversary forming itself slowly before his eyes: face, then neck, then two shoulders and a chest, then a trunk and two legs, until the narrator finds himself face to face not with his adversary but with himself: "This is not Mustafa Sa'eed – it's a picture of me frowning at my face from a mirror."[40] What is an uncanny

---

[37] Salih, 134.   [38] Salih, 134.   [39] Salih, 135.   [40] Salih, 135.

transposition serves to replicate the devices of self-as-other that we have seen repeatedly in the novel. The image disappears and he strikes another match that suffuses him in an oasis of light, and he looks about him to see an extraordinary room with an English fireplace, "with all the bits and pieces, above it a brass cowl and in front of it a quadrangular area tiled in green marble," and on each side of the fireplace "two Victorian chairs covered in a figured silk material, while between them stood a round table with books and notebooks on it."[41] He also sees paintings of Jean Morris and of people in the village, including Wad Rayyes, as well as several pictures of Mustafa Sa'eed in different poses: laughing, writing, swimming, in a gown and mortar-board, rowing on the Serpentine, in a Nativity play, and so on. The rendition of mundane activities that are registered in the pictures must be set alongside the immense narcissism that has created this detailed shrine to Western knowledge in the very heart of a village in Sudan. For even though the physical dimensions of the study may be small, the idea that animates it is anything but. There is an immense scale that has already been hinted at in the sensorial triggers of dampness and sandal-wood but that are reaffirmed in the suggestiveness of fireplace and furniture with all their attendant symbolism of a Western study. And it is finally the books in the library that encapsulate this dialectic of shifting chronotopic scales most poignantly. The passage where the narrator comes upon the books is worth attending to in some detail:

> Though I sought revenge, yet I could not resist my curiosity. First of all I shall see and hear, then I shall burn it down as though it had never been. The books – I could see in the light of the lamp that they were arranged in categories. Books on economics, history and literature. Zoology. Geology. Mathematics. Astronomy. The Encyclopaedia Britannica. Gibbon. Macaulay. Toynbee. The complete works of Bernard Shaw. Keynes. Tawney. Smith. Robinson. *The Economics of Imperfect Competition.* Hobson *Imperialism.* Robinson *An Essay on Marxian Economics.* Sociology. Anthropology. Psychology. Thomas Hardy. Thomas Mann. E. G. Moore. Thomas Moore. Virginia Woolf. Wittgenstein. Einstein. Brierly. Namier. Books I had heard of and others I had not. Volumes of poetry by poets of whom I did not know the existence. *The Journals of Gordon. Gulliver's Travels.* Kipling. Housman. *The History of the French Revolution* Thomas Carlyle. *Lectures on the French Revolution* Lord Acton. Books bound in leather. Books in paper covers. Old tattered books. Books that looked as if they'd just come straight from the printers. Huge volumes the size of tombstones. Small books with gilt edges the size of packs of

---

[41] Salih, 136.

playing cards. Signatures. Words of dedication ... Owen. Ford Madox Ford. Stefan Zweig. E. G. Browne. Laski. Hazlitt. *Alice in Wonderland.* Richards. *The Koran* in English. *The Bible* in English. Gilbert Murray. Plato. *The Economics of Colonialism* Mustafa Sa'eed. *Colonialism and Monopoly* Mustafa Sa'eed. *The Cross and Gunpowder* Mustafa Sa'eed. *The Rape of Africa* Mustafa Sa'eed. *Prospero and Caliban. Totem and Taboo.* Doughty. Not a single Arabic book. A graveyard. A mausoleum. An insane idea. A prison. A huge joke. A treasure chamber. "Open Sesame, and let's divide up the jewels among the people."[42]

The narrator's essentially telegraphic impressions mime the character of browsing, but in a context shaped by feelings of anger and resentment toward what he is looking at. Despite its appearance of being fleeting and random, the browsing also conveys a tellingly rhythmic patterning as it is registered within the library itself. Entire subject headers (zoology, economics, mathematics) are listed alongside author names that stand as paradigmatic signatures in and of themselves (Gibbon, Smith, Macaulay). These are mixed in with non-attributed book titles. The roughly rhythmic sequencing of disciplinary subject headers, paradigmatic author names, and bare titles is interrupted briefly with references to the material characteristics of the books on display (leather-bound, paperback, gilt-edged), their relative sizes (large and small), and their specific location in the room (in boxes, strewn around the floor as opposed to being stacked upon the shelves). There are also references to inscriptions and paratextual traces (signatures and dedications) that suggest that the browsing narrator has paused to look inside some of the books. This also hints at a modicum of perambulation, as though the narrator was actually walking through the library as he browsed, invoking to a certain degree, the sense of walking and fleeting observation that is famously encapsulated in W.H. Auden's "Musée des Beaux Arts," where, like the narrator of *Season of Migration to the North,* the browsing triggers a number of reflections on larger questions relating tragedy to obliviousness and ignorance.

Significantly, the four books of Mustafa Sa'eed's that are listed in sequence toward the end of the passage serve to break the patterned randomness that appears to have governed the browsing so far. Rather, their sandwiching between the prior list of book titles and a short list of postcolonial and ethno-cultural classics – *Prospero and Caliban, Totem and Taboo,* all unattributed – immediately raises the question of the status of Mustafa Sa'eed's treatises between colonial and postcolonial knowledge

---

[42] Salih, 113–114.

economies. Are the books he authored, as suggested by their titles, thoroughgoing critiques of the colonial library, or are they like the two unattributed titles that follow them, already coopted additions to the monumental archive? The chink of ambiguity exposed by the location of Mustafa Sa'eed's books within the sequence of impressions is further accentuated by the narrator's scornful observation that there is not a single Arabic text in the entire library. His disdain is augmented by a series of negative epithets. The library is at once a form of play-acting, an insane idea, a prison, a graveyard, a mausoleum, and a joke. This, we might conclude with the narrator, is no ordinary library, but an archaeology of knowledge as Foucault might have described it, one that frames the colonized within the epistemic constraints of a particular and exclusionary colonial order despite the implicit claims to universalism contained within it.

Beyond the revelation that Mustafa Sa'eed is an avid intellectual and thinker, his library may also be read as the consummate condensation of a gallery of mirrors: it is a chronotope simultaneously of colonial knowledge and of colonial space-making, and one into which Mustafa Sa'eed, and in his turn the narrator, have been discursively inserted as colonized intellectuals. The library becomes a chronotope of a discursive encounter that makes visible the epistemic ravages of colonialism. It sutures several dimensions of colonial space-time and stages the myriad dynamics of encounter inherent to them. The narrator's report on the library also marks a deep degree of ambivalence. He appears to want to disavow the assumed incorporation of his nemesis into the archive, yet is propelled by the force of his curiosity to browse the library before attempting to set it on fire. That he ends up not burning it down is a sign of his own ambiguous attachment. Even as he disavows it, he is no less interpellated by the colonial episteme. When he codifies his browsing around two apparently contradictory spatio-temporal metaphors – the tombstone/mausoleum and the mythographic *Arabian Nights* ("Open Sesame, and let's divide up the jewels among the people")[43] – he also invokes another dimension of the library chronotope that inheres at once in death and in its elusive narrative deferrals. The question also arises: whose mausoleum is this? Is it that of the Western tradition or of Mustafa Sa'eed's Faustian ambition in attempting to consume and then be a part of the colonial library? And who is it that attempts to divide the jewels amongst the people?

[43] Salih, 138.

The entry into Mustafa Sa'eed's study enacts in a concentrated form the fundamental split in the narrator's consciousness. For, by the time he enters the study he is already no longer at ease in the old dispensation of the provincial village in which he grew up and to which he has returned with unexamined, romantic views. But all the mirrorings within Mustafa Sa'eed's study also tell him that there is no resolution to the ambiguities that he experiences because they come as much from inside himself as from the outside world of interpersonal relations. Like Mustafa Sa'eed, the narrator is no ordinary colonial subject but a fully Westernized one, even if he does not have the same implacable desire for self-authorship that motivated his alter-ego. The narrator has been content to live and let live by ignoring the larger local and colonial contexts in which life is a series of choices that involve knowledge and freedom as well as alienation and death. The degree of existential ambiguity is given final confirmation at the end of the novel when the narrator appears to be drowning in the Nile:

> Though floating on the water, I was not part of it. I thought that if I died at that moment, I would have died as I was born – without any volition of mine. All my life I had not chosen, had not decided. Now I am making a decision. I choose life. I shall live because there are a few people I want to stay with for the longest possible time and because I have duties to discharge. It is not my concern whether or not life has meaning. If I am unable to forgive, then I shall try to forget. I shall live by force and cunning. I moved my feet and arms, violently and with difficulty, until the upper part of my body was above water. Like a comic actor shouting on stage, I screamed with all my remaining strength, "Help! Help!"[44]

The entire drowning sequence starts with him rehearsing the typical aspects of his life of not choosing, but by the end of it, his declaration to live by force and cunning brings him close to a disavowal of Mustafa Sa'eed's position. One of the amazing things about this ending is that the narrator choosing life might be said to be the equivalent of Sa'eed choosing death. Had he drowned himself in a copy-cat suicide, it would not have truly been a decision in the way that Sa'eed's drowning was. It would have been yet another example of him allowing himself to be swept up by inspiration and carried along down a path that is not real or original to him. But if he does not die and is rescued, he will return to his old life a completely changed person. We may assume that he will become morose and despondent, but that this will be the measure of his alienation and indeed his choice of life after near-death.

[44] Salih, 168–169.

Season of Migration to the North gives us two different themes essential to understanding the canon of postcolonial tragedy. The first theme has to do with the vagaries of self-authorship as the product of conditions that enlist choice into the domain of interlocution between colonizer and colonized. At this level, it is an interlocution where archetypes are rendered important instruments for choice-making but that then come to distort the entire process of self-authorship for the colonized himself. The second theme pertains to the apparatus of the life-long identification with ego-ideals in which the splitting and reconfiguration of the ego is tied to different forms of melancholic introjection and thus to the ultimate distortion of the ego. That these two themes are delivered to us as mutually enforcing dimensions of the Self/other dialectic, exploring the realities of existence within the racial economy of the colonial metropolis along with those in the remotest parts of empire, make the novel one of the most resonant for thinking about what it means for a work to be postcolonial. And tragic.

CHAPTER 6

Form, Freedom, and Ethical Choice in Toni Morrison's Beloved

Any comparison between texts that are conventionally taken to be postcolonial (from Africa, India, South America, etc.), with those from the African American tradition has to proceed with Edward Said's advice in mind. As he points out in *Culture and Imperialism*, "we must be able to think through and interpret together experiences that are discrepant, each with its particular agenda and pace of development, its own internal formations."[1] John Cullen Gruesser echoes similar sentiments with reference to the relations among postcolonialism, African American literary studies, and the Black Atlantic, noting that their joint study requires "comprehensive engagement with the history of anticolonial struggles, a history that ought to take account of African American experience and cultural productions but must not minimize the extent to which these diverge from those of colonized and formerly colonized peoples."[2]

In many ways, Henry Louis Gates and Kwame Anthony Appiah's *Race, Writing, and Difference* and Gates's own introduction to the PMLA's special issue on African and African American literature are totemic for helping us to think through the implications not just of putting the two fields together, but also for the shaping of postcolonial studies in general.[3] The *Race, Writing, and Difference* volume introduced readers to some of the most seminal texts in postcolonial studies including those by Edward Said, Homi Bhabha, Gayatri Spivak, Abdul JanMohamed, Mary Louise Pratt, Patrick Brantlinger, and several others, along with pieces by Gates and Appiah themselves. Gate's PMLA piece addresses the genealogy of the

[1] Edward Said, *Culture and Imperialism* (London: Vintage, 1994), 36.
[2] John Cullen Gruesser, *Confluences: Postcolonialism, African American Literary Studies, and the Black Atlantic*, (Athens: University of Georgia Press, 2005), 132.
[3] Henry Louis Gates, Jr. and Kwame Anthony Appiah, *Race, Writing, and Difference*, (Chicago: Chicago University Press, 1986) and Henry Louis Gates, Jr., "Introduction: 'Tell Me, Sir ... What is 'Black' Literature?," *PMLA*, 105.1, Special Topic: African and African American Literature, (1990): 11–22.

literary criticism of African American and African literature and recognizes the need for combining the predominantly sociological accounts from the civil rights era with more formalist and structuralist accounts from the mid-1970s onward. This focus is pertinent to this day in pedagogical contexts not only in the USA but also in Africa, where the imperatives of finding pathways for interpreting the vagaries of postcolonial nation building through whatever means are available still exerts a strong influence on what passes for literary criticism.

For my own part, I think that the comparative account of colonial space-making I laid out in the Introduction allows us to see the relevance of a postcolonial lens for understanding the conditions of the United States as emerging from the historical confluence of settler colonialism and plantation slavery. The steady rise of diverse cultural diasporas and their literary expression from the late nineteenth century onward have also come to decenter and diversify what we understand by American literature. Gates correctly points out in his PMLA introduction that when we engage with African American literature, it ought to be read and reread from inside the logic of its own long literary tradition. Thus, the comparative payout that might come from crossing that tradition with a postcolonial perspective emerges only with a contrapuntal reading practice. But in doing this we must acknowledge that a writer with the complexity and reach of Toni Morrison consistently transcends any framework that we might want to place her in. This is definitely the case with her tragic vision as encapsulated in *Beloved*, a work that encompasses much pain, grief, and suffering, and yet is so exquisitely rhythmic in its narrative cadences as to recall the "terrible beauty" of Yeat's invocation in "Easter, 1916."[4] It may not be a story to pass on, and yet what we discover about the factors that lead a mother to kill her own child instigates repeated return to the novel to find a pathway to our understanding. And in these repeated returns, we discover that Sethe's case cannot be understood on its own but must be read alongside other literary examples of infanticide from sources as varied as the Bible, Aeschylus, Euripides, George Eliot, Eugene O'Neill, Sam Shepherd, Chinua Achebe, and many others.

***

In 1855, Margaret Garner, an enslaved African American woman affectionately known as "Peggy," escaped from Kentucky to Cincinnati with her

---

[4] W. B. Yeats, "Easter Rising"; www.poetryfoundation.org/poems/43289/easter-1916, last accessed July 6, 2020.

four children. When she was caught, she murdered her two-year-old with a butcher's knife in an attempt to spare her from a life of slavery. She attempted to kill the other children as well but was subdued in the process. 1863 is the year of Abraham Lincoln's Emancipation Declaration, which marked the beginning of the end of slavery but still, only the beginning. That all the events in Toni Morrison's *Beloved* take place in 1873–1874, just a decade after this declaration and with the historical infanticide of 1855 haunting its pages through Sethe's choice, means that slavery still casts a baneful influence, seen not just in the enduring signs of violence and injustice toward black folk, but in the dark shadow that it continues to place upon the psyches of the free, particularly in the southern states of Virginia, Kentucky, Alabama, Carolina, and Georgia, mentioned at different times in the novel as staging posts for the worst instances.[5] As we are reminded by Stamp Paid: "Eighteen seventy-four and whitefolks were still on the loose. Whole towns wiped clean of Negroes; eighty-seven lynchings in one year alone in Kentucky; four colored schools burned to the ground; grown men whipped like children; children whipped like grown men; black women raped by the crew; property taken, necks broken."[6]

Each of the characters in *Beloved* is personally, corporally, marked by this brutality. Baby Suggs, having sustained a hip injury on a Carolina plantation of her youth, at sixty years still "jerked like a three-legged dog when she walked" and suffered constant pain.[7] Sethe, along with the three Pauls and Sixo, has her "animal" features listed by schoolteacher on Sweet Home farm, her breast milk forcibly extracted from her by his nephews, and also has a chokecherry tree planted on her back with the furious lash of the slaver's whip. Paul D has the iron bit put in his mouth while Sethe's mother is recalled as having a permanent smile implanted on her face because of it. Paul D is subsequently sold by schoolteacher to an owner whom he tries to kill and who in his turn sells him to a chain-gang of other slaves, the forty-five members of which are buried nightly in wooden boxes dug deep into the ground. For many months he suffers a silent and invisible trembling, "A flutter of a kind, in the chest, then the shoulder blades" that sometimes he felt in his legs, then again in the base of his spine but that was visible to no one."[8] Sixo is burnt alive for organizing a breakout from Sweet Home and singing an indecipherable song when they are caught. Then there are the many, many fragments of stories about the rape of slave women, the children that they barely know and refuse to

[5] All references are from Toni Morrison, *Beloved* (London: Picador, 1988).
[6] Morrison, *Beloved*, 180.   [7] Morrison, *Beloved*, 139.   [8] Morrison, *Beloved*, 106–107.

love, and the burdens these mothers have to bear in constructing community whilst struggling to keep the past at bay.

These details of both a historical and personal kind about the violence of slavery form a potent background to our reading of the novel. And yet, for all its descriptions of inflicted violence on black folk, *Beloved* is neither ethnography nor history. It delivers all these horrifying details piecemeal and no matter how horrifying they are, the novel does not allow us to lose our focus on the emotional challenges that the characters face in reconstructing their lives. The system of slavery places sadness at the center of their lives, "the desolated center" as Morrison tells us in her description of Baby Suggs, "where her real self that was no self made its home."[9] This description may be extended to all the survivors of slavery that we are introduced to in the novel, for the desolation at their core is tied to a no less momentous question, namely: what does freedom mean to persons previously unfree whose entire world was crafted with them as objects to be dehumanized, bought, whipped, sold, captured, whipped, and sold again? We are told more than once in the course of the novel that to be free is one thing but what to do with that freedom is the real question, and each character provides a different answer. For Baby Suggs the initial challenge is to learn how to love each part of her body slowly and individually, and to teach others how to do the same. As she puts it to the people that gather on Saturday afternoons to hear her secular sermons at the Clearing:

> Here, in this here place, we flesh; flesh that weeps, laughs; flesh that dances on bare feet in grass. Love it. Love it hard. Yonder they do not love your flesh. They despise it. They don't love your eyes; they'd just as soon pick em out. No more do they love the skin on your back. Yonder they flay it. And O my people they do not love your hands. Those they only use, tie, bind, chop off and leave empty. Love your hands! Love them. Raise them up and kiss them. Touch others with them, pat them together, stroke them on your face 'cause they don't love that either. You got to love it, you![10]

But it turns out that claiming the body after bondage is not so straightforward, because entailed in that claiming of the self is also the relationship that one has with others. As Sethe shows us, the claim that she makes of her own self extends to her children, such that in her mind she comes to hold the power not only of salvation but also of life and death. Rather than give us an ethnography or history of slave life, Toni Morrison places at the center of *Beloved* an event that acts as the emotional vortex for both the characters within the novel and us, its readers. As we shall see, Sethe's

[9] Morrison, *Beloved,* 140.   [10] Morrison, *Beloved,* 88.

killing of her "crawling-already?" baby and the contrasting responses that it adduces from different characters who bear witness, places the event in the vicinity of the deeply elusive ethical choices that we find in the Greeks and Shakespeare, and also, as we have already seen, in several other postcolonial tragedies. The extreme choice that Sethe exercises in attempting to take her children away from the slaver opens up questions of what it means to be free after such bondage, what such freedom means in reshaping the terms of access to *philia* – both familial and friendly – and the ethical choices that derive from these questions.

What I propose to do in in this chapter is to isolate the terms of the ethical *topos* that Morrison so suggestively lays out with respect to Sethe's terrible choice and to connect this to two other interrelated aspects of the novel. The first is the problem of moral residue that is seen most tellingly in Baby Suggs's response to Sethe's choice. Following James Phelan's careful detailing of the variant focalizations on Sethe's choice provided in the novel through schoolteacher, Stamp Paid, and Paul D, and the positional shifts that these impose upon the reader, my own procedure will also be narratological. I will be paying close attention to the rhetorical devices within the text and the ways in which these induct the reader into the heart of the ethical *topos* and adduce for Baby Suggs the crisis of ethical dilemma and moral residue.[11] In contrast to what Phelan demonstrates for the other characters that attempt to make a judgment on Sethe, I shall show that it is only Baby Suggs who truly recognizes the total impossibility of moral judgment. So profound is this recognition that it destroys her big heart, undermines her faith, and makes her retreat to her bed to contemplate colors. Baby Suggs's recognition of the undecidability of ethical choice may be interpreted in terms of Aristotle's category of *anagnorisis* (recognition), but, in this instance, it is enacted through a discursive displacement – as she takes on what should, strictly speaking, have been Sethe's own *anagnorisis*. This transposition of *anagnorisis* from the central actor to a key witness is at the heart of the moral residue that Baby Suggs has to contend with. She has to contend with it because, unlike the characters that Phelan writes about, all of whom are men, she is, like Sethe, also a mother as produced by the system of slavery, and thus is the only one really able to empathize with the younger woman while still refusing to endorse her terrible act. The simultaneous expression and atrophying of maternal instincts that are placed on

---

[11] James Phelan, "Sethe's Choice: *Beloved* and the Ethics of Reading," *Style*, 32.2 special edition on Literature and Ethical Criticism (1998): 318–333.

view by Sethe's choice are what split Baby Suggs both ways and what fatally prevent her from either condemning or approving that choice.

Form and Narration: Proximity and Distance

The first three pages of *Beloved* are highly instructive in establishing narrative expectations. It is clear from the outset that the third-person narrator adopts different relations of proximity and distance to the consciousness of different characters and that these relations define a series of narrative vectors pertaining to rhythm and pacing, and most importantly, to the different orientations of foreground and background within the text. This is how the novel opens:

> 124 was spiteful. Full of a baby's venom. The women in the house knew it and so did the children. For years each put up with the spite in its own way, but by 1873 Sethe and her daughter Denver were its only victims. The grandmother, Baby Suggs, was dead, and the sons, Howard and Buglar, had ran away by the time they were thirteen years old – as soon as merely looking in a mirror shattered it (that was the signal for Buglar); as soon as two tiny hand prints appeared in the cake (that was it for Howard). Neither boy waited to see more; another kettleful of chickpeas smoking in a heap on the floor; soda crackers crumbled and strewn in a line next to the door-sill. Nor did they wait for one of the relief periods: the weeks, months even, when nothing was disturbed. No. Each one fled at once – the moment the house committed what was for him the only insult not to be borne or witnessed a second time.[12]

As noted earlier, the years 1855–1874 bookend the historical framework that resonates at various levels of the text. We will later come to learn that the spitefulness of 124 comes from Sethe's desperate attempt to escape her slave past when it materializes at her door in Cincinnati in the persons of schoolteacher and three other slave catchers from Sweet Home. Like the historical Margaret Garner, who Toni Morrison uses as an inspiration for her fictional character, Sethe cuts the throat of her then two-year-old "crawling-already?" daughter with a handsaw and almost succeeds in killing her three other children before the horror of what she has done stops the slave catchers in their tracks. The spitefulness of the house we are introduced to at the start of the novel comes from the spirit of the murdered child manifesting herself as a vengeful poltergeist. The uncanny phenomenology that this implies sharply contradicts the "house" that

---

[12] Morrison, *Beloved*, 3.

Gaston Bachelard elaborates in *The Poetics of Space* as a guarantor of daydreams, solitude, and even boredom.[13] None of that pertains to 124. Writing from the African American gothic tradition of which she is an exemplar, Morrison gives us a house whose history is steeped in violence, betrayal, and unresolved pain.[14] Over the next two pages we get prime examples of how the spitefulness of the baby was "known" by both the women and the children that lived there. What will later be expanded into various forms of digression that are aligned specifically to the consciousness of individual characters is signaled in these first paragraphs in minimal parenthetic remarks ("that was the signal for Buglar"; and "that was it for Howard" [that's it, I am outta here!]) but with a slight differentiation in the mirrored syntactical structure that also helps to convey in compressed form the characterological difference between the young brothers. In the early pages of the novel, the different character perspectives are rendered as minimal interpositions within the narration of background information which is delivered by the third-person narrator, and against which the diegetic foreground of unfolding events will take place. The relation between background and foreground, and between perspectival interposition and the provision of information by the narrator is not at all straightforward or indeed predictable in *Beloved* but becomes more varied and complex as the novel progresses.

Witness, for example, the relationship of past and present and the interposition of digressions in one of the most suggestive passages in the entire novel:

> Unfortunately [Sethe's] brain was devious. She might be hurrying across a field, running practically, to get to the pump quickly and rinse the chamomile sap from her legs. Nothing else would be in her mind. The picture of the men coming to nurse her was as lifeless as the nerves in her back where the skin buckled like a washboard. Nor was there the faintest scent of ink or the cherry gum and oak bark from which it was made. Nothing. Just the breeze cooling her face as she rushed toward water. And then sopping the chamomile away with pump water and rags, her mind fixed on getting every last bit of sap off – on her carelessness in taking a shortcut across the field just to save a half mile, and not noticing how high the weeds had grown until the itching was all the way to her knees. Then

---

[13] Gaston Bachelard, *The Poetics of Space*, trans. Maria Jolas (Boston: Beacon Press, 1958).

[14] On the literary tradition of the Southern gothic, see especially, Susan Castillo Street and Charles L. Crow, eds., *The Palgrave Handbook of the Southern Gothic* (London: Palgrave, 2016); Kathleen Brogan, *Cultural Haunting: Ghosts and Ethnicity in Recent American Fiction* (Charlottesville: University of Virginia Press, 1998); and Jeffrey Andrew Weinstock, *The Cambridge Companion to the American Gothic* (Cambridge: Cambridge University Press, 2017).

something. The plash of water, the sight of her shoes and stockings awry on the path where she had flung them; or Here Boy lapping in the puddle near her feet, and suddenly there was Sweet Home rolling, rolling, rolling out before her eyes, and although there was not a leaf on that farm that did not make her want to scream, it rolled itself out before her in shameless beauty. It never looked as terrible as it was and it made her wonder if hell was a pretty place too. Fire and brimstone all right, but hidden in lacy groves.[15]

Toni Morrison wrote her MA thesis on Virginia Woolf and William Faulkner, so it is useful to recall what Paul Ricoeur writes about *Mrs Dalloway* as a welcome window to Morrison's narrative technique.[16] As Ricoeur points out with reference to the many stream-of-consciousness digressions that occur in Woolf's novel:

> These long sequences of silent thoughts – or what amounts to the same thing, of internal discourse – not only constitute flashbacks that, paradoxically, make the narrated time advance by delaying it, they hollow out from within the instant of the event in thought, they amplify from within the moments of narrated time, so that the total interval of the narrative, despite its relative brevity, seems rich with an implied immensity.[17]

There are however some fundamental differences to be noted between Woolf and Morrison's novels. The first is that whereas the third-person narrators of *Mrs Dalloway* and *Beloved* both orchestrate a switch between the internal consciousness of different characters, what Ricoeur later on describes as the "resonance" of Woolf is often replaced in Morrison by a series of ruptures. For Ricoeur, resonance pertains to the cues found within specific spaces that allow different characters to follow the same trail of implications triggered by their shared spatial contexts, even if these implications are often taken in completely different directions. In Ricoeur's terms, the third-person switches between streams of consciousness in *Mrs Dalloway* are facilitated primarily by relations of spatial proximity, that is to say, the switches almost always occur when the characters are located within the same geographical location. However, as we can also see from *Mrs Dalloway*, it is not only spatial proximity within

---

[15] Morrison, *Beloved*, 6.
[16] Chloe Ardelia Wofford, aka Toni Morrison, "Virginia Woolf's and William Faulkner's Treatment of the Alienated," MA thesis, Cornell University Press, 1955. On Morrison's MA thesis and the influences that might be discerned of Woolf and Faulkner in her work, see Barbara Christian, "Layered Rhythms: Virginia Woolf and Toni Morrison," *Modern Fiction Studies*, 39, 3 & 4 (1993): 483–500; Alessandra Vendrame, "Toni Morrison: A Faulklerian Novelist?," *American Studies*, 42.4 (1997): 679–684; and Lorie Watkins Fulton, "A Direction of One's Own": Alienation in *Mrs Dalloway* and *Sula*," *African American Review*, 40.1 (2006): 66–77.
[17] Paul Ricoeur, *Time and Narrative* vol. 2 (Chicago: University of Chicago Press, 1984), 103–104.

specific geographical locations that facilitates the switches. The switches between characters are also produced through a variety of what we might more broadly label as spatial correlatives. In *Mrs Dalloway*, the resonance effect that Ricoeur writes of is generated throughout by varied spatial correlatives such as the striking of Big Ben and other clocks, the Queen's stalled vehicle, the airplane assiduously writing letters in the sky, the park bench at Regent's Park, the ambulance that carries Septimus Warren Smith to hospital, and finally Clarissa's party. What facilitates the switch across proximate as well as distant spaces (say in the case of the airplane early in the novel) is that for the narrative switch to work different characters have to actively *think* about what they are hearing or seeing, thus immediately inflecting their thought processes in the direction of the spatial correlative. In *Beloved* the only such example of spatial resonance for the switching between the minds of different characters occurs when Sethe and Paul D are in bed early in the novel after making love, and they return individually to the same conjoined moment of memory in their shared past. This shared past is when Sethe and her newly married husband Halle first consummated their new marriage in the cornfields, presumably to show respect for the other four men who had desperately desired Sethe when she was first brought to the farm, but who had restrained themselves in letting her choose for herself. The thoughts of Sethe and Paul D in the present moment of narration are intimately traced back by the narrator, with the shift between each character's thoughts cued in by the movements they make on the bed as they suppress an involuntary laugh, stretch an arm or a leg, or mutually adjust themselves for comfort. So subtly has the narrator treated the entire sequence that when she steps back to describe the events in the third person it is impossible to distinguish narrator from characters. In contrast to the switches in *Mrs Dalloway*, in this scene what facilitates the switches is not a spatial correlative in the shape of an external object, but their shared intimacy of ephemeral gestures and actions, which then serves to transport them back to the same emotional moment in their shared past.

In all other instances in *Beloved*, we find that the switch between consciousnesses is constituted not through resonance but through rupture. That is to say, even when occupying the same geographical space, the take-off point in the present for each character does not appear to have any direct relationship to the spatial correlatives within their immediate environment, but is rather the sudden interposition of a completely different thought-moment for each individual character, and thus of a different texture of temporality.

The passage of Sethe walking down the field encapsulates several of the main devices of sudden temporal interposition that we will become accustomed to throughout the novel. Note first of all that the difference between present and past is obliterated within her consciousness, not through the simple juxtaposition of the two, but by the rendition of the present as somehow being surrogate to the past and vice-versa in a restless oscillation between the two. Furthermore, the past is rendered as a trace-effect of different affective intensities that come to intrude upon the present. In this passage, the intrusion is conveyed through two key devices that come to be reiterated throughout the novel. The first is the intensification of Sethe's perspectival sensorium and thus of her consciousness of her immediate surroundings: the faintest scent of ink or of the cherry gum and oak bark (smell, present in its absence); not noticing how high the weeds had grown until the itching was all the way to her knees (tactile sensation); the plash of water (sound); the appearance of her stockings (sight). Second is in the sudden replacement of the contents of the heightened sensorium in the present with an equally intensified set of sensual contents from the past that are also coupled with an uncanny aesthetic judgment: "and although there was not a leaf on that farm that did not make her want to scream, it rolled itself out before her in shameless beauty. It never looked as terrible as it was and it made her wonder if hell was a pretty place too. Fire and brimstone all right, but hidden in lacy groves . . ."

This terrible beauty also indicates a crucial difference between Woolf and Morrison. In *Mrs Dalloway,* Clarissa Dalloway's reminiscences involve awkward but not traumatic or painful memories from the past. We see the effects of trauma in the novel predominantly with respect to Septimus Warren Smith, but even then his memories from the war institute a form of epistemological disorientation, articulated not in the form of pain but in that of schizophrenic panic, such that he feels himself *compelled* to act rather than to surrender to the "slings and arrows of outrageous fortune," as Hamlet memorably put it. In *Beloved,* the procedure by which the past is incorporated into the present, whether as a momentary fragment or as a larger digression, appears to be specifically designed to attribute sensual and affective intensity to stray thoughts and observations. In other words, Sethe may be doing something entirely banal in the present-time of the narration, when suddenly there is a tangential digression in her thought processes whose main effect is to attach affective intensity to her present moment. It is these modes of sudden affective intensification that make her want to keep the past at bay. Furthermore, it is not always that she returns from her digressive reveries to the precise moment from which the digression took off; quite often she is relocated to a different biographical moment within the narration.

In *Beloved*, the interposition of thought digressions seems not merely to introduce immensity, as Ricoeur notes with respect to *Mrs Dalloway*, but rather to render the past dense with affect, and thus to register its unassimilability to the present or indeed to a simple order of temporality. This process of intensification also raises difficulties for identifying the referential locus of the past in Morrison's novel. As we shall see presently, the instability of the referential locus becomes central to the problematic of ethical choice for Sethe as well as for Paul D and Baby Suggs, the two other tragic slave survivor characters who, like Sethe, struggle the most to contain the past. Denver too has a tragic quality to her but, having grown up outside of slavery, her main concern is in how to interpret her mother's love, which has been contaminated for her by the knowledge that her mother killed her sister. Sethe's maternal instincts provide no sense of safety for Denver but only a nebulous and insistent existential anxiety. The arc of temporality in the novel is thus not from the past to the present, but from memory to the present and vice-versa. And since memory is depicted as essentially traumatic, it becomes not the reservoir of inert impressions, but rather the composition of intense affective traces that serve to destabilize the referential locus of the past and to introduce serious questions about where the past resides. The past may be past, but how past is it really? To return to the memorable quote by William Faulkner already mentioned in the Introduction, "The past is never dead. It's not even past."[18]

What we have seen in *Beloved* as the subtle narrative mechanism for intensifying the past, making it both subtend and intrude upon the present, is then materialized in the fantastical emergence of Beloved. A preamble of the device of materialization is given to us when, right after the ruminations on Sweet Home in the passage above, Sethe arrives home to find Paul D, "the last of the Sweet Home men" sitting on her steps. She has not seen him in eighteen years, and his physical reappearance at that precise moment foreshadows another imminent reincarnation from the past. This is Beloved, who emerges from a lake nearby:

> A fully dressed woman walked out of the water. She barely gained the dry bank of the stream before she sat down and leaned against a mulberry tree. All day and all night she sat there, her head resting on the trunk in a position abandoned enough to crack the brim in her straw hat. Everything hurt but her lungs most of all. Sopping wet and breathing shallow she spent those

[18] William Faulkner, *Requiem for a Nun* 73.

hours trying to negotiate the weight of her eyelids. The day breeze blew her dress dry; the night wind wrinkled it. Nobody saw her emerge or came accidentally by. If they had, chances are they would have hesitated before approaching her. Not because she was wet, or dozing or had what sounded like asthma, but because amid all that she was smiling. It took her the whole of the next morning to lift herself from the ground and make her way through the woods past a giant temple of boxwood to the field and then the yard of the slate-gray house. Exhausted again, she sat down on the first handy place – a stump not far from the steps of 124. By then keeping her eyes open was less of an effort. She could manage it for a full two minutes or more. Her neck, its circumference no wider than a parlor-service saucer, kept bending and her chin brushed the bit of lace edging her dress.[19]

There are no witnesses to Beloved's emergence from the water; the information of her emergence is conveyed to us strictly by the third-person narrator. Shortly after her emergence out of the lake, she makes her way to 124 and is taken in by Sethe, Denver, and Paul D. Sethe and Paul D ask Beloved several questions as to where she might be coming from, but this means of verification adduces only vague answers from her that are somehow considered satisfactory (at least in the moment for Sethe, if not necessarily for Paul D). What we see as a fantastical intrusion into the narrative is thus naturalized by being set against the other characters' observance of the protocols of civility that have been imposed by the post-slavery environment (every black person had something they would prefer not to reveal so why ask too many questions?). As the narrative progresses, Beloved makes her esoteric nature known to each of the other characters in different ways, but Paul D's barely disguised incredulity is repeatedly counter-balanced in the narrative by Denver's complete acceptance of her sister's strange nature. Later on, a different modality for judging her sister's uncanny significance is focalized through Denver when Beloved begins to sap Sethe's will through her capricious demands for exclusive affirmations of her mother's love, something that Sethe is all too happy to give her as a way of demonstrating the consistency of her motivations, as if the infanticide were another form of nourishment, generosity, of giving to Beloved all that Sethe herself was not fortunate enough to have. She feeds Beloved and starves herself as if to say: *I would give you anything, the meat on my bones, the energy in my blood, a life free away from the horrors of slavery, or – if I cannot manage that – a quick death; I feed you now, just as I killed you then, out of love.* In this later stage of the narrative, Denver adjudges Beloved to be destroying their mother and breaks the cycle of enchanted

[19] Morrison, *Beloved*, 50.

captivity by stepping out of the house into the neighborhood to seek a means of sustenance and help.

The different motivations for introducing a fantastical element in the narrative raise implications for how we interpret Morrison's novel as tragedy. The character of Beloved is revealed to us first as a poltergeist and then as a returnee spirit. But in waylaying and then forcing Paul D to sleep with her she is also depicted as a succubus, that is to say, a female demon that has sexual intercourse with men. By the end of the novel, Beloved completely drains Sethe's willpower, drawing on her to feed her own insatiable desire for affirmation of her mother's love but also infantilizing Sethe in the process. This first cluster of esoteric significations may all be said to be motivated by the disjuncture of the family saga that is the direct product of slavery. Each of the elements in this cluster can be traced to a particular aspect of that disjuncture and thus interpreted as the correlation of cause to consequence and of familial infraction to punishment. However, the novel also provides another genealogy for this fantastical characteristic, by suggesting that Beloved is the spirit of the 12.5 million that were carried in the hold of slave ships from Africa into slavery. This genealogy is conveyed much later, and primarily in the chapter of poeticized discourse that appears in the last third of the novel, when Beloved reveals that she has been formed in the hold of a slave ship. Unlike the first cluster of fantastical significations, the reference to the Middle Passage has no direct narratological motivation from within the familial relationships outlined within the text and seems to be Morrison's attempt to shift the scale of the tragedy from the personal to the socio-historical.

The importation of the idea of the slave ship and of the consequences that this entails are never worked out explicitly within the novel, except perhaps as a form of overdetermining and suggestive innuendo about the collective responsibility for the historical traumas of the past that have shaped America and made it what it is today. Nevertheless, since Beloved's return does not serve to punish the slave master but only to discombobulate the slave family centered around her mother, it is not clear where the responsibility for her murder is thought to lie. When adjusting our moral valuations of individual actions in the novel, how much background circumstance do we allow into view? Put another way, how much is ethical action the function of individual choice and how much is it overdetermined by historical forces beyond such choices? This has a Greek tincture to it, and prompts a persistent question: is ethical action the product of determinism or free will, and where does the responsibility lie for individual choice? The answer that Morrison provides to this question entails reflections on individual choice as well as on the status of the temporality of slave history.

The Monadology of Rememory

The instability of the referential locus of the past and its materialization in the present are given a philosophical interpretation by Sethe. In answering a question posed by Denver, Sethe delivers a distinctive interpretation of history:

> "What were you praying for, Ma'am?"
> "Not *for* anything. I don't pray any more. I just talk."
> "What were you talking about?"
> "You won't understand, baby."
> "Yes I will."

> "I was talking about time. It's so hard for me to believe in it. Some things go. Pass on. Some things just stay. I used to think it was my rememory. You know. Some things you forget. Other things you never do. But it's not. Places, places are still there. If a house burns down, it's gone, but the place – the picture of it – stays, and not just in my rememory, but out there, in the world. What I remember is a picture floating around out there outside my head. I mean, even if I don't think it, even if I die, the picture of what I did, or knew, or saw is still out there. Right in the place where it happened."
> "Can other people see it?" asked Denver.
> "Oh, yes. Oh, yes, yes, yes. Someday you be walking down the road and you hear something or see something going on. So clear. And you think it's you thinking it up. A thought picture. But no. It's when you bump into a rememory that belongs to somebody else. Where I was before I came here, that place is real. It's never going away. Even if the whole farm – every tree and grass blade of it dies. The picture is still there and what's more, if you go there – you who never was there – if you go there and stand in the place where it was, it will happen again; it will be there for you, waiting for you. So, Denver, you can't never go there. Never. Because even though it's all over – over and done with – it's going to always be there waiting for you. That's how come I had to get all my children out. No matter what."[20]

Note that, in answer to her daughter's question, Sethe says she does not pray for anything. She just talks to herself. This talking to herself proves to be highly significant for interpreting her character, for it shows that far from being the mere victim of thoughts from the past, she also attempts to

[20] Morrison, *Beloved*, 35–36.

make sense of her life through the examination of deeply metaphysical categories such as time. Thus, her talking is a form of thinking, but her thinking is also in pictures or images, as we have already noted. The fact that Sethe no longer believes in time does not prevent her from think-talking about it. This brings to mind Baby Suggs's desire to retire to her bed to contemplate color after she witnesses Sethe's terrible choice, for color is something that invokes for Baby Suggs the inoffensive, building blocks of creation. Sethe's view of time is of a different and more complex order.

It is evident that in *Beloved* the past moment is not simply one of a once-and-unrepeatable time. On the contrary, precisely because of the traumas of slavery, each and every moment of the characters' lives is pregnant with tensions that engender flashes of affective intensity. As Sethe tells it to her daughter, the past moment that is pregnant with the intensities that shaped her as a slave exists as an isolable entity in space-time, and this can be reencountered even by those in her family that did not experience that past moment. The recognition provided by Sethe's concept of rememory is that time is essentially granulated and does not flow like a river. For Sethe, there is none of Heraclitus's idea that "No - woman steps into the same river twice, for it is not the same river and she is not the same woman."[21] The granulation of time is the product of an affective leakage into history and as such, the concept of rememory bears resemblance to Walter Benjamin's reflections on historical time. In "Theses on the Philosophy of History," Benjamin is at pains to establish a distinction between traditional historiography, what he terms universal history, and a more radical form of historical interpretation. XVII of the "Theses" illustrates the crux of his views:

> Historicism rightly culminates in universal history. Materialistic historiography differs from it as to method more clearly than from any other kind. Universal history has no theoretical armature. Its method is additive; it musters a mass of data to fill the homogenous, empty time. Materialistic historiography, on the other hand, is based on a constructive principle. Thinking involves not only the flow of thoughts, but their arrest as well. *Where thinking suddenly stops in a configuration pregnant with tensions, it gives that configuration a shock, by which it crystallizes into a monad.* A historical

---

[21] This oft-quoted line from Heraclitus (here revised for gender) is thought to have been derived not from the philosopher directly but from Plato, Cleanthes, Arius Didymus, Eusebius, and Plutarch; all trying to interpret things that he said at different times regarding time as flux. For a handy discussion of this aspect of Heraclitus's thought, see the entry on him by Daniel W. Graham in the *Stanford Encyclopedia of Philosophy*, https://plato.stanford.edu/entries/heraclitus/; last accessed Nov. 28, 2019.

materialist approaches a historical subject only where he encounters it as a monad. In this structure he recognizes the sign of a Messianic cessation of happening, or, put differently, a revolutionary chance in the fight for the oppressed past. He takes cognizance of it in order to blast a specific era out of the homogenous course of history – blasting a specific life out of the era or a specific work out of the lifework.[22]

Benjamin is theorizing in his own distinctive way the aporia of time and thus its referential instability, and examining the implications this raises for historical interpretation. Three strands of thought may be isolated for comparison to the concept of rememory: 1) the constructive principle behind materialist historiography is precisely an epiphanic recognition of the historical moment as pregnant with tensions; 2) this moment pregnant with tensions is a configuration (Benjamin calls it elsewhere a constellation) of present and past, and of conceptual frameworks and the world of individual ideas; 3) the moment presents the materialist historian, acting as an interpreter, with the means by which to perceive the past as a monad and to recuperate it for radical uses. Underpinning all these is the recognition of history as an almost religious experience that serves to reconfigure both past and present simultaneously. As Benjamin elaborates his ideas in the *Theses*, he is at pains to establish a distinction between traditional historiography, what he terms here, universal history, and a more radical form of historical understanding that would serve to "blast open the continuum of history."[23]

Gottfried Wilhelm Leibniz, from whom Benjamin drew inspiration for his theory of historical time, conceived of matter as essentially made up of monads. Leibniz's inspiration came partly from the discovery of the microscope, but in *The Monadology* of 1714 he added the dimension of persistent change and evolution to his monadic structure of the universe.[24] For Leibniz, each monad is a distinct entity possessing its own kind or degree of consciousness and existence. And in his account, monads are not materialistic but possess a subtle and ultimately transcendental content. But in *The Origin of German Tragic Drama*, Benjamin adds an important distinction to Leibniz's monadology, suggesting that "The idea is a monad. The being that enters into it, with its past and subsequent history, brings – concealed in its own form – an indistinct abbreviation of the rest of the world of ideas, just as, according to Leibniz's *Discourse on Metaphysics*

---

[22] Walter Benjamin, *Illuminations*, trans. Harry Zohn (London: Fontana Press, 1992), 254, emphasis added.
[23] Benjamin, *Illuminations*, ibid.
[24] Lloyd Strickland, *Leibniz's Monadology: A New Translation and Guide* (Edinburgh: Edinburgh University Press, 2014).

(1686), every single monad contains, in an indistinct way, all the others."²⁵
For Benjamin, the purpose of the representation of the idea is "nothing less
than an abbreviated outline of this image of the world."²⁶ The idea is
a monad and, as the monad contains an indistinct abbreviation of the
world, every idea contains the image of the world.

This Neoplatonist strand, which might easily be mistaken to rest upon
a notion of the visible world as postlapsarian and therefore spiritually
tarnished, is turned by Benjamin to radical usage in terms of a quest for
revolutionary action. In its Neoplatonist strain, monadology allows
Benjamin access to a crucial religious component of the theory of ideas,
namely, *anamnesis*. *Anamnesis* is the notion that truth is already and
eternally present in the world, and that in order to get it we need only
recognize it in the flow of existence. Benjamin's monadic ideas then emerge
as a vehicle for generating *anamnesis*; for blasting open the possibility of
accessing truth beyond the confines of form.²⁷ The implication of all cases
of historical interpretation with the potential for rupture, is that transcendence is always immanent inside of history, but that it requires the specific
recognition of such transcendence. Thus, it is that for Benjamin, the
moment of potential transcendence must be seized upon as it flashes out
of the structures of historical reality, and it is seizing it that helps push
reality beyond the confines of calcified thought.

To read the monad through Sethe's concept of rememory requires us to
see it as divulging nothing less than the indistinct outline of the image of
the slave's world. This spin to Benjamin's concept seems apposite, yet
requires at least one significant qualification. As we just noted, one implication of Benjamin's thought is that history is never innocent of a degree of
transcendence and that this is what constitutes the flashpoint inherent to
the monad. Sethe's account of time is, unlike Benjamin's, not one of
revolution, but of the persistent recalcitrance of past moments to being
subsumed within any simple framework of temporality. It is an active
constitutive principle of time that is independent of the interpreter's
intentionality or viewpoint and thus not a déjà vu but something that
waits in its chronotopic singularity to be reencountered rather than merely
reinterpreted. For rememory implies both epistemological and ontological
realities deriving from the slave's world. Rather than flowing freely like
a river, time for Sethe is granulated like grains of sand, with each granule

²⁵ Walter Benjamin, *The Origin of German Tragic Drama*, trans. John Osborne (London: BLB, 1977), 47.
²⁶ Benjamin, *The Origin of German Tragic Drama*, 48.
²⁷ On *anamnesis*, see Julian Roberts, *Walter Benjamin* (London: Macmillan, 1982).

(monad) containing the abbreviation of past violence that persists in history to be reencountered again and again.

Monad, from the Greek word *monas*, implies singularity or oneness. The monad, even when taken as a reflection of some aspect of the world, seems to operate as a singular and perhaps even unified entity. But how can the historian and the literary writer deploying history and choosing to be deeply steeped within the moment of radical perception, remain coherent enough in his or her cognition to extract a history from the monadic debris that is past? With the concept of rememory, Morrison instigates a recognition both of the different frames of monadic encounter for individual characters and also of the stakes for interpretation in recognizing it. The significance of rememory ramifies not just for the characters within the text but also in direct relation to the ethics of reading enjoined for the reader. For if rememory is a requirement for acknowledging slavery's affective leakage into history, then it also raises implications for how we read the text and interpret the real historical record out of which Morrison has produced this consummate condensation. Interpretation has to thus be experiential as much as epistemological and must issue in praxis in the present rather than merely in knowledge of the past.

No. No. Nono. Nonono: The Instability of the Referential Locus and the Problem of Ethical Choice

The problem of the referential locus is rendered differently when looked at not from Sethe's viewpoint but from other characters such as Paul D. For him, a persistent elusiveness is attached to Sethe. This elusiveness is raised as a key question on at least two different occasions in the novel, once when he asks her directly how she came to kill her daughter, and before that when Stamp Paid shows him the artist's impression of her from the old newspaper article that had reported the infanticide. Seeing the drawing in the newspaper, Paul D expresses incredulity not about the news item itself, but about the shape of Sethe's mouth as it is conveyed in the drawing. As he looks at it he keeps repeating the refrain "That ain't her mouth" throughout as if to suggest that the stubborn disavowal of such a detail is an insurance against mimesis itself. For the refrain also suggests that the drawn picture with a false mouth cannot be an adequate condensation and thus a mirror of the entire life process of the Sethe he thought he knew so well. But in response to his query about whether she was the one in the picture, and by extension was the one being reported for killing her daughter, something different transpires:

> She was spinning. Round and round the room. Past the jelly cupboard, past the window, past the front door, another window, the sideboard, the keeping-room door, the dry sink, the stove – back to the jelly cupboard. Paul D sat at the table watching her drift into view then disappear behind his back, turning like a slow but steady wheel. Sometimes she crossed her hands behind her back. Other times she held her ears, covered her mouth or folded her arms across her breasts. Once in a while she rubbed her hips as she turned, but the wheel never stopped.[28]

The series of spatial and gestural fragments we see in this excerpt (the pieces of furniture, Sethe's disjointed gestures) are focalized through the eyes of Paul D, but there is also another process of fragmentation taking place throughout the chapter that turns on Sethe's steady refusal to actually answer the question she has been asked.

Rather, as Phelan notes in his essay, Sethe focuses mainly on her motivation in taking her children out of Sweet Home Farm and her love in rescuing them from schoolteacher. At no time in her answer does she actually name the sordid details of the moment of infanticide itself: the bloody handsaw at the throat of her daughter, her attempt at swinging one of the boys against the wall of the shed, and the chaotic crying and screaming that must have saturated the entire scene. Rather, her answer may be interpreted as being conducted around a series of metonymic displacements, partly rationalized as maternal motivation and partly apparent in her attempt at evacuating the shed where the deed occurred of all its referential content. Since all the details of the scene have already been provided for us in the previous chapter through the perspective of Stamp Paid, we know exactly what Sethe is leaving out. Every affective charge within the moment that might be called forth by a specific image (the handsaw, the child's cut throat) is systematically evacuated from her account. For someone whose consciousness is normally triggered by casual sensorial detail, her answer to Paul D seems entirely uncharacteristic and carefully obliterates any specific detail that might trigger the sensorial intensifications that we know her mind to be capable of. It is only in a tangential thought to herself, an internal pause in her answer to Paul D, that she admits to any affective or emotional intensity. But even then, the admission does not invoke any particular detail or image but only tries to

---

[28] Morrison, *Beloved*, 159.

define metaphorically the feeling of panicked possession that had seized her then:

> Sethe knew that the circle she was making around the room, him, the subject, would remain one. That she could never close in, pin it down for anybody who had to ask. If they didn't get it right off – she could never explain. Because the truth was simple, not a long-drawn-out record of flowered shifts, tree cages, selfishness, ankle ropes and wells. Simple: she was squatting in the garden and when she saw them coming and recognized schoolteacher's hat, she heard wings. *Little hummingbirds stuck their needle beaks right through her headcloth into her hair and beat their wings. And if she thought anything, it was No. No. Nono. Nonono.* Simple. She just flew. Collected every bit of life she had made, all the parts of her that were precious and fine and beautiful, carried, pushed, dragged them through the veil, out, away, over there where no one could hurt them.[29]

What she designates here as simple truth is also a profound collapse of language, for the "No. No. Nono. Nonono" also shows that in the precise moment of the event she is powered exclusively by a singular emotional motivation that refutes at once both language and referentiality. Nothing matters either in the past (flowered shifts) or in the present (schoolteacher's hat) but the implacable demand to take her children beyond the vale of death that a return to Sweet Home would have definitively entailed. The collapse of language and referentiality we see here is also replicated for different characters in Morrison's other novels such as Consolata in *Paradise* and Pilate in *Song of Solomon*, where the moment of extreme emotional shock is registered through the rhythmic repetition of single words or phrases that are themselves emptied of any particular referentiality. In *Jazz*, the narrator refers to Violet's experience of these moments' referential collapse as "cracks because that is what they were. Not openings or breaks, but dark fissures in the globe of light of the day . . . . But the globe of light is imperfect too. Closely examined it shows seams, ill-glued cracks and weak spaces beyond which is anything. Anything at all."[30] But unlike in the cases of Consolata, Pilate, and Violet, for Sethe this collapse of language and referentiality is an accompaniment to her extreme tragic choice.

[29] Morrison, *Beloved*, 163; emphasis added.
[30] In Morrison's *Paradise*, Consolata's "*Sha sha sha. Sha sha sha*" denotes this collapse of language after she bites Deacon's lip and sucks his blood and has to return deeply contrite to the convent. In *Song of Solomon*, it is encapsulated in Pilate's distraught "My baby girl" intoned repeatedly at her daughter's funeral. *Jazz* is narrated by a first-person narrator who is a non-participant in the events that we see, thus folding in the perspective of third-person omniscience with that of the first-person focalizer. Her description of the gaps in reality that Violet experiences seem at once an objective description as well as the free-indirect focalization of Violet herself. See *Paradise* (London: Chatto and Windus, 1998), 226 and 240–241; and *Song of Solomon* (London: Chatto and Windus, 1978), 318–319; and *Jazz* (New York: Plume, 1993), 23.

While Sethe is unrelenting in evading the question posed by Paul D, in contrast, with Beloved, she feels a compulsion to explain. This is strongly seen in the alacrity with which she surrenders to Beloved's every whim when it "clicks" in her mind that she is her returned daughter: "I thought you were mad at me. And now I know that if you was, you ain't now because you came back here to me and I was right all along: there is no world outside my door. I only need to know one thing. How bad is the scar?"[31] It is impossible to read this without realizing that somewhere beneath her lack of hesitation in the infanticide, somewhere beneath her inability to address what she has done even to herself, there is – if not guilt then, extreme discomfort. It seems clear from her answer to Paul D's question that Sethe does not believe she made a wrong choice in killing Beloved. But why then might she be feeling discomfort or even a tinge of guilt in facing her returned daughter? Why feel guilt for something if you firmly believe you could not have acted otherwise? When Sethe says "I thought you were mad at me," perhaps it is not exactly guilt she is feeling, but rather an anxiety that Beloved would not understand her own murder as the highest act of maternal love.

This is a good place to recall our observations in the Introduction about how historical conjunctures such as colonialism or slavery that reverse the logic of social and familial relations make impossible Judith Butler's idea of giving-an-account-of-oneself. In other words, maybe Sethe remains confident in the ethical rightness of her own behavior, but at the same time, she remains aware of her inability to provide an account of herself through a language that will make sense to anyone who does not already intuitively understand what she has done: "If they didn't get it right off – she could never explain," and which is why she could not answer Paul D's question. Perhaps what Sethe is rejecting then, is language, since what she has done can never be put into words to anyone who does not already share her own viewpoint about the necessity and inescapability of her tragic choice. Sethe seems to be suffering here from a crisis of intelligibility to others – and more specifically to her daughter. So rather than saying sorry to Beloved, she must show her love through more and more outlandish demonstrations of love and self-sacrifice (feeding her while wasting away herself, etc.).

Even though Sethe's killing of her daughter is inspired by the real-life choice of Margaret Garner, the represented action in Morrison's novel also immediately serves to invoke a series of other literary infanticides such as Agamemnon's sacrifice of Iphigenia, Medea's killing of her two sons in Euripides' play, and of course Okonkwo's killing of Ikemefuna, who as we

[31] Morrison, *Beloved*, 184.

saw in Chapter 3 called him father. But more important than its long literary lineage is that the infanticide in *Beloved* unleashes a vortex of emotional responses to the event within the novel itself, which then registers for us the ethical conundrum that Sethe's choice represents for others as well as herself. Sethe persistently invites comparison to Greek tragic characters because of the way her face is described:

> A face too still for comfort; irises the same color as her skin, which, in that still face, used to make [Paul D] think of a mask with mercifully punched-out eyes ... Even in that tiny shack, leaning so close to the fire you could smell the heat in her dress, her eyes did not pick up a flicker of light. They were like two wells into which he had trouble gazing. Even punched out they needed to be covered, lidded, marked with some sign to warn folks of what that emptiness held.[32]

And at the moment when she kills her daughter, this Greek-mask quality is invoked again, but this time from the viewpoint of schoolteacher:

> Enough nigger eyes for now. Little nigger-boy eyes open in the sawdust; little nigger-girl eyes staring between the wet fingers that held her face so her head wouldn't fall off; little nigger-baby eyes crinkling up to cry in the arms of the old nigger whose own eyes were nothing but slivers looking down at his feet. But the worst ones were those of the nigger woman who had looked like she didn't have any. Since the whites in them had disappeared and since they were as black as her skin, she looked blind.[33]

If in Athenian theatre, the mask guaranteed the conversion of an actor into the character of the role he was to play, it also, in instances such as the mask of Dionysus in Euripides' play, invoked the sense of a god's fateful implacability. For Sethe, however, it is the depth of her suffering as a slave that has hollowed out her eyes. But the mask-like character of her face also suggests something else that is central to her self-definition, namely, a streak of absoluteness that allows her to be extraordinarily determined in pursuit of her role as mother, and, as we see in the exercise of her terrible choice, in interpreting that role as the power to protect the life of her children precisely by taking it.

Euripides' Medea has correctly been compared to Sethe in that they both subvert our anticipations of how maternal instincts are expressed.[34] However, unlike Medea, who attempts to rationalize to the chorus her decision to kill her sons, Sethe's decision is taken on the spur of the

---

[32] Morrison, *Beloved*, 9.   [33] Morrison, *Beloved*, 150.
[34] On this point, see especially Hilary Emmett "The Maternal Contract in *Beloved* and *Medea*," in Heike Bartel and Anne Simon, eds., *Unbinding Medea: Interdisciplinary Approaches to a Classical Myth from Antiquity to the 21st Century* (London: Legenda Press, 2010), 248–260.

moment, and, as we saw, almost as if she was possessed by a force beyond her own consciousness. Unlike Medea, she lacks the language to describe or reason about the event, much less the capacity to directly confront its full effects. It is precisely Sethe's precipitousness, which is strictly speaking a species of spontaneity, that alerts us to the fact that her action requires rigorous contextualization in sociological conditions, which in the novel are amply provided for in the many descriptions of the infantilization of the slaves at Sweet Home by Mr. and Mrs. Garner and the ways in which their expression of any natural adult human impulses is curtailed by the arrival of schoolteacher. Sethe's terrible action is the one that cannot be understood without grasping the context of slavery itself, which totally organizes her existence and circumscribes her every action, "natural" or otherwise. Thus, in *Beloved,* unlike in Medea, the "natural" is put under erasure and is shown to embody its dialectical negation as a constitutive part of its ultimate expression. This is foundational to the ways that human impulses are expressed in the novel especially during the period of slavery, but sometimes even afterward in the phase of freedom. And again, in contrast to Medea, the responses to Sethe's action by the other characters that bear witness to the event cover a range of emotions and interpretations, the most significant of which is that of Baby Suggs, as we shall see shortly.

Split Anagnorisis and the Transfer of Moral Residue

To revisit our discussion of Aristotle's views on tragedy from the Introduction, in the *Poetics* he notes his preference for complex as opposed to simple plots. A complex plot must have two key dimensions. First, is a clear measure of ineluctability that is primarily conveyed in the plot's tightly sequential structure (beginning, middle, and end is how Aristotle frames it) and second, is that the moment of ethical reversal should ideally coincide with that of *anagnorisis* or recognition. The first element suggests the requirement of causal intelligibility while the second indicates the relation between ethically significant reversals and moral residue. We should note that in both classical and Shakespearean tragedy, *anagnorisis* is never a boon of insight but always the signal of cognitive limitations which may have previously been masked to the tragic protagonist. Moral residue is typically expressed as a byproduct of *anagnorisis*; as an aspect of regret and deep guilt, such as we see in the cases of Sophocles' Ajax and Oedipus; Aeschylus' Orestes, especially in the second half of the *Choephori* but also in *The Eumenides*; and for

Othello, King Lear, and Lady Macbeth. In all these instances, the regret and guilt that are triggered at the moment of *anagnorisis* are tied specifically to the tragic protagonists and not to those that bear witness to their tragedies. This is not the case in *Beloved*. (We shall pick up the thread on moral residue more fully in our discussion of J. M. Coetzee's *Waiting for the Barbarians* in the next chapter.)

All the nodal points of perspectivization on Sethe's choice that James Phelan identifies in his essay have to be juxtaposed to that of Baby Suggs, for it is her response that shows the relation of *anagnorisis* and moral residue inherent not to the tragic actor but to the one who bears witness to the tragedy. The shock that Baby Suggs experiences on bearing witness to Sethe's tragic choice (the killing of a child) and that then breaks her big heart and makes her lose her faith is a mutual product of Akan *musuo* and Aristotelian *anagnorisis* but of a different order. The horror of the infanticide is like a *musuo* because it threatens in its very simplicity to undo all the bounds of sociality pertinent to the community. When it occurs, it is immediately perceived by everyone but Sethe as a form of rupture and contamination. However, whatever *anagnorisis* might be adduced for the scene is significant not from Sethe's perspective but from the way it is transposed onto Baby Suggs. The split in *anagnorisis* and its transfer from one female character to the other operates along the same mechanisms of both resonance and rupture we saw earlier in Ricoeur's reading of *Mrs Dalloway*. For the transposition is discursively generated from the spatial proximity of Sethe and Baby Suggs, both of whom are located within the same scene that reads almost like a tragic painting or tableau. They, along with schoolteacher, Stamp Paid, and of course the hapless children, occupy the same spatial location within which the traumatic event unfolds. However, unlike the other focalizers to the scene – namely Paul D, Stamp Paid, and schoolteacher – Baby Suggs's response is shaped by her grasp of the utter impossibility of exercising maternal instincts from within the habitus of slavery. For her, the event completely ruptures her known world. Earlier in the text we are told that the exercise of maternal instincts is a distinct problem for mothers like her and Sethe, and indeed for all mothers:

> It made sense for a lot of reasons because in all of Baby's life, as well as Sethe's own, men and women were moved around like checkers. Anybody Baby Suggs knew, let alone loved, who hadn't run off or been hanged, got rented out, loaned out, bought up, brought back, stored up, mortgaged, won, stolen or seized. So, Baby's eight children had six fathers. What she called the nastiness of life was the shock she received upon learning that

nobody stopped playing checkers just because the pieces included her children. Halle she was able to keep the longest. Twenty years. A lifetime. Given to her, no doubt, to make up for *hearing* that her two girls, neither of whom had their adult teeth, were sold and gone and she had not been able to wave goodbye. To make up for coupling with a straw boss for four months in exchange for keeping her third child, a boy, with her – only to have him traded for lumber in the spring of the next year and to find herself pregnant by the man who promised not to and did. That child she could not love and the others she would not.[35]

Baby Suggs is the only one of the four focalizers who responds to the event not as a lover (Paul D), a helpful neighbor (Stamp Paid), or a "theorizing sadist" (schoolteacher), but as a mother.[36]

Like Elektra in Aeschylus' *Choephori*, at this moment Baby Suggs is "struck through, as by the cross-stab of a sword."[37] In the case of Elektra, she is responding to the sight of a lock of hair on her father's gravesite, which she mistakenly assumes to have been taken from his head before his death at the hand of Clytemenestra, her mother, but that is really a lock from her brother Orestes' head. The metaphor of feeling as though stabbed by a sword encapsulates the intense welling of emotion on seeing what seems to be a material correlative of the absent presence of both male relations. At this very early stage in the *Choephori*, the lock of hair also acts as a mnemonic token of the entire bloody and cursed history of the House of Atreus, of which Elektra is of course a part. But the point to note is the dialectical relationship between the perceived object and the internal state of recognition that it triggers. In the scene from the *Choephori*, the recognition is by no means that of an Aristotelian *anagnorisis*, since the lock only serves as a memory prompt rather than the recognition of an ethical state of things. For Baby Suggs, her witnessing of Sethe's choice also induces the sensation of a stab in the flesh, not from a material token or object as in the case of Elektra, but from bearing witness to the tragic tableau of which she herself is a part. What Baby Suggs witnesses induces a deep existential crisis that she will never recover from. Her entire world is discombobulated.

[35] Morrison, *Beloved*, 23, emphasis in original.
[36] This completely apposite description of schoolteacher is used by Thomas R. Edwards in his review of *Beloved* shortly after it was published. See his "Ghost Story," *New York Review of Books*, 5 November, 1987, www.nybooks.com/articles/1987/11/05/ghost-story/, last accessed Jan. 17, 2020.
[37] Aeschylus, *Choephori*, line 184.

"What I have to do," she tells Stamp Paid, as he tries to encourage her to go back to the Clearing, "is get in my bed and lay down. I want to fix on something harmless in this world." The conversation continues:

> "What world you talking about? Ain't nothing harmless down here."
> "Yes it is. Blue. That don't hurt nobody. Yellow neither."
> "You getting in bed to think about yellow?"
> "I likes yellow."
> "Then what? When you get through with blue and yellow, then what?"
> "Can't say. It's something can't be planned."[38]

For someone whose entire life has been spent healing others and giving of her mighty heart, this is an extremely painful moment. But the point is that for Baby Suggs neither judgment nor *catharsis* is available to her; she recognizes that Sethe's act is both necessary and repugnant, both fated and willed, a gesture of freedom and its destruction at one and the same time. It is not at all clear to me whether the splintering and transfer of *anagnorisis* from the tragic protagonist to the one that bears witness to the tragic act is to be found in other tragedies, but Morrison definitely gives us the means for reviewing this idea.

Conclusion: A Story to Pass On

There is much in *Beloved* that might cause discomfort and that would qualify it as tragic in the ordinary sense we often find in newspapers and the popular media. As I noted at the beginning of this chapter, we are never meant to forget the many acts of violence perpetrated against black folk both during the period of slavery and in its long aftermath. But against this background of weariness and woe is set a series of actions that disclose the deep problem of freedom after bondage, the instability of ethical choice, and the persistence of moral residue for those that bear witness to Sethe's action. Each of these themes is conveyed in prose of extraordinary lyricism that captures the internal states of the central characters as well as the improbable beauty of their memories that are so firmly entangled in the ways in which they attempt to carve a place to live in the present. In contrast to the communal incantations that we find at the end of *Beloved*, I would like to say this *is* a story that must be passed on. The incantations have a ritual quality to them that has often made me think of Toni Morrison's work as bearing a congregational quality, as if inviting her

[38] Morrison, *Beloved*, 179.

readers to participate in the contemplation of something transcendent that is nonetheless mired in the messiness of constrained lives. And so, in closing our reading of the novel, we feel like saying a quiet yet tremulous Amen. But not for long, because it is a story that we will have to return to, again and again and again.

CHAPTER 7

On Moral Residue and the Affliction
of Second Thoughts
J. M. Coetzee's Waiting for the Barbarians

The description that Paul Rayment gives of himself in J. M. Coetzee's *Slow Man* is the inspiration behind the phrase "affliction of second thoughts" in the title to this chapter. At the end of a letter to the husband of his in-house caregiver for whom he has developed romantic feelings, he writes: "I am going to seal and stamp this missive now, and before I have second thoughts make the trek to the nearest mailbox. I used to have lots of second thoughts, I had second thoughts all the time, but now I abhor them."[1] Later, Elizabeth Costello points out to him that his habit of waiting for second thoughts is part of his "tortoise character" because "[he] sniff[s] the air for ages before [he] stick[s] [his] head out. Because every blessed step costs such an effort."[2] The tortoise character Elizabeth Costello attributes to Paul Rayment is no mere species of prevarication, however, but rather comes from the ontological burden of making any choice in the first place. Many of Coetzee's central figures exemplify forms of thought affliction similar to Paul Rayment's. Whether with the Magistrate in *Waiting for the Barbarians*, as we shall see more fully; Magda in *In the Heart of the Country*; David Lurie in *Disgrace*; Susan Barton in *Foe*; or even the nicknamed JC or Señor C (a surrogate for Coetzee himself) in the reflective and largely essayistic *Diary of a Bad Year,* the affliction of second thoughts are readily in evidence.

Part of the inspiration for the affliction of second thoughts that we find in Coetzee's novels may be glimpsed from the remarks in St. Augustine's *Confessions* with which Coetzee opens his discussion of fictional and autobiographical confessions in the aptly titled "Confession and Double Thoughts."[3] After describing the moment in the *Confessions* where he and

---

[1] J. M. Coetzee, *Slow Man* (London: Penguin, 2006), 225.   [2] Coetzee, *Slow Man*, 228.
[3] J. M. Coetzee, "Confession and Double Thoughts: Tolstoy, Rousseau, Dostoevsky," *Doubling the Point: Essays and Interviews*, ed. David Attwell (Cambridge, MA: Harvard University Press, 1992), 251–293.

his friends go out to steal a large load of pears from a neighbor's garden, Augustine reflects upon the shame that he felt afterwards and the realization that he lacked self-knowledge about his attraction to committing evil deeds. What is significant in this episode for Coetzee, however, is that Augustine "wants to know what lies at the beginning of the skein of remembered shame, what is the origin from which it springs, *but the skein is endless*, the states of self-searching required to attain its beginning infinite in number."[4] Furthermore, he continues, "The truth about the self that will bring an end to the quest for the source within the self for that-which-is-wrong . . . *will remain inaccessible to introspection.*"[5] The inaccessibility of the sources of the self to introspection and the endless skein of remembrances are dual processes encapsulated by the affliction of second thoughts. Skepticism, self-scrutiny, self-division, as well as fundamental doubt about the basis of action itself, are all aspects of the affliction of second thoughts. In Coetzee's novels, choice-making appears to be an enervating and almost contaminating process and is designed to emphasize the difficulty of both adopting moral positions and then acting from them.[6]

What I am describing here as the affliction of second thoughts is not exclusive either to Coetzee or indeed to postcolonial writing in general. In fact, when seen as a device for the existential examination of the self, the affliction of second thoughts is an aspect of self-interlocution that can be traced back to the writings of Augustine himself. While he was not the first to deploy self-interlocution as a modality of spiritual exercise, Augustine is the first to have reflected upon a narrative theory of the self as derived from the nature of inner dialogue. Brian Stock argues in *Augustine's Inner Dialogue* that the Bishop of Hippo, in what is today's Algeria, considered the self to be temporally and narratively conceived. Augustine's reflections in both the *Confessions* and in the *Soliloquies* before it, typically entailed a demonstration of the historical or biographical trigger for inner dialogue, a description of the dramatis personae that the self was to debate, and a sense of the temporal and durational depth of the contradictions that were to be worked out within such dialogue. As Stock goes on to note,

[4] Coetzee, *Slow Man*, 251; emphasis added.   [5] Coetzee, "Confession," 252; emphasis added.
[6] Significantly different in this regard is the aforementioned Elizabeth Costello. She is first introduced as a mouthpiece character in *The Life of Animals* and subsequently in the eponymously named *Elizabeth Costello* and immediately establishes herself in world literature as a firm and clear-sighted animal rights activist. Her sudden entry into the narrative of *Slow Man* immediately imports a sense of purposefulness and desire for closure, something that she tries to instill unsuccessfully in Paul Rayment.

Augustine's form of inner dialogue has inspired a long line of philosophers, including Descartes, Pascal, and Wittgenstein. The soliloquy, that inner dialogue rendered external, is listed in the OED as first appearing in 1613 (Stock gives the date of first appearance as 1604), and, as Stock rightly notes, it derived from the repeated use of soliloquies in Renaissance drama. Stock points out that examples of dramatic soliloquies incorporating philosophy were to be found in Calderon, Racine, Lessing, Schiller, and of course most notably, in Shakespeare.[7] Scholars have drawn on William James, Michel Foucault, Mikhail Bakhtin, and Jacques Lacan among others to elaborate varying frameworks for reflecting upon inner dialogue, internal monologue, and stream of consciousness, the cognate terms by which self-interlocution has been discussed. Self-interlocution illustrates the different internal rhythms of consciousness, the shifting relationships between the self and the external world that these imply, and the varying ways in which the mind binds thoughts to emotions and to images in sustaining the subterranean murmur that always accompanies thought.

Coetzee's *Waiting for the Barbarians* is distinctive from the many other novels in postcolonial literature and elsewhere that deploy forms of self-interlocution because of the way in which it also consistently ties this to forms of moral residue. Narrated by the Magistrate and exclusively from his perspective, the subterranean murmur in his mind is directed mainly at himself, even if the murmur is dialectically strung between opposing and often shifting and incompatible moral principles. Given that the novel is set in the outpost of an unnamed Empire that is gathering its resources for a potential war with the so-called barbarians of the title, the material conditions that trigger the affliction of second thoughts in the Magistrate also serve as signifiers of a classic colonial condition. But the novel also lays out something much more complicated than the hydraulic relationship between oppression and resistance found in many other postcolonial novels; rather, the Magistrate's crisis derives from the negotiation between contradictory moral choices that proliferate subsidiary contradictions, and leave him in a limbo of regret irrespective of what choice he makes. Having to exercise choice from within an unideal and brutally violent political context is only one part of his problem. His somewhat futile internal struggle to extricate himself from the contagious cynicism of Empire is compounded first by his attraction to the benefits of civilization that the

---

[7] Brian Stock, *Augustine's Inner Dialogue: The Philosophical Soliloquy in Late Antiquity* (Cambridge: Cambridge University Press, 2010), 64.

Empire represents, and second by the peculiar relationship he has with the barbarian girl, who has been subjected to torture and whom he rescues and keeps in his rooms as an object of simultaneous desire and revulsion.

Colonial Conditions and Moral Isolation

The entire action of *Waiting for the Barbarians* is set in a remote and sleepy outpost of an unnamed Empire. The roughly 3000-person township is a walled and gated fortress whose residents live on cultivating corn, trapping and hunting bush animals, and trading with the fisher folk who reside not far from the settlement and come in periodically to exchange their fish for goods at the township's market. Some three days southeast of the outpost lies "a plain of wind-eroded clay terraces merging at its extremes into banks of red dust-clouds and then into the yellow hazy sky," along with flat marshland, belts of reeds, and a large salty lake upon which in winter lies a central ice-sheet.[8] Nothing grows in certain regions of the salty lake floor, "which in places buckles and pushes up in jagged crystalline hexagons a foot wide."[9] Ten days beyond the settlement in the same direction lie the blue mountain ranges where the nomadic barbarian tribes reside. The areas around the settlement, both near and far, are extremely inhospitable and have become correlated in the social imaginary of the town's residents with the barbarian tribes as equal bearers of potential danger and destruction. When the Magistrate crosses the lake region to return the barbarian girl to her people, he wonders what would become of the settlement if the lake grew into a dead sea. Given that the town's residents depend largely on "nature's cornucopia," this question itself becomes a thematic refrain later on in the novel when food supplies are cut off by the barbarian tribes in response to the military campaign launched against them by Colonel Joll, the military leader of the imperial center, and his soldiers.[10]

Seen through the Magistrate's eyes, life at the outpost seems utterly dull and predictable. He spends quiet hours collecting tithes and taxes, administering communal lands, seeing that the garrison is provided for, supervising the junior officers, keeping an eye on trade, and presiding over the law-court twice a week, followed by evenings hunting game, going to dinner with friends, or frequenting young prostitutes with whom he has been regularly consorting as he grows old and into "placid concupiscence."[11] He

---

[8] Coetzee, *Waiting for the Barbarians*, 59.   [9] Coetzee, *Waiting for the Barbarians*, 60.
[10] Coetzee, *Waiting for the Barbarians*, 57.   [11] Coetzee, *Waiting for the Barbarians*, 9.

yearns for "the familiar routine of [his] duties, of the approaching summer, the long dreamy siestas, the conversations with friends at dusk under walnut trees, with boys bringing tea and lemonade and the eligible girls in twos and threes promenading before [them] on the square in their finery."[12] None of the social interactions that the Magistrate has with his friends are described in in the novel, and even those with the young prostitute he consorts with during the course of the narrative are barely delineated. All this gives the impression that the Magistrate is a social anchorite among the outpost's population. The appearance of social isola-tion is accentuated when he takes in the barbarian girl, for his exclusive obsession with her becomes the background against which his larger state of isolation is further defined. On his return to the outpost after delivering her to her people, the Magistrate is detained by the security officers and undergoes lengthy physical humiliations – and through his punishment is thus further isolated, but now it is an enforced isolation rather than a chosen one. In this period of detention, the distinction between choice and imposition is one that he reflects upon at great length. It is also during this period that he experiences what it must feel like to be a colonial Other subject to disdain, mockery, demonization, and incomprehension. His status is also partially converted into that of a *pharmakos* or sacrificial figure; this conversion can only be said to be partial because the full symbolic cycle of becoming a *pharmakos* requires that he be the represen-tative of a wider communal sensibility, something which his social isolation clearly precludes. Unlike the *pharmokoi* we encountered earlier in the Greeks, Achebe, Soyinka, and to a certain degree in Morrison, the Magistrate does not represent any larger communal standpoint but only his own sense of moral rightness. Each of the elements just described – the physical environment, his social isolation, the range of humiliations he suffers, and most importantly his relationship to the barbarian girl – become themes of reflection in his mind, the objects of the affliction of second thoughts.

Until the arrival of Colonel Joll and the soldiers from the imperial center at the start of the novel, few people in the outpost had ever encountered any barbarians directly. In fact, until Joll's arrival, the township did not even have facilities to hold prisoners; the detention of the first captives requires that the old granary be converted into a makeshift prison cell. In the thirty years the Magistrate has governed the township there has never been any direct problem or indeed confrontation with the barbarians. And

---

[12] Coetzee, *Waiting for the Barbarians*, 75.

yet in every generation without fail, there has been an episode of hysteria regarding them. As the Magistrate notes:

> But last year stories began to reach us from the capital of unrest among the barbarians. Traders travelling safe routes had been attacked and plundered. Stock thefts had increased in scale and audacity.
>
> . . .
>
> Of this unrest I myself saw nothing. In private I observed that once in every generation, *without fail*, there is an episode of hysteria about the barbarians. There is no woman living along the frontier who has not dreamed of a dark barbarian hand coming from under the bed to grip her ankle, no man who has not frightened himself with visions of the barbarians carousing in his home, breaking plates, setting fire to the curtains, raping his daughters. These dreams are the consequence of too much ease. Show me a barbarian army and I will believe.[13]

The relationship between the outpost and the barbarians has rightly been interpreted by commentators as expressing the dialectic between self and Other that is commonplace in colonial relations.[14] However, we must also take account of the overall spatial topography of the novel, both in terms of the internal social dynamics within the outpost settlement, and, more importantly, between the settlement and the external natural environment of which the barbarians are seen to constitute an essential aspect. Many African novels set nature in apparent opposition to the spaces of civil settlement. Thus, for Achebe's Umuofia in *Things Fall Apart* there is the Evil Forest full of the unappeased spirits of the dead that have been cast out, and for the village at the beginning of Amos Tutuola's *My Life in the Bush of Ghosts* there is the "bush" teeming with various grotesque and malevolent spirits. A similar relationship can be found in Ben Okri's *The Famished Road*, Ngũgĩ wa Thiong'o's *A Grain of Wheat*, and even in more recent works such as Chigozie Obioma's *The Fishermen*. Writing about Achebe's Evil Forest, Ainehi Edoro-Glines cautions us, however, not to view such spaces simply as zones of prohibition or civilizational voidance. Rather, approaching the question via a reading of Hobbes, Locke and Agamben, she argues that the state of wild nature represented in African literature is not "a chronological datum" to be consigned to a life of the

[13] Coetzee, *Waiting for the Barbarians*, 8; emphasis added.
[14] Homi Bhabha, "Signs Taken for Wonders: Questions of Ambivalence and Authority under a Tree outside Delhi, May 1817," *Critical Inquiry*, 12.1 (Autumn, 1985), 144–165; also Derek Attridge, *J. M. Coetzee and the Ethics of Reading: Literature in the Event* (Chicago, IL: University of Chicago Press, 2004).

past, but is always contemporaneous with the constitution of sovereignty as such.[15]

While the topography of *Waiting for the Barbarians* is quite different from that of *Things Fall Apart*, following Edoro-Glines' argument we may argue that once the barbarians are incorporated into the threatening geographical landscape that surrounds the settlement they come to perform a similar function as the Evil Forest in Achebe's novel. The unfriendly landscape and the barbarians are Others to the civilization, and yet they are nevertheless required for the assertion of the key terms of that civilization. Even though he is skeptical of their sources, the periodic episodes of hysteria that the Magistrate refers to translate the contemporaneous threat of the breakdown of civilizational values into flashpoints within the social imaginary of the townsfolk. Taken in this way, the interpretations that Colonel Joll and his officers make about the imminent threat from the barbarians only represent an upgrade to the familiar dialectic of civilization versus nature and colonizer versus colonized, with the essential idea of a state of emergency becoming the ploy by which to rationalize the operations of a delirious sovereignty. In the novel, each installment of capturing so-called barbarian enemies (often not barbarians at all but merely innocent fisher folk), their interrogation and torture, and the very public acts of abuse and humiliation against them are designed to affirm the Empire's sovereign dominion, not just over the barbarians, but also over the settlement's internal populations. The displays are for the benefit of the population and demonstrate the necessary spectatoriality that Empire requires to get its citizens to acquiesce to the violent form by which it procures its civilizational guarantees. This is one way to interpret what the Magistrate says about the Time of Empire:

> What has made it impossible for us to live in time like fish in water, like birds in air, like children? It is the fault of Empire! Empire has created the time of history. Empire has located its existence not in the smooth recurrent spinning time of the cycle of the seasons but in the jagged time of rise and fall, of beginning and end, of catastrophe. Empire dooms itself to live in history and plot against history. One thought alone preoccupies the sub-merged mind of Empire: how not to end, how not to die, how to prolong its era. By day it pursues its enemies. It is cunning and ruthless, it sends its bloodhounds everywhere. By night it feeds on images of disaster: the sack of cities, the rape of populations, pyramids of bones, acres of desolation. A mad vision yet a virulent one: I, wading in the ooze, am no less infected with it

---

[15] Ainehi Edoro-Glines, "Achebe's Evil Forest: Space, Violence, and Order in *Things Fall Apart,*" *The Cambridge Journal of Postcolonial Literary Inquiry*, 5.2 (2018): 176–192.

than the faithful Colonel Joll as he tracks the enemies of Empire through the boundless desert, sword unsheathed to cut down barbarian after barbarian until at last he finds and slays the one whose destiny it should be (or if not he then his son's or unborn grandson's) to climb the bronze gateway to the Summer Palace and topple the globe surmounted by the tiger rampant that symbolizes eternal dominion, while his comrades below cheer and fire their muskets in the air.[16]

The Empire controls history by manipulating a series of catastrophes by day and by night, thus establishing a particular man-made rhythm to history. Thus, the exercise of imperial sovereignty is set in opposition to the natural cycle and constitutes a temporality of history that is celebrated through the rhythms of war and conquest. This is also a template for establishing absolutisms and a principle of sovereign right that is grounded exclusively in the logic of power, the necropolitical right, as Achille Mbembe notes, of deciding who is to live and who is to die.[17] That by the end of the novel, this logic is directly defeated by the very cycles of nature that Empire sets itself against shows its fundamental futility. But it does not obviate the play of the dialectic between sovereignty and nature, since there is no indication that the demands of the periodic episodes of hysteria regarding the barbarians are ever going to be attenuated within the social imaginary of the outpost's dwellers. In fact, we would not be wrong in surmising that, after the events that have been described in the novel, the episodes of hysteria might be multiplied in both frequency and intensity. The Magistrate's disavowal of the rationale for the hysteria, then, comes from the same source as his social isolation.

Moral Conflict and Moral Dilemma

The Magistrate's sense of isolation has a direct bearing on how he experiences moral conflict, and concomitantly, of moral residue. Moral conflict and moral dilemma are closely interrelated concepts that have been much discussed by philosophers interested in the question of moral residue.[18]

---

[16] Coetzee, *Waiting for the Barbarians*, 133–134.
[17] Achille Mbembe, "Necropolitics," *Public Culture*, 15.1 (2003): 11–40.
[18] The literature on this is quite extensive. For a representative sample of the debates, see Bernard Williams's "Ethical Consistency" in *Problems of the Self* (Cambridge: Cambridge University Press, 1973), 166–186; Michael. J. Zimmerman, "Lapses and Dilemmas," *Philosophical Papers*, 17.2 (1988): 103–112; Patricia Greenspan, *Practical Guilt: Moral Dilemmas, Emotions, and Social Norms* (New York: Oxford University Press, 1995); Terrance McConnell, "Moral Residue and Dilemmas" in H. E. Mason, ed., *Moral Dilemmas and Moral Theory* (Oxford: Oxford University Press, 1996), 36–47; Terrance McConnell, "Moral Dilemmas," *Stanford Encyclopedia of Philosophy*,

Moral residue is often used in reference to an agent's experience of doubt, regret, remorse, guilt, or shame as generated from making an ethically significant choice. It is the retrospective equivalent or extension of second thoughts, which are themselves *prospective*; in other words, the anxiety, doubt, hesitation, and self-interrogation which precedes a difficult moral decision is inevitably followed by guilt, remorse, and more uncertainty after the fact, such that the moment of choosing, the moment of *action*, is temporally cushioned or mirrored on either side by emotional and psychological unease. This is especially the case if the subject is in a true moral dilemma, rather than simply a moral conflict. As a shorthand for the distinction between moral conflict and moral dilemma, from which we can go on to stipulate a further understanding of moral residue, consider this formulation by Terrance McConnell:

> A moral dilemma is a situation in which each of two things ought to be done but both cannot be done. Restricted to single agents, a dilemma is a situation in which a person ought to do A, ought to do B, and cannot do both A and B. In order for a moral conflict to count as a genuine dilemma, the conflicting obligations or moral requirements must at least be such that neither overrides the other. If one moral requirement does override another, we have a resolvable conflict but not a dilemma. But in a genuine dilemma, not only must the conflicting requirements both be non-over-ridden, they must also both issue in ought-all-things-considered moral judgements. Also, genuine moral dilemmas are ontological, not merely epistemic; the truth of the conflicting ought-statements is independent of the agent's beliefs.[19]

Moral conflict comes from a situation where a person believes him or herself obligated to do A and also to do B, but cannot do both at the same time. In a moral conflict once one of the two options is decided upon, it is perceived as annulling the moral claim of the other option, but in the case of moral dilemma, the moral force of the rejected claim is not considered to have been attenuated simply on being rejected.

We can conclude from McConnell's discussion that moral conflict is a precondition of moral dilemma since one must first be faced with two (or more) moral choices of relatively equal strength before determining

https://plato.stanford.edu/entries/moral-dilemmas/, last accessed July 14, 2018; Lisa Tessman, *Moral Failure: On the Impossible Demands of Morality* (Oxford: Oxford University Press, 2015); Lisa Tessman, *When Doing the Right Thing is Impossible* (Oxford: Oxford University Press, 2017). Tessman's second book covers the same questions as her first but is targeted at a more general and lay audience and is very useful as a primer to the key questions.
[19] Terrance McConnell, "Moral Residue and Moral Dilemmas," 36; see also, Tessman, *When Doing the Right Thing*, 27–42.

whether or not the fulfillment of one cancels out the others. What is not clear from McConnell's account is why in a case of moral dilemma where there is no annulment of the claims of a rejected option (A or B), the rejected option still retains its moral force, its force of *oughtness*, and by implication, that the choice of either option may result in moral residue. It appears on the face of it that moral dilemma is inherently linked to something other than facts or information. Rather, moral dilemma seems linked to emotional attachments and desires that transcend mere facts. Furthermore, emotional attachments and desires may be linked to *both choice options* rather than merely being dictated by the facts pertaining to either one. That is to say, an objective course of action that is invested with some desire or cluster of desires may not necessarily be annulled in its moral claim simply on the disclosure of some relevant fact pertaining to it, or on its being rejected as an option for action. Rather, the desire that was part of the option in the first place may be temporarily attenuated on not being chosen, only to be forcefully restored in a different form or as a residual regret within memory.

Even though Bernard Williams does not use the term moral dilemma, his discussion of the problem of ethical (in)consistency is relevant to the overall question of the relationship between moral conflict, moral dilemma, and desires. As Williams notes:

> What is normally called conflict of *desires* has, in many central cases, a feature analogous to what I have been calling conflict of beliefs: that the clash between the desires arises from some contingent matter of fact. This is a matter of fact that makes it impossible for both the desires to be satisfied; but we can consistently imagine a state of affairs in which they could both be satisfied . . . . A more fundamental difficulty arises with conflicts of desire and aversion towards one and the same object. Such conflicts can be represented as conflicts of two desires: in the most general case, the desire to have and the desire not to have the object, where "have" is a variable expression which gets a determinate content from the context and from the nature of the object in question . . . . Thus, it seems that for many cases of conflict of desire and aversion towards one object, the basis of the conflict is still, though in a slightly different way, contingent, the contingency consisting in the co-existence of the desirable and the undesirable features of the object.[20]

Williams is pointing here to two situations that are each differently inflected by the impact of facts and desires. One has to do with the

[20] Bernard Williams, *Problems of the Self*, 167–168.

emergence of facts contingent upon the status of desires, and the other has to do with the implications of the same object being the source of both attraction and revulsion depending on the aspect of it that is brought into view. But we may even add a third: that some strong desire is invested in each of the options being considered in the first place, such that the sequence of their consideration is obscured by the fact that they share something in common, that is to say, desire. Among the many matters of fact that may interfere in the fulfillment of a desire for example, are the insuperable realities of space and time. The fulfillment of desire A or desire B may require that you be present at completely different locations but this fact may not have been known when the two options were first being considered. The emergence of the relevant fact may in certain instances allow you to prioritize between the two options, but in the instances where such a prioritization is impossible you have a case of moral dilemma.

Take, for example, this scenario: your favorite aunt has just died and a date for her funeral has been set. You definitely want to be at her funeral; it is very important for you and the rest of the family. But it turns out that the date of your aunt's funeral happens to coincide with the date of a major international environmental conference to which you have been invited to address. At this conference will also be several heads of states, thus presenting you with an excellent opportunity to make your impassioned call for our collective responsibility for taking care of the planet on which we live. You had often discussed your environmentalist views with your aunt and she had always seemed to understand you intuitively. That is why you loved her so much. But you are jarred by the fact that the date of the conference falls on the same day as your aunt's funeral. Plus, the conference is being held in another country, which means you will have to travel a long distance to be there. You cannot be at both your aunt's funeral and the conference at the same time. But whichever one you decide on you are going to feel bad afterwards. The reason for this, as I see it, is not merely because of the oughtness of the two choices placed before you, or even the factual details of time and distance pertaining to them, but the fact that each of them represents a cluster of emotions that cannot be attenuated simply by taking the other option. This is a moral dilemma that is guaranteed to produce a moral residue, of guilt, regret, self-blame, or something similar. Notwithstanding the source of the moral conflict (A or B), in a moral dilemma the emergence of a relevant fact pertaining to any relevant detail of the two options does not necessarily limit the attraction of either of them. The fact that A and B cannot be satisfied without you being in two places at once does not attenuate the moral force of either because the moral force is also the product of the strong feelings and desires attached to them. In contrast, a conflict of beliefs does not automatically imply a moral conflict, since the conflict of beliefs may be merely due to the absence of some factual piece of information, the appearance of which renders one belief less believable or viable than another without raising the question of moral valence. Thus, not all beliefs entail morally significant choices.

Reading McConnell's account of moral conflict and moral dilemma through Williams's discussion of moral (in)consistency we can then conclude that it is the entanglement of morally significant beliefs with desires and feelings that converts them into moral dilemmas and ultimately to moral residue, since their satisfaction can only be achieved on the exhaustion (as in the energetic dissipation) of that which is desired. Whether it is chosen as an option or not, the morally significant belief that is also invested with desire does not cease to stake its claim simply by not being chosen, but persists in drawing attention to itself. It demands to be satisfied and is simultaneously retrospective and proleptic to the process of choice-making in the way we noted earlier.

It is possible to suggest then that desires are central to moral dilemma and concomitantly to the persistence of moral residue and that they are at the heart of the endless skein of soul-searching that Coetzee refers to in his comments on Augustine. What Williams further points out as the oscillation between desire and rejection provoked by the same object is directly relevant to the Magistrate's fraught relationship with the barbarian girl. As we shall see shortly, the Magistrate's moral dilemma – the equal oughtness of two apparently incompatible choices of action – is triggered not just by the conflict between two seemingly incompatible beliefs, but by the fact that, for him, ethically held beliefs proliferate contradictions that persist in his mind irrespective of what action he takes or does not take on the basis of those beliefs. Whatever course of action he undertakes does not resolve his internal conflict, since the satisfaction of one course of action does not annul the proliferating and contradictory claims inherent to the beliefs and feelings that sustained the course of action in the first place. Thus, what might appear in *Waiting for the Barbarians* as a straightforward binary opposition – to side with the Empire or to side with the barbarian girl – also includes contradictions that multiply because of his different emotional attachments to each option. The Magistrate's moral dilemma is compounded by the fact that he has two warring sets of desires within him: on the one hand, he completely detests the instruments of torture that Colonel Joll and the security agents of Empire deploy in their quest for truth, and yet he is also completely enamored of the historical future of civilization that the form of life represented by his imperial outpost guarantees; and on the other hand, he is sexually invested in the barbarian girl, but in a way that moves in turn between possessiveness and disavowal, attraction and repugnance, both for her as his female captive and for the very thought of his desire for her. It is these contrasting sets of dialectically constituted moral standpoints invested with contradictory desires that ultimately underlie his moral residue. While the first-person narrative by which *Waiting for the Barbarians* unfolds has been much commented upon, it seems to me that it is the affliction of second thoughts as a structural form tied to moral residue that encapsulates the narrative conflicts and contradictions most strongly and makes this such a powerful exemplar of postcolonial tragedy and world literature.

Examples from the Greeks

To illustrate the differences between moral dilemma and moral residue more fully we need to make a detour through examples from classical tragedy before returning to *Waiting for the Barbarians* for comparison. Literature has historically been a handy source for thinking about questions of moral philosophy. The most widely referenced illustration of moral dilemma is that of Aeschylus' Agamemnon. As the military leader of the Greek army, Agamemnon is asked to sacrifice his daughter Iphigenia in appeasement of the goddess Artemis so their naval fleet can sail off on their campaign to Troy. The military choice he faces is equally balanced against the requirement that, as a father, he not destroy the foundation of *philia*, this time familial rather than friendly. This is the moral dilemma Agamemnon is faced with; however, one might argue that, while the two claims may be equivalent in an abstract sense, they are rendered asymmetrical in the specific material conditions under which the choices are presented to him. Agamemnon's moral dilemma is set within the vortex of a military emergency. Let us set out the context for greater clarification. The Greeks are ready to sail from the port of Aulis, but Agamemnon seems to have incurred the wrath of Artemis. The reasons given for her wrath vary, but, in Aeschylus' *Agamemnon* the goddess is angry that young soldiers will wantonly be killed in battle, while in Euripides' *Elektra,* Artemis is angry that Agamemnon slayed an animal sacred to her and subsequently boasted of being a better hunter than her. Hubris seems to be at the heart of each account. A plague and lack of wind prevent the army from sailing out from Aulis, so the army consults the prophet Calchas who informs them that the goddess will only be propitiated if Agamemnon sacrifices his daughter. Philip Vellacott's translation of the play renders quite vividly the material conditions faced by the Greek army at this point:

> So it was then. Agamemnon, mortified,
> Dared not, would not, admit to error; thought
> Of his great Hellene fleet, and in his pride
> Spread sail to the ill wind he should have fought.
> Meanwhile his armed men moped along the shores,
> And cursed the wind, and ate his dwindling stores;
> Stared at white Chalkis' roofs day after day
> Across the swell that churned in Aulis Bay.
> And still from Strymon came that Northern blast,
> While hulks and ropes grew rotten, moorings parted,
> Deserters slunk away,
> All ground their teeth, bored, helpless, hungry, thwarted.
> The days of waiting doubled. More days passed.
> The flower of warlike Hellas withered fast.[21]

Soldiers bored and moping, some deserting, stores depleting, hulks and ropes rotting, and the palpable murmur of mutiny; these are not signs to be easily set aside by any military general. It is perfectly conceivable that, had Agamemnon been faced with the options whilst still at home with his family, his decision might have turned out quite differently. Be that as it may, his decision to go ahead and sacrifice his daughter does not annul the moral claims of the *oikos* upon him, the full force of which is articulated in Aeschylus' play through the fearsome Clytemnestra, his wife and Iphigenia's mother. He is thus faced with a stark moral dilemma.

There is no evidence, however, that Agamemnon suffers any form of moral residue after he kills his daughter, at least not in Aeschylus' account. As we have already noted, it is not merely the equivalence of *oughtness* for the two options that constitutes a moral dilemma, but also the equivalence of the *desire* invested in both options. The fact that Agamemnon eventually makes peace with his decision to sacrifice his daughter and, following the infanticide, does not appear to suffer any moral residue suggests that the pull of military or communal duty was in fact much stronger than his familial ties. Some might even argue that in Aeschylus' account the question is more that of moral conflict (A or B) than of moral dilemma (that neither option is attenuated in its moral claim). In Euripides' *Iphigenia at Aulis*, Agamemnon does suffer some second thoughts in the

---

[21] Aeschylus, *Agamemnon, The Oresteian Trilogy*, trans. Philip Vellacott (London: Penguin Books, 1959), lines 185–199.

early stages regarding the rightness of killing his daughter and even sends a message to his wife Clytemnestra to that effect. The letter is intercepted by his brother Menelaus, who is enraged at his change of heart and worries that if Agamemnon does not go ahead with the plan to kill his daughter there might be mutiny in the ranks. The section in which the two brothers meet to discuss the question ultimately leads to them changing each other's minds, so that Menelaus now thinks that the Greek army should be disbanded so as to avoid the sacrilege to family life, while Agamemnon now becomes fully determined to sacrifice his daughter. By the time he goes ahead with the decision he seems to have purged himself of any sense of doubt regarding his choice. In Aeschylus' account, too, Agamemnon briefly debates his choices with heavy heart:

> My fate is angry if I disobey these,
> but angry if I slaughter
> this child, the beauty of my house,
> with maiden blood shed staining
> these her father's hands beside the altar.
> What of these things go without disaster?[22]

However, as the chorus reports it, "necessity's yoke is put upon him/ he changed, and from the heart the breath came bitter and sacrilegious, utterly infidel,/ to warp a will now to stop at nothing."[23] This implies that his character was transformed by a form of possession, the effect of which was to make him hubristic and determined to stop at nothing. And yet we might also say that the "yoke of necessity" becomes the conduit for intensifying already existing dispositions inherent to his character. In fact, on his return home to Argos the entire scene in which he is persuaded by Clytemnestra to stride upon the red tapestries to enter his palace is a symbolic reenactment of his hubris and utter lack of remorse for what he has done, whether it is the wanton shedding of the blood of vanquished Trojans or that of his daughter.

Sophocles' *Oedipus Rex* shows more promise for the question of moral residue. The choices for Oedipus seem initially to be easy to resolve: he is determined to find Lauis's murderer and thus also to guarantee his security as the king of Thebe. He experiences extreme regret and shame only on finally discovering that he has committed both incest and fratricide. But his regret is tied securely to the progressive revelation of fresh facts that emerge

---

[22] David Grene and Richmond Lattimore, Aeschylus, *Agamemnon* in *Greek Tragedies: Volume 1* (Chicago: Chicago University Press, 1991), lines 206–211.
[23] Grene and Lattimore, *Agamemnon*, lines 217–220.

slowly and enigmatically throughout the action of the play and that are
relayed by different agents including Tiresias, Jocasta, and the Theban and
Corinthian shepherds. Oedipus' moral residue is thus ultimately a function
of the emergence of facts mediated by a slow temporal contingency. Their
progressive discovery serves to increase his level of anxiety, but it is only on
the full disclosure of the choices he has made that he is drowned in sorrow
and shame. But Oedipus' moral residue manifests only after a time lag,
even though each stage of the action reveals new perspectives that put
already-existing facts into shadow and relief. We might argue that
Oedipus' original actions in killing his father and marrying his mother
were both invested with certain clusters of desires (anger in the first
instance, passion and relief in the second) but that these desires are recoded
on the discovery of the infractions of fratricide and incest that were
implicitly buried in his previous, ignorant actions. This suggests then
that desires-in-ignorance can be overturned and replaced by desires-in-
fact, which then become the real producers of moral residue. On this
reading, temporality becomes critical to the appearance of moral residue
and cannot be assumed to appear immediately in the weighing of different
courses of action that might each have a moral claim to one's attention.

A contrast to the representation of the relationship between choice and
temporality in *Oedipus Rex* is provided by Sophocles' *Philoctetes*. For
Neoptolemus, the time lag between choice and the onset of moral
residue is obscured by the fact that he makes the relevant moral choice
early in the play but only realizes its real significance upon fulfilling the
demands of that choice as he interacts with Philoctetes. At the start of the
play, Odysseus presents the young Neoptolemus with the stratagem for
stealing Herakles' magic bow from Philoctetes, who has been marooned
on the island of Lemnos for nine years by the Greek army prior to the
start of the action. Herakles' bow has been prophesized as critical to
winning the war. "If you don't do this," Odysseus warns ominously,
"you will inflict suffering on all Greeks."[24] Neoptolemus initially balks at
the thought of lying to gain the bow but is persuaded on the promise of
winning "a reputation for wisdom, as well as bravery" among the
Greeks.[25] Even though he finally pledges himself to the stratagem, it
cannot be achieved without him having to replicate a series of subsidiary
choices that subtend the original one and that also serve to amplify the
moral implications of original choice. Each subsidiary choice
Neoptolemus makes, such as lying about his mistreatment at the hands

[24] Sophocles, *Philoctetes*, lines 65–66.   [25] Sophocles, *Philoctetes*, lines 23–24.

of Odysseus and Menelaus, creating a false sense of camaraderie and friendship with Philoctetes by invoking Greek heroes of the older man's generation that have fallen in battle, and adducing the reasons of awe and respect for wanting to first touch the bow, all come to magnify the moral implications of the initial choice he makes in using deception. But the overall effect of both original and subsidiary choices is to expose him to contingent facts about Philoctetes that he could not have anticipated beforehand. Neoptolemus knows when he arrives on the island that Philoctetes is badly injured from an incurable sore on his foot and that he walks with a bad limp. He and the chorus of sailors also find ample evidence of Philoctetes' bare existence and impaired mobility from looking at the rudimentary utensils and pus-filled cloths left to dry at the mouth of his cave. But it is only in interacting with the older man that Neoptolemus realizes the true implications of the moral choice he has made.

The fairly straightforward stratagem for seizing the bow (a lie augmented by more lies in an ever-upward spiral) is progressively converted into a process by which Neoptolemus becomes an unwilling witness to Philoctetes' pain. This he does not anticipate. Neoptolemus first asks to touch the bow in admiration in lines 633–650 but then hands it back. Philoctetes returns the bow to him a second time without being prompted in lines 768–781, at which point the original stratagem of getting the bow may, to all intents and purposes, be thought to have been satisfied. But the second handing over of the bow occurs *after* the onset of the unbearable pain that racks Philoctetes' body, undermines his capacity for coherent speech, and makes him momentarily lose consciousness. The hiatus between the two moments is crucial, for when Philoctetes hands over the bow to Neoptolemus the second time, it is for safekeeping and after he has extracted from him a solemn oath, by which time the bow is arguably not the same trophy that Neoptolemus had asked to touch in the first place. The bow is now a charged object and has been resignified as an instrument born from bearing witness to the older man's pain. While the process of being converted into a witness comes only piecemeal for Neoptolemus, it is inextricably tied to the very process by which he seeks to actualize the original stratagem for taking the bow. Hence, at each step Neoptolemus also comes to learn more about Philoctetes' anxious nostalgia for home, the conditions under which he has survived alone all these years, and, most importantly, the terms of his extreme infirmity. The excruciating pain in Philoctetes's foot is the last instalment of this process of discovery. The sequence of conversion is well conveyed in Judith Affleck's translation of

the play, which mixes a modern-day colloquial English with Greek ono-
matopoeic sounds at all the critical junctures.

PHILOCTETES: It's all over for me, child. I can't keep it hidden from you.
    Attattai!
    It goes through me, through me. Ah, misery. It's all over, I'm finished, child.
        I'm being eaten alive.
    Papai! Apappapai! Papa! Papa! Papa! Papai!
    By the gods, child, if you have a sword to hand, strike at my foot. Cut it off,
        quick as you can. Don't spare my life. Go on, boy.
NEOPTOLEMUS: What is it that's suddenly making you scream and cry out like
    this!?
PHILOCTETES: Do you know, child?
NEOPTOLEMUS: What?
PHILOCTETES: Do you know, boy?
NEOPTOLEMUS: What do you want? I do not know.
PHILOCTETES: How can you not know? *Pappapappapai!*
NEOPTOLEMUS: The burden of this sickness is terrible.
PHILOCTETES: Terrible it is, beyond words' reach. But pity me.
NEOPTOLEMUS: What shall I do?[26]

While there is some level of disagreement among Greek scholars as to
whether the sounds *Papa! Pappai! Pappapappapai* and *Attattai* signify
a breakdown of sound and sense, or simply just of the meter of the lines,
all agree that they represent the moments at which the extreme pain
Philoctetes is experiencing annuls coherence and concomitantly afflicts
Neoptolemus with confusion about what course of action to take in the
face of what he is witnessing.[27] At one point he says to Philoctetes: "I've
been feeling your pain, upset by your troubles all this time."[28] The moral
residue we see in Neoptolemus comes from being reluctantly drawn into
feelings of compassion for Philoctetes, a compassion which is at the heart of
what Martha Nussbaum has interpreted as the superlative ethico-cognitive
construction of Sophocles' play, and which she holds up as exemplary for
thinking about pity, fear, and our responsibility to others.[29] Its implications are directly relevant to how we might understand the interaction

---

[26] Sophocles, *Philoctetes*, lines 742–758.
[27] For a review of interpretations regarding Philoctetes' cry in the context of such linguistic break-
    downs in Greek tragedy in general, see Sarah Nooter, *The Mortal Voice in the Tragedies of Aeschylus*
    (Cambridge: Cambridge University Press, 2017), 42–45.
[28] Sophocles, *Philoctetes*, lines 809–810.
[29] Martha Nussbaum, "Tragedy and Self-Sufficiency: Plato and Aristotle on Fear and Pity,"; "The
    'Morality of Pity': Sophocles's *Philoctetes*," 148–169; and *The Fragility of Goodness: Luck and Ethics in
    Greek Tragedy and Philosophy*.

between moral dilemma and moral residue in *Waiting for the Barbarians*, as we shall see presently.

The Genesis of Moral Residue for the Magistrate

Unlike Oedipus and Agamemnon, the Magistrate "knows what he is doing" before he does it. The skepticism he feels about Colonel Joll's interrogation methods at the beginning of the novel quickly turns into disdain and even anger after he has to put into effect the instructions Joll leaves behind on his departure. Instead, the Magistrate goes about systematically freeing the captured fisher folk and nomads left in his care and, by giving instructions to make the young boy who has been brutally tortured by Joll's soldiers more comfortable, he also tries to make practical amends for the mindless violence that has been visited upon the prisoners. And his skepticism becomes more pronounced after he himself is detained and tortured on his return from delivering the barbarian girl, by which point his every instinct is to actively distinguish himself from the Empire's cynicism. What looks like a moral conflict with respect to serving the Empire does not relate to what to do or not to do, but is rather to be seen at the more abstract level of his belief system.

There seems to be something persistently attractive to the Magistrate about the civilizational values that the Empire guarantees. It is this that he finds himself instinctively defending even when he clearly cannot subscribe to their brute exercise of power. Even in the sections in which he becomes an explicit rebel against the Empire's authority, the Magistrate is afflicted by second thoughts about the significance of his opposition, wondering what exactly he stands for "besides an archaic code of gentlemanly behaviour towards captured foes" and an opposition to "the new science of degradation that kills people on their knees, confused and disgraced in their own eyes."[30] More pertinently, he worries endlessly about what implications a barbarian lifestyle might raise when contrasted to the hitherto unacknowledged civilizational values that have always undergirded his lifestyle:

> And do I really after all believe what I have been saying? Do I really look forward to the triumph of the barbarian way: intellectual torpor, slovenliness, tolerance of disease and death? If we were to disappear would the barbarians spend their afternoons excavating our ruins? Would they preserve our census rolls and our grain-merchants ledgers in glass cases, or

---

[30] Coetzee, *Waiting*, 108.

devote themselves to deciphering the script of our love-letters? Is my
indignation at the course that Empire takes anything more than the peev-
ishness of an old man who does not want the ease of his last years on the
frontier disturbed?[31]

Ironically, the civilizational deficit implied in "intellectual torpor, sloven-
liness, tolerance of disease and death" and attributed to the barbarian way is
directly contradicted by the cache of wooden slips he unearths on his
amateur archeological digs from the dunes that lie two miles south of the
settlement. The 256 wooden slips are painted in a script he is not familiar
with, but whether syllabary or pictograph they trigger a fascination with
what they might mean; "a map of the barbarians in olden times, or
a representation of a lost pantheon."[32] The Magistrate's response to the
Empire is thus formally structured through a binary opposition – Empire/
barbarian – in which each term of the opposition is then recoded as
dialectically incorporating aspects of the opposite term – Empire-
civilization/Empire-barbarianism, but also barbarian-barbarianism/bar-
barian-civilization. This essentially proliferating structure is then replicated
along a second axis that also exercises his consciousness in the novel,
namely, the barbarian girl and the feelings he has toward her.
This second axis, however, has more profound consequences for him in
terms of the choices he makes because it is invested with strong desire and
emotional attachment, which is not what we find in the Empire axis. It is
the barbarian girl axis that becomes both the subject of the affliction
of second thoughts and engenders moral residue for the Magistrate.

The Magistrate's relationship with the barbarian girl is extraordinarily
complicated. At the simplest level, he is merely her benefactor for having
found her on the streets and taken her in to give her shelter, food, warmth,
and protection. She has been badly tortured by the agents of Empire: her
ankles are broken, she shuffles along on walking sticks, and is partially
blind from having had a heated fork held close to her eyeballs. This would
make her dependent on any benefactor not just for food and board, but
also for aid in physically navigating her way around. This baseline of
dependency is complicated in the relationship with the Magistrate, however, because on taking her in he immediately converts her into an object of
almost sacred veneration and sexual desire. This combination proves
highly problematic; try as he might, he can neither use her as a vehicle
for his own absolution nor have sex with her. When he eventually does
have sex with her on the way to returning her to her people it brings no

---

[31] Coetzee, *Waiting*, 52.   [32] Coetzee, *Waiting*, 16.

exhilaration but only a feeling of flaccid regret. Rather, the relationship he has with the barbarian girl while holding her captive in his room is reduced to a series of cleansing rituals inflected by possessive intimacy:

> I dry the right foot, shuffle to the other side, lift the leg of the wide drawers above her knee, and, fighting against drowsiness, begin to wash her left foot. "Sometimes this room gets very hot," I say. The pressure of her leg against my side does not lessen. I go on. "I will find clean bandages for your feet," I say, "but not now." I push the basin aside and dry the foot. I am aware of the girl struggling to stand up; but now, I think, she must take care of herself. My eyes close. It becomes an intense pleasure to keep them closed, to savour the blissful giddiness. I stretch out on the carpet. In an instant I am asleep. In the middle of the night I wake up cold and stiff. The fire is out, the girl is gone.
>
> But more often in the very act of caressing her I am overcome with sleep as if poleaxed, fall into oblivion sprawled upon her body, and wake an hour or two later dizzy, confused, thirsty. *These dreamless spells are like death to me or enchantment, blank, outside time.*[33]

It is useful to recall at this point the moment when Okonkwo beheads the *kotma* toward the end of *Things Fall Apart* where we are told that instead of springing into action the people of Umuofia are merged into the natural background, waiting. It is a moment in Achebe's novel that represents the staging of elemental time when it appears that anything at all is possible. This trope of elementalness is also seen in the moment the Magistrate describes to the barbarian girl of the time he is out hunting a ram but cannot bring himself to shoot it when the ram is caught in his rifle's cross-hairs:

> My pulse quickens: evidently it is not important to me that the ram die.
>
> He chews again, a single scythe of the jaws, and stops. In the clear silence of the morning I find an obscure sentiment lurking at the edge of my consciousness. With the buck before me suspended in immobility, there seems to be time for all things time even to turn my gaze inward and see what it is that has robbed the hunt of its savour: the sense that this has become no longer a morning's hunting but an occasion on which either the proud ram bleeds to death on the ice or the old hunter takes aim; *that for the duration of this frozen moment the stars are locked in a configuration in which events are not themselves but stand for other things.*[34]

It is not entirely insignificant that, a few pages earlier, the Magistrate likens the barbarian girl to the little silver-fox cub he also keeps in his

[33] Coetzee, *Waiting*, 28–29, 31, emphasis added.   [34] Coetzee, *Waiting*, 39–40, emphasis added.

rooms, telling her people will gossip that he keeps two animals in his room, a "fox and a girl." She is understandably not amused by this comparison and the fox is never mentioned again, but the point of the analogy, when set alongside the suspended moment when he stands before the ram, and the one in which he describes himself falling into a slumber like death, enchantment, blankness, and outside time, is to notify us that the barbarian girl also functions for him as an irruption of the elemental, of the once-and-repeated-time of endless possibilities. But unlike the moment we saw in *Things Fall Apart*, in *Waiting for the Barbarians* the elemental is not resolved in favor of the assertion of certainty (for Okonkwo), but rather as the nodal point for the proliferation of endless contradictions. Is it, as he muses to himself, that he wants to possess the barbarian girl whole and unmarked, that is to say, not scarified by a violent history, or is it precisely "the traces of a history that her body bears" that make her attractive to him?[35] In different lights the Magistrate feels either sexually attracted or completely revolted by what he sees as her gross barbarian body, thus allowing the incipient and always-present implications of the Empire's civilizational values that he subconsciously defends to also influence his aesthetic judgment regarding her sexual desirability. His attitude toward her is inflected by his subliminal ascription to the civilizational guarantees of the Empire, which are, in their turn, subtended by the impulse toward aesthetic judgment and control. Something of Edward Said's *Orientalism* and the ways in which under imperial regimes knowledge and aesthetic judgment often subserve power seems pertinent to the Magistrate's attitude toward the barbarian girl.[36]

When he returns her to her people, the Magistrate is filled with what seems like a sense of ontological regret and shame, of moral residue. As he says, he has wanted to make reparation, irrespective of the fact that this has been mixed with other questionable motives: "there must always be a place for penance and reparation," for he "will not be touched with the contagion and turned into a creature that believes in nothing."[37] But penance and reparation for what exactly, we might ask? Is it for the fact that as a servant of Empire, he is automatically implicated in their attitudes to the barbarians? Or that he arrives in her life when she has ceased believing in fathers and benefactors? Or is it for the fact that he had effectively been keeping her as a sex slave and had been emotionally abusive when he went off to sleep with a prostitute and thus effectively denigrated her

[35] Coetzee, *Waiting*, 64.   [36] Edward Said, *Orientalism* (London: Vintage, 1979).
[37] Coetzee, *Waiting*, 81.

womanhood and sexuality? All these motives coalesce into a crisis of liberal humanist consciousness, something that has been amply remarked upon by commentators on the novel.[38] But the Magistrate's desire for penance and reparation may also be read as essentially features of moral residue that pertain not only to his conflicted impulses toward the barbarian girl, but also to his inherent impulse toward revision, an aspect of the affliction of second thoughts.

It is the Magistrate's impulse toward revision that instils in him the desire to both possess the barbarian girl and also efface her as a material body. But part of this impulse of revision requires that he convert substantive facts about her into contingent ones. Substantive facts of her body, such as her broken ankles and scars, are re-transcribed by him as possibly contingent and thus potentially substitutable by other features, not necessarily present, even if imaginable (such as a ponytail, say). In his mind, this would then allow her to transcend the brutal history composed on her body by the violations of Empire. But the things the Magistrate seeks to interpret as contingent are not incidental to her identity by the time he interacts with her; rather, they are fundamental to her body's being-in-time and thus to Empire's history. At an earlier point in her life, she would not have borne the scars he sees on her, and at a later time she might well have appeared more beautiful. But those moments are not the ones in which he interacts with her.

The process of converting substantive facts into contingent ones is part of the Magistrate's impulse toward revision and is undertaken through various devices of interpretation. It requires that the barbarian girl be reconstituted as something other than she really is, which is a girl who has been separated from her people and suffered immense trauma by seeing her father tortured to death before her, a girl who herself has endured gross physical torture that reduced her to blindness and begging, and a girl who is practically held captive by a man who for unclear reasons (he never shares his sexual fantasies and doubts with her) repeatedly subjects her to the process of sexual arousal but never quite gets to the point of actually sleeping with her while she is his captive. The Magistrate's impulse toward revision, which is not a singular impulse but an entire process for the interpretative disassembling and reassembling of the barbarian girl as an

---

[38] See Sue Kossew, "The Politics of Shame and Redemption in J. M. Coetzee's *Disgrace*," *Research in African Literatures* (2003): 155–162; but most poignantly, Teresa Dovey, *The Novels of J. M. Coetzee: Lacanian Allegories* (Johannesburg: Ad. Donker, 1988) where Dovey reads the Magistrate's dreams as symbolizing different stages of the crisis in his liberal humanist consciousness.

object of interpretation, is the means by which his guilt is rationalized and for which he requires penance and reparation.

The contrast here with Neoptolemus's response to Philoctetes is instructive. For, as we may recall, once Philoctetes is afflicted by the pain in his foot and becomes incoherent from that pain, his body-in-pain becomes a brute material fact that Neoptolemus can no longer ignore. Philoctetes' screams force Neoptolemus to completely reverse his plans to trick him of the bow. Not only that, they also afflict Neoptolemus with deep emotional pain. For the Magistrate, whatever emotional disturbance he experiences on seeing the tortures the barbarian girl has been exposed to is grafted onto the complex process of revision by which everything potentially proliferates further questions and those questions even more questions, in a dizzying spiral of self-interrogations. The barbarian girl's axis of signification poses a stark moral contrast to the one signified by Empire, but both of them are rendered dialectically unstable by the Magistrate's predisposition toward revision and second thoughts. This is where his crisis resides.

"But what gray man among the vines is this?"[39]

All the characters we have encountered thus far do not suffer the plague of doubt. Okonkwo is decisive and that leads him to contravene explicit codes of behavior within his community, while if Ezeulu is afflicted by doubts about his role as chief priest, they do not prevent him from taking controversial decisions that no one either in his family or his tribe can fathom. Soyinka's Professor is essentially a lunatic who governed by the phantasms inside the theatre of his own mind, while for Sethe, the decision to kill her children is one she never veers from or tries to explain, even when her mind becomes saturated with traumatic images from the past as a consequence of that decision. None of them suffer any form of moral residue for the decisions that they take. The Magistrate's character is different from all these in that, for him, it is the very act of choosing that produces the crisis. It is choice that proliferates doubt, and not the reverse,

---

[39] These are the lines that the young lady uses to describe the gray man in John Crowe Ransome's poem "Piazza Piece," www.poetryfoundation.org/poems/49146/piazza-piece, last accessed July 6, 2020. The poem is fascinating for being simultaneously a love poem that turns on the carpe diem conceit ("your ears are soft and small/and listen to an old man not at all") and also a poem about Death coming for his maiden ("For I shall have my lovely lady soon"). The Magistrate strikes me very much as a "gray man" in the first sense, but only to the degree that his thoughts have to be constantly revised even to himself.

for his tortoise character ensures that nothing can be asserted without being subjected to a series of revisions codified in the affliction of second thoughts. This process may be interpreted ultimately as a painful process of verification of his own self, of his political and natural environment, and, most importantly, of the single most important social relationship he participates in in the course of the novel.

Perhaps it is not the characters themselves that must be examined but the authors who created them. None of Achebe's, Soyinka's, or Morrison's characters that I can think of are hesitant or uncertain of their choices. They seem propelled by absolute certainty. They believe – and we are made to believe with them – that whatever decision they made was *the only one possible under the circumstances.* In contrast, Coetzee's entire literary project seems to be devoted to putting characters in impossible ethical conundrums and then watching them struggle under second thoughts. None of his protagonists make decisions they are entirely confident of or simply satisfied with. The difference between Coetzee and the others may be due to him never being entirely at ease as a spokesperson of any ethico-political community. Achebe was famous for writing what has been described by Harry Garuba as "teacherly texts," that is to say, texts that while not didactic, aimed to teach Achebe's African readers something specific about what it was to be an African after colonialism.[40] This is a point also amply elaborated upon by Simon Gikandi in his book on Achebe. The same sense of teacherliness may be extended to Soyinka and Morrison, where in each instance they are proclaimed to be the spokespersons of their African and African American communities respectively. But Coetzee would find it extremely difficult to make such an assured proclamation. Unlike them, having been formed within the emotionally exhausting milieu that was apartheid South Africa, he is bereft of any secure community upon whose behalf he might deign to speak. His fictional characters express this difficulty by not just being representatives of their own personal crises, but also by being divided as to what exactly those crises might entail. The problem is as much epistemological as it is ontological. But the effect of it is to generate a contrastive model for working out what the terms for thinking about postcolonial tragedy might be. It is a model continually to be reflected upon, and as in the case of his characters, one that is regularly subject to revision. We shall return to this question more fully in the final chapter.

---

[40] Harry Garuba, "Teacherly Texts: Imagining Futures in Nuruddin Farah's Past Imperfect Trilogy," *Boundary 2*, 244: 2 (2017): 15–30.

CHAPTER 8

Enigmatic Variations, Language Games, and the Arrested Bildungsroman
Arundhati Roy's The God of Small Things[*]

Amidst motifs of time, temporality, and the eternal instant in T. S. Eliot's "Burnt Norton," there also appear the recurring appeals of a bird drawing attention to the laughter of children amongst foliage:

> Footfalls echo in the memory
> Down the passage which we did not take
> Towards the door we never opened
> Into the rose-garden . . .
> . . .
>
> Go, said the bird, for the leaves were full of children,
> Hidden excitedly, containing laughter.
> . . .
>
> Sudden in a shaft of sunlight
> Even while the dust moves
> There rises the hidden laughter
> Of children in the foliage
> Quick now, here, now, always —[1]

While the entire first movement of the *Four Quartets* has many philosophical reflections on time, various motifs that invoke the world of fairy tale also present themselves: the rose garden, leaves and foliage, children's laughter, the door not taken, and a speaking (or singing) bird. By linking the deserted rose-garden to the world of children and fairy tales, Eliot also introduces a favorite theme in depictions of children in literature, namely, the garden as the microcosm of both pattern and wildness where children are invigorated in their potential for re-dreaming the world. And yet, given that children are

---

[*] The title to this chapter is inspired by Lissa Paul's "Enigma Variations: What Feminist Theory Knows about Children's Literature," *Signal*, 54 (September 1987): 186–202, in which she attends to the variations of characterization, storyline, and plot in the criticism of children's literature.

[1] T. S. Eliot, "Burnt Norton," in *The Poems of T. S. Eliot*, eds., Christopher Ricks and Jim McRue (Baltimore: Johns Hopkins University Press, 2015), 179–184.

hinted at in the poem only fleetingly through the metonymic implication of their laughter, their innocence is registered as a sign of what is hoped for yet remains elusive and ephemeral. All that is present in reality is the invitation proffered by the bird, never quite taken up in "Burnt Norton," to cross the threshold into the garden of imagined possibilities.

Gardens also provide philosophical templates of nature and time, as both Michel Foucault and Jorge Luis Borges have instructed us. In contrasting heterotopias to utopias, Foucault suggests that the latter "are something like counter-sites, a kind of effectively enacted utopia in which the real sites, all the other real sites that can be found within the culture, are simultaneously represented, contested, and inverted."[2] Heterotopias for him juxtapose a single real place with several spaces that may themselves be incompatible. He recommends the oriental garden as one privileged example of heterotopia, for it has "very deep and seemingly superimposed meanings," among which is the fusion of the sacred and the secular as they are reflected by the cardinal points of the world, and the navel or umbilicus of the universe as it is encapsulated in the fountain at the center of the garden. The superimposition of universal space upon the material design of the oriental garden also means that the garden becomes a microcosm of simultaneities, at once a category of space and an invitation for speculation about the reiterating patterns of divine or specular time – much like Aristotle's description in *De Anima* of the interconnection of the celestial spheres and their correlation to the animation of the world itself. For Aristotle, all the elements that comprise the universe are in some sense "animate" in that they encompass a principle of movement that is linked to an internal symmetry that they each possess. In this Aristotelian model, the eleven spheres of the universe orbit the earth in a geocentric model that, and while this model was centuries later replaced by the heliocentrism of Galileo and others, it is still residually retained in the idea that events within the natural world are ultimately interlinked with elements of the universe. Material locations such as Foucault's oriental garden encapsulate this interlinkage.

For its part, in Borges's "The Garden of Forking Paths," the mystical garden of Yu Tsun provides occasion for contemplating the confluence of all temporal paths including those both taken and not taken. The story does not replicate the Aristotelian geocentric model but rather that of the infinite layering of all time and temporality in a non-repeatable instant.

---

[2] Michel Foucault, "Of Other Spaces: Utopias and Heterotopias," *Architecture/Mouvement/ Continuité*, (October 1984): 1–9.

Borges's story implicitly echoes the enigma posed by Eliot in "Burnt Norton": "If all time is eternally present/ All time is irredeemable." But the contradiction in this statement may also be thought to derive from its direct opposite. For if time can be conceived of as eternally present then it can also be imagined as never annulled in its individual instantiations, as we saw in Sethe's concept of rememory, for example. Time does not flow like a Heraclitan river but is composed of granulation, with each granule harboring the potential for intensifying the effects of choice as composed within the crucible of events.

The God of Small Things may be read against the background of the many literary representations of gardens as enigmatic locations of epistemological confluences. However, if the novel echoes any of the previous literature on gardens, it does so not directly but by taking on the themes of childhood and the cycles of history and employing them as elements with concentric ramifications that interlink the sphere of human action and the domain of nature in a single continuum. The garden that appears in the novel is only a surrogate of nature itself, which is depicted as volatile and excessive, a capricious agent within the domain of the tragic plot itself. As we shall see, the concentric interlinkage depicted in the novel is accomplished via a series of metonymic transfers that go in several directions at once and encompass the movement from social relations to the volatility of nature, and from the domain of privacy to that of representation in one chaotic and ultimately tragic series of events.

Child-Talk and Small Things

The God of Small Things tells the story of the Ipe family in the town of Ayemenem. The story is related predominantly from the perspective of Rahel and her fraternal twin brother Estha and interlaces two diegetic timeframes. The first unfolds during the course of two fateful weeks in 1969 when the twins are seven, and the family is visited for Christmas by Sophie Mol and Margaret Kochamma, their cousin and her mother from London. Sophie Mol drowns in a storm whilst accompanying the twins to the History House across the swollen Meenachal river. The second timeframe takes place over a few hours some twenty-three years later, when Rahel returns from a failed marriage in America to be reunited with her twin brother, who she hears has been "Re-Returned" after being sent away to live with his estranged father following the tragic events of the earlier timeframe. The series of incidents that lead to Sophie Mol's death coincide in the earlier timeframe with the beating to death by police of Velutha, the untouchable lover of Ammu, the twins' mother. Because the children had also grown to love Velutha, his death affects them badly. In the chaotic aftermath of their cousin's death, Estha is tricked by his grandaunt Baby Kochamma into answering yes to a seemingly innocuous question posed to him by a policeman at the Kottayam station where the badly beaten Velutha is being detained. It turns out Estha has answered yes to the question of whether they had been abducted by Velutha. It is Baby Kochamma's accusation that Velutha had raped Ammu that provided the excuse used by the policemen to beat him up mercilessly. The beating occurred at the History House where the twins themselves had been hiding after their boat capsized, and Sophie Mol was lost. As a consequence of all these unhappy events, Estha suffers unspeakable pangs of guilt for the rest of his days, while Rahel, in complete emotional identification with her twin brother, is voided of all motivation and is instead filled with a numbing sense of chaos. Thus, as adults, "Quiet" and "Emptiness" come to mark Rahel and Estha's existential responses to the trauma they had experienced as seven-year-olds.

In *The God of Small Things*, the stories about the deaths of Sophie Mol and Velutha are relayed piecemeal across several chapters and from different vantage points. Each instance of retelling provides us with a fragment of the two stories as if to incite our curiosity and keep us fixated on unravelling the details surrounding the family's trauma. As Baneth-Nouailhetas puts it: "The narrative thus stretches in two directions, first towards the past and reminiscence, then towards the outcome of the story, constantly referred to in proleptic hints, that ultimately come together like the pieces of a puzzle."[3] But the focalization of the two deaths through the eyes of Rahel and her brother also serves to give us progressive, if fragmentary, instalments of the collapse of their own internal emotional landscapes. We find in the second timeframe that the now thirty-year-olds replicate the same structure of feeling conveyed in the language games of their childhood some twenty-three years earlier, and that this replication is a means of holding on to the best of their childhood, where, as we shall see, they were profoundly creative in their use of language.

Even though the distribution of the children's story across two timeframes immediately suggests the shape of a fractured bildungsroman, the traumatic events of their childhood seal them so firmly into the discourse of tragedy that theirs becomes not the story of growing up but rather the teleology of an arrested development. The arrested development is signaled for us in the distinctive language of the novel, which combines several

---

[3] Emilienne Baneth-Nouailhetas, *The God of Small Things: Arundhati Roy* (Delhi: MLBD, 2000), 49.

linguistic quirks in an evocative and superbly poetic discourse and maintains the perspective of childhood across the two temporal frames. The novel mimes a childlike tone not only within the predominant focalization through Rahel's perspective when events occur in the vicinity of her and her brother, but also through the omniscient third-person narrator's voice, when events and historical information are conveyed that do not necessarily connect to the twins' immediate experiences. The consistency of this linguistic register not only helps cast a puerile inflection upon the world of adults but also reveals the implacable escapism that childhood innocence performs for the twins. In Roy's novel, the hermeneutic of child's play, which effectively shapes both the narrative form as well as the specific structure of memory, is progressively overwhelmed by the grave impositions of a history that has itself been shaped by the catastrophic interdictions of politics, the caste system, and what the novel calls the Love Laws. All these then amount to "the distribution of the sensible," in the terms outlined by Jacques Rancière. For as Rancière notes, the aesthetic itself is "the delimitation of spaces and times, of the visible and the invisible, of speech and noise, that simultaneously determines the place and the stakes of politics as a form of experience."[4] The social policing of the boundaries of what is desirable and what is repugnant, of who can be loved and by how much that we find amplified in *The God of Small Things*, is also part of what Rancière describes as "the politics of the aesthetic," for such politics entails questions of choice, agency, and their interdiction as much as questions of visibility and desire. Even though the novel is consistent in its deployment of a humorous, child-centered linguistic register, by the end, this register reveals itself to be the mark not of play and plenitude but of nostalgia and melancholia. The consistency of the childlike voice becomes both boon and burden because it shows that the twins are, in a sense, sheltered from the full realization of their trauma and stunted in a perpetual juvenility from which there is no end and no escape. Their bodies continue to grow into adulthood but psychically they remain trapped in the minds of children.

The novel also outlines the limitation of choices that are imposed upon Ammu, and yet despite her centrality to the tragic events she is only one of a number of female figures in the text that have constraints placed upon their freedom of self-expression. To a large degree the novel illustrates what Lissa Paul says about the representation of women in literature: "Women

---

[4] Jacques Rancière, *The Politics of Aesthetics: The Distribution of the Sensible* (London: Continuum, 2004), 13.

in literature are disproportionately shown as physically trapped in rooms, attics, in their father's houses, or in their husband's. In those enclosed spaces women go mad or silent, or they die."[5] Roy illustrates all three aspects of the entrapment and deterioration of the lives of women in *The God of Small Things* but adds an extra aspect that is more profound for the overall tragedy of the novel. This is the idea that women's entrapment also serves to fundamentally atrophy their character and make them depleted in their capacity for either self-care or the care of others, thus echoing what we saw in the Introduction about the effects of the reversal of fortune in Aristotle's *Nicomachean Ethics* and the *Poetics*. For, as we might recall, Aristotle argues that the obstruction of access to worldly goods, which include access to the succor of *philia* among other things, leads to the incapacitation for undertaking ethically salient choices, and thus ultimately, to tragedy. The atrophying of the self is also depicted in the character of Baby Kochamma, who is actively malicious and instrumental in implanting unbearable guilt in the young Rahel and Estha. Baby Kochamma suffers an episode of unrequited adolescent love that extends into her adulthood. The burden of her loveless life and her permanent residence in her parents' home turns her into a source of ambient menace to anyone she deems less fortunate than her, which in the immediate context of the Ipe household means Ammu, Rahel, Estha, then Velutha. As we shall see, this ambient menace comes to tincture the world of the children and their mother and swells to become an active agent in their ultimate destruction as a close-knit unit.

The title of the novel sets up a series of contrasts between small and big things. This is given specific expression several times throughout the novel but especially in the statement that the Ipe household is a place where "only the Small Things were said. The Big Things lurked unsaid inside."[6] Given the fact that the novel's tragedy is intricately tied to over-determining processes that go beyond individual characters while at the same time also coinciding with their personal hopes, fears, and vague ideas, Small Things and Big Things may also be transposed onto a register of causalities. Big Things pertain to large social realities such as caste, religion, patriarchy, and (communist) politics. These imply deterministic codes that seek to regulate individual behaviour and social relations according to

<hr/>

[5] Lissa Paul, ibid; see also Baneth-Nouailhetas, *The God of Small Things: Arundhati Roy* and Catherine Lanone, "Seeing the World Through Red-Coloured Glasses: Desire and Death in The God of Small Things," in Jean-Pierre Durix and Caroline Durix, eds. *Reading Arundhati Roy's* The God of Small Things (Paris; Dijon: Editions Universitaires de Dijon, 2002), 125–144.

[6] Arundhati Roy, *The God of Small Things* (London: Vintage, 1997), 165.

imponderable rules that come with attendant threats of punishment and exclusion. For their part, Small Things reveal themselves mainly in the domain of feelings, emotions, and internal states that color the characters' personal dispositions and agendas. The ethically consequential individual choices that shape the tragedy may be traced from the domain of Small Things as they contingently interact with that of Big Things. Something of the domain of distinctions implied by Small Things and Big Things is echoed through Larry McCaslin, Rahel's American husband, who signally fails to grasp the significance of the chaos in Rahel's eyes during lovemaking. As the narrator tells us:

> He didn't know that in some places, like the country that Rahel came from, various kinds of despair competed for primacy. And that *personal* despair could never be desperate enough. That something happened when personal turmoil dropped by at the wayside shrine of the vast, violent, circling, driving, ridiculous, insane, unfeasible, public turmoil of a nation. That Big God howled like a hot wind and demanded obeisance. Then Small God (*cosy and contained, private and limited*) came away cauterized, laughing numbly at his own temerity. Inured by the confirmation of his own inconsequence, he became resilient and truly indifferent. Nothing mattered much. Nothing much mattered. And the less it mattered, the less it mattered. It was never important enough. Because Worse Things had happened . . . So Small God laughed a hollow laugh . . . He climbed into people's eyes and became an exasperating expression.[7]

The large scale of Big Things, which in this case is the chaos of India itself, not only renders the Small Things of inner life unremarkable but also threatens to entirely abrogate the possibility of their expression. It is this abrogation that makes the Small Things climb into people's eyes, registering in them a distant look of bewilderment and despair. This collocation of historical scale and the impossibility of personal expression is instituted as a structuring device within the novel, and as we shall see, ramifies at different levels of its vision of tragedy.

Small Things are also repeatedly emblematized in the narrative through certain identificatory items and motifs: the leaf on Velutha's back that predicts the monsoons, the moth that flutters inside Rahel whenever she feels nervous or unloved, Estha's Elvis Presley puff, Sophie Mol's thimble, Chacko's skyblue Packard, Baby Kochamma's garden, and Mammachi's violin. Each item is incrementally echoed and repeated throughout the narrative so as to create a series of resonances around the individual

---

[7] Roy, *The God of Small Things*, 19; emphasis added.

characters that they are attached to. They become for the reader the indices of emotional states. Broader nature for its part falls in the domain of Big Things, and yet nature's beauty also harbors a volatility that does not subtend human action but rather seems to fundamentally confound it. When Baby Kochamma goes to America to be trained as a landscape artist and returns with a vengeful and domineering spirit to raise "a fierce, bitter garden" that she later leaves wild, the motif of the untended garden attached to her falls within the domain of Small Things and is in sharp contrast to the larger landscape of monsoon winds, the Ayemenem river, and the thick tropical foliage that for much of the novel provides a backdrop of natural cycles to the unfolding events.[8] This natural cycle later on joins the mess of multiple causalities that coalesce together to shape the tragic events.

Enigmatic Variations, Child Egos, and Trapped Women

It is worth examining some other novels which foreground enigmatic variations in order to contrast them with *The God of Small Things* and further work out their implications. Unless adults are directly involved in the adventure or mystery that children are pursuing, novels for children and young adults typically represent the adult world as a series of often bewildering enigmas that the children are obliged to navigate in their fraught process of social evolution.[9] These enigmas may or may not impose

---

[8] Roy, *The God of Small Things*, 26.
[9] There were significant differences in what "growing up" meant for girls and boys from the mid-1900s, considered as the period that marked a boom and transformation in the world of children's literature. Thus, Louisa M. Alcott's universally beloved *Little Women* (1868) framed the difficulties in Jo's navigation of the demands of girlhood and housework with reference to motifs from Bunyan's *The Pilgrim's Progress*, while Mary Sewell's *Patience Hart's First Experience* (1862) was a morality tale of instruction for young girl readers burdened with the care of others. The most popular titles for boys in the period on the other hand, such as those by Captain Marryat, G. A. Henty, R. A. Ballantyne, H. Rider Haggard, and Anthony Hope, typically set masculine adventure narratives in the outer reaches of empire where boys figured out the rules for becoming men. Mark Twain's *Tom Sawyer* and *Huckleberry Finn* provided a more local and domestic context for achieving adulthood, but in doing so also implicitly entangled the plots with questions of American settler colonialism. Even though the landscape of children's literary publishing has changed substantially in the twentieth and twenty-first centuries, such that by the 2000s Philip Pullman's *His Dark Materials Trilogy* (1995–2000) establishes equal male and female roles for the multiverse fantasy adventure and Suzanne Collins's *The Hunger Games Trilogy* (2008–2010) features a lead female character amongst a team of both boys and girls in a complicated dystopian context, the literary division in emphases for boys and girls still remains strangely resolute. The history of children's writing is now a large and highly complicated academic field and I make no pretense of having a thorough grasp of it. Instead I have taken my cues from Peter Hunt, ed. *Children's Literature: The Development of Criticism* (London: Routledge, 1990); Roderick Cave and Sara Ayad, *A History of Children's Books in 100 Books* (London: Fidelity Books, 1997); Seth Lerer, *Children's Literature: A Reader's History, from Aesop to*

direct threats to the world of childhood. In a children's novel such as Twain's *Tom Sawyer*, for instance, all the enigmas of the adult world have a largely benign and non-threatening character that Tom navigates through the performative mode of the trickster hero. His crafty mischief-making acts as a guarantee of his capacity to control the outcomes of events in which he is a participant – all of them except the ones surrounding Injun Joe. Injun Joe's introduction into the novel triggers a different set of emotional responses in Tom and his friend Huck Finn and is categorically different from all the other adult enigmas they are obliged to navigate. One night, Tom and Huck chance upon Injun Joe's murder of Dr. Robinson and for their own safety swear to keep it a tight secret between them. But Tom steps forward during Injun Joe's trial at the courthouse to stand witness against him. When Injun Joe jumps out of the courthouse window and escapes, he immediately becomes a menacing threat to Tom and Huck. This fundamentally unsettles the sense of freedom and adventure that the two boys have enjoyed up to that point. The terror and dread looming over them are only alleviated at the very end of the novel when Injun Joe is found to have died trapped inside the abandoned catacombs.

Significantly, however, the Injun Joe thread in the novel also serves to interweave the colonized Other into the novel's settler colonial social imaginary. The real town of Hannibal, where Mark Twain spent his childhood, is the inspiration behind the township where both Tom Sawyer and Huckleberry Finn live. Hannibal's Wikipedia site informs us quite simply that, "The site of Hannibal was long occupied by various cultures of indigenous Native American tribes."[10] This is delivered without any further elaboration about the presence of Native Americans. The town was also, like many such towns at the time, the site of slave auctions and slave owning practices. Notices in the *St. Louis Republican* of 1849 that reached Hannibal in the period had listings for the sale of slaves, so, as Shelley Fisher Fishkin notes, even if theirs may not have been the overtly

---

Harry Potter (Chicago: Chicago University Press, 2008); and Perry Nodelman, *The Hidden Adult: Defining Children's Literature* (Baltimore: Johns Hopkins University Press, 2008). I have also benefited tremendously from many conversations over the past decade on this and other subjects with Siobhan O'Flynn from the University of Toronto. O'Flynn's blogpost on the differences in the aesthetics of compassion and children's refusal to sacrifice others as a concession to arguments about the greater social good in *Tom Sawyer*, *Huckleberry Finn*, *Harry Potter*, and *The Hunger Games* (http://siobhanoflynn.com/why-the-hunger-games-is-not-harry-potter-why-we-should-care/; last accessed Dec. 23, 2019) was particularly helpful in shaping my own thinking on the relationship between children and the enigmas posed by the adult world.

[10] "Hannibal, Missouri," see https://en.wikipedia.org/wiki/Hannibal,_Missouri; last accessed Feb. 25, 2020.

brutal kind, "it was slavery nonetheless, with the all too familiar mix of pain and powerlessness."[11] The town's slaving background is of course pertinent to the descriptions of the life of slavery in *Huckleberry Finn*. In *Tom Sawyer*, however, by positing Injun Joe as a vengeful criminal and a liar, the Native American is assigned the role of moral deficit and thus provides a stark contrast to the young Tom, whose heroism is a functional aspect of his position as part of American settler colonialism. Since the bildungsroman represented in *Tom Sawyer* is arguably focalized through a white settler sensibility, one of its objectives is to show the white boy's induction into adulthood through the exercise of civilized impulses and moral choices. The romantic thread encapsulated in the relationship of Tom and Becky Thatcher is a crucial aspect of Tom's maturation process and ends in the retention of the benefits of childhood amply leavened by the adulation from the town's adults. The security provided by his share of the wealth from Injun Joe's recovered loot also means that Tom's future access to adult respectability is guaranteed. Whereas Tom Sawyer is progressively grafted into the values of the adult settler colonial world, in contrast, *Huckleberry Finn* shows Huck's trajectory moving in the opposite direction. From the very beginning of the novel, Huck completely renounces the values of the adult world, repeatedly declaring them as constraining, confusing, and outright oppressive. His defense of the black servant Jim against Tom's several mischievous schemes also marks the two boys as different in their adoption of the values of the adult world. For Huck, these values are not to be investigated for whatever enigmatic qualities they might possess but rather must be completely disavowed, since to understand them is also to concede to their rationalization of unthinking injustice toward people such as Jim and himself. That Huck's father Pap seeks to kidnap him so as to benefit from the $6,000 he was awarded from Injun Joe's loot also shows that Huck's life is marked by unresolvable menace from the most intimate of familial sources, again in complete contrast to

---

[11] Shelley Fisher Fishkin, *Lighting Out for Territory: Reflections on Mark Twain and American Culture* (Oxford: Oxford University Press, 1996), 19. Fishkin has a detailed account of the conditions of slavery in Hannibal but does not mention Native Americans either, except in her discussion of Joe Douglass, the real-life half-Indian inspiration behind the character of Injun Joe, who was, unlike his fictional alter-ego, a man of perfectly good standing in the community and not the evil murderer depicted in *Tom Sawyer*. For his part, Mark Twain had a thoroughly ambivalent attitude toward Native Americans. This covered the entire gamut from bigotry to curious charitableness, especially following his trip to New Zealand and Australia in 1895, where he got to learn at first hand the degree of dispossession that the aboriginal populations had suffered. On Twain's attitudes to Native Americans, see Kerry Driscoll, *Mark Twain Among the Indians and Other Indigenous Peoples* (Berkeley: California University Press, 2018).

the family life of his friend Tom Sawyer. For each of the two boys, however, the enigmas of the adult world are ultimately resolved in such a way as to protect their ego-formation from any existential damage. Rather than challenging their sense of their own moral positionality, whatever bafflement the adult world offers Tom and Huck ultimately only serves to validate their ego-formation.[12]

In contrast to Mark Twain's novels, Rudyard Kipling's *Kim* shows us the eponymous child protagonist's progressive introduction to the mysteries of India as a mode of induction into the dynamics of colonial surveillance, of which he becomes an accomplice. Kim navigates the mysteries of India with a confidence that draws on his race as the inflection of larger historical significance. If the thirteen-year-old Kim becomes the focal point of the quest for colonial assurance in a world of bewildering variety, he already arrives at this quest with the advantages of the ethnographic know-how that derives from his privileged position as an unwitting agent of imperial geopolitical scheming.[13] Unlike Tom or Huck, the stakes are much higher for Kim, so that what appear to be enigmas of the adult world are merely the thresholds for his display of epistemological mastery. As S. P. Mohanty notes: "Kim's marvellous facility in inhabiting India – in being able to navigate its social mores just as easily as the narrow and confusing corridors of its urban bazaars, to score points over a small-town policeman by outdoing him in verbal abuse – is underscored from the

[12] Shelley Fisher Fishkin also makes the intriguing argument that the first-person narrative voice of *Huckleberry Finn*, with its innocence and distinctive speech forms, was subliminally inspired by the black oral traditions that Mark Twain was exposed to in his childhood in Hannibal and that he celebrated throughout his life. However, her argument about the inspiration of African American voices behind Huck Finn goes directly counter to what Mark Twain himself states about his inspiration for the character, whom he says was based on Tom Blakenship, an "ignorant, unwashed, insufficiently fed" white kid with the utmost unrestricted liberties who grew up in Hannibal when Twain was a child there. See her, *Was Huck Black? Mark Twain and the African American Voices* (Oxford: Oxford University Press, 1993). The quotation about Tom Blakenship is taken from Twain's autobiography cited on p. 14 of Fishkin's book.

[13] *Kim* was published in 1901, in the same year that the census of India revealed that there were 170,000 Europeans on the subcontinent, including soldiers, with another half as many Eurasians. This was in comparison to 294 million Indians. The novel illustrates what historians of India have termed "information anxiety" by which is meant the colonial desire to "know" the native, to map them, and by various instruments such as censuses, schools, and the postal system, to ultimately gain more assured control over them. The period in which *Kim* is set compounds this form of colonial desire because it also coincides with the rise of a resurgent Russia during the last days of the Ottoman Empire. The geopolitics of the region were something to be carefully considered for any of European powers that sought to gain dominance in the region at the collapse of the Ottomans. On colonial information anxiety, see C. A. Bayly, *Empire and Information: Intelligence Gathering and Social Communication in India, 1780–1870* (Cambridge: Cambridge University Press, 1996) and Bernard Cohn, *Colonialism and its Forms of Knowledge: The British in India* (Princeton: Princeton University Press, 1996).

beginning." For Kim will effortlessly become what his guiding lama, "and for that matter, most of the Indian characters in the novel – cannot quite become: a competent and reliable reader of texts, ultimately, in fact, of society as text."[14]

Whereas *Tom Sawyer* and *Kim* are recounted by third-person narrators that establish different relations of proximity and distance from the young characters being represented, *Huckleberry Finn* is firmly rooted in the speech forms and worldview of childhood. For a contrasting example of a novel narrated directly by a child narrator but with an essentially adult world thematic, consider NoViolet Bulawayo's *We Need New Names*.[15] Crucial to the first part of Bulawayo's novel is the translation of the enigmas of the adult world into the children's universe of play. Even though the slum world of Paradise where Darling and her friends live is full of the most ghastly details of AIDS, suicide, political violence, rapacious evangelical Christianity, rape, childhood pregnancy, and even a primal scene in which ten-year-old Darling, the child narrator, hears her mother having sex with a stranger while she hides under their small bed, the entire narrative is designed to translate everything into the hermeneutic of children's play. None of the nasty things that take place in Paradise pose a direct threat to the ego-integration of the children.[16] Furthermore, the rules of each game that Darling and her friends play are the subject of intense debates amongst themselves. These debates come to establish a reiterated agonistic structure of raucous interlocution, that is to say, the rules of each game are established through debate and negotiation rather than being the imposition of one or other of the children, no matter how well-intentioned or forceful they might be. In the few instances where one of the children seeks to impose their version of rules, the others refuse to play along. This hermeneutic is then directly applied to the enigmas of the adult world. The results are uniformly funny and often poignant. This,

---

[14] S. P. Mohanty, "Kipling's Children and the Colour Line," *Race & Class*, 31.1 (1989), 25, 24. See also Sara Suleri, "The Adolescence of Kim," in *The Rhetoric of British India* (Chicago, IL: University of Chicago Press, 1992), 117–131.

[15] NoViolet Bulawayo, *We Need New Names* (New York: Little, Brown and Company, 2013).

[16] In two of what are perhaps the most potentially damaging events to the children in *We Need New Names* – the rape of Chipo by her grandfather and her subsequent pregnancy and the death of Bornfree – the children negotiate the traumas of these experiences through role-playing games that provide different forms of closure for them. But by incorporating Chipo's pregnancy into their world of play, the children also seem to avoid confronting what threat the adult world might pose to them as children; the fact that they may not be entirely safe from the sexual predatoriness of adults within their world. Chipo goes around for a long time refusing to speak, and this can only mean that she is suffering some serious form of trauma. See the titular chapter and "For Real" for how they accommodate the difficult questions of childhood pregnancy and political violence respectively.

for example, is what we see when the children sing a song over Darling's dying father:

> Me, when I die I want to go where there's lots of food and music and a party that never ends and we're singing that Jobho song, Godknows says.
>
> When Godknows starts singing Jobho, Sbho joins in and we listen to them sing it for a while and then we're all scratching our bodies and singing it because Jobho is a song that leaves you with no choice but to scratch your body the way that sick man Job did in the Bible, lying there scratching his itching wounds when God was busy torturing him just to play with him to see if he had faith. Jobho makes you call out to heaven even though you know God is occupied with better things and will not even look your way. Jobho makes you point your forefinger to the sky and sing at the top of your voice. We itch and we scratch and we point and we itch again and we fill the shack with singing.
>
> Then Stina reaches and takes Father's hand and starts moving it to the song, and Bastard moves the other hand. I reach out and touch him too because I have never really touched him ever since he came and this is what I must do now because how will it look when everybody is touching him and I'm not. We all look at one another and smile-sing because we are touching him, just touching him all over like he is a beautiful plaything we have just rescued from a rubbish bin in Budapest. He feels like dry wood in my hands, but there is a strange light in his sunken eyes, like he has swallowed the sun.[17]

Darling's father has returned to Paradise after many years working in a South African mine during which he broke off all communication with his family. He returns with terminal AIDS, effectively to die at home. Because Darling is required to stay home and care for her father she can no longer go out and play with her friends. Her deep embarrassment at this turn of events prevents her from telling them the truth about the situation, so each time they come calling her out to play she stands at the door of her shack and tries to shield the inside from their prying eyes while making increasingly unconvincing excuses about why she is not able to come out and join them. One day her friends push past her and enter the room to find her father on the bed inside the dimly-lit room. In what can only be described as a benediction of innocence, they anoint him with the Jobho song and elevate him momentarily to the status of the well-known symbol of Christian fortitude in suffering.

In *We Need New Names*, the agonistic structure of the children's relationships amongst themselves is fundamental to the character of Part I of the novel. In Part II, Darling moves from the slum of Paradise to go

[17] NoViolet Bulawayo, *We Need New Names*, 105.

and live in "Destroyedmychigan" with her aunt Fostalina. The consequent loss of her childhood friends marks the complete attenuation of the agonistic structure and also the candid reinscription of the conventional bildungsroman that renders this second part much less interesting than Part I. What were adult enigmas that could be converted into the hermeneutics of play now just pose irritations to the fourteen-year-old Darling. Much that she finds confusing lies in the peculiarities of American cultural life, of which she holds an increasingly dim opinion. Even though Part I of the novel has many bewildering examples of suffering and confusion, the children's egos are somehow insulated from the threats implied in the pain and bewildering traumas of the adult world. Despite living in a slum and amidst terrible living conditions, the children do not experience suffering as the sign of an intractable epistemological crisis and their imagination is not limited by the desperate material conditions in which they are immersed. Rather, these conditions provide the grounds upon which the world is reimagined through the games that they play.

As in *We Need New Names*, *The God of Small Things* shows Rahel and Estha interpreting the enigmas of the adult world through a hermeneutic of imaginative children's play, but with one fundamental difference; from the very beginning the adult world of *The God of Small Things* poses variant threats of embarrassment, humiliation, and, finally, emotional devastation on the twins and their mother. When Ammu's marriage collapses, she returns in disgrace from the tea estate in Assam with her two-year-olds to her parents' house. She knows that in the background to her life in Ayemenem will always be "the constant, high, whining mewl of local disapproval."[18] As a response to this incessant mewl of disapproval Ammu develops an Unsafe Edge, a mixture of the "infinite tenderness of motherhood and the reckless rage of a suicide bomber."[19] Ayemenem's public disapproval is not limited to gossip but is also expressed in the most cynical and humiliating ways. When Ammu goes to the Kottayam police station with the twins to complain that some mistake has been made in arresting Velutha, Inspector Thomas Matthew looks at her with eyes full of slyness and greed and tells her that the Kottayam police do not "take statements from *veshyas* [prostitutes] or their illegitimate children."[20] Then he proceeds to tap her breasts with his baton "*Tap, tap*. As though he was choosing mangoes from a basket."[21] When they step out of the police station and the children see their mother crying they do not ask her what *veshya* means, or for that matter *illegitimate*, for they correctly intuit that the

---

[18] Roy, *The God of Small Things*, 43.   [19] Roy, *The God of Small Things*, 44.
[20] Roy, *The God of Small Things*, 8.   [21] Roy, *The God of Small Things*, ibid.

words are meant to denigrate them along with their mother. It is the first time they have seen their mother cry. Just before she dies in a grimy room alone many years later, Ammu will wake up from a recurrent nightmare in which policemen approach her "with snicking scissors, wanting to hack off her hair."[22] This was what policemen did to prostitutes when they caught them in the bazaar so they would be easily recognizable in the land "where long, oiled hair was only for the morally upright."[23] This form of branding is a way of separating the saved from the damned so that Inspector Matthew's reference to her as a *veshya* was no ordinary jibe but rather the means of imposing hierarchy in a world he judged to have gone mad. At home, Ammu's brother Chacko repeatedly reminds her that she has no "Locusts Stand I" to take any decisions regarding the family's Paradise Pickles & Preserves business or about any other family property, for that matter. As he tells her: "What's yours is mine and what's mine is also mine."[24] In this stifling, patriarchal context, the lack of a husband renders Ammu a social outcast and the regular references to their mother's complete lack of social status reminds the twins of their own precarity.

A further threat to the twins' sense of security comes from what they see as their mother's sometimes volatile and seemingly unreliable love for them. This is registered early on when Ammu reprimands Rahel for her petulant remark about the Orange-drink man at the movie theatre. Because the twins have always intuitively felt each other's experiences, Rahel knows that Estha has been molested by the Orange-drink man when Estha steps out of the *Sound of Music* to get something to drink. So, when Ammu later praises his molester for being "surprisingly sweet with Estha" it triggers a petulant "So why don't you marry him then?" from Rahel.[25] The result is an immediate chill in her mother's attitude:

> "Rahel," Ammu said.
> Rahel froze. She was desperately sorry for what she had said. She didn't know where those words had come from. She didn't know that she'd had them in her. But they were out now, and wouldn't go back in. They hung about that red staircase like clerks in a Government office. Some stood, some sat and shivered their legs.
> "Rahel," Ammu said. "Do you realize what you have just done?"
> Frightened eyes and a fountain looked back at Ammu.
> "It's alright. Don't be scared," Ammu said. "Just answer me. Do you?"
> "What?" Rahel said in the smallest voice she had.
> "Realize what you've just done?" Ammu said.

---

[22] Roy, *The God of Small Things*, 161.   [23] Roy, *The God of Small Things*, ibid.
[24] Roy, *The God of Small Things*, 57.   [25] Roy, *The God of Small Things*, 112.

Frightened eyes and a fountain looked back at Ammu.

"D'you know what happens when you hurt people?" Ammu said. "When you hurt people, they begin to love you less. That's what careless words do. They make people love you a little less."

A cold moth with unusually dense dorsal tufts landed lightly on Rahel's heart. Where its icy legs touched her, she got goose bumps. Six goose bumps on her careless heart.

A little less her Ammu loved her.[26]

Following this rebuke Rahel immediately begins to look out for signs of being less loved and finds them readily in the attention that everyone, including her mother, bestows on Sophie Mol when she arrives on her visit to Ayemenem a day after the scene at the movie. But the volatility of their mother's love is turned to more disastrous effect after the discovery of her relationship to Velutha. Baby Kochamma conspires to have Chacko lock Ammu up in her room and when the twins come to find out what has happened, their mother turns her full anger and frustration on them:

> "Because of you!" Ammu had screamed. "If it wasn't for you I wouldn't be here! None of this would have happened! I wouldn't be here! I would have been free! I should have dumped you in an orphanage the day you were born! You're the millstones around my neck!"
>
> . . .
>
> "Just go away!" Ammu had said. "Why can't you just go away and leave me alone?"
>
> So they had.[27]

Already the children had been secreting supplies away in the History House across the river in order to Always Be Prepared so when their mother snaps at them they realize their incipient plans for testing how long they might be missed by the adults and thus how much they were really loved. But it is in that last fateful crossing of the Meenachal river that their boat capsizes and Sophie Mol dies.

Baby Kochamma's slow-burning resentment also poses an ambient threat to Rahel and Estha's wellbeing. At first, this is not experienced by them as a threat but only as a source of amusement and no one in the family really pays any attention to Baby Kochamma in her many attempts at getting the kids into trouble. And yet her slow-burning resentment comes to deadly fruition during the Terror, when everything goes awry and the worst human motivations contribute to the unfolding tragedy. That her resentment comes from the lovelorn

---

[26] Roy, *The God of Small Things*, 112.   [27] Roy, *The God of Small Things*, 253.

nostalgia she has shared with no one but nurses throughout her life, means that the resentment is consistently refueled by an internal sense of loss. As a young girl many years earlier, Baby Kochamma had fallen in love with the dashing Father Mulligan, the young Catholic priest who frequently came to visit her father, himself a priest of the local Syrian Christian Church. Undeterred by Father Mulligan's lack of interest, Baby Kochamma converted to Catholicism and asked to become a nun in his convent in Madras in hopes of seeing more of him. This proved inadequate for gaining his attention, and years later Father Mulligan converts to Hinduism and joins an ashram. That he had left Catholicism not for her but due to an independent change of faith solidified her bitterness. In the years that followed, Baby Kochamma developed a ritual that she adhered to unerringly for the rest of her life. Every day she picked up her maroon diary that came with its own pen and writes simply, *I love you*:

> Every page in the diary had an identical entry. She had a case full of diaries with identical entries. Some said more than just that. Some had the day's accounts, To-do lists, snatches of favourite soaps, But even these entries all began with the same words: *I love you I love you.*[28]

In what is a classic case of melancholia, Baby Kochamma refuses to let go of her lost love-object but continues to renew her ties to it through the repeated formulaic declarations she writes in her diary. Religion and love, which should ideally have provided an internal state of grace, are in her case transmogrified into a feeling of deep resentment for those in society that happen to be less fortunate than her. That the genesis of her resentment derives from such a private source but also coincides with the social demonization of single women means that her negative feelings toward the children and their mother also automatically channels the harsh social judgement of which she herself is a victim. To ward off her own sense of social ostracization she becomes the agent for victimizing others. And so it is that she becomes the pitiless agent of Ammu and the twins' emotional devastation, like an implacable vengeful goddess seeking capricious retribution for an offence that is not theirs. Baby Kochamma's social entrapment is the trigger for the atrophying of any nurturing instincts she may have had to start with.

[28] Roy, *The God of Small Things*, 297.

Unlike the other children's novels we discussed earlier, in *The God of Small Things,* the character of patriarchal social conventions regarding single women and fatherless children translates inexorably into the entrapment of women such as Ammu, Baby Kochamma, and also Mammachi, Ammu's mother. And because these are the primary care-givers to Rahel and Estha, these women's unsatisfactory position in society provides a backdrop of uncertainty to the children's lives that then gets converted and internalized by them as extreme feelings, first of rejection, then of guilt during the Terror. Even as adults some twenty-three years later, the enigmas of their childhood remain unresolved, and so they continue to return to that childhood for answers and thus psychically cannot move on.

History, Tragic Causality, and the Domain of Privacy

The brief love affair between Ammu and Velutha instigates the rapid unraveling of social boundaries. For Mammachi, Baby Kochamma, and Chacko, Ammu's transgressive love for the untouchable Velutha represents a form of pollution that they feel they must insulate the Ipe family name from. Every step they take after the details of the affair are made known is to establish a form of containment from the perceived social pollution. First Chacko locks Ammu up in her room, then Baby Kochamma marches to the police station to make up the accusation of rape against Velutha. Her accusation serves to move Ammu and Velutha's relationship from the domain of love to that of law-and-order, thus providing the police a perfect excuse for cleansing the community from what they now con-veniently describe as a crime. In reality, however, each of the characters in the Ipe household is insinuating their obeisance to the Love Laws, whose ancient regimen defines who will be loved and by how much in a veritable distribution of the sensible in Rancière's terms:

> Still, to say that it all began when Sophie Mol came to Ayemenem is only one way of looking at it.
>
> Equally, it could be argued that it actually began thousands of years ago. Long before the Marxists came. Before the British took Malabar, before the Dutch Ascendency, before Vasco da Gama arrived, before the Zamorin's conquest of Calicut. Before three purple-robed Syrian Bishops murdered by the Portuguese were found floating in the sea, with coiled sea serpents riding on their chests and oysters knotted in their tangled beards. It could be argued that it began long before Christianity arrived in a boat and seeped into Kerala like tea from a teabag.

> That it really began in the days when the Love Laws were made. The laws
> that lay down who should be loved, and how.
> And how much.[29]

Each historical arrival listed in this passage (Marxists, the British, the
Dutch Ascendency, Vasco da Gama, etc.) represents the intrusion of
a mode of social hierarchy upon the locals. In other words, the Love
Laws over-determine interpersonal relationships well before the start of
recorded history or of local Christian legend. They cast the shadow of
determinism over the schema of choice and also proliferate multi-causal
relations through the contingent political and personal agendas that come
to define such social relationships.

When all the scores are settled, the social contamination that Baby
Kochamma and the Ipe family attach to Ammu is discursively converted
onto their victims as unspeakable feelings of guilt that Ammu and the twins
come to labor under. Mother and children are transformed from social
pariahs – due to their status as unmarried woman and fatherless children –
into *pharmakoi* (sacrificial carriers), charged with taking on the responsibility for not one but two deaths. In this process they are burdened with the
internalized inflection of the social judgement that attaches to whoever
transgresses the Love Laws. What was their socially peripheral status is now
re-transcribed by the rest of the family into a form of segregation. Even at
the church service for Sophie Mol, "Though Ammu, Estha and Rahel were
allowed to attend the funeral, they were made to stand separately, not with
the rest of the family. Nobody would look at them."[30] Their social
segregation is rendered complete when they are separated even from each
other: Ammu is sent off to a far-away town where she eventually dies alone;
Estha is Returned to his father; and Rahel remains in the Ayemenem
house, but only to slip into an ontological void that defines the rest of
her life.

***

Even though the world of Small Things is, as we have already noted, always
represented in the novel in the discourse of ineffable emotions, from
a literary perspective, individual human sentiments are detached from
the domain of privacy and transferred onto the domain of representation,
thus coming to constitute a parallel vector to the blind forces of nature. If
in *The God of Small Things* nature is from the opening pages depicted as
lush, fecund, and full of vitality, during the Terror it is also shown to be

[29] Roy, *The God of Small Things*, 330.   [30] Roy, *The God of Small Things*, 5.

a Big Thing that transcends the human capacity for comprehension. It is nature's overwhelming and confounding volatility that triggers the social crisis in the first place, for it is this incomprehensibility that makes Vellya Paapen feel compelled to go and report to Mammachi the abomination he has seen: his untouchable son Velutha standing naked with the touchable Ammu, Mammachi's daughter. Vellya Paapen's compulsion is triggered by his own attempt at containing the polluting effects of the social transgression he has reluctantly borne witness to, which he thinks is somehow connected to the unruliness of the weather. As we are told:

> Though it was December, it rained as though it was June. *Cyclonic disturbance*, the newspapers called it the next day. But by then nobody was in any condition to read the papers.
>
> Perhaps it was the rain that drove Vellya Paapen to the kitchen door. To a superstitious man, the relentlessness of that unseasonal downpour could have seemed like an omen from an angry god. To a drunk superstitious man, it could have seemed like the beginning of the end of the world. Which, in a way, it was.[31]

The narrator does not explain her enigmatic "which, in a way, it was" but gives us enough clues from her anthropomorphic descriptions of natural events during the Terror for us to see that nature is indeed an angry god. The question, however, is why? Why is nature "angry"? And if it is angry, why with the human world? While we are given no direct answer, it is possible to interpret nature's anger as the figural product of a series of metonymic transfers that flow in several directions at once. The first transfer is from the direction of disruptive social relations related to transgression of the Love Laws and how they get discursively projected onto the natural register of the monsoon and the Menachal river, which are themselves shown to be tumultuous in that period. Together, the disruptive social relations and the volatility of nature come to act as the signal of ontological disturbance, "the beginning of the end of the world," as Vellya Paapen interprets it. The second flow of metonymic transfers is more elusive but is keyed into the narrative through the character of Velutha, who is symbolically connected to nature through the emblematic sign of the small leaf on his back said to predict the coming of the monsoon. During the Terror, the narrator keeps referring to Velutha as a god of small things as well as a god of loss, but given that he has already been symbolically connected to Big Things (predicting the monsoon), this suggests that he represents both the worlds of large historical causalities as well as of

---

[31] Roy, *The God of Small Things*, 254.

feelings and emotions. And through the image of the leaf on his back, the violent suffering that is inflicted upon him is effectively cathected onto the disruptions of the natural cycle, as though he is a son of nature and the two are an inseparable single part of the same continuum.

When Velutha was summoned to the Ayemenem house after the news breaks of the affair, "Mammachi lost her bearings and spewed her blind venom, her crass, insufferable insults," first at a panel in the sliding-folding door and then, after Baby Kochamma tactfully turns her around to face in the right direction, at Velutha. "Out!" she screamed. "If I find you on my property tomorrow I'll have you castrated like the pariah dog that you are! I'll have you killed!"[32] The last threat comes to fruition in the worst way imaginable. By the time Velutha walks to the gate of the house all his senses are heightened. And they are heightened in order to deliver him into the elemental heart of all things, much as we found in *Things Fall Apart*, *Waiting for the Barbarians*, and *Beloved* at comparable moments of crises for the central characters:

> As he walked away from the house, he felt his senses had been honed and heightened. As though everything around him had been flattened into a neat illustration. A machine drawing with an instruction manual that told him what to do. His mind, desperately craving some kind of mooring, clung to details. It labelled each thing it encountered.
>
> *Gate*, he thought, as he walked out of the gate. *Gate. Road. Stones. Sky. Rain.*
>
> Gate.
> Road.
> Stones.
> Sky.
> Rain.
>
> The rain on his skin was warm. The laterite rock under his feet jagged. He knew where he was going. He noticed everything. Each leaf. Each tree. Each cloud in the starless sky. Each step he took.[33]

Velutha begins to count, as if in an attempt to return to a secure calming practice from childhood. He counts *one, two, three, four, five, six,* and up to *twenty-nine*, and then:

> The machine drawing began to blur. The clear lines to smudge. The instructions no longer made sense. The road rose to meet him and the

---

[32] Roy, *The God of Small Things*, 284.   [33] Roy, *The God of Small Things*, 284–285.

darkness grew dense. Glutinous. Pushing through it became an effort. Like
swimming underwater.
It's happening, a voice informed him. *It has begun.*
His mind, suddenly impossibly old, floated out of his body and hovered
high above him in the air, from where it jabbered useless warnings.[34]

What appears to Velutha as a form of sensorial intensification is also the
means by which he is enveloped by an elemental sense of his surroundings.
The ekphrastic implications of everything around him being flattened into
a neat illustration with an instruction manual of what to do also signifies
the momentary transubstantiation of reality into the realm of the fantastical and thus of an essential conflation of ontological categories with him
at their center. Throughout the novel, Rahel and Estha have played with
the sounds of words, breaking words up into their constituent phonemes
(Lay Ter, Locusts Stand I, Bar Nowl [for Barn Owl]) in such a way as to
highlight the strangeness of words and their re-constitutability into new
forms. A similar thing is implied in their habit of reading backwards, which
endlessly irritates Baby Kochamma. Even though Velutha's experience of
the collapse of language into its phrasal constituents is similar to what we
see with the twins, it is not tied to any games of linguistic reconstitution
but rather to the intensification of his perspectival sensorium. He is
delivered into the womb of space-time and becomes at-one with the primal
and the elemental around him. And it is this at-one-ness that is then
discursively transposed onto nature and magnified into a clashing of the
spheres. The violent monsoon rains that precede and indeed trigger the
Terror and then swell the Menachal river to drown Sophie Mol also
continue into the scene where the policemen arrive at the History House
to systematically beat the emotionally drained Velutha. The violent monsoon winds and the river are both an omen and metonymic displacement
of the events that take place at the domain of social relations. Because the
leaf on Velutha's back is always recorded in the narrative as predictive, the
"*It has begun*" that he hears as he floats out of his body upon leaving the Ipe
household may be interpreted as nature itself voicing the sense of an ending
by way of his heightened consciousness. Nature is symbolically routed
through him but also takes him as an object of sacrifice, thus joining him to
the other *pharmakoi* in the novel represented by Ammu, Rahel, and Estha.
The two processes of metonymic displacement during the Terror – from
disruptive social relations to the volatility of nature and from the tribula-
tions of Velutha to the monsoon's unseasonal disruptions and the swollen

---

[34] Roy, *The God of Small Things*, 286.

river – then carry the implication of the entire universe being out of joint, as if to echo Aristotle's geocentric model which we noted at the beginning of this chapter.

The specific form of pathetic fallacy that we find in *The God of Small Things* also calls to mind the figural processes commonly found in Shakespeare, where, for example, in the separate assassinations of Julius Caesar and Duncan and during the run of King Lear's madness, the states of political upheaval are also simultaneously registered in the disruptions of nature, and sometimes even noted in dreams and premonitions.[35] The contrast with Shakespeare's characters is of course that Velutha is no epic hero or high-ranking protagonist. Even though he is someone who amply illustrates Aristotle's notion of *eudaimonia* (virtue, living consciously) that we saw in the Introduction, Velutha is not directly responsible for any shifts in the action of the plot. He is primarily the victim and not the progenitor of events. In the implied geocentrism of *The God of Small Things*, nature's indifference to the human realm is ultimately terrifying, since it cannot be shown that nature establishes any codes of restitution for the oppressed. And even if, as I have suggested, Velutha is discursively represented as a child of nature and on a symbolic continuum with it, what is left for us after the various metonymic displacements is a residue of bewilderment and even horror, something that itself echoes the collapse of innocence represented in the characters of Rahel and Estha.

Conclusion: Innocence, Loss, and the Entrapment of Childhood

If *The God of Small Things* invokes the trope of children in a lush garden, it does so not through any direct invocations of peaceful nature, but predominantly through the language games in which Rahel and Estha recreate their sense of the world. Their variant play with the codes of language is a means of corralling language's potential for imagining different possibilities. It is their Edenic practice of renaming everything using the constituent sounds and textures of language, its idiosyncrasies and potential for confusion, that signifies both the vitality and pitfalls of the various garden figurations we noted at the start of this chapter. The twin's devices for unleashing the inherent possibilities of language are many: palindromes, reverse reading, breaking up words into constituent sounds, assembling

---

[35] See for example, Calpurnia's premonitory dream in *Julius Caesar* act 2, scene 2, the strange and unnatural events that take place after Macbeth's murder of Duncan in *Macbeth* 2.4, and the large section in the central parts of *King Lear*, acts 2–4, during Lear's madness.

fragmentary word lists and anagrams, and the random capitalization of words, among others. Significantly, the various language games that the children play seem to apply only to English, and not to the Malayalam which is also a common part of the Ipe household. In other words, the novel's linguistic hybridity does not apply to the local language itself, as if to suggest that it is English, in its inherent hegemony, that requires constant dismembering and reconstitution.

Crucial to any interpretation of *The God of Small Things*, however, must be the fact that this play of language applies as much to the diegetic focalization we see through Rahel's perspective as it does to the discourse of the omniscient third-person narrator. The suggestion here is not only that the third-person narrative viewpoint is permanently grafted onto Rahel's, but that the essential tenor of Rahel's perspective is consistently ratified throughout the narrative. And as we saw with respect to Velutha, in his moment of existential crisis even he reverts to the device of language discombobulation which we had up until then associated with the twins. However, what appears in the earlier narrative timeframe of 1969 as a sign of imaginative effervescence can only be interpreted in the later timeframe of the adult twins as a sign of entrapment. For the uniformity of linguistic register across both narrative timeframes, and also between the third-person narrator and the child characters, suggests that the tragic events they are a part of have sealed them into a world of innocence from which they cannot hope to escape. It is as if Rahel and Estha are permanently fixed at the primal moments of their ego-constitution. Thus, the narrative's continual return to divulge different aspects of Sophie Mol and Velutha's deaths in a process of enigmatic relays may then be read as a narrative form of repetition compulsion, that is to say, not the repetition of specific details, but of entire structural ensembles tied inextricably to the feelings and emotions of childhood. The predominance of childlike language games at different levels of the text is thus the mnemonic of a quest for wholeness, which of course is unavailable to the twins within the social terms that have been established throughout the narrative. As Baneth-Nouailhetas adroitly notes, there is for them essentially a tyranny of memory and an "identity-shaping struggle to 'live with' what happened."[36] All their actions in the later timeframe of the novel "gravitate around the incapacity to forget . . . the aim is not so much to reveal a story as to measure the tensions between individual memory and social heritage, history."[37] The tragedy comes from their entrapment by the traumatic events they have experienced in a state of endless repetition, a repetition enabled by the same linguistic devices through

[36] Baneth-Nouailhetas, 149.   [37] Baneth-Nouailhetas, 148.

which they had attempted to imagine a world of new possibilities. But the social history of which they are ultimately victims has shown that it is implacable in its demands for obeisance. What the policemen do to Velutha as the twins watch in horror in the History House is "human history masquerading as God's purpose" and revealed to them as "Necessity."[38] In that sense, the language games that they play from childhood and which might be interpreted as signifiers of an Edenic plenitude and of their capacity to rename their reality by renegotiating all the terms of naming inherent within language, only lapse into a form of entrapment once they are routed through the crucible of tragic events. What several commentators have noted as the second sexual transgression in the novel, when brother and sister embrace each other as sexual beings and make love, is to my mind the despairing sign of a desire to return to their mother's womb. And because this sexual transgression is entirely private and never revealed to anyone but us readers it lacks any of the dire consequences of their mother's love for Velutha within the diegetic context of familial and social relations. Theirs is not the sign of transgression but rather the retreat into the imagined comfort of the "I am not yet Born; O hear me," of Louis MacNeice's declaration in "Prayer Before Birth":

> I am not yet born; O hear me.
> Let not the bloodsucking bat or the rat or the stoat or the
>
> club-footed ghoul come near me.
> I am not yet born; forgive me
> For the sins that in me the world shall commit, my words
> when they speak me, my thoughts when they think me,
> my treason engendered by traitors beyond me,
> my life when they murder by means of my
> hands, my death when they live me.[39]

For Rahel and Estha, it is the testament of an arrested bildungsroman and a tragedy of the transformation of childhood innocence out of the garden and into the prison house of language.

In focusing its tragedy on the implications that the enigmas of the adult world have on the world of childhood, *The God of Small Things* produces a new inflection to the themes we had hitherto examined. Except for Toni Morrison's *Beloved*, much of what we saw in earlier chapters relate primarily to the world of men and of public affairs. Those works are focused

---

[38] Roy, *The God of Small Things*, 309.
[39] Louis MacNeice, "Prayer Before Birth," www.poemhunter.com/poem/prayer-before-birth/, last accessed July 6, 2020.

mainly on an ethnography of the public sphere, of grand gestures and impassioned speeches. What Roy illustrates for us is that the world of Small Things is as much the domain of postcolonial tragedy as that of Big Things. As we are told when the policemen come to beat Velutha, history is telescoped into one evanescent moment. But it is from within the evanescent emotions that the most durable human values are born and against which is lined up the terrifying universe of politics, laws, and even nature. *The God of Small Things* instructs us that to come to a fuller grasp of postcolonial tragedy we have to pay as much attention to Small Things as we pay to Big Things, even if the latter cloud the foreground and make it seem as if god (God?) only appears within the grander domains of public expression.

CHAPTER 9

Distressed Embodiment and the Burdens
of Boredom
Samuel Beckett's Postcolonialism

The first time I read a Beckett play, I recognized the Egyptians in it immediately. In the post-revolution limbo, rampant unemployment, the sudden depreciation of the Egyptian pound, as well as increased difficulty gaining travel visas and immigration opportunities, means that many young Egyptians feel trapped. There is an overwhelming sense of future-lessness. The days roll around and into each other. Time is not forward-facing, but loose, and circling. People smoke too much, take risks. Insofar as it is possible to speak of a national mood, it is one of desensitization, nihilism, idleness, but also levity and jocularity. There is a Beckettian recognition of, and appreciation for, the absurd on every level. Conversations revolve around minutiae, get more and more cartoonlike with every orbit. Out of sheer boredom and desperation, people make hot decisions based on a why-not? attitude. Should we get high? Let's get high. You want some corn? Let's walk to the Corniche for some corn. Let's go to Sinai for a swim. Let's cartwheel on the balcony railing. Should we kill ourselves? Why not? Let's cartwheel off the balcony railing.

Noor Naga[1]

[O]ne need not propose that an analysis of postcolonial regimes and their bases for authority constitutes the "true" or "secret" intent of his work. The broader or more universal claims of a typical "modernist" reading of Beckett are in no way compromised by a postcolonial reading pursued along these lines. To the contrary, the overlap between the two should be understood as comprising a key aspect of such a postcolonial reading in its suggestion of the importance of empire and its accelerating dissolution as a driving

---

[1] Noor Naga is a gifted Egyptian American writer and winner of the 2017 RBC Browen Wallace Award for Emerging Writers for an excerpt from her verse-novel *Washes, Prays* which is being published by McClelland & Stewart in 2020. She also won the 2019 Graywolf Press Africa Prize for her novel *American Girl and Boy from Shobrakheit*. Naga has been published in *Granta*, *The Common* and *POETRY*. I was very lucky also to have her as the copy editor for *Tragedy and Postcolonial Literature* before it went to CUP. Her creative intelligence is only matched by her patience for my frequent changes of direction.

264

force behind modernism's twin impulses of fragmentation and
renewal.

Mark Quigley, "Unnaming the Subject: Samuel Beckett
and Colonial Alterity"[2]

Of all the chapters in the book, this one on Beckett presented me with the
most difficulties. An early conundrum came from a question I tried to clear
up with several colleagues that study Beckett, but not with much success. It
was simply this: the most explicitly postcolonial text in Beckett's oeuvre
seems to me to be *Murphy*, which alas does not appear to be especially
tragic, at least not in the terms established by the likes of Okonkwo,
Ezeulu, Elesin Oba, Sethe, or even the Magistrate, all of whom we have
encountered so far. And on the other hand, the most tragic of his works,
namely *Waiting for Godot*, *Endgame*, and *Krapp's Last Tape*, don't seem to
be especially postcolonial, at least not in any explicit sense that we can
readily point to. And even these exhibit a clear mix between tragedy and
comedy, making their tragic vision far from straightforward. I realized only
several months into my struggles with the chapter that I had been asking
the wrong questions entirely with respect to both tragedy and postcolonialism. For even while several scholars have persuasively argued that
Beckett's work is indeed postcolonial, the terms by which this has been
established in specific relation to the Ireland of his birth produce a different
requirement for postcolonial analysis. This is because of the semi-colonial
yet also advanced Western cultural characteristics of Ireland, made
increasingly evident at least from the late nineteenth century onward.
But it is precisely this admixture of advanced economy and colonial
backwardness that makes of Ireland such an interesting prospect for
a postcolonial analysis. That the Irish nationalist movement was inspired
by distant anticolonial struggles such as the South African Anglo-Boer
War helps clarify what Elleke Boehmer describes as the imperial framework of "interrelating margins," and thus suggests the inextricable intertwining and refraction of resistance to colonialism from different parts of
the world.[3] Robert Young's entirely reasonable question as to why there
has not yet been a study of the role of violence in Ireland's nineteenth and
twentieth century history to compare with Fanon's analysis of the fundamental role of violence in Algeria's struggle for independence raises

---

[2] Mark Quigley, "Unnaming the Subject: Samuel Beckett and Colonial Alterity," *Samuel Beckett Today/Aujourd'hui*, 15, Historicising Beckett (2005): 87–100, 88.
[3] The point about the Boer War's inspiration for Irish decolonization struggles is made in *Empire, the National, and the Postcolonial, 1890–1920* (New York: Oxford University Press, 2002), 2.

another area of comparative interest, while the fact that Irish writers have long influenced writers from diverse parts of the postcolonial world such as Wole Soyinka, Athol Fugard, Ayi Kwei Armah, Chinua Achebe, Christopher Okigbo, José Triana, along with Ariel Dorfman, and others, makes Ireland a fertile source for any comparative postcolonial investigation.[4]

One of the preliminary realities of Beckett's work I had to contend with in specific reference to tragedy, had to do with the terms by which we might establish the Aristotelian terms of causal plausibility. It is clear from the outset that all of Beckett's work is marked by modes of randomization between causes and effects, so that he comes to pose a fundamental challenge to the issue of causal plausibility and thus to the ways in which we evaluate the tragic status of his characters. Also pertinent to the discussion in this chapter, however, is the degree to which Beckett's work illustrates different relations between the body, embodiment, and boredom, which I now see as the inescapable building blocks of the elusive meanings of his texts. While I now recognize with Mark Quigley that Beckett's modernism is inextricably intertwined with his postcolonialism, it seems to me that it is in the location of the body in pain and in different forms of constraint that he is most productively to be understood. This takes me back to earlier pieces I wrote on Beckett from the perspective of Disability Studies, where my objective was to show how the brute objective facts of physical impairments in his work served to impede or forestall the original protocols of representation in which the characters attempted to express their identities. *Aesthetic Nervousness* was the book in which I first engaged with Beckett, but that book was neither explicitly postcolonial nor indeed tragic. My second prolonged engagement with Beckett was in an essay I wrote on *Murphy*, where, without making any explicit connections between the novel and any idea of postcoloniality, I noted how the eponymous protagonist exhibits some key features of autistic spectrum disorder, such as his habit of strapping himself to the rocking chair and rocking his mind to calmness and also in his almost compulsive attraction to patterns.[5] I am going to be drawing broadly on the argument of that essay for rethinking the relationship between Murphy's quest for patterns

---

[4] Robert Young poses and attempts a preliminary profile for just such a comparison in *Postcolonialism: An Historical Introduction* (Oxford: Blackwell, 2001), 299–307. Nathan Suhr-Sytsma traces some of the confluences between Irish, African, and other postcolonial literatures in his *Poetry, Print, and the Making of Postcolonial Literature* (Cambridge: Cambridge University Press, 2017).

[5] Ato Quayson, "Autism, Narrative, and Emotions: On Samuel Beckett's Murphy," *University of Toronto Quarterly*, 79.2 (2010): 838–864.

and the collapse of the mode of self-validation he is attracted to. These now seem to me to be interrelated aspects of Murphy's situation as a diasporic Irishman in early twentieth-century London. I am hoping that the return to my earlier engagements with Beckett's work will help me redefine the terms by which to extract a sense of the central theme of postcolonial ethical choice-making that has been at the core of our discussions thus far.

The final critical vector I find relevant for my reengagement with Beckett has to do with the phenomenology of boredom. The theme of boredom and the plot of inertia that I discussed in Chapter 4 with respect to Wole Soyinka's *The Road* is also directly pertinent to Beckett, for in his work the constraints placed on the mobility of the characters links directly to the uncertainty of hermeneutical frameworks by which they might interpret their condition. Whereas in *The Road*, Professor and the unemployed touts attempt to imagine grand modes of action while they wait for something to happen, in Beckett, waiting is often its own condition that refuses to grant any guarantees of either solace or futurity. As we shall see with respect to *Murphy*, his embodied disability, in this case of an autistic spectrum disorder, is combined with a quest for analogical validation that produces the perceived disintegration of self-identity, and subsequently, of a tragic diminuendo that devolves into an accidental death.

The Randomization of Causal Plausibility

As we noted in the Introduction, when Aristotle notes in the *Poetics* that the plot of tragedy must have a beginning, a middle, and an end, he is not simply calling for the mechanical, temporal sequencing of the tragic action but rather for the establishment of what Martha Nussbaum has glossed elsewhere as "causal plausibility."[6] Whether with respect to literary tragedy or to real life, for the victim of suffering to elicit sympathetic identification from the witness to their suffering, it has to be shown, first, that the sufferer was not culpable for the catastrophe that befalls them, second, that even if they were somewhat culpable, that the scale of the catastrophe vastly outstrips their degree of culpability, and third and most importantly, that the catastrophe has undermined the sufferer's capacity to undertake ethically informed actions. It is these elements that collectively define causal plausibility and thus elicit sympathy for the sufferer in literary tragedy. And similarly, in real life another's undeserved suffering may also trigger an ethically cognizant response from us. Sometimes, the

---

[6] Nussbaum, "Tragedy and Self-Sufficiency: Plato and Aristotle on Fear and Pity," 266.

question of ethical response goes beyond the context of individual relations and encompasses the complex apparatuses of transitional justice. In the 1990s and early 2000s, truth and reconciliation commissions in South Africa, Sierra Leone, and East Timor established transitional justice frameworks to link suffering and witnessing to their nation-building projects after civil war, genocide, and the long-term inequitable distribution of political and social rights. But causal plausibility also implies a predictable horizon of expectations regarding the correlation of causes and effects. While in the *Poetics* Aristotle places human agency at the center of causality through the implications of *hamartia*, in real-life human affairs it is recognized that even if certain events occur beyond the purview of individual agency, compassion may still be appropriate in the face of suffering. Sometimes the relationship between terrible things and human agency may also be acknowledged as being dispersed and lacking direct causal relationship to the sufferer's choice-making. While we recognize that war, genocide, and even natural environmental disasters occur due to the poor short- and long-term decision making of those in power that we think ought to know better, the impact of such disasters on the lives of ordinary people still manages to elicit our proper sympathy for them.

Beckett appears to pose a direct challenge to the entire Aristotelian apparatus of causal plausibility, and so, we might say, to the very categories of pity and fear and how they might be applied as responses to the unhappy plight of the characters in his work. To find a pathway to understanding what constitutes suffering in Beckett requires that we engage with a series of seemingly irresolvable antinomies. As Ronan McDonald and others have noted, Beckett's drama is "too concerned with the uncertain and the remorselessly squalid, to reach tragic status."[7] For he presents us with characters that do not aspire and for whom he provisions no ready closure or means of relief. Most importantly, as McDonald goes on to note, the fusion of tragic and comic elements in Beckett's work produces an inherent disorientation of mood and the interpenetration of such elements does not serve the function of contrapuntal contrast. Comedy is not the momentary relief of the tragic that we find in, say, the gravediggers' scene in *Hamlet* or the gatekeeper's scene in *Macbeth*, but rather comic and tragic are fused into a form of generic inter-modality, with each element canceling out the other. The generic inter-modality in Beckett's works has consequences

---

[7] Ronan McDonald, *Tragedy and Irish Literature: Synge, O'Casey, Beckett* (London: Palgrave, 2001), 128.

both at the level of the characters' actions and choice-making and for how we might come to understand what constitutes their suffering.

The challenge from Beckett to any sense of causal plausibility comes from different sources. In plays such as *Waiting for Godot* and *Endgame*, the characters are rarely able to establish the correlation between their current conditions of pain and squalor and the decisions that they made in the past. For Nagg and Nell, trapped in dustbins on stage in *Endgame*, there is a fundamental disagreement even on what constituted particular sequences of memorable events in their shared past. And in *Krapp's Last Tape*, Krapp's melancholic disavowal of what he was as he listens to tapes of himself from thirty years' previously is mediated through the tape recorder to reveal the subject to be pluralized, disembodied, decentered, and altogether fractured. His past may have preceded his present, but he nonetheless impatiently seeks to disconnect himself from that past.

On Waiting, Exhaustion, and Boredom

The waiting that Noor Naga describes for the post-Arab Spring Egyptian youth of her generation is inherently Beckettian in its dissociative and dislocated aspects and replicates something of what we see in much of his work. For the sense of being on the edge that we noted in the Introduction is translated by these Egyptian youth into the so-what of ordinary decision-making to produce an absurd equivalence between going down to the Corniche for roasted corn and turning cartwheels on the balcony railing in contemplation of suicide. As we noted with respect to the unemployed Lagosian lorry park workers of Soyinka's *The Road* and the *kòbòlòi* of Accra, the rich have leisure but the urban poor have free time. Free time is never the same as freedom. For free time is the product of disjunctive economies in which the poor, the unemployed, and the semi-employed strive strenuously to exchange their free time for labor time, that is to say, for wages and the organization of time that the wage economy concomitantly brings along with it. The long-term absence of work not only leads to lack of opportunities and a sense of futurelessness, but also makes time itself become progressively circular, repetitive, and seemingly pointless and oppressive. Waiting around for opportunities then comes to be experienced as the burdensome elapse of temporal circularity that generates a sense of exhaustion.[8] The apparent entrapment in the pointless and

---

[8] Ronan McDonald argues that the trope of idleness commonly found in modernist texts is, in Irish literature, specifically tied to "a history of withdrawal from useful masculine citizenry to be traced to

repetitive circularity of waiting for something, anything, to happen is a species of boredom and exhaustion that Deleuze describes for Beckett:

> Exhaustion is something entirely different: one combines the set of variables of a situation, on the condition that one renounce any order of preference, any organization in relation to a goal, any signification . . . . One was tired of something, but one is exhausted by nothing. The disjunctions subsist, and the distinction between terms may become ever more crude, but the disjointed terms are affirmed in their nondecomposable distance, since they are used for nothing except to create further permutations.[9]

"One was tired by something, but one is exhausted by nothing." This tantalizing formulation suggests that for Beckett's characters, the doing of nothing against a horizon of elusive expectations can be as exhausting, if not more so, than being tired of something that drains the attention. The horizon of frustrated expectations against which Beckett's characters undertake various futile acts is echoed in the lives of the postcolonial unemployed burdened by free time. Why not turn cartwheels on the balcony railings of the thirtieth floor, or join a caravan across the desert from West Africa to try and make it aboard the many dinghies that attempt the crossing over the Mediterranean into Europe? And what if the dinghies capsize and everyone drowns? So what? To these youth, life in the post-colony in the early twenty-first century is bereft of hope anyway, so achieving meaning through some decisive form of action, any action, is preferable to exhaustion by waiting.[10]

It is the body itself that in Beckett registers diminishment, mobility impairment, and physical decay and is also the means by which his characters experience the circular, slow, and steady elapse of time, which is the specific source of exhaustion for them. However, going slow and "slow going" are distinct formulations of time and temporality that carry

---

the literary Revival, despite the contradictory emphasis on the necessarily muscular project of nation building." See his "Nothing to Be Done: Masculinity and the Emergence of Irish Modernism," Natalya Lusty and Julian Murphet, eds., *Modernism and Masculinity* (Cambridge: Cambridge University Press, 2014), 71–86, 71. Apart from the fact that the malaise I am describing here for postcolonial youth equally applies to both males and females, their idleness and malaise illustrates the perceived collapse of the postcolonial nation-state project rather than a withdrawal from the premises of its construction.

[9] Gilles Deleuze, *Essays Critical and Clinical* (Minneapolis: Minnesota University Press, 1997), 153.
[10] A landmark UN migration study published in October 2019 show that 93 percent of Africans making the journey to Europe along perilous and irregular routes would do it again despite experiencing life-threatening danger. See https://news.un.org/en/story/2019/10/1049641; last accessed March 2, 2020.

different implications in his work. Steven Connor describes the two modes in this way:

> Slowness is indeterminable, since in order to know the absolute limit of slowness, we would need to know how long the universe is going to last . . . . Slowness is of course relative. Slowness is slow by comparison with the right speed, or relative to expected or desired promptness or despatch; relaxed slowness is relative to hurry or pressure to speed up. We mistake the experience of slowness as a simple negative measure; if only things could go more quickly, in the queue, on the end of the line, during pain or unhappiness. But slow going is not quite this. It is the experience of a loss of temporal relativity; when things are going slowly, the scale of measurement itself begins to elongate, to attenuate, to dissolve.[11]

For Connor, duration in Beckett is dissociative rather than accretive, "the ordinary, fundamental, terrifying topple of time's slow foot into the next moment, the *disfazione* (unfolding, unworking, working out, falling out, dissolution, decomposition) of sheer elapse that never resolves into anything as dramatic and determinate as collapse or relapse, the pitiless passing away, in soft and imperceptible torrent, that passes understanding."[12] We see then that Beckett's work does shed light on the phenomenology of waiting – the slow going of Connor's formulation – that helps us see what death-like grip pointless waiting has on the psyches of the postcolonial youth and unemployed. The final part of this chapter will specifically calibrate some ways in which we might use a Beckettian perspective to think through the conditions of slow durational elapse, boredom, and the sense of futurelessness in many parts of the postcolonial world, but especially in Africa.

Disability and Distressed Embodiment

Embodiment, it has been suggested by Omar Lizardo, is "the bodily substrate of meaning and experience."[13] Lizardo discusses embodiment in relation to Pierre Bourdieu's concept of habitus, and argues that from a cognitive sociological perspective there is evidence of both hard and soft embodiment of culture that shows that the body acts as a "living memory

---

[11] Steven Connor, *Beckett, Modernism, and the Material Imagination* (Cambridge: Cambridge University Press, 2014), 118.

[12] Connor, 120.

[13] Omar Lizardo, "Pierre Bourdieu as Cognitive Sociologist," Wayne H. Brekhus and Gabe Ignatow, eds., *The Oxford Handbook of Cognitive Sociology* (Oxford: Oxford University Press, 2019), 65–80, 70.

pad" and "the substrate of the cognitive unconscious where culture is embodied in a particularly durable way." He suggests that "there is a systematic nonarbitrary link between the meaning (encoded in 'analog' or 'iconic' form) in bodily posture and the abstract high-level meaning (or emotional quality) elicited by that posture."[14] What Lizardo illustrates with the ample support of cognitive linguists such as George Lakoff and Mark Johnson, Arthur Glenberg and David Robertson, and others is that our bodily postures encode responses to frames of sociocultural signification that themselves imply social hierarchies and sundry forms of acquiescence or rebellion against these hierarchies.[15] While the bodily postures of Beckett's characters are not directly correlated to abstract high-level social meanings as set out by Lizardo, they still reveal physical signs of bewildered responses to the absence of any meaningful structural frameworks that might be adduced by and for them. Thus, modes of distressed embodiment register a central and nonnegotiable crisis for Beckett's characters. In *Happy Days,* Winnie is buried up to her bosom in a mound at the center of the stage. Her half-burial is the simultaneous invocation of womb and tomb that gives visual credence to the sin of having been born, as McDonald points out.[16] Vladimir suffers from a painful hernia while Hamm is confined to a wheelchair; Molloy seems to have one leg slightly shorter than the other; while Murphy, Clov, and Watt appear to be on different points of the autistic spectrum, which is to be seen in their penchant for routine and repetition and their difficulty in relating to others on a basic emotional level. Watt hears voices,

> singing, crying, stating, murmuring, things unintelligible, in his ear . . . .
> Now these voices, sometimes they sang only, and sometimes they cried only, and sometimes they stated only, and sometimes they murmured only, and sometimes they sang and cried, and sometimes they sang and stated, and sometimes they sang and murmured, and sometimes they stated and mur-mured, and sometimes they sang, and cried and stated, and sometimes they sang and cried and murmured

And so on and so forth, as if his mind itself was a theatre of changeable and distracting character parts.[17]

---

[14] Lizardo, 71.
[15] George Lakoff and Mark Johnson, *Philosophy in the Flesh: The Embodied Mind and Its Challenge to Western Thought* (New York: Basic Books, 1999); Arthur M. Glenberg and David A. Robertson, "Symbol Grounding and Meaning: A Comparison of High-Dimensional and Embodied Theories of Meaning," *Journal of Memory and Language,* 43.3 (2000): 379–401.
[16] McDonald, "Nothing to Be Done: Masculinity and the Emergence of Irish Modernism," 153–171.
[17] Samuel Beckett, *Watt* (New York: Grove Press, 1953), 29.

And yet, because we are almost never given the precise cause of the characters' impairments, their mode of distressed embodiment also serves to destabilize any ready links that we might seek to establish between cause and effect. All we are left with are the idiosyncratic gestures by which the characters attempt, and repeatedly fail, to make sense of the conditions in which they are located. The Beckettian characters' quest for meaning is repeatedly frustrated and this is accompanied by various gestures and bodily postures as an aspect of that frustration. We need only think of Vladimir and Estragon's frequent peering into their bowler hats, Clov's stiff walk, Hamm's regular yawns, Molloy's neurotic distribution of sucking stones in his four pockets so as not to suck the same two stones in succession, and Murphy's habit of tying himself with seven scarves into his rocking chair and rocking himself into oblivion to see that the negotiation of distressed embodiment is indeed a central concern for Beckett's characters. As Ulrika Maude notes, Beckett's literature is a literature of the body in which there is "a striking emphasis on seeing, hearing, smelling, touching, falling, rolling, crawling, limping, ailing, and aging" that serves as "a rebuttal of philosophical idealism."[18] And this distressed embodiment is inescapable in any experience of slow going, whether in Beckett or elsewhere. What Zoe Wool points out with reference to an injured American soldier's hopes of return to ordinary married life, and in an unwitting variation on Connor's observations, seems to me entirely apposite in this respect: "the essential difference is that *waiting for* is productively attached to an other and a future legible within heteronormative regimes of sociality; *waiting around just uselessly circles a relentless present*, a negative evocation of the temporalities of disability that refuse the productive organization of lifetimes essential to heteronormative and capitalist fantasies of the good life."[19]

Without attempting to make too strong a link between the details of his own life and that of the characters in his writing, it is instructive to also note that Beckett encountered people with disabilities throughout his lifetime. As background research to the writing of the Mercyseat scenes in *Murphy*, he closely questioned his friend Geoffrey Thompson, who in February 1935 had started working as a senior house physician at the Royal Hospital in Beckenham in Kent, a place for the treatment of mental illness. And from August to December 1945 he worked as a "Quartermaster/

[18] Ulrika Maude, "Beckett, Body and Mind," *The New Cambridge Companion to Samuel Beckett* (Cambridge: Cambridge University Press, 2015), 170–184.
[19] Zoe H. Wool, "In-durable Sociality: Precarious Life in Common and the Temporal Boundaries of the Social," *Social Text*, 130 (2017): 79–90; emphasis added.

Interpreter" for the Normandy Hospital at St.-Lô. Furthermore, Beckett's aunt, Cissie Sinclair, is acknowledged to have been the model for Hamm. Beckett used to wheel her around in her wheelchair when she was crippled with arthritis; she frequently used to ask him to "straighten up the statue." She also had a telescope with which she used to spy out the ships in Dublin Bay.[20] Furthermore, *Endgame* was completed shortly after the death of his brother Frank, after a period of cancer that left Beckett devastated. James Knowlson describes *Endgame's* "flintlike comedy" as being "sparked out of darkness and pain."[21] Perhaps what is even more pertinent to the discussion of Beckett and the disabled body is that he himself suffered endless illnesses, ranging from an arrhythmic heartbeat and night sweats to numerous cysts and abscesses on his fingers, the palm of his left hand, the top of his palate, his scrotum and, most painfully later in life, on his left lung. These led to regular bodily discomfort for him.[22] It seems, then, that the deteriorating body had a special attraction for Beckett because his own body reminded him of its pain and mortality in a forceful way. He was thus able to use the disabled, maimed, and decaying body as a multiple referent for a variety of ideas that seem to have been at least partially triggered by encounters with others with impairments and by his own personal experience of pain and temporary disability. The impaired and distressed body also becomes a useful vector for thinking about his attitudes to the certitudes of nation, whether these emanated from the specific case of Ireland in the early twentieth century, or were articulated in their generic forms after the crisis in Europe during World War II and its aftermath.

Postcolonialism and London's Irish Diaspora

Even though several of Beckett's works illustrate the fractured nature of distressed embodiment and slow temporal elapse that we have been discussing so far, it is to *Murphy* that I want to turn for linking these features specifically to postcolonial tragedy and to the larger question of ethical choice that has been a central concern throughout this book. Peter Bixby has usefully set out the terms by which we might consider Beckett's critique of Irish nationalism, its relation to the increased migration of Dublin's youth into London in the late nineteenth and early twentieth centuries, and the overall sense of "unhomeliness" that we find in *Murphy* as a register

---

[20] James Knowlson, *Damned to Fame: The Life of Samuel Beckett* (New York: Simon and Schuster, 1996), 367; James Knowlson and John Haynes, *Images of Beckett*, (Cambridge: Cambridge University Press, 2012), 52.

[21] Knowlson, *Damned to Fame,* 367.   [22] Knowlson, *Damned to Fame,* 484–508.

of its postcolonial sensibility: "a growing Irish population in the British metropolis experienced the unhomely condition of postcolonial migration, which mingles separation from the wholeness of a national community with a longing for home, if not a homeland."[23] The social conditions that Bixby describes for Murphy and his fellow diasporic Dubliners suggests grounds for comparison with later postcolonial works such as Sam Selvon's *The Lonely Londoners,* Amy Tan's *The Joy Luck Club,* Dionne Brand's *What We All Long For,* Hanif Kureishi's *My Beautiful Launderette,* Mohsin Hamid's *The Reluctant Fundamentalist,* and Chimamanda Adichie's *Americanah,* among many others. In all these works, as in *Murphy,* the homeland that has been left behind is reconfigured in the consciousness of the characters by way of a contradictory process of nostalgia and disavowal that serves not simply to attenuate the grip of the homeland on their imagination but rather to institute diaspora as an intractable problem of identity-formation and place-making.

It has to be noted, however, that there had always been a steady stream of Irish and indeed European migration into London, but that even though the number of such immigrants increased considerably throughout the nineteenth century, it was the Jewish and the Irish that became the targets of public opprobrium. As Peter Ackroyd tells us:

> They were the object of derision and disgust because they lived in self-contained communities, popularly regarded as squalid; it was generally assumed, too, that they had somehow imported their disorderly and insanitary conditions with them. Philanthropic visitors to the Irish rookeries discovered such scenes "of filth and wretchedness as cannot be conceived." Somehow these conditions were considered to be the fault of the immigrants themselves, who were accustomed to no better in their native lands. The actual and squalid nature of London itself, and the social exclusion imposed upon the Irish and Jews, were not matters for debate. The question – where else are they to go? – was not put. Similarly, the fact that immigrants were willing to accept the harshest and most menial forms of employment was also used as another opportunity for clandestine attack, with the implied suggestion that they were good for nothing else.[24]

From the purview of modern diaspora studies there are different categories of postcolonial diasporas. Among these we may count victim diasporas, which are defined by two key principles, namely the violent dispersal of a population to at least two locations, coupled with the

---

[23] Patrick Bixby, *Samuel Beckett and the Postcolonial Novel* (Cambridge: Cambridge University Press, 2009), 87.
[24] Peter Ackroyd, *London: A Biography* (London: Vintage, 2001), 709.

interdiction against return back to the homeland. These principles are amply illustrated in the Jewish, African American, and Armenian diasporas, among others. Labor diasporas imply what is conventionally referred to in popular discourse as economic migrants. By the height of empire in the nineteenth century these included the indentured labor diasporas of Indians in Africa, the Caribbean, and other parts of the world, as well as the many soldiers from outside of Europe that were conscripted to fight wars on its behalf. Then there are also trade diasporas, composed primarily of traders and their families that settle outside of their homelands for purposes of trading and commerce. Chinatowns everywhere illustrate this type of diaspora. Ethno-nationalist diasporas are formed out of dispersed cultural populations that then organize themselves to either seize power back in their homelands or to influence political frameworks and institutions there. The important thing to note is that these diaspora categories are not mutually exclusive but can be co-constitutive depending on historical configuration.[25] Thus, the Irish diaspora after the Potato Famine of the 1840s may be said to have combined features of a victim diaspora with that of environmental diaspora (another cause of violent dispersal), but with a steady stream of economic migration to different parts of the world. That by the early part of the twentieth century the Irish also had a highly active ethno-political diaspora, especially in the United States, cannot be discounted. However, while the negative responses to the Irish in London that Ackroyd speaks of were to continue well into the twentieth century, it has to be noted that it is not the conditions of Irish denigration that Beckett focuses upon in *Murphy*. Rather, as Bixby notes, the unhomeliness of the characters in the novel is produced simultaneously by their attempts at differentiating themselves from the implicit demands of the Irish Revival and Irish nationalism, as well as by their attempts at making their way in metropolitan London. They are economic migrants with a highly sophisticated yet ironic attitude to the politics of their homeland as well as to their city of sojourn. Their postcolonial condition requires them to think of themselves continually from dual homeland and diasporic perspectives at once, much like in the many other postcolonial diasporic novels we noted earlier.

[25] The literature on modern diasporas is now quite substantial. For a useful sampling, see especially Robin Cohen's *Global Diasporas: An Introduction*, 2nd edition (London: Routledge, 2008); Gabriel Sheffer, *Diaspora Politics: At Home Abroad* (Cambridge: Cambridge University Press, 2006); Stéphane Dufoix, *Diasporas* (Berkeley: California University Press, 2008); and Ato Quayson and Girish Daswani, eds., *Companion to Diaspora and Transnational Studies*, (New York: Blackwell, 2013).

At the same time, the intermixing of tragic and comic elements that saturates *Murphy* requires us to read it quite differently from any other postcolonial novel in the same diasporic category. For one thing, Beckett goes to great pains to ensure that his central character is not taken too seriously. In a letter to Thomas McGreevy, he writes:

> The point you raise is one that I have given a good deal of thought to. Very early on, when the mortuary and Round Pond scenes were in my mind as the necessary end, I saw the difficulty and danger of so much following Murphy's own "end." There seemed two ways out. One was to let the death have its head in a frank climax and the rest be definitely epilogue (by some such means as you suggest. I thought for example of putting the game of chess there in a section itself). And the other, which I chose and tried to act on, was to keep the death subdued and go on as coolly and finish as briefly as possible. I chose this because it seemed to me to consist better with the treatment of Murphy throughout, with the mixture of compassion, patience, mockery and "tat twam asi" that I seem to have directed on him throughout, with the sympathy going so far and no further (then losing patience) as in the short statement of his mind's fantasy on itself. There seemed to me always the risk of taking him too seriously and separating him too sharply from the others.[26]

Beckett writes this in response to McGreevy's observation that the characters in the novel are all essentially lovable. The contrast between what Beckett sought to do with Murphy and what an astute reader such as McGreevy saw in him and in the other characters is instructive, because it suggests that, in spite of Beckett's best efforts, he could not prevent a degree of sympathy and indeed identification with the plight of these fictional characters, especially from a fellow Irishman. But the possibility of sympathy and identification goes beyond being Irish and is due to what we recognize as Murphy's extreme solitude, that nevertheless is also firmly coupled to a desire to seek one much like himself. As Beckett notes in another letter to McGreevy just over a week earlier: "I shall have to go into TCD after Geulincx, as he does not exist in National Library. I suddenly see that Murphy is break down [sic] between his *ubi nihil vales ibi nihil velis*

---

[26] Letter to Thomas McGreevy, June 7, 1936, *The Letters of Samuel Beckett, 1929–1940*, eds., Martha Dow Fehsenfeld and Lois More Overbeck (Cambridge: Cambridge University Press, 2009), 350. "Ta tam aswasi," from the Sanskrit, meaning "that thou art" is a phrase drawn from the *Chandogya Upanishad* and taken up by Arthur Schopenhauer in the essay "Character" where he differentiates between two ways of regarding the world. The first understands all others with indifference as "not ourselves," and the second, which he calls the "Tat-twam-asi – this-is-itself principle," understands all others as identical with ourselves. This helpful gloss to the phrase is provided in fn. 3 to the letter to McGreevy of June 7. The footnote is on page 350 of *The Letters of Samuel Beckett*.

(position) & Malraux's *il est difficile à celui qui vit hors du monde de ne pas rechercher les siens* (negation)."[27] The first phrase Beckett refers to here is from Geulincx, who in discussing "Contempt of Self" in the *Ethica* suggests that "Where you are nothing, may you also wish for nothing," while the second, from Malraux's *La Condition Humaine* translates as "The ultimate solitude, for it is difficult for one who lives isolated from the everyday world not to seek others like himself."[28] Thus solitude and quest are two essential motivations to Murphy's character. But unlike the other tragic, postcolonial characters we have encountered so far, Murphy's quest is not for any concrete bid for freedom from either political or social oppression, but rather derives from his relentless attraction to patterns and patterned behavior in what disability scholars will readily recognize as characteristic of autistic spectrum disorders. As I noted earlier, when I first wrote on *Murphy* some years ago my focus was, unlike Bixby's, not on its diasporic and postcolonial credentials. Nor did I in any sense emphasize its tragic aspects. To revisit *Murphy* again through the framework of postcolonial *tragedy*, as I wish to do now, is to reinterpret Murphy's attraction to patterns not just as an aspect of his location on the autistic spectrum but rather as a central feature of his failed quest for analogical validation of his own mind in the *unheimlich* context of London.

Autistic Spectrum Disorders and Murphy's Failed Analogical Validation

I take my cue for the idea of analogical validation from Thomas Owens' fine discussion of the subject in *Wordsworth, Coleridge, and "The Language of the Heavens."* There Owens suggests that the two poets developed "a relational way of seeing the world which was indebted to a language of shapes drawn from natural, geometric, celestial, and scientific sources."[29] In what was a special species of analogical thinking, Wordsworth and Coleridge did not simply imagine one thing in terms of another, as would be the case in thinking metaphorically, but saw the shapes and patterns that were

[27] Letter to McGreevy, 16 January, 1936, *The Letters of Samuel Beckett*, 299.
[28] Geulincx, *Ethica*, Tract I, Cap. II, S. II., paragraph 3, *Arnoldi Geulincx antverpiensis Opera Philosophica. Sumptibus providerunt Sortis spinozianae curatores*, vol 1., ed. Jan Pieter Nicolas Land (The Hague: apud Martinum Nijhoff, 1891–1893), 37; and Andre Malraux, *La Condition Humaine* (Romans, Paris: Gallimard, 1947), 353. Both translations are from *The Letters of Samuel Beckett*, fn. 5, 302.
[29] Thomas Owens, *Wordsworth, Coleridge, and "The Language of The Heavens"* (Oxford: Oxford University Press, 2019), 4.

depicted in mathematics and astronomy as directly fructifying their own poetry. As Owens adroitly shows, anatomical shapes discovered in nature, such as circles, dewdrops, crescents, and centrifugal and centripetal forces, found mimetic analogies in Wordsworth and Coleridge's poetics. The argument for analogical thinking of the mathematical type that Owens describes is also relevant to understanding Murphy's quest for patterns and the autistic spectrum disorder that inspires it. The moment when the quest is simultaneously fulfilled and frustrated occurs toward the end of the novel, in the chess game that takes place between Murphy and the imperturbable Mr. Endon at the Magdalen Mental Mercyseat. Murphy's frustrated quest is the ultimate marker of the unhomeliness that Bixby writes of, for it replicates the foundational quest for home that the Irish characters pursue in London that, in its turn, is discursively aligned to the sense of a hermeneutical crisis, not just for Murphy, but for his friend Neary, and even to some degree for Celia, his girlfriend. With specific reference to Murphy, however, he pursues analogy not through forms of mirroring of like with like but rather through the attempt at parallel replication of complicated patterns from world to mind and vice-versa. This bears resemblance to the type of analogical thinking that Owens describes for Wordsworth and Coleridge. Murphy's attraction to patterns is the means by which he attempts to "free his mind" as a way of asserting his solitude and freedom from all dependencies while at the same time seeking one like himself. The claim to solitude is grounded especially on his active disavowal of any materialist dependencies that might serve to yoke him to a given identity, whether this be national, capitalist, or even amorous, as it pans out in his relationship with Celia. And yet his affirmation of solitude is fundamentally undermined precisely because, in the true nature of Geulincx's lonely man, Murphy is compelled to seek one like himself and mistakenly thinks he has found this in the person of Mr. Endon. But Mr. Endon is not like Murphy; he refutes analogy completely. As we shall see shortly, Mr. Endon too is wedded to patterns but not ones that reflect anything from the outside world but only as pure image-shapes within his own peculiar schizophrenia. Hence to Mr. Endon, Murphy can be nothing but a figment of individual imagination – both Mr. Endon's and Murphy's. That Murphy's analogical quest is staged in the context of a diasporic sojourn in London is relevant to his tragedy, as we shall see. Bixby as well as David Lloyd, Sean Kennedy, Emilie Morin, and various others have amply shown that the Dublin he and his friends left behind, in the doldrums of a semi-colonial identity crisis, was rife with its own nationalist analogical quests.[30]

Aspects of autistic spectrum disorders, but especially of Asperger's syndrome, are pertinent to an analysis of Murphy's analogical quests. Uta Frith, one of the best-known authorities on autism, provides a working definition of the condition:

> Autism is due to a specific brain abnormality. The origin of the abnormality can be any of three causes: genetic fault, brain insult [injury] or brain disease. Autism is a developmental disorder, and therefore its behavioral manifestations vary with age and ability. Its core features, present in different forms, at all stages of development and at all levels of ability, are impairments in socialization, communication and imagination.[31]

Asperger's syndrome (AS) on the other hand is generally marked by fluent if unusual speech, along with different degrees of social ineptitude and a fascination with patterns and systems, either linguistic, numeric, or alphanumeric. Of the eleven features of persons with AS listed by Simon Baron-Cohen, the most pertinent to a reading of *Murphy* are 1) their fascination with systems, be they simple (light switches, water taps), a little bit more complex (weather fronts), or abstract (mathematics); 2) their tendency to follow their own desires and beliefs rather than paying attention to, or indeed acknowledging, others' desires and beliefs; and 3) their preference for experiences that are controllable rather than unpredictable. Aligned with their fascination with systems is also a strong attraction toward repetition, whether in patterns and systems, or rhythmic actions of particular kinds – something that is arguably inherent in patterns and systems in the first place. The overarching and central aspect of the autistic/Asperger's syndrome continuum, however, is silence and lack of communication. While these features may be said to be common in different degrees to many non-autistic people, what differentiates the autist is the fact that the features are mutually reinforcing and become central aspects of the autist's identity as such.[32]

---

[30] See David Lloyd, *Anomalous States: Irish Writing and the Post-Colonial Moment* (Duke University Press, 1993); Sean Kennedy, ed., *Beckett and Ireland* (Cambridge: Cambridge University Press, 2010), Emilie Morin, *Beckett's Political Imagination* (Cambridge: Cambridge University Press, 2019).

[31] Uta Frith, "Asperger and His Syndrome," *Autism and Asperger Syndrome*, Uta Frith, ed. (Cambridge: Cambridge University Press 1991), 2.

[32] Simon Baron-Cohen provides the list of symptoms in "Is Asperger's Syndrome Necessarily a Disability?," *Development and Psychopathology*, 12 (2000): 489–500. But see also his *Mindblindness: An Essay on Autism and Theory of Mind*, (Cambridge, MA: MIT Press, 1995) and also Simon Baron-Cohen, Helen Tager-Flusberg and Donald Cohen, eds. *Understanding Other*

Stillness is a central part of Murphy's character and provides an important dimension to what I want to argue is his autistic syndrome. When we first meet him, he has tied himself up with seven scarves to a rocking chair and desires to rock himself into a state of absolute stillness:

> He sat in his chair in this way because it gave him pleasure! First it gave his body pleasure, it appeased his body. Then it set him free in his mind. For it was not until his body was appeased that he could come alive in his mind, as described in section six.
>
> . . . he fastened his hand back to the strut, he worked up the chair. Slowly he felt better, astir in his mind, in the freedom of that light and dark that did not clash, nor alternate, nor fade nor lighten except to their communion, as described in section six. The rock got faster and faster, shorter and shorter, the iridescence was gone, the cry in the mew was gone, soon his body would be quiet. Most things under the moon got slower and slower and then stopped, a rock got faster and faster and then stopped. Soon his body would be quiet, soon he would be free.[33]

This was to me the first clue to his location on the autistic spectrum. The connection between feeling "astir in his mind" and the rhythm of motion-to-stillness encapsulated in rock, cry, and most sublunary objects, embeds Murphy within a diurnal order specifically yoked to the progressive dissolution of life. As the novel progresses, we get more evidence of Murphy's fascination with patterns and systems. We are provided with two main nodal points for exploring this fascination. First, is his fascination with his lunch biscuits and the permutations he considers eating them in and second is the game of chess with Mr. Endon toward the end of the novel. Suk's astrological chart provides a third nodal point, but this is less well focused than the previous two examples. The five biscuits – a Ginger, an Osborne, a Digestive, a Petit Beurre and one anonymous – present a peculiar problem for Murphy. The variety of sequences in which he contemplates ingesting them in order to achieve the highest number of permutations is hampered by the fact that he always eats the Ginger biscuit first. This is despite recognizing that "were he to take the final step and overcome his infatuation to the ginger, then the assortment would spring to life before him, dancing the radiant measure of its total permutability, edible in a hundred and twenty ways!"[34] The biscuits are seen by Murphy not as mere digestibles but as ciphers of concealed numeric patterns. He does not want to free himself from desire; rather his desire is precisely to

---

Minds: Perspectives from Developmental Cognitive Neuroscience (Oxford: Oxford University Press 1993).
[33] Beckett, *Murphy*, 2, 9.   [34] Beckett, *Murphy*, 96–97.

translate the mundane act of eating into an avenue for accessing mathematical possibilities. One is reminded of Molloy's intent effort at distributing his six sucking stones among his four pockets so that he will be able to suck each stone in sequence and without repetition. It is a major mathematical conundrum that runs continuously for six pages of *Molloy*.[35]

One of the discursive features that comes to ramify at different levels of *Murphy* is the splitting or reluctant attribution of perspectival ascription, or what we might describe as referential equivocation, as if the narrative in general is mimicking the social reluctance of the autistic character himself.[36] Even though the novel is told through the viewpoint of a third-person narrator, this narrator's perspective is itself firmly tied to the consciousness of the characters themselves, such as Celia, Mr. Kelly, Neary, and of course Murphy. However, it is not always possible to clearly identify what perspective particular segments of the narrative are being told from. Focalization is blurred, and the narrative voice seems to be sardonic and satirical in its refusal to clearly locate the source of narrative perspective. Consider this example:

> Miss Carridge's day had a nucleus, the nice strong cup of tea that she took in the afternoon. It sometimes happened that she sat down to this elixir with the conviction of having left undone none of those things that paid and done none of those things that did not pay. Then she would pour out a cup for Celia and tiptoe with it up the stairs. Miss Carridge's method of entering a private apartment was to knock timidly on the door on the outside some time after she had closed it behind her on the inside. Not even a nice hot cup of tea in her hand could make her subject to the usual conditions of time and space in this matter. It was as though she had an accomplice.[37]

The deadpan tone in which the narrator relates what is a physical impossibility is a hint to the fact that he wants to convey Miss Carridge's furtiveness (he calls it timidity) from two perspectives at once. It is as if Miss Carridge wishes to be able to surprise the tenants in the private

---

[35] Samuel Beckett, *Molloy*, in *Three Novels: Molloy, Malone Dies, The Unnamable* (New York: Grove Press, 1958), 69–74.

[36] The difficulties of perspectival ascription in *Murphy* is noted by J. M. Coetzee in *Doubling the Point: Essays and Interviews*, ed. David Attwell; Coetzee wrote his doctoral dissertation on Samuel Beckett and returned to the older writer many times in the course of his own career. See for instance, "Eight Ways of Looking at Samuel Beckett," in Minako Okamura, Naoya Mori, and Bruno Clement, eds., *Samuel Beckett Today/Aujourd'hui*, vol. 19, Borderless Beckett/Beckett sans frontières: Tokyo 2006 (2008), 19–31; "The Making of Samuel Beckett," *New York Review of Books*, 56:7 (30 April 2009); www.nybooks.com/articles/2009/04/30/the-making-of-samuel-beckett/, last accessed June 3, 2018. On referential equivocation, see Jacques Derrida's highly suggestive discussion of Kafka's *The Trial* in Derek Attridge, ed., *Acts of Literature* (London: Routledge, 2015).

[37] Beckett, *Murphy*, 67–68.

apartments by entering the apartments completely unnoticed while also satisfying the basic courtesy of knocking on the outside of the door before entering. What seems to be a wish inside of Miss Carridge's mind is described by the narrator as taking place in real space-time yet with a tone of mild incredulity. But what we see as the splitting of perspectival ascription here also represents a formal constitutive gap that is manifested at different discursive levels of the text. Miss Carridge's almost magical capacity to knock on the outside of a door when she is already inside behind the closed door is just one species of this gap.

Referential equivocation and the refusal of perspectival ascription also pertain to Murphy's silence and the decidedly aporetic character of his speech. This is related to his impulse toward stillness, an aspect of his autistic spectrum disorder. Murphy is less silent than other characters in Beckett's novels such as say, Molloy, Malone, Watt, and others; yet what makes his speech ultimately baffling is its elusive nature and the ways in which it appears consistently to generate aporia rather than meaning. Whereas the progressively complicated lines of the plot ultimately lead all the characters to Murphy, he seems to have more speech attributed to him by others than spoken by himself. It is more often the case that the narrator and the other characters will impute or report Murphy's opinions than that he will speak them himself, making him one of the most silent characters in the novel. Celia and Miss Counihan are midpoint between Neary and Wylie (the most talkative), while Murphy, Cooper, and Endon (the least talkative) are on the other extreme of the speech/silence spectrum. One thing shared by the more silent group is that they all carry illnesses and impairments of various sorts. They each represent forms of fraught embodiment. Thus, we are told, for example, that Cooper has "a curious hunted walk, like that of a destitute diabetic in a strange city," and also that his "only visible humane characteristic was a morbid craving for alcoholic depressant."[38] In addition he has only one good eye, never sits down, and never takes off his hat. (He does both toward the end of the novel, when they are returning in the taxi after identifying Murphy's burnt-up corpse at the morgue.)

The significance of Murphy's silence stems not from his speechlessness per se but from the endemic aporetic elusiveness of his utterances. Celia in particular finds this most baffling:

---

[38] Beckett, *Murphy*, 54.

> They said little. Sometimes Murphy would begin to make a point, some-
> times he may have even finished making one, it was hard to say. For
> example, early one morning he said: "The hireling fleeth because he is an
> hireling." Was this a point? And again: "What shall a man give in exchange
> for Celia?" Was that a point?[39]

Mr. Kelly, the paraplegic uncle to whom Celia is reporting her difficulties
with Murphy, thinks that these are undoubtedly points. But that, we
might say with her, is not the point. For this is how Murphy's speech
ultimately strikes her:

> She felt, as she felt so often with Murphy, spattered with words that went
> dead as soon as they sounded; each word obliterated, before it had time to
> make sense, by the word that came next; so that in the end she did not know
> what had been said. It was like difficult music heard for the first time.[40]

The description of the effects of Murphy's language are emblematic of
Beckett's work as a whole, for it is a good summation of the language of
*Endgame, Waiting for Godot, Krapp's Last Tape, Happy Days, The
Unnamable,* and of much of his narrative fiction in general. Ultimately,
what these works generate is an epistemological impasse rather than any
sense of certainty so that we as readers or spectators are required to work as
hard as the characters themselves in trying to make any sense of the worlds
that are laid out before us. Murphy's words come at Celia like stray drops
of paint from the brush of an artist whose works she cannot understand, or,
perhaps more disturbingly, like blood. When Celia says she "felt" spattered
with his words, it can safely be assumed that the word "felt" couples
emotive perception with cognitive misunderstanding. In trying to grasp
the meaning of Murphy's words, Celia seems to want to *feel* her way to
understanding them. And yet, with Murphy, both emotional and cognitive
understanding are rendered nearly impossible because of the enigmatic and
aporetic character of his speech.

In spite of what Beckett says in his letter to McGreevy regarding his
progressive loss of patience with Murphy as encapsulated in "the statement
of his mind's fantasy of itself," what is immediately noticeable in chapter 6
of the novel is, in fact, the equivocation of perspectival ascription pertaining to the standpoint from which the description of his mind emerges. In
exploring the description of "Murphy's mind," it is important to recognize
the oscillation between the omniscient narrator and the thoughts of the
character himself, which are subtly mediated through the narrator's voice

---

[39] Beckett, *Murphy*, 22.   [40] Beckett, *Murphy*, 40.

by way of free indirect discourse. The narrator first describes Murphy's mind as if it were an entity separate and autonomous from the rest of Murphy's being. It is referred to as "this apparatus," which is concerned "solely with what it pictured itself to be":

> Murphy's mind pictured itself as a large hollow sphere, hermetically closed to the universe without. This was not an impoverishment, for it excluded nothing that it did not itself contain. Nothing ever had been, was or would be in the universe outside it but was already present as virtual, or actual, or virtual rising into actual, or actual falling into virtual, in the universe inside it . . .
>
> The mind felt its actual part to be above and bright, its virtual beneath and fading into dark, without however connecting this with the ethical yoyo.[41]

Even though there seems to be a degree of overlap between the narrator's conception of Murphy's mind and Murphy's own self-conception of this entity, the description provided here makes it unclear whether Murphy is fully conscious of what "this apparatus" pictures itself to be. The distinction between the two will later prove useful when we come to explore the significance of Murphy's attempted analogy with Mr. Endon's mind, as well as the metonymic transfers that take place following the chess game between him and Mr. Endon. The two-part scheme pictured by the mind itself is later qualified by Murphy into a tripartite schema, not exclusively defined by the virtual or the actual, but rather by shades of light. Even though the narrator's reference to Murphy's mind as an apparatus is in line with the overall humorous tone of the narrative in general, it is salient for the discussion of the autistic dynamic in the novel because of the image of a hermetically sealed system that is used to represent it. The hermetically sealed and systematic dimension of "Murphy's mind" later becomes a trope of isolation that is illustrative of the text's autistic dynamic that shifts discursively between Murphy and Mr. Endon after their chess game.

In true Leibnizian mode, Murphy's mind is described first and foremost as an interface between inside and outside, "the big world and the little world," as Richard Begam put it.[42] With respect to the autistic dynamic, however, what is of interest here is that Murphy's mind is being described in the first instance as a self-determining and autonomous entity while also being represented as interactive with what lies outside its boundaries. Later,

---

[41] Beckett, *Murphy*, 107–108.
[42] This is Richard Begam's description of the dynamic inside/outside nature of Murphy's mind in *Samuel Beckett and the End of Modernity* (Stanford: Stanford University Press, 1996).

when Murphy reflects upon his own mind (as opposed to the mind reflecting upon itself in the voice of the narrator), we are told that Murphy "felt himself split in two, a body and a mind."[43] Since his understanding of his mind does not generate any particular emotional response from him, the word "felt" as it is used here appears more cognitive than emotional and is in accordance with the narrator and Murphy's general attempt to objectively anatomize his mind.

In the description of Murphy's mind, a series of dialectical movements are defined between mind and body: the relationship between the inside and the outside of his hermetically sealed mind is at a primordial level, with the outside creating imagistic residues that reside inside of the mental sphere. This primary inside/outside dimension is then augmented by Murphy's own affective cognition (a thought-feeling or a feeling-thought) of an apparent intercourse between body and mind. In other words, the inside/outside dialectic is augmented by a supplementary one, that between body and mind. But where, then, do inside and outside reside spatially? The relationship between mind and body itself retains the quality of a perennial enigma in the novel since Murphy also considers his mind to be exclusively "bodytight" and by implication impervious to the dictates of his body. To the inside/outside, and mind/body dialectical set is added a third, which is registered as the opposition between autonomous mind and externally integrated system. Does this mean that Murphy feels his mind as an entity inextricably entangled with the mortal coil of his body yet autonomous in and of itself, or does he consider it to be part of a larger integrated apparatus that includes his body as an aspect of an externally generated system? Most commentators have settled on the former explanation, but, strictly speaking, it is impossible to decide conclusively between the two. This ambiguity, I suggest, creates a significant gap within the text – a gap that is inextricably connected to the workings of the autistic dynamic, for it speaks directly to the difficulty that the autistic character has in acknowledging emotion if it is not tied to the expression of a clearly reproducible pattern or system. The difficulty for the character translates into a difficulty for the critic since it is not possible to decide from the evidence of chapter 6 what the exact relationships are between Murphy's mind, body, and the external world.

The description of Murphy's mind does not stop at these dialectical sets (of inside/outside, mind/body, and autonomy of mind and body/integration with external system) but is augmented by another set of metaphors,

[43] Beckett, *Murphy*, 109.

this time drawing on the spatial relations between light and shade. Murphy imagines his mind as divided into three zones of light, half-light, and dark, "each with its specialty." With respect to the three zones and their distinctive qualities, the light zone embodies the "forms with parallel," the residues from physical experience that make themselves available for fresh rearrangements. The main pleasure inherent in this zone is the possibility of reversing his own experiences, so that "the whole physical fiasco became a howling success."[44] In the second zone, of half-light, the forms are without parallel, and the pleasure is derived mainly from contemplation. In both of these worlds Murphy feels himself to be free, able to be satisfied without regard to potential "rival initiatives." The third zone, the dark, is "a flux of forms, a perpetual coming together and falling asunder of forms."[45] It is also a space of constant becoming where all forms, sentiments, and feelings are liminal and therefore rapidly changeable without his conscious intervention:

> He distinguished between the actual and the virtual of his mind, not as between form and the formless yearning for form, but as between that of which he had both mental and physical experience and that of which he had mental experience only … The mental experience was cut off from the physical experience, its criteria were not those of the physical experience, the agreement of part of its content with physical fact did not confer worth on that part.[46]

It is the third zone, where Murphy is "not free, but a mote in the dark of absolute freedom" for which he consciously yearns and for which the rhythmic motion of his rocking chair is a necessary conduit:

> Thus as his body set him free more and more in his mind, he took to spending less and less time in the light, spitting at the breakers of the world; and less in the half light, where the choice of bliss introduced an element of effort; and more and more and more in the dark, in the will-lessness, a mote in its absolute freedom.[47]

But is this an attempt to free himself from thought into pure feeling or the other way round? And what insights about himself does he hope to achieve with the rhythmic diminuendo provided by the motions of the rocking chair? There does not seem to be a clear answer, at least not directly. Rather, we now find that the trope of the hermetically sealed mind has been augmented by a map-like and patterned system of light,

[44] Beckett, *Murphy*, 111.   [45] Beckett, *Murphy*, 112.   [46] Beckett, *Murphy*, 108.
[47] Beckett, *Murphy*, 113.

shade, and imagistic residues. Furthermore, the map itself is both conceptual and spatial since the movement is ultimately toward the dark, which is
both a zone and a mental quality. The metaphors that Beckett deploys in
describing Murphy's mind generate something akin to a Borgesian
enigma, in which the initial terms of the narrative puzzle begin to shift
and proliferate further contradictions as soon as they are set against one
another in any attempt at categorical clarity. The effort to solve the puzzle
is thoroughly defeated by the simultaneous orderliness and chaos of the
enigma, something that we see amply exemplified in stories by Borges such
as "The Garden of Forking Paths," or "Tlön, Uqbar, Orbis Tertius." In the
case of Beckett's text, we may take the proliferation of metaphors specifically relating to inside/outside, mind/body, autonomy/system integration,
and map/zone distinctions as a narrative dimension of the autistic
dynamic. The textual patterning at this stage as it relates to the mentalscape
of a character who is arguably autistic mimes, at a wider discursive level, the
determined principles of patterned ordering that have been noted as
features of autistic spectrum disorders. In each instance of the description
of Murphy's mind, the emotions are completely excised from account.
Like an autistic person, Murphy appears to tie his emotions exclusively to
ordered patterns and systems. His emotions return devastatingly into play
only when he perceives an analogy between his own mindscape and
Mr. Endon's but fails to secure a mirrored recognition of his own identity
from the latter. This failure triggers a crisis of self-perception and ultimately leads to Murphy's accidental death.

Analogical Displacements and the Game of Chess

Of the various loci of patterns within the novel it is the game of chess that
has attracted the most critical attention, and for good reason. It takes place
on Murphy's first night shift at the MMM, where his duties involve
making rounds of the ward at regular intervals and turning on and off
the lights in patients' cells to ascertain that none of the inmates has come to
harm in the interval between the rounds. The purpose of turning on the
light switches is also to record each cell visit on the electric switchboard
located in Bom's (the boss's) apartment. On arriving at Endon's cell that
night, a strange sight meets Murphy's eyes:

> Mr. Endon, an impeccable and brilliant figurine in his scarlet gown, his crest
> a gush of vivid white against the black shag, squatted tailor-fashion on the
> head of his bed, holding his left foot in his right hand and in his left hand his

right foot. The purple poulaines were on his feet and the rings were on his fingers. The light spurted off Mr. Endon north, south, east, west and in fifty-six other directions. The sheet stretched away before him, as smooth and taut as a groaning wife's belly, and on it a game of chess was set up. The little blue and olive face, wearing an expression of winsome fiat, was upturned to the judas.[48]

In the game of chess that follows, Mr. Endon plays Black and Murphy, White. Since the two of them have already been conducting intermittent games of chess during the course of Murphy's daylight rounds of the ward, the nocturnal setup is not entirely surprising. What is surprising is the peculiar character of the game they play on this occasion. Endon is interested only in constructing a private system of play with his own pieces. But this is not something that Murphy realizes until it is too late. Despite opening with White, Murphy ends up imitating Endon's moves, who plays in such a way as to ultimately return all of his Black pieces to their starting positions on the back rank. The only pieces that cannot be so returned are the pawns, only two of which Endon moves. Murphy's imitation of Endon's chess moves operates at two levels simultaneously: first, at the level of the movement of the pieces themselves and second, at the level of mirroring Endon's mind. As Taylor and Loughrey put it, "The imperfect attempt at mirror-symmetry is thus an expression of the relationship between Black and White. It is also a comment on Endon and Murphy as individuals: Endon is pursuing temporal symmetry for its own sake; Murphy is committed to the pursuit of temporal symmetry because Endon is pursuing it, and to mirror-symmetry because he is pursuing Endon."[49] In attempting an imitation of Endon's moves, Murphy's engagement is "not with the movements of the inanimate chess pieces, but with the movements of an animate mind, Endon's."[50] However, Murphy's mimetic effort is inherently imperfect because he assumes that Endon is actually playing chess with him, when, in fact, the system that Endon pursues is one of utter chaos, even if it is masked by way of the chess moves. Endon is not playing against White but only using White's moves as a trigger for elaborating his exclusive and ultimately inimitable private system. Murphy resigns on the forty-third move.

---

[48] Beckett, *Murphy*, 241.
[49] Neil Taylor and Bryan Loughrey, "Murphy's Surrender to Symmetry," *Journal of Beckett Studies*, 11/12 (1989): 5. See also, Thomas J. Cousineau, "Demented vs. Creative Emulation in *Murphy*," *Samuel Beckett Today/Aujourd'hui*, vol. 18 (2007): 355–365.
[50] Taylor and Loughrey, 7.

Not only is the game of chess the most significant focalization of Murphy's fixation with patterns and systems, it is also the point at which the narrative performs a series of switches and transfers along the entire rhetorical plane, and more specifically, on the metonymic axis. And since it is the point at which Murphy, the autistic character, is pitted against Endon, the mild schizophrenic, it is also the juncture at which the process of analogical patterning becomes most pronounced. However, as we can see throughout the novel in general, the process of analogical patterns is not limited to this primary level but is augmented by tensions refracted across other levels of the text such as the disposition of spatial motifs, the overall reluctance of perspectival ascription, and the constitutive aporia of both speech and plot structure. The conclusion of the game of chess is the moment when Murphy's emotional confusion is made fully evident, thus subtly tying autistic dynamic, emotion, and analogical quest together within a singular discursive ensemble.[51] In the game of chess they play, Endon's mind may be said to replicate the hermetically sealed system dimension of Murphy's mental space that we encountered in chapter 6. Thus, Murphy's failed imitation of Endon's mind is actually his failed imitation of the hermetically sealed and system-like aspect of "Murphy's mind," which is elaborated by the narrator but to all intents and purposes is not reflexively revealed to Murphy's own consciousness. For despite playing against an opponent, what Endon does is essentially use his opponent's moves as a cue for the elaboration of his own hermetic personal system, thus effacing the opponent and converting him into a mere function of Endon's own system. This exemplification of the system-like dimension of the "mind of Murphy" by Endon is crucial to what happens directly after their chess game, since it implies a displacement of significations along the metonymic axis such that, after the chess game Murphy becomes Endon and Endon, Murphy.

Directly after Murphy resigns from the chess game he is overwhelmed by an irresistible desire to sleep. He drops his head amongst the chess pieces, perceiving as he does so a series of fragmentary images not dissimilar to what might be adduced as existing in the dark zone of his own mind:

---

[51] This section of metonymic displacements between the two characters fundamentally alters the largely realist basis of the text and satisfies the principle of aesthetic nervousness through which I read the scene in "Autism, Narrative, and Emotions." For a fuller definition and account of the concept of aesthetic nervousness, see Ato Quayson, *Aesthetic Nervousness: Disability and the Crisis of Representation.*

Following Mr. Endon's forty-third move Murphy gazed for a long time at the board before laying his Shah on his side, and again for a long time after that act of submission. But little by little his eyes were captured by the brilliant swallow-tail of Mr. Endon's arms and legs, purple, scarlet, black and glitter, till they saw nothing else, and that in a short time only as a vivid blur, Neary's big blooming buzzing confusion or ground, mercifully free of figure. Wearying soon of this he dropped his head on his arms in the midst of the chessmen, which scattered with a terrible noise. Mr. Endon's finery persisted for a little in an after-image scarcely inferior to the original. Then this also faded and Murphy began to see nothing, that colourlessness which is such a rare postnatal treat, being the absence (to abuse a nice distinction) not of *percipere* but of *percipi*.[52]

The reference to "Neary's big blooming buzzing confusion or ground" is to his friend's Pythagorean system of which we get various hints in the course of the novel. It is not clear how long Murphy sleeps, but when he wakes up "in the familiar variety of stenches, asperities, ear-splitters and eye-closers," Mr. Endon has gone missing.[53]

Now, for anyone with experience of playing chess, Murphy's sudden slumber is extraordinary. Chess is the direct opposite of a soporific; rather it tends to arouse the mind. Whether they win or lose, chess players generally tend to mentally replay the game after it ends in order to review their strengths and weaknesses. The hypnotic sleep Murphy falls into should not be taken as just an "unrealistic" detail; it also marks what I think is a subtle yet decisive shift in the largely realist discourse that has been operational up to this point. The unrealistic detail of the post-chess-game slumber marks a shift from the overall realist mode toward a supplementary set of relations based on discursive displacements along the metonymic axis of the text. I use the term supplementary because the essential logic of realism is not entirely overthrown. Rather, the metonymic shifts are generated as a new underlying logic that remains partially concealed by the realist discourse. This shift is not at all straight-forward but defines itself via a rhythmic pattern of oscillations, in what we might describe as a metonymic circle.

On escaping the cell, Endon,

> had been drifting about the corridors, pressing here a light-switch and there an indicator, in a way that seemed haphazard but was in fact determined by a mental pattern as precise as any of those governed by chess. Murphy found him in the south transept, gracefully stationed before the hypomaniac's pad, ringing the changes on the various ways in which the indicator could be

---

[52] Beckett, *Murphy*, 246, emphasis in original.   [53] Beckett, *Murphy*, ibid.

pressed and the light turned on and off. Beginning with the light turned off to begin with he had: lit, indicated, extinguished; lit, extinguished, indicated; indicated, lit, extinguished. Continuing then with the light turned on to begin with he had: extinguished, lit, indicated; extinguished, indicated, lit; indicated, extinguished and was seriously thinking of lighting when Murphy stayed his hand.[54]

Mr. Endon is here performing Murphy's role after the articulation of the imperturbable symmetry of his "Murphy's mind" in the chess game just completed. He has switched places with Murphy across the chess board, whose discursive function has partially been to enable the initiation of metonymic transfer and the progressive shaping of the metonymic circle that will follow the game.

After returning Endon to his cell, Murphy clutches Endon's face between his hands and gazes deep into his eyes. He finds himself "stigmatized in the eyes that did not see him."[55] For Murphy is merely a "speck in Endon's unseen."[56] This generates an emotional crisis for Murphy since it proves to him once and for all that not only does he remain unrecognized by Endon but also that he is not admitted to what he supposed was a higher state of stillness that he thought Endon represented. To the reader, it suggests that all along Murphy has actually been on a quest for a form of analogical validation, something that is hermeneutical as well as emotional. As we just saw, Endon's mind is an exemplum of the closed system of "Murphy's mind," but without reference to the three zones of light, half-light, and darkness that so preoccupy Murphy. Even though Endon is a mild schizophrenic, the point to remember is that his "Murphy's mind" is still illustrative of one part of Murphy's – the hermetically sealed and autonomous part that unsees the Other of the big world. The other part refracts residual images within its own internal matrix, but this part is sealed off by Mr Endon, thus enacting the hermetically sealed dimension of "Murphy's mind" without any possibility of refraction or acknowledgment of the real world, in this particular case, of Murphy himself.

After this moment of startling Aristotelian *anagnorisis*, Murphy runs out of the ward in a highly distraught state, strips off his clothes, and lies on the grass in the half dawn trying to evoke images of proximate and distant social interlocutors. He starts off by trying to visualize Celia. Nothing. His mother. Nothing. His father. Again, nothing. He goes through a list of friends and associates, then moves on to men, women, and animals unfamiliar to him. Alas, all is in vain: "Scraps of bodies, of landscapes,

---

[54] Beckett, *Murphy*, 246–247.   [55] Beckett, *Murphy*, 249.   [56] Beckett, *Murphy*, 250.

hands, eyes, lines and colors evoking nothing, rose and climbed out of sight before him, as though reeled upward off a spool level with his throat."[57] It is almost as if the hermetically sealed dimension of his "Murphy's mind," the part most associated with Endon, has taken over such that his attempts at invoking the images of sociality end up producing only fragmentary imagistic residues of persons, places, and things. He rushes up to his room to desperately avail himself of the rocking chair to make his body go quiet. The quiet of his body coincides, however, with the explosion of gas in the WC that he has precariously hooked up to the radiator in his garret. The "excellent gas, superfine chaos" is then the final element that is associated with Murphy's mind going quiet, thus recalling the chaos of Endon's chess moves, and beyond that the universal fiasco Murphy has been trying to escape from since the beginning of the novel.[58] What Mr. Endon induces in Murphy is a deep quest for analogical validation. This is not available, since Endon is only playing with a reflection of his own self.

But if we ascribe a causal relation between the autistic patterns that Murphy exhibits and is attracted to throughout the novel and his ultimate disappointment and death, does this not appear to be somewhat mechanistically determinist? (Are we not thinking like Murphy?) And is this enough for us to suggest that Murphy suffers and thus must elicit our sympathy? Or is it the progressive collapse of his hermeneutical quest for patterns that justifies the application of the label of tragedy? Where does his *hamartia* lie, if at all? In spite of the mixture of comic and tragic characteristics that we find throughout the novel, there is enough to suggest that Murphy is a tragic rather than a comic character. This comes not from any attempt of his at forms of epic action, which are of course entirely out of his purview, but from the very nature of his struggle against personal disintegration. His primary interest is to arrive at a certain mental quietude that would not only bring him peace but would also permit him to integrate all aspects of inside and outside as he emerges from light and half-light "fading into dark, without however connecting this with the ethical yoyo." The terms of the ethical yoyo have been established for him throughout the novel as those of amorous love, which in their turn are tied to particular forms of economic rationality and thus to the requirement that he "be a man and find a job for himself." These are aspects of the regimes of normalcy that govern everybody else. By leaving his and Celia's apartment each morning and returning at exactly the same time each evening, he seems to be conceding to the external ritual form of economic discipline

---

[57] Beckett, *Murphy*, 252.　　[58] Beckett, *Murphy*, 254.

and yet not to its content. He fills the hiatus between daily departure from their apartment and arrival back there with sundry meanderings around London and earnest reflections upon the various permutations by which he might eat his biscuits. The five biscuits, as we noted earlier, present a peculiar problem for Murphy that is by far more engaging than the protocols of finding a job. In other words, what gives him peace is the active quest for patterns wherever they might be found and not the pointless searching for work. And it is this pattern-quest that ultimately leads him to the imperturbable Mr. Endon, with very unhappy consequences, as we have seen.

The collapse of Murphy's analogical quest is of a piece with what we might describe as a hermeneutical delirium. Hermeneutical delirium ramifies both at the level of interactions between the characters and between us and the text in such a way as to persistently frustrate any attempts at meaning-making. But the defeat or frustration of the quest for meaning situates hermeneutical delirium as a product of repeated circling, as though to replicate the slow going of time at the level of textual signification itself. When Murphy lies on the grass after the chess game and attempts to recall images of his friends and others he has known, it is as if in an attempt to identify a possible mode of integration into the sociality of *philia* different from his futile attempt at identification with Mr. Endon. But he fails here too, for in the ultimate instance whatever principle the sociality of *philia* represents cannot replicate the desire for patterns that is the first principle of the autistic spectrum. Thus, we return to echo Malraux; solitude necessitates the quest for one like one's lonely self, and yet in the autist's case the quest is always going to be defeated because what is required is the analogical reflection of patterns and not the sociality of *philia*. Murphy's accidental death at the end is only a formal discursive confirmation of what had already taken place inside his mind.

Postcolonial Illuminations: Free Time and the Plot of Inertia

What we just saw in *Murphy* as a process of analogical validation may also be extrapolated into a form of reading from Beckett in general to the postcolonial condition of waiting. To turn to Beckett for illuminating the burdens of free time requires us to recall our discussion of Wole Soyinka's *The Road* in Chapter 4, and beyond that to a thorough review of what is conventionally characterized as the informal economy. What is normally described by commentators as the entrepreneurial spirit demonstrated by people who, by the fact of under- or unemployment, have to subsist through informal economic networks is a sign not of enterprise but necessity. For the vagaries of the informal economy engender a tense preparedness for action at all times, even if this action is simply that of being constantly alert to various options and possibilities that may become available but that do not necessarily lead to the relief of the boredom and waiting that are a central part of the informal economy. This is what makes those under- and unemployed in Africa and elsewhere seem so entrepreneurial; they take up any opportunities that become available to them. It is also not unusual for the under- or unemployed to move deftly between short-term, low paying jobs, the defining condition here being not the jobs themselves, but the existential condition of impermanence that they generate by being both low-paying and transitory. Unlike the fictional Murphy, in the informal economy *not* doing anything is not really a choice available to the unemployed. The phenomenology of boredom, waiting, and the seemingly pointless circling of time that are definitive of the informal economy marks the condition of the Egyptian youth of Naga's description, of the *kòbòlòi* of Accra, the motor park workers in Soyinka's play, and of the unemployed and homeless denizens of Johannesburg that come to the soup kitchens organized by churches in that city. It is also the condition that drives the despairing youth of Guatemala City into drugs, and ultimately into the routines of rehabilitation regimes that are partially funded by religious organizations and partly by American charitable groups and security apparatus.[59] In each instance, the long-term waiting around for something to happen engenders acts of a what-if variety that may also tip over into acts of desperation.

Even though the conditions of the informal economy in Africa and other parts of the postcolonial world seem to be as far from *Waiting for Godot* or any of Beckett's works as can be imagined, waiting and the desperation to extract some semblance of meaning from that waiting is not dissimilar to the scenarios I have just enumerated. However, unlike any of these, because *Waiting for Godot* is ultimately free of economic rationality, the language games that characters such as Vladimir and Estragon play to while away their boredom end up being utterly devoid of any vestiges of

[59] For a discussion of the semi- or unemployed youth of Accra (*kòbòlòi*), see Quayson, *Oxford Street*, 183–212, 239–250; for those dependent on the soup kitchens of Johannesburg and the cycles of waiting that this defines, see Alex Wafer, "Informality, Infrastructure and the State in Post-apartheid Johannesburg," PhD dissertation, Department of Geography, Open University, 2011. On the youth of Guatemala City, see Kevin O'Neill, *Secure the Soul* (Berkeley: University of California Press, 2015). For a fine discussion of boredom as it appears on the edges of Europe following the fall of the Berlin Wall, see also Bruce O'Neill, *The Space of Boredom: Homelessness in the Slowing Global Order* (Durham: Duke University Press, 2017).

practicality. Had Beckett, for example, been a hypothetical Lagosian or
Guatemalan he would very well have had Vladimir and Estragon turn
themselves into entrepreneurial artisans of waste, recycling not just language, but any objects by which they might productively negotiate the
vagaries of free time. In this respect, their interaction with Lucky and Pozzo
might have been conceived quite differently. From the perspective of
a semi- or unemployed person in Cairo, Mumbai, or Accra, what greater
missed opportunity than that Vladimir and Estragon do not even *try* to sell
Estragon's recalcitrant boots to the evidently wealthy and self-involved
Pozzo when he enters the action in the middle of act 1? Vladimir and
Estragon's choices of action are not dominated by any form of economic
rationality and so their waiting can only be navigated through the language
games they play. As we noted in Chapter 4, while *The Road* is Beckettian it
is also thoroughly Lagosian, because along with their Yorùbá turns of
language and ritual, the unemployed motor park workers also participate
in cycles of epic dreaming that involves imagining themselves as drivers of
powerful trucks and lorries, and making money across Nigeria. Soyinka's
characters are economic beings first and last. But it is through the circularity and dissociative character of waiting and the burdens of free time that
the characters of *The Road* mirror Beckett's plays, and by implication,
provide the ways in which Beckett might be taken to illuminate Lagos in
the 1960s; in his turn, Soyinka might be used to examine Dublin or Irish
London in the 1920s. And Naga's Cairo of the early 2010s shares something
with both Beckett and Soyinka.

Conclusion

There is one further question we need to answer before we leave this
chapter, and that is in what ways does Murphy's condition divulge
a specific problematic for thinking about postcolonial tragedy? What, in
the end, is fundamentally tragic about *Murphy* and how might this be
related to Beckett's postcolonialism? The answer to the tragic quality of the
novel requires us to compare Murphy's crisis to those of the other tragic
characters we have encountered so far. Unlike Okonkwo, Ezeulu, Elesin
Oba, Sethe, and Baby Suggs, Murphy does not have any *grand récit* of
empire, colonialism, colonial modernity, or slavery against which he has to
define his own responses in rebellion or refutation. He is closest to the
Magistrate in that what appears to be an essentially unruly and self-
revisionary affective economy that does not issue forth in any decisive
gesture of revolt by which he might be memorialized for us readers. But

even the Magistrate has the scale of the cynical ideology of Colonel Joll and the Empire to contend with, and the dialectical relations between civilization and barbarism that preoccupy him echo forcefully for any real or even imagined imperial context we might think of. Murphy is also unlike Mustafa Sa'eed and Othello in that he does not make recourse to the guarantees of epic iconicity that are provided by orientalist metaphors and symbols. And yet to dismiss Murphy only on the terms of his lack of grand gesture is to signally ignore the lesson we learned from Arundhati Roy's novel about the salience of Small Things for helping us grasp the foundational basis of ethical choice-making. As we saw in the previous chapter, Big Things stand for grandly impacting social details such as politics, the Love Laws, and even nature, while Small Things stand for the domain of emotion, affect, and sentiment. It is from the world of Small Things that Murphy's quest for analogical validation gathers its force, since it also defines the terms by which he enacts being one thing (silent, introspective, pattern oriented) and not another (an economic subject). But it is this internal world of Small Things that also goes awry when the means of analogical validation rebounds on him and shows itself to be defective as a route to the comforts of *philia*, friendly rather than familial, unlike in *The God of Small Things*.

Furthermore, unlike in any of the other tragedies we have looked at, Beckett's work aims at fundamentally usurping any form of causal plausibility, thus wreaking havoc on the relation between cause and effect, past and present, language and referent, and signifier and signified. What we find in Beckett's Murphy is the minimal synopsis of an incipient self that is nevertheless waylaid by various systems – national, identitarian, religious – that seek to corral the Self to a pre-given order of things, to echo the title of Foucault's book. The price that Murphy pays for the rebuttal of this order is not as a consequence of any direct confrontation with it, but rather, like other Beckettian characters, is the direct product of being born at all in the first place. That is the "sin" that Beckett often refers to, the burden of which requires a constant circling and the repetition of disavowals against despair that nonetheless proves futile in the final instance. But even if one cannot go on, one must go on.

CHAPTER 10

Conclusion
Postcolonial Tragedy and the Question of Method

One of the primary motivations behind this book has been how to diversify the focal points by which we establish what passes for literary value. But for me, the issue of literary value does not simply imply the switching of contents, that is to say, replacing a Western text with a postcolonial one in our reading or pedagogical practices. Rather, it entails the primary question of how we read in the first place. And because both postcolonialism and tragedy are highly complex constellation concepts, they instigate the necessity for thinking closely about the dynamics of comparison, critical theory, interdisciplinarity, and the ethics of reading.

The historical contexts in which the literature we read were produced, and those in which our reading takes place are both of serious concern in postcolonial studies. This concern has undergone a series of shifts in both form and content. The relation between literary and historical context had already been suggested early in the gestation of the field by Aimé Césaire, Albert Memmi, Frantz Fanon, and other decolonial thinkers writing in the 1950s. In 1955, Aimé Césaire outlined the earliest form of what was later to be known as colonial discourse analysis in his monumental *Discours Sur Le Colonialisme*. He was followed in rapid succession by Albert Memmi and Frantz Fanon in setting out a mode of cultural analysis that was rhetorically sophisticated as well as refracting fresh revolutionary, political, and cultural ideals deriving from the decolonial moment. From the Caribbean, the works of C. L. R. James, Édouard Glissant, George Lamming, Wilson Harris, and V. S. Naipaul each raised key questions about nation-and-narration and the struggle between universalism and localism in the literature of the newly independent nations. The fraught intersections of the aesthetic, the ethical and the political dimensions of these new forms of writing were at the center of their concerns. While political and social formations had been significant vectors for understanding the literary historical context of literatures from erstwhile colonies in the model of

Commonwealth literature, they became a much more robust area of interest in postcolonial studies.[1]

From the 1980s, the concerns with the historical contexts of postcolonial literary studies that had drawn on Memmi, Fanon, and others were given a more complicated theoretical inflection by Edward Said, and further consolidated in the 1990s in the work of Gayatri Spivak, Homi Bhabha, and Abdul JanMohamed, among others. The analytical models of colonial discourse analysis that these critics elaborated were by the 2000s being joined to influential interdisciplinary offerings provided by non-literary scholars such as Arjun Appadurai (*Modernity at Large*; social anthropology), Dipesh Chakrabarty (*Provincializing Europe*; history), and Achille Mbembe (*On the Postcolony*; African political theory) to lay out a heady theoretical and cultural mix that inspired many lively debates in the field of postcolonial studies in general.[2] However, throughout the 1990s and into the 2000s, the collocation of colonial discourse analysis and the interdisciplinary infusions from outside of literary studies proper had the net effect of decisively shifting emphasis in the field away from the examination of literary and aesthetic products as such and toward the exploration of their discursive contexts and conditions of production. The study of rhetorical devices made way for that of discursive ensembles, but discursive ensembles were not couched necessarily in either literary or historical terms. Literature itself was resorted to only as an excuse for illustrating other things. It almost became an embarrassment to pay close attention to the specific details of the literary text itself.

At the same time, literary analysis proper was also gradually being transferred to the study of culture, whether of the highbrow or popular variety. One remembers, for example, the signal impact of James Clifford and George Marcus's now classic *Writing Culture* of 1986, which applied modes of literary analysis to the reading and interpretation of ethnography.[3] The essays there by Vincent Crapanzano, James Clifford, Mary Louise Pratt, Paul Rabinow, and others were highly stimulating in my own formation as an interdisciplinary postcolonial literary critic. In postcolonial cultural studies the device of the expressive fragment that was

[1] For more on these genealogies see, Ato Quayson, "Introduction: Postcolonial Literature in a Changing Historical Frame," and "The Journal of Commonwealth Literature: the 1980s."

[2] See Arjun Appadurai, *Modernity at Large* (Minneapolis: Minnesota University Press, 1996); Dipesh Chakrabarty, *Provincializing Europe: Postcolonial Thought and Historical Difference* (Princeton: Princeton University Press, 2000); and Achille Mbembe, *On the Postcolony* (Berkeley: California University Press, 2000).

[3] James Clifford and George Marcus, *Writing Culture: The Poetics and Politics of Ethnography* (Berkeley: California University Press, 1986).

taken to somehow reflect the social totality of which it was a part became commonplace, and the intercourse between discourse analysis and the study of culture was firmly established. By the end of the early 1990s, context had become folded into text in certain branches of postcolonial literary studies such that the literary text, shorn of its expressly literary features, was taken to illuminate history and culture. While historical contexts and the history of ideas were put to many good uses in postcolonial studies, strictly speaking, after Said's signal *Orientalism* (1979) and *Culture and Imperialism* (1993), Benita Parry's *Conrad and Imperialism* (1983), Abdul JanMohamed's *Manichean Aesthetics* (1984), and Paul Carter's *The Road to Botany Bay* (1987), the interdisciplinarity of postcolonial studies did not manage to provide a persuasive account of literature (*qua* literature, and not literature as a stand-in for something else) *and* history at the same time.[4] The distance of this vein of cultural studies from the Marxist-inspired version practiced by scholars at the University of Birmingham's Centre for Contemporary Cultural Studies – founded in 1964 by Richard Hoggart and with Stuart Hall and Paul Gilroy among its later luminaries – was soon being lamented by various observers.[5]

It has to be noted, however, that the trends that were manifested in the study of postcolonial literatures in the 1980s and into the 1990s and 2000s were of a piece with similar reorientations evident in literary studies more generally, which from at least the early 1980s had been heavily impacted by the poststructuralist and neo-formalist approaches of Michel Foucault, Jacques Lacan, Pierre Bourdieu, and Mikhail Bakhtin. For me, however, the source of constant regret was the progressive, one might say almost decisive, retreat from the rigorous reading of literature that came to pass under the rubric of postcolonial literary criticism. Reading literature for its literariness was regarded as almost an admission of moral deficiency.[6]

---

[4] Edward Said, *Orientalism* and *Culture and Imperialism;* Abdul JanMohamed, *Manichean Aesthetics: The Politics of Literature in Colonial Africa* (Boston: University of Massachusetts Press, 1983); Benita Parry, *Conrad and Imperialism: Ideological Boundaries and Visionary Frontiers* (London: Palgrave, 1983); Paul Carter, *The Road to Botany Bay* (Minneapolis: Minnesota University Press, 1987).

[5] For a detailed critique of the overlapping yet dramatically different tendencies between cultural and postcolonial studies, see especially E. San Juan, Jnr., *Beyond Postcolonial Theory* (London: Palgrave Macmillan, 2000); also Nicholas Thomas's fine essay, "Becoming Undisciplined: Anthropology and Cultural Studies," Henrietta Moore, ed., *Anthropological Theory Today* (Cambridge: Polity Press, 1999), 262–279.

[6] The typology I have described here is necessarily summative and polemical and does not take into account the many fine works that continued to be produced on different literatures from the Global South but without any specifically postcolonial or indeed theoretical inflection. These were, however, not the texts that drove the heady and most influential claims of postcolonial theorizing in general.

The study of tragedy, however, raised a different set of problems for me. As already noted in the Introduction, all serious discussions of literary tragedy in the twentieth century made almost no reference either to what was happening outside of Euro-America or indeed to postcolonial literary examples. This is in spite of the growing and steady popularity of texts outside the Euro-American geopolitical enclave from the 1960s onward, with various postcolonial writers steadily winning the most prestigious prizes and awards. In the discussion of the absences in Terry Eagleton's *Sweet Violence* (2005) in the Introduction, I limited myself to mentioning only the best-known examples of Nobel Prize winners from the late 1980s onward, but in truth, their ranks could be much augmented with postcolonial writers as diverse as Rabindranath Tagore, Miguel Ángel Asturias, Taha Hussain, Leopold Sedar Senghor, H. I. E. Dhlomo, Nawal El-Sadawi, Alejo Carpentier, Louise Bennett, Julio Cortázar, and Gabriela Mistral (a hitherto unsung Chilean poet who actually won the Nobel Prize for Literature in 1945), and many, many others.

Tragedy raised another problem for me, which was how to think of it not as a form whose contours were permanently set by the Greeks, Shakespeare, and the Renaissance tradition (George Steiner's view, which I clearly do not share), but rather as offering a series of tragic morphologies that could be detected in operation in various contexts, fields, and genres beyond the theatre. Most important for me, however, was to devise a critical practice of reading by which to oscillate between the tragic tradition and the postcolonial texts I was interested in, by paying equally serious attention to both in terms of their modalities of expression, their material conditions, and other multidimensional qualities inherent to the two domains. When I turned to Aristotle and Fanon and augmented them with my own account of the Akan concept of *musuo*, it was to elaborate a critical apparatus supple enough to take account of the wide variety of texts I was looking at. But each text also called forth its own subcategories of concepts and necessary theoretical inflections: the contradictions of cosmopolitanism, the problem of self-accounting, the metonymic transfers between the social and the natural worlds, the affliction of second thoughts, disputatiousness and unruly affective economies, moral residue, the volatile proximity between different historical epochs, split *anagnorisis*, causal plausibility, hermeneutical delirium, and analogical verification were the most prominent that came up for elaboration. My central focus on the impediments to ethical choice-making was a way of organizing a diverse set of materials into a more-or-less coherent frame of analysis. At the same time all critical concepts were adduced from the close-reading of the texts in question, with such reading being closely attentive to the literary and discursive texture of individual texts as much as to the disposition of the characters through whose perspectives the arrangements might best be seen.

Throughout the book, my interest in rectifying what I take to be variant forms of Eurocentric parochialism has been not necessarily to write *against* the Western tradition of literary tragedy but *through* postcolonial texts to illuminate the ways in which Western tragedy might be reread via postcolonial examples, and postcolonial texts might in their turn be animated from the comparison and contrasts with those from the Western tradition. *Tragedy and Postcolonial Literature* is thus thoroughly comparative in completely abjuring hierarchies between literary traditions and texts. Rather, my reading method requires a form of the "interleafing" of texts.

The idea of an interleafed reading is best understood in terms of how we read well-known canonical texts from any tradition. Each well-known text you encounter is always read as if for the second time, even if it is your very first time of encountering the text. Interleafing also means that to take any literary text seriously you have to read it with the subliminal or explicit knowledge of all the various ways in which it is impinged upon by other texts and, may in its turn, impinge upon others. This should be the preliminary starting point, even if you have no idea how these interrelations might be established. In other words, every text is to be read as a portal to other things of literary value and not simply to confirm already-established cultural experiences and dispositions. In this type of reading, attitude is incipient action, that is to say, to read as if what you are reading is part of a larger set of cross-cultural illuminations is to be open to finding out more about how such cross-cultural illuminations occur in the first place. To transfer this to the shaping of a reading practice specifically around postcolonial tragedy meant for me interleafing, say, Achebe's *Things Fall Apart* with Sophocles' *Oedipus Rex* and *Philoctetes* (few people notice that Okonkwo has a disability; he has a very bad stammer) as well as with Aeschylus' *Agamemnon* (infanticide, anyone?), and Conrad's *Heart of Darkness*. J. M. Coetzee's *Waiting for the Barbarians* can productively be interleafed with Samuel Beckett (Coetzee wrote his doctoral dissertation on Beckett), Ngũgĩ wa Thiong'o (especially with respect to Mugo's confused reticence in *The Grain of Wheat*), or even Michael Ondaatje's *The English Patient* (for the scarred landscape of both geography and the mind). That we read Toni Morrison's *Beloved* as interleafing Euripedes' *Medea* is an obvious option, but what if we think of her as animating methods for establishing the interconnectivity we also find in Virginia Woolf's *Mrs*

Dalloway (Morrison wrote her MA thesis on Faulkner and Woolf). Morrison can also be read alongside Yvonne Vera's *Without a Name* (in the uncontrolled proliferation of symbolization compulsions due to trauma), and Amos Tutuola's *The Palm-Wine Drinkard* (is Beloved not much like Tutuola's "the perfect gentleman" from the ghost town who borrows body parts wherever he can find them?). But because my reading of postcolonial tragic texts interleaf all the others before and alongside them, it also means that when I go back to reread, say, Sophocles, Aeschylus, or Woolf, Achebe and Morrison are going to be automatically entailed in my (re)reading of them. I perform a slightly different type of interleafing in relation to my chapter on Shakespeare's *Othello* and the question of cosmopolitanism, where I calibrate an interpretation of the modules of image-making and self-management inherent to the play and relate these to the contradictory attraction and revulsion to ideas of otherness in our own times. The point is that I never read postcolonial literary tragedy or literature in general as illustrative of some exclusive enclave mentality, but rather attend to the ways in which it serves to illuminate fertile ethico-aesthetic questions and conundrums, many of which have already been present in the larger tradition of tragedy. To understand Sophocles, I tell my students, read Achebe!

A skeptic might launch a completely understandable objection to this kind of reading practice: is interleafing not the lazy man's attempt at establishing relations among all texts, no matter how tenuous? How about the differences in the material contexts in which the texts were first produced? And does this form of reading practice not ultimately distort the integrity of different texts by transposing too readily between texts of completely different provenance and traditions? (Achebe and Sophocles? Like, really? Come on!) This is where the capacious nature of tragedy provides an answer. For any study of tragedy that does not limit itself to a specific period or author (Renaissance tragedy, tragedy in the works of Tolstoy, etc.), must always proceed on the assumption that what is being compared, whether of genre, form, thematic emphasis, ethical disposition, or particular tragic morphological element, has to be assigned an explicit place within the framework of comparison, with an acknowledgement that it is the act of comparison itself that renders elements commensurable between texts in the first instance. Commensurability is not always antecedent to the process of comparison, as we might readily conclude from looking, say, exclusively at adaptations of Greek tragedy, where the adaptations are wedded as closely as possible to the dramaturgical and conceptual features of the originals, with variations for the new cultural contexts of production.[7] Rather, it is the *processual quality* of comparison established in the juxtaposition of unlikely literary worlds that renders one element commensurable to another and converts the incommensurable into something stimulating and fertile, whether this is characterological, cultural, conceptual, or otherwise.

The emphasis I am laying here on the processual quality of comparison in postcolonial tragedy is to avoid the potential pitfall of straining to track the anxiety of comparative influence, to echo the title of Harold Bloom's book.[8] This is essentially the idea that a later text within a tradition is necessarily imitative of a previous one, and that its creativity has to be measured primarily in relation to how cleverly it evades the explicit marks of influence while invoking enough to recall the previous literary iteration. However, as Michael Baxandall has argued with respect to art criticism, the anxiety of influence model implies a reversal of what really happens in the relationship between later and earlier practitioners within the same field. He points out that it is rather the case that later writers and artists "draw on, resort to, avail [themselves] of, appropriate from, have recourse to, adapt, misunderstand, refer to, pick up, engage with, react to, quote . . ." Baxandall's list of words and phrases denoting the agency of later writers and artists in relation to earlier ones runs up to forty-six. For him, the relationships between earlier and later artists requires a vocabulary that demonstrates the agency of the succeeding ones.[9] Indeed, it is arguable that literary influence is more like an act of perception that triggers further literary action. If, in the study of tragedy, adaptations have been taken to illuminate mimetic influence, what I have in mind in my practice of interleafing, is the redistribution of influence(s) between and among texts in such a way as to invoke multiple and competing creative genealogies that make of them simultaneously part of a tradition and yet each irreplaceably a new articulation of older problems. And for the critic, the challenge is to be alive to all the many overlaps, references, and counter-references within the larger body of tragedy, even if these are not rendered explicit within the postcolonial texts in question.

---

[7] African adaptations of the classics seem to loom large in the postcolonial world. Twelve of the nineteen pieces in Lorna Hardwick and Carol Gillespie's *Classics in Post-Colonial Worlds* (Oxford: Oxford University Press, 2007) center on African examples.

[8] Harold Bloom, *The Anxiety of Influence: A Theory of Poetry* (Oxford: Oxford University Press, 1997).

[9] See his *Patterns of Intention: On the Historical Explanation of Pictures* (New Haven and London: Yale University Press, 1985), 58–59.

Characterological Types and the Question of Freedom: Attached and Unattached

On a final note, and this time to demonstrate the practice of interleafing by comparing various characters in the postcolonial texts we have already looked at, what might the characters we have encountered so far tell us about the relationship between tragedy, freedom, and community? Furthermore, are there any conclusions we might draw from them about freedom in the world in which we live today? These are questions I first alluded to in the chapter on Coetzee and which I now want to engage with more fully. As we have already seen, Othello, Okonkwo, and Sethe are totally headstrong and absolute. They believe, and make us want to believe, in the absolute justness of their causes, that is, until they are shown to have been fundamentally mistaken. In contrast, the Magistrate and Murphy are not given to any epic or heroic orientations and are often afflicted by second thoughts, or, in the case of Murphy, of the desire to be insulated from the outside world. Mustafa Sa'eed sits somewhere between Okonkwo and the Magistrate in being full of dash and certainty to begin with, but then being afflicted by serious loss of certainty after he kills his English wife, Jean Morris. What do we make of these stark differences in characterological dispositions? Can we perhaps move beyond the texts themselves and trace these differences in characterological types to the different relations between their various authors' proximity or distance from their imagined communities? And if so, what are their overall implications for the question of freedom?

The most appropriate comparison in answering these questions are the characters from J. M. Coetzee, as alluded to in Chapter 7. As already noted, Coetzee wrote his PhD on Beckett in the late 1960s and we can see the Beckettian influence in Coetzee especially in his many characters who are given to self-revision and the affliction of second thoughts, such as, say, the Magistrate in *Waiting for the Barbarians*, Paul Rayment in *Slow Man*, and David Lurie in *Disgrace*. But there is something else that Coetzee's characters share with Beckett's Murphy, Molloy, Watt, Hamm, and Estragon that goes beyond their nervous self-doubt, self-revision, and even endemic anxiety. This is the fact that both sets of characters are also wedded to small physical gestures, as if in an effort not to expend too much energy in the accomplishment of any individual objective. For Coetzee, as for Beckett's characters, we find none of the grand physical gestures and actions of, say, an Okonkwo, an Elesin Oba, or even a Baby Suggs. Coetzee and Beckett's characters are not given to any epic actions or grand statements either. And yet at the same time, they tend to be capacious in their intellect and able to range widely inside of their own minds. Why are their external gestures minimalist, but their minds so large in sweep and scale? What accounts for this disjuncture?

One provisional answer might be found in the fact that, unlike those of Achebe, Soyinka, and Morrison, the Coetzean and Beckettian character is devoid of a community on whose behalf he or she might speak. We are required to qualify this observation somewhat with specific reference to Salih's Mustafa Sa'eed, who is extremely intelligent and as thoughtful (full of thought) as any of Coetzee's or Beckett's characters, but given to large rather than diminutive gestures and yet also utterly bereft of any community on whose behalf he might be presumed to speak. However, I want to suggest that in his escapades with the various white women in London before he meets with Jean Morris, Sa'eed is at pains to channel the epic grandeur he thinks are guaranteed by the orientalist archetypes he deploys. This process, as we saw in the chapter on *Season of Migration to the North*, is essentially co-constitutive, that is to say, both him and the white women he consorts with glory in the same set of orientalist archetypes. He is the spirit of the Nile, a son of Africa, man of the jungle, and representative of all the wanton forces of raw nature. My suggestion is that, since he is not part of any Sudanese or African diasporic community in London of his time, the orientalist archetypes act as guarantors of epic if not community values. However, once Jean denudes him of these props and incites him to fulfil the one grand, tragic archetype of Othello that he then fails to realize, he is left floundering. His recourse to the village of Wad Hamid and the activities he participates in as a member of the local agricultural committee are all attempts at reimagining an engagement with community, precisely what he was denied by his sojourn in London. The denial of any form of community in London is, of course, because of his supreme egotism and his insistent suppression of any form of emotion except hedonistic ones, symbolized specifically in the image of the cold knife that he repeatedly uses to represent his mind. The contents of his library as reviewed by the unnamed narrator suggests that his mind seeks a form of validation through an immersion in the scholarly traditions of intellectual engagement and self-writing inherent to the colonial archive, of which he is both exemplar and critic. But this dimension of his identity clearly does not satisfy his desire for community. I would say then, that even though Mustafa Sa'eed shares something of the non-communal isolation of the Coetzean or Beckettian character, he subliminally pines for the guarantees and comforts of community, typified in the first instance by his recourse to orientalist archetypes in London and in the second by the choices he makes whilst in Wad Hamid. The question, ultimately, is about freedom, and whether this is to be attained purely through individual agency or in conjunction and alliance with the determinants of a wider community. The either/or nature of the question might seem a bit distortive, but that is what we see when we contrast Othello, Okonkwo, Elesin Oba, and Sethe to the Magistrate and Murphy, with Mustafa Sa'eed providing the contradictions inherent to each orientation.

This then brings us to two definitions of freedom that Tejumola Olaniyan had begun to explore in an interview he gave a year or so before his untimely passing in November 2019. In the interview, conducted and filmed by Phyllis Taoua and Jean-Marie Teno on the fringes of the African Studies Association conference in 2018, Olaniyan was asked about his definition of freedom and its relation to modernity.[10] He noted two definitions: the first he termed "attached freedom," which was the freedom of being part of a larger community. This was what defined the precolonial and early colonial societies illustrated in Achebe's works and among the Yorùbá of Olaniyan's own heritage. All struggles for freedom in those colonial periods had to do with collective and individual efforts at integrating self with community and it was the impediments to that integration that triggered revolutionary upheavals. The second mode of freedom, which to Olaniyan, develops alongside the first mode but also during the phase of colonial modernity, is that of "unattached freedom." This is the freedom of expressing oneself as an autonomous individual and not necessarily by way of attachment to a collectivity. The spread of Christianity among the Yorùbá in the nineteenth century, and the fissures brought by internal wars that triggered the founding of hybrid states such as Ibadan, concomitantly served to qualify the terms of attached freedom. This contradiction, Olaniyan points out, is pertinent to many parts of the Global South to this day.

It is clear that in the conditions of apartheid under which Coetzee wrote, and in those of semi-colonial Ireland that was the background to Beckett's formation and subsequently for his work as a writer in exile, they both, as individuals, were severed from being able to speak with any clear-cut communal sensibility. That Coetzee was a white descendant of the Boers in South Africa and developed his sensibility bearing witness to the

---

[10] Tejumola Olaniyan interview with Phyllis Taoua and Jean-Marie Teno, https://vimeo.com/3767 08021?fbclid=IwAR29UeF8fO7l4eyEcuS-K2PjLpCUxajOijZEolzzrIQAOc8OyfbpYuh8-Eo; last accessed Dec. 4, 2019.

oppression of the black population in his country is not entirely to be discounted in his inability to speak for any particular community. This is not what we see from the work of colored and black South African writers such as Zakes Mda and Dennis Brutus, who write with a clear and explicit consciousness of their role as representatives of their oppressed communities. Something similar might be adduced for Beckett. Raised as a member of a wealthy Anglo-Irish group in Dublin, he progressively grew uneasy with his own social dispensation, and indeed with the collective nationalist claims that the Irish Revival sought to make on behalf of the Irish people. The point to be noted here is that characters such as Murphy, Watt, Molloy, Estragon, Vladimir, Hamm, Clov, and Krapp, among others, are avatars of the unattached freedom that Olaniyan speaks of, which is the direct product of a contradictory modernity, colonial or otherwise. The inverse is what we find for Achebe, Soyinka, and Morrison, where the confidence and large gestures of their characters derive from their sense of being representative figures of larger communal sensibilities.

However, sometimes what passes for communal sensibilities may also be internally contradictory. Both Sethe and Beloved represent a sense of larger communal sensibilities; Sethe for all mothers whose maternality and nurturing instincts are rendered unnatural and void by slavery, and Beloved for the six million and more of the Black Atlantic (to echo only the number we find in the epigraph to the novel). For much of *Beloved,* Sethe is shown to be an isolated pariah in her small community of Cincinnati, Ohio; by the time we encounter her, the "natural" has been put under severe pressure from slavery and shown to embody its ever-present negation. But in the novel other mothers, such as Baby Suggs and Ella, recognize that Sethe represents something more than just herself. Like her, they are also distorted in their maternal instincts by slavery. In contrast, the six million and more as represented by Beloved are shown to be fundamentally inimical to the well-being of Sethe and whatever communal function she stands for.

Which, then, is the true freedom: attached or unattached? And in what instances do impediments in the face of either produce the grounds for the tragic alienation of the individual? In Olaniyan's brief comments he was at pains to suggest that the onset of colonial modernity rendered the attached variety of freedom almost impossible as a mode by which to operationalize a quest for greater public goods in the modern world. Rather, what we find is that different historical epochs in the twentieth and twenty-first centuries illustrate collective modes of action that seek to subsume individual aspiration under a larger order. And yet these modes of collective action find themselves obliged to reach into the domain of historical exemplars so as to define what such actions might mean for the collective and the individual. History thus repeats itself as a collective morphology. And so, the impulses of decolonization from different parts of the world, from the 1940s through the 1960s, are still pertinent to us today for how to battle the many forms of existing neo-colonialism. The anti-nuclear demonstrations of the 1960s and 1970s bear salutary lessons for the environmentalist warriors of today, while the Civil Rights movement provides insights for Black Lives Matter and the various Occupy battles that flare up sporadically in different parts of the world. The killings of several African Americans in very recent memory from Trayvon Martin to George Floyd remind us that at least for this racial group, forms of attached freedom are the only conduits for gaining unattached freedom. But from the continuing conflagrations in places such as Syria, Turkey, Nigeria, Myanmar, to the delirious sovereignty that we now see expressed by the United States and the United Kingdom, we know that the struggle for freedom is by no means over. Whether we turn for examples from Othello, Okonkwo, Sethe, the Magistrate, or Murphy, they each provide us with templates by which to think and rethink fresh modalities of freedom. For ultimately, agency and freedom must be seen as items in a chain of significations that entangle both, rather than simply being their origins or destinations. This, it seems to me, is what postcolonial tragedy teaches us.

Bibliography

Achebe, Chinua. "An Image of Africa: Racism in Conrad's *Heart of Darkness*," *Massachusetts Review*, 18.4 (1977): 782–794.
 "An Image of Africa: Racism in Conrad's *Heart of Darkness*," Robert Kimbrough, ed., *Heart of Darkness: An Authoritative Text, Background Sources and Criticism*, 3rd edition. London: W. W. Norton, 1988.
 Arrow of God. London: Penguin, 2016.
 No Longer at Ease. London: Heinemann, 1964.
 Things Fall Apart. London: Heinemann, 1958.
Achebe, Nwandwo. *The Female King of Colonial Nigeria: Ahebi Ugbabe*. Bloomington: Indiana University Press, 2011.
Ackroyd, Peter. *London: A Biography*. London: Vintage, 2001.
Aeschylus. *Agamemnon, The Oresteian Trilogy*, trans. Philip Vellacott. London: Penguin Books, 1959.
Afigbo, A. E. *The Warrant Chiefs: Indirect Rule in Southeastern Nigeria, 1891–1929*. London: Longman, 1972.
Agamben, Giorgio. *Homo Sacer: Sovereign Power and Bare Life*. Stanford: Stanford University Press, 1998.
Al-Musawi, Muhsin. "The Republic of Letters: Arab Modernity? Part I," *Cambridge Journal of Postcolonial Literary Inquiry*, 1.2 (2014): 265–280.
 "The Republic of Letters: Arab Modernity? Part II," *Cambridge Journal of Postcolonial Literary Inquiry*, 2.1 (2015): 115–130.
Alcott, Louisa M. *Little Women*. New York: Signet Classics, 2004.
Althusser, Louis. "Ideology and Ideological State Apparatuses: Notes Toward An Investigation," *Lenin and Philosophy and Other Essays*. London: Verso, 1971, 85–125.
Altman, Joel. *The Improbability of Othello: Rhetorical Anthropology and Shakespearean Selfhood*. Chicago: Chicago University Press, 2010.
Amadiume, Ifi. *Male Daughters, Female Husbands: Gender and Sex in an African Society*. London: Zed Books, 1989.
Anderson, Perry. "From Progress to Catastrophe," *The London Review of Books*, 33.15 (2011): 24–28.
Andrews, Travis M. "Police held 'Mission Impossible' actor Ving Rhames at gunpoint for entering his own home," *Washington Post*, July 29, 2018; www.washington post.com/news/arts-and-entertainment/wp/2018/07/29/police-held-mission-im

possible-actor-ving-rhames-at-gunpoint-for-entering-his-own-home/?noredirec
t=on&utm_term=.baed6144a29e, last accessed Sept. 7, 2018.

Annas, Julia. *The Morality of Happiness*. New York: Oxford University Press, 1993.

"Anthropophagi," Oxford English Dictionary Online; www.oed.com/view/Entr
y/8472?redirectedFrom=anthropophagi#eid, last accessed Oct. 30, 2019.

Appadurai, Arjun. *Modernity at Large*. Minneapolis: Minnesota University Press,
1996.

Appiah, Anthony K. *Cosmopolitanism: Ethics in a World of Strangers*. New York:
Norton, 2007.

Aristotle. *Poetics*, ed., T. S. Dorsch. London: Penguin Classics, 1965.

The Nicomachean Ethics, trans. J. A. K. Thomson. London: Penguin, 2004.

Attridge, Derek. *J. M. Coetzee and the Ethics of Reading: Literature in the Event*.
Chicago, IL: University of Chicago Press, 2004.

Atwood, Margaret. "In Search of *Alias Grace*: On Writing Canadian Historical
Fiction," *The American Historical Review*, 103.5 (1998): 1503–1516.

Auerbach, Erich. "Odysseus' Scar," *Mimesis: The Representation of Reality in
Western Literature*. Princeton: Princeton University Press, 1953, 3–23.

Bachelard, Gaston. *The Poetics of Space*, trans. Maria Jolas. Boston: Beacon Press,
1958.

Badawi, M. M. "Shakespeare and the Arabs," *Cairo Studies in English* (1963/1966):
181–196.

Baneth-Nouailhetas, Emilienne. *The God of Small Things: Arundhati Roy*. Delhi:
MLBD, 2000.

Barber, Karin. "*Oríkì*, Women and the Proliferation and Merging of *Orìṣa*,"
Africa, 60.3 (1990): 313–336.

I Could Speak Until Tomorrow: Oriki, Women, and the Past in a Yorùbá Town.
Edinburgh: Edinburgh University Press, 1991.

Baron-Cohen, Simon. "Is Asperger's Syndrome Necessarily a Disability?"
Development and Psychopathology, 12 (2000): 489–500.

Mindblindness: An Essay on Autism and Theory of Mind. Cambridge, MA: MIT
Press, 1995.

Baron-Cohen, Simon, Helen Tager-Flusberg, and Donald Cohen, eds.,
*Understanding Other Minds: Perspectives from Developmental Cognitive
Neuroscience*. Oxford: Oxford University Press, 1993.

Battersby, John D. "The Drama of Staging *Othello* in Johannesburg," *New York
Times*, Oct. 26, 1987; www.nytimes.com/1987/10/26/theater/the-drama-of-
staging-othello-in-johannesburg.html, last accessed Aug. 6, 2018.

Baxandall, Michael. *Patterns of Intention: On the Historical Explanation of Pictures*.
New Haven and London: Yale University Press, 1985.

Bayly, C. A. *Empire and Information: Intelligence Gathering and Social
Communication in India, 1780–1870*. Cambridge: Cambridge University
Press, 1996.

"BBC On This Day, 1950–2005," BBC; http://news.bbc.co.uk/onthisday/hi/yea
rs/default.stm, last accessed Jan. 15, 2018.

Beckett, Samuel. *Murphy*. New York: Grove Press, 1957.

The Letters of Samuel Beckett, 1929–1940, eds., Martha Dow Fehsenfeld and Lois More Overbeck. Cambridge: Cambridge University Press, 2009.

Three Novels: Molloy, Malone Dies, The Unnamable. New York: Grove Press, 1958.

Watt. New York: Grove Press, 1953.

Begam, Richard. *Samuel Beckett and the End of Modernity*. Stanford: Stanford University Press, 1996.

Bellini, Gentile. *Miracle of the True Cross at the Bridge of S. Lorenzo*. Tempera on canvas, 1500; en.wikipedia.org/wiki/Miracle/of/the/Cross/at/the/Bridge/of/S./Lorenzo#/media/File:Accademia/-/Miracolo/della/reliquia/della/Croce/al/ponte/di/San/Lorenzo/-/Gentile/Bellini/-/cat.568.jpg, last accessed July 7, 2020.

Benjamin, Walter. *Illuminations*, trans. Harry Zohn. London: Fontana Press, 1992.

The Origin of German Tragic Drama, trans. John Osborne. London: BLB, 1977.

Berger, Harry, Jr. *A Fury in Words*. New York: Fordham University Press, 2013.

Bhabha, Homi. "Signs Taken for Wonders: Questions of Ambivalence and Authority under a Tree outside Delhi, May 1817," *Critical Inquiry*, 12.1 (Autumn 1985): 144–165.

Billings, Joshua. *Genealogy of the Tragic: Greek Tragedy and German Philosophy*. Princeton: Princeton University Press, 2014.

Bixby, Patrick. *Samuel Beckett and the Postcolonial Novel*. Cambridge: Cambridge University Press, 2009.

Bloom, Harold. *The Anxiety of Influence: A Theory of Poetry*. Oxford: Oxford University Press, 1997.

Boal, Augusto. *Theatre of the Oppressed*. New York: Theatre Communication Group, 1985.

Borges, Jorge L. "The Garden of Forking Paths," *Labyrinths*, trans. Andrew Hurley. New York: Penguin, 1998, 119–128.

Bowie, Malcolm. *Lacan*. Cambridge, MA: Harvard University Press, 1993.

Bradley, A. C. *Oxford Lectures on Poetry*. Oxford: Oxford University Press, 1909.

Brantlinger, Patrick. "Victorians and Africans: The Genealogy of the Myth of the Dark Continent." *Critical Inquiry*, 12.1 (1985): 166–203.

Briggs, Julia. *This Stage-Play World: Texts and Contexts, 1580–1625*, revised edition. Oxford: Oxford University Press, 1997.

Broadie, Sarah. "What Should We Mean by 'The Highest Good,'" *Aristotle and Beyond: Essays in Metaphysics and Ethics*. Cambridge: Cambridge University Press, 2007, 153–165.

Brogan, Kathleen. *Cultural Haunting: Ghosts and Ethnicity in Recent American Fiction*. Charlottesville: University of Virginia Press, 1998.

Brown, Jacqueline N. *Dropping Anchor, Setting Sail: Geographies of Race in Black Liverpool*. Princeton: Princeton University Press, 2005.

Brown, Nicholas. *Utopian Generations: The Political Horizon of Twentieth-Century Literature*. Princeton: Princeton University Press, 2005.

Bulawayo, NoViolet. *We Need New Names*. New York: Little, Brown and Company, 2013.

Bunyan, John. *The Pilgrim's Progress*, eds., Roger Sharrock and J. B. Wharey. Oxford: Oxford University Press, 1975.

Burrow, Colin. *Imitating Authors: Plato to Futurity*. Oxford: Oxford University Press, 2019.

Burton, Jonathan. "'A Most Wily Bird': Leo Africanus, *Othello* and the Trafficking in Difference," Ania Loomba and Martin Orkin, eds., *Post-Colonial Shakespeares*. London: Routledge, 1998, 23–42.

Butler, Judith. *Giving an Account of Oneself*. New York: Fordham University Press, 2005.

Butler, Judith. *The Psychic Life of Power: Theories in Subjection*. Stanford: Stanford University Press, 1997.

Cabanel, Alexandre. Ophelia. Oil on canvas, 1883; www.art.com/products/p122 79955-sa-i1657523/alexandre-cabanel-ophelia.htm, last accessed, July 6, 2020.

Calhoun, Craig. "A Cosmopolitanism of Connections," Paula Lemos Horta and Bruce Robbins, eds., *Cosmopolitanisms*. New York: New York University Press, 2017, 189–200.

Callahan, James M. *Great Hatred, Little Room: The Irish Historical Novel*. Syracuse, NY: Syracuse University Press, 1983.

Calvino, Italo. *Invisible Cities*. New York: Harcourt, 1974.

Camus, Albert. *The Myth of Sisyphus*. Paris: Gallimard, 1942.

Carpaccio, Vittore. *Hunting on the Lagoon*. Oil on panel, 1490; www.getty.edu/ art/collection/objects/686/vittore-carpaccio-hunting-on-the-lagoon-recto-le tter-rack-verso-italian-venetian-about-1490-1495/, last accessed July 6, 2020.

Carter, Paul. *The Road to Botany Bay*. Minneapolis: Minnesota University Press, 1987.

Castoriadis, Cornelius. *The Imaginary institution of Society*. Cambridge: Polity, 1975.

Cavarero, Adriana. *Relating Narratives: Storytelling and Selfhood*. London: Routledge, 2000.

Cave, Roderick, and Sara Ayad. *A History of Children's Books in 100 Books*. London: Fidelity Books, 1997.

Chakrabarty, Dipesh. *Provincializing Europe: Postcolonial Thought and Historical Difference*. Princeton: Princeton University Press, 2000.

Cheah, Pheng. *Inhuman Conditions: On Cosmopolitanism and Human Rights*. Cambridge, MA: Harvard University Press, 2006.

Cheng, Anne. *The Melancholy of Race: Psychoanalysis, Assimilation, and Hidden Grief*. Oxford: Oxford University Press, 2001.

Christian, Barbara. "Layered Rhythms: Virginia Woolf and Toni Morrison," *Modern Fiction Studies*, 39.3 & 4 (1993): 483–500.

Cleary, Joe. *Literature, Partition, and the Nation-State: Culture and Conflict in Ireland, Israel, Palestine*. Cambridge: Cambridge University Press, 2002.

"Postcolonial Ireland." Kevin Kenny, ed., *Ireland and the British Empire.* Oxford: Oxford University Press, 2005.

Clifford, James, and George Marcus. *Writing Culture: The Poetics and Politics of Ethnography.* Berkeley: California University Press, 1986.

Coates, Ta-Nehisi. "The First White President," *The Atlantic,* Oct. 2017; www .theatlantic.com/magazine/archive/2017/10/the-first-white-president-ta-nehi si-coates/537909/, last accessed Aug. 17, 2018.

Coetzee, J. M. "Confession and Double Thoughts: Tolstoy, Rousseau, Dostoevsky," David Attwell, ed., *Doubling the Point: Essays and Interviews.* Cambridge, MA: Harvard University Press, 1992, 251–293.

"Eight Ways of Looking at Samuel Beckett," Minako Okamura, Naoya Mori, and Bruno Clement, eds., *Samuel Beckett Today/Aujourd'hui,* vol. 19, Borderless Beckett/Beckett sans frontières: Tokyo 2006 (2008): 19–31.

Slow Man. London: Penguin, 2006.

"The Making of Samuel Beckett," *New York Review of Books,* 56: 7, April 30, 2009; www.nybooks.com/articles/2009/04/30/the-making-of-samuel-beck ett/, last accessed June 3, 2018.

Waiting for the Barbarians. New York: Penguin, 1980.

Cohen, Robin. *Global Diasporas: An Introduction,* 2nd edition. London: Routledge, 2008.

Cohn, Bernard. *Colonialism and Its Forms of Knowledge: The British in India.* Princeton: Princeton University Press, 1996.

Collins, Suzanne. *The Hunger Games Trilogy.* New York: Scholastic, 2008–2010.

Connor, Steven. *Beckett, Modernism, and the Material Imagination.* Cambridge: Cambridge University Press, 2014.

Cooper, Fred. *Colonialism in Question: Theory, Knowledge, History.* Berkeley: California University Press, 2005.

Coryat, Thomas. *Coryat's Crudities reprinted from the edition of 1611. To which are now added his letters, from India. Together with his orations, character, death, &c. with copper plates,* vol. 1. London: printed for W. Carter, Samuel Hayes, J. Wilkie, and E. Easton at Salisbury, 1776.

Coundouriotis, Eleni. *Claiming History: Colonialism, Ethnography, and the Novel.* New York: Columbia University Press, 1999.

Cousineau, Thomas J. "Demented vs. Creative Emulation in *Murphy,*" *Samuel Beckett Today/Aujourd'hui,* vol. 18 (2007): 355–365.

Curran, Angela. "Brecht's Criticisms of Aristotle's Aesthetics of Tragedy," *The Journal of Aesthetics and Art Criticism,* 59.2 (2001): 167–184.

Curzer, Howard J. "The Supremely Happy Life in in Aristotle's *Nicomachean Ethics,*" *Apeiron,* 24 (1991): 47–69.

Dalley, Hamish. "Postcolonialism and the Historical Novel: Epistemologies of Contemporary Realism," *The Cambridge Journal of Postcolonial Literary Inquiry,* 1.1 (2014): 51–68.

Davis, Robert C. *Christian Slaves, Muslim Masters: White Slavery in the Mediterranean, The Barbary Coast, and Italy, 1500–1800.* London: Palgrave Macmillan, 2003.

de la Campa, Román. *Latin Americanism*. Minneapolis: Minnesota University Press, 1999.

Deleuze, Gilles. *Essays Critical and Clinical*. Minneapolis: Minnesota University Press, 1997.

Dennett, Daniel. *The Intentional Stance*. Cambridge, MA: MIT Press, 1989.

Derrida, Jacques. *Acts of Literature*, ed., Derek Attridge. London: Routledge, 2015.

Dovey, Teresa. *The Novels of J. M. Coetzee: Lacanian Allegories*. Johannesburg: Ad. Donker, 1988.

Driscoll, Kerry. *Mark Twain Among the Indians and Other Indigenous Peoples*. Berkeley: California University Press, 2018.

Dufoix, Stéphane. *Diasporas*. Berkeley: California University Press, 2008.

Eagleton, Terry. *Sweet Violence: The Idea of the Tragic*. Malden, MA: Blackwell Publishing, 2003.

Eagleton, Terry, Fredric Jameson, and Edward W. Said. *Nationalism, Colonialism, and Literature*. Minneapolis: Minnesota University Press, 1990.

Edoro-Glines, Ainehi. "Achebe's Evil Forest: Space, Violence, and Order in *Things Fall Apart*," *The Cambridge Journal of Postcolonial Literary Inquiry*, 5.2 (2018): 176–192.

Edwards, Thomas R. "Ghost Story," *New York Review of Books*, Nov. 5, 1987; www.nybooks.com/articles/1987/11/05/ghost-story/, last accessed Jan. 17, 2020.

Elias, Taslim O., S. N. Nwabara, and C. O. Akpamgbo. Abolition of Osu System Law, Eastern Regional House of Assembly, 1963, 1956.

Eliot, T. S. "Burnt Norton," Christopher Ricks and Jim McRue, eds., *The Poems of T. S. Eliot*. Baltimore: Johns Hopkins University Press, 2015.

"The Love Song of J. Alfred Prufrock," *The Wasteland and Other Poems*. London: Faber, 2001.

Ellman, Maud, ed., *Psychoanalytic Criticism*. London: Routledge, 1994.

Emmett, Hilary. "The Maternal Contract in *Beloved* and *Medea*," Heike Bartel and Anne Simon, eds., *Unbinding Medea: Interdisciplinary Approaches to a Classical Myth from Antiquity to the 21st Century*. London: Legenda Press, 2010. 248–260.

Esslin, Martin. *The Theatre of the Absurd*. New York: Anchor Books, 1961.

Ezeanya, Stephan N. "The Osu (Cult-Slave) System in Igbo Land," *Journal of Religion in Africa*, 1.1 (1967): 35–45.

Fanon, Frantz. *Black Skin, White Masks*, trans. Charles Lam Markmann. New York: Grove, 1967.

Faulkner, William. *Requiem for a Nun*. New York: Vintage, 2011.

Fishkin, Shelley Fisher. *Lighting out for Territory: Reflections on Mark Twain and American Culture*. Oxford: Oxford University Press, 1996.

Was Huck Black? Mark Twain and the African American Voices. Oxford: Oxford University Press, 1993.

Foucault, Michel. "Of Other Spaces: Utopias and Heterotopias," *Architecture/ Mouvement/Continuité* (October 1984): 1–9.

French, J. M. "Othello among the Anthropophagi," *PMLA*, 49.3 (1934): 807–809.

Freud, Sigmund. "Mourning and Melancholia," *The Standard Edition of the Complete Works of Sigmund Freud*, vol. XIV, trans. James Strachey. London: Hogarth Press, 2014, 243–258.

Frith, Uta. "Asperger and His Syndrome," Uta Frith, ed., *Autism and Asperger Syndrome*. Cambridge: Cambridge University Press, 1991.

Fryer, Peter. *Staying Power: The History of Black People in Britain*. London: Pluto Press, 1984.

Fulton, Lorie Watkins. "A Direction of One's Own": Alienation in *Mrs Dalloway* and *Sula*," *African American Review*, 40.1 (2006): 66–77.

Garuba, Harry. "Teacherly Texts: Imagining Futures in Nuruddin Farah's Past Imperfect Trilogy," *Boundary 2*, 244: 2 (2017): 15–30.

Gates, Henry Louis, Jr. "Introduction: 'Tell Me, Sir... What Is 'Black' Literature?" *PMLA*, 105.1, Special Topic: African and African American Literature (1990): 11–22.

The Signifying Monkey: A Theory of African-American Literary Criticism. Oxford: Oxford University Press, 1988.

Gates, Henry Louis, Jr., and Kwame Anthony Appiah. *Race, Writing, and Difference*. Chicago: Chicago University Press, 1986.

Geulincx, Arnoldi. *Arnoldi Geulincx antverpiensis Opera Philosophica. Sumptibus providerunt Sortis spinozianae curatores*, vol 1., ed., Jan Pieter Nicolas Land. The Hague: apud Martinum Nijhoff, 1891–1893.

Ghazoul, Ferial. "The Arabization of *Othello*," *Comparative Literature*, 50.1 (1988): 1–31.

Gibbons, Luke. *Transformations in Irish Culture*. Cork: Cork University Press, 1996.

Gikandi, Simon. *Reading Chinua Achebe: Language and Ideology in Fiction*. London: James Currey, 1991.

Glenberg, Arthur M., and David A. Robertson. "Symbol Grounding and Meaning: A Comparison of High-Dimensional and Embodied Theories of Meaning," *Journal of Memory and Language*, 43.3 (2000): 379–401.

Glendinning, Simon. "Europe, for Example?" *LSE Europe in Question Discussion Paper Series* (LEQS), 31 (2011): 1–22.

Goldmann, Lucien. *Racine*. Cambridge: Rivers Press, 1972.

Goldstuck, Arthur. *The Ink in the Porridge*. London: Penguin, 1994.

Graham, Daniel W. "Heraclitus," *Stanford Encyclopedia of Philosophy*; https://plato.stanford.edu/entries/heraclitus/, last accessed Nov. 28, 2019.

Greenspan, Patricia. *Practical Guilt: Moral Dilemmas, Emotions, and Social Norms*. New York: Oxford University Press, 1995.

Grene, David, and Richmond Lattimore. *Greek Tragedies: Volume 1*. Chicago: Chicago University Press, 1991.

Gruesser, John Cullen. *Confluences: Postcolonialism, African American Literary Studies, and the Black Atlantic*. Athens: University of Georgia Press, 2005.

Gumbrecht, Hans U. *In 1926: Living at the Edge of Time*. Cambridge, MA: Harvard University Press, 1997.

Gyekye, Kwame. *An Essay on African Philosophical Thought: The Akan Conceptual Scheme*, revised edition. Philadelphia: Temple University Press, 1995.

Unexamined Life: Philosophy and the African Experience. Accra: Ghana Universities Press, 1988.

Hadfield, Andrew. *A Routledge Literary Sourcebook on William Shakespeare's Othello*. London: Routledge, 2003.

Hall, Kim F. *Things of Darkness: Economies of Race and Gender in Early Modern England*. Ithaca: Cornell University Press, 1995.

Halpern, Richard. *Eclipse of Action: Tragedy and Political Economy*. Chicago: Chicago University Press, 2017.

Hardwick, Lorna, and Carol Gillespie. *Classics in Post-Colonial Worlds*. Oxford: Oxford University Press, 2007.

Hart, Keith. "Bureaucratic Form and the Informal Economy," Basudeb Guha-Khasnobis, Ravi Kanbur, and Elinor Ostrom, eds., *Linking the Formal and Informal Economy: Concepts and Policies*. Oxford: Oxford University Press, 2006, 19–23.

"Informal Income Opportunities and Urban Employment in Ghana," *The Journal of Modern African Studies*, 11, no. 1 (1973): 61–89.

Hassan, Wail. *Tayeb Salih: Ideology and the Craft of Fiction*. Syracuse: Syracuse University Press, 2003.

Hazlitt, William. *Characters of Shakespeare's Plays*. Boston: Wells and Lilly, 1818.

Hecter, Michael. *Internal Colonialism: The Celtic Fringe in Britain's National Development*, 2nd edition. London: Routledge, 1998.

"Henry Louis Gates Controversy," Wikipedia; https://en.wikipedia.org/wiki/Henry_Louis_Gates_arrest_controversy, last accessed Sept. 7, 2018.

Heywood, Annemarie. "The Fox's Dance: The Staging of Wole Soyinka's Plays," Biodun Jeyifo, ed., *Perspectives on Wole Soyinka: Freedom and Complexity*. Jackson: University of Mississippi Press, 2001, 130–138.

Horta, Paulo, and Bruce Robbins, eds. *Cosmopolitanisms*. New York: New York University Press, 2017.

Howard, Jean, and Marion F. O'Connor, *Shakespeare Reproduced: The Text in History and Ideology*. London: Routledge, 1988.

Hoxby, Blair. "What Was Tragedy? The World We Have Lost, 1550–1795," *Comparative Literature*, 64.1 (2012): 1–31.

Hughes, Derek. *Culture and Sacrifice: Ritual Death in Literature and Opera*. Cambridge: Cambridge University Press, 2007.

Hunt, Peter, ed., *Children's Literature: The Development of Criticism*. London: Routledge, 1990.

Idowu, Bolaji. *Olodumare: God in Yorùbá Belief*. London: Longman, 1962.

The Informal City Dialogues; http://nextcity.org/informalcity, last accessed Feb. 8, 2018.UN report on African immigrants making the perilous journey to Europe; https://news.un.org/en/story/2019/10/1049641, last accessed Mar. 2, 2020.

Irele, Abiola. "Preface," Amadou Hampate Bâ. *The Fortunes of Wangrin*. Bloomington: Indiana University Press, 1999.

Isichei, Elizabeth. *A History of the Igbo People*. London: Macmillan, 1976.

"The Quest for Social Reform in the Context of Traditional Religion: A Neglected Theme in African History," *African Affairs*, 77.309 (1978): 463–478.

Jameson, Fredric. *The Political Unconscious: Narrative as a Socially Symbolic Act.* Ithaca: Cornell University Press, 2011.

JanMohamed, Abdul. *Manichean Aesthetics: The Politics of Literature in Colonial Africa.* Boston: University of Massachusetts Press, 1983.

Jeyifo, Biodun. "The Hidden Class War in *The Road,*" *The Truthful Lie: Essays in a Sociology of African Drama.* London: New Beacon, 1985, 11–22.

Johanyak, Debra. "'Turning Turk,' Early Modern English Orientalism, and Shakespeare's *Othello,*" Debra Johanyak and Walter S. H. Lim, eds., *The English Renaissance, Orientalism, and the Idea of Asia.* London: Palgrave, 2009, 77–96.

Jones, Eldred. *Othello's Countrymen: Africans in English Renaissance Drama.* Oxford: Oxford University Press, 1965.

Kennedy, Sean, ed., *Beckett and Ireland.* Cambridge: Cambridge University Press, 2010.

Kettie, Bellis, "The Last Innocent Person to Be Hanged in Wales," Wales Online: www.walesonline.co.uk/news/wales-news/last-innocent-person-hanged-wales-14860984, last accessed Dec. 4, 2018.

Kiberd, Declan. *Inventing Ireland: The Literature of the Modern Nation.* London: Verso, 1996.

Kimble, David. *A Political History of Ghana: The Rise of Gold Coast Nationalism, 1850–1928.* Oxford: Clarendon Press, 1963.

Kipling, Rudyard. *Kim.* Orinda, CA: Seawolf Press, 2020.

Kirk-Greene, Anthony. *Principles of Native Administration in Nigeria: Selected Documents, 1900–1947.* Oxford: Oxford University Press, 1965.

Kleingeld, Pauline. *Kant and Cosmopolitanism: The Philosophical Idea of World Citizenship.* Cambridge: Cambridge University Press, 2012.

Kleingeld, Pauline, and Eric Brown. "Cosmopolitanism," *Stanford Encyclopedia of Philosophy*; https://plato.stanford.edu/entries/cosmopolitanism/, last accessed Aug. 7, 2018.

Knowlson, James. *Damned to Fame: The Life of Samuel Beckett.* New York: Touchstone, 1996.

Knowlson, James, and John Haynes. *Images of Beckett.* Cambridge: Cambridge University Press, 2012.

Koebner, Richard. *Empire.* Cambridge: Cambridge University Press, 1962.

Kortenaar, Neil ten. *Postcolonial Literature and the Impact of Writing.* Cambridge: Cambridge University Press, 2011.

Kossew, Sue. "The Politics of Shame and Redemption in J. M. Coetzee's *Disgrace,*" *Research in African Literatures,* 34.2 (2003): 155–162.

Lacan, Jacques. "The Mirror Stage as Formative of the Function of the I," Écrits: A Selection, trans. Alan Sheridan. London:Tavistock, 1977, 1–7.

"The Mirror Stage," Écrits, trans. Bruce Fink. London: Routledge, 2007, 502–509.

Lakoff, George, and Mark Johnson. *Philosophy in the Flesh: The Embodied Mind and Its Challenge to Western Thought.* New York: Basic Books, 1999.

Lanone, Catherine. "Seeing the World Through Red-Coloured Glasses: Desire and Death in *The God of Small Things*," Jean-Pierre Durix and Caroline Durix, eds., *Reading Arundhati Roy's* The God of Small Things. Paris: Dijon: Editions Universitaires de Dijon, 2002, 125–144.

Law, Robin. "Human Sacrifice in Pre-Colonial West Africa," *African Affairs*, 84.344 (1985): 53–87.

Lazarus, Neil. "Introduction," *The Cambridge Companion to Postcolonial Literary Studies*. Cambridge: Cambridge University Press, 2004.

Lee, Spike. *The BlacKkKlansman*. Universal City, CA: Universal Pictures Home Entertainment.

Leonard, Miriam. *Tragic Modernities*. Cambridge, MA: Harvard University Press, 2015.

Lerer, Seth. *Children's Literature: A Reader's History, from Aesop to Harry Potter*. Chicago: Chicago University Press, 2008.

Lévi-Strauss, Claude. *From Honey to Ashes*, trans. John and Doreen Weightman. London: Jonathan Cape, 1973.

Tristes Tropiques. Paris: Librairie Plon, 1955.

Lizardo, Omar. "Pierre Bourdieu as Cognitive Sociologist," Wayne H. Brekhus and Gabe Ignatow, eds., *The Oxford Handbook of Cognitive Sociology*. Oxford: Oxford University Press, 2019, 65–80.

Lloyd, David. *Anomalous States: Irish Writing and the Post-Colonial Moment*. Duke University Press, 1993.

Loomba, Ania. *Colonialism/Postcolonialism*, 2nd edition. London: Routledge, 2005.

Shakespeare, Race, and Colonialism. Oxford: Oxford University Press, 2002.

Loomba, Ania, and Martin Orkin. "Introduction," *Post-Colonial Shakespeares*. London: Routledge, 1998.

Lovejoy, Paul E. *Transformations in Slavery: A History of Slavery in Africa*, 3rd edition. Cambridge: Cambridge University Press, 2012.

Lowe, Kate. "Black Gondoliers and Other Black Africans in Renaissance Venice," *Renaissance Quarterly*, 66.2 (2013): 412–452.

Lukács, Georg. *Soul and Form*. Cambridge, MA: MIT Press, 1978.

The Historical Novel. Nebraska: University of Nebraska Press, 1983.

Lynch, Kevin. *Image of the City*. Boston: MIT Press, 1966.

MacNeice, Louis. "Prayer Before Birth"; www.poemhunter.com/poem/prayer-before-birth/, last accessed July 6, 2020.

"Mahmood Hussein Mattan: A Man Wrongly Accused of Murder in 1952," African Stories in Hull and East Yorkshire; www.africansinyorkshireproject.com/mahmood-hussein-mattan.html, last accessed Dec. 4, 2018.

Malraux, Andre. *La Condition Humaine*. Romans, Paris: Gallimard, 1947.

Mamdani, Mahmood. *Citizen and Subject: Contemporary Africa and the Legacy of Late Colonialism*. Princeton: Princeton University Press, 1997.

Define and Rule: Native as Political Identity. Cambridge, MA: Harvard University Press, 2012.

Divide and Rule; Citizen and Subject: Contemporary Africa and the Legacy of Late Colonialism. Princeton: Princeton University Press, 1996.

Mann, Kristin. *Slavery and the Birth of an African City: Lagos, 1760–1900.* Bloomington: Indiana University Press, 2007.

Mark, Peter. "Africans in Venetian Renaissance Painting." *Renaissance 2. A Journal of Afro-American Studies*, 4 (1975): 7–11.

Márquez, Gabriel G. Nobel Lecture, 8 December, 1982, *Nobel Lectures: Literature 1981–1990*, ed., Sture Allén. Singapore: World Scientific Publishing Company, 1993, 11–14.

Maude, Ulrika. "Beckett, Body and Mind," Dirk Van Hulle, ed., *The New Cambridge Companion to Samuel Beckett.* Cambridge: Cambridge University Press, 2015, 170–184.

Mbembe, Achille. "Necropolitics," *Public Culture*, 15.1 (2003): 11–40.

Necropolitics. Durham: Duke University Press, 2019.

On the Postcolony. Berkeley: California University Press, 2000.

"The Planetary Library: Notes on Theory Today." *Out of the Dark Night: Essays on Decolonization.* New York: Columbia University Press, forthcoming.

McCallum, Pamela. "Introduction," Raymond Williams, ed., *Modern Tragedy.* New York: Broadview Press, 2006.

McClintock, Anne. "The Angel of Progress: Pitfalls of the Term 'Postcolonialism,'" Francis Barker, Peter Hulme, and Margaret Iversen, eds., *Colonial Discourse/Postcolonial Theory.* Manchester: Manchester University Press, 1994, 253–256.

McConnell, Terrance. "Moral Dilemmas," *Stanford Encyclopedia of Philosophy;* https://plato.stanford.edu/entries/moral-dilemmas/, last accessed July 14, 2018.

"Moral Residue and Dilemmas," H. E. Mason, ed., *Moral Dilemmas and Moral Theory.* Oxford: Oxford University Press, 1996, 36–47.

McDonald, Ronan. "Nothing to Be Done: Masculinity and the Emergence of Irish Modernism," Natalya Lusty and Julian Murphet, eds., *Modernism and Masculinity.* Cambridge: Cambridge University Press, 2014, 71–86.

Tragedy and Irish Literature: Synge, O'Casey, Beckett. London: Palgrave, 2001.

Meek, Richard, and Erin Sullivan, eds., *The Renaissance of Emotion: Understanding Affect in Early Modern Literature and Culture.* Manchester: Manchester University Press, 2014.

Mgbobukwa, Jude A. *Osu and Ohu in Igbo Religion and Social Life.* Nsukka: Fulludu Publishing Company, 1996.

Millais, John E. *Ophelia.* Oil on canvas, 1852; www.tate.org.uk/art/artworks/millais-ophelia-no1506, last accessed July 6, 2020.

Mohanty, S. P. "Kipling's Children and the Colour Line," *Race & Class*, 31.1 (1989): 21–40.

Moraes Farias, P. F. de, and Karin Barber, eds., *Self-Assertion and Brokerage: Early Cultural Nationalism in West Africa.* Birmingham: Centre for West African Studies, 1990.

Morin, Emilie. *Beckett's Political Imagination.* Cambridge: Cambridge University Press, 2019.

Morrison, Toni. *Beloved*. London: Picador, 1988.

Jazz. New York: Plume, 1993.

Paradise. London: Chatto and Windus, 1998.

Song of Solomon. London: Chatto and Windus, 1978.

Mukherjee, Ankhi. *What Is a Classic: Postcolonial Rewriting and Invention of the Canon*. Stanford: Stanford University Press, 2014.

Neill, Michael. "Othello and Race," Peter Ericson and Maurice Hunt, eds., *Approaches to Teaching Shakespeare's* Othello. New York: MLA Publications, 2005, 37–52.

Nietzsche, Friedrich. *The Birth of Tragedy and the Genealogy of Morals*, trans. Francis Goffling. New York: Doubleday, 1956.

Nkemngong, John N. "Samuel Beckett, Wole Soyinka, and the Theatre of Desolate Reality." *Journal of African Literature and Culture* (2006): 153–175.

Nodelman, Perry. *The Hidden Adult: Defining Children's Literature*. Baltimore: Johns Hopkins University Press, 2008.

Nooter, Sarah. *The Mortal Voice in the Tragedies of Aeschylus*. Cambridge: Cambridge University Press, 2017.

Nordstrom, Carolyn. *Global Outlaws: Crime, Money, and Power in the Contemporary World*. Berkeley: University of California Press, 2007.

Nussbaum, Martha. *The Fragility of Goodness: Luck and Ethics in Greek Tragedy and Philosophy*. Cambridge: Cambridge University Press, 2001.

"The 'Morality of Pity': Sophocles's *Philoctetes*," Rita Felski, ed., *Rethinking Tragedy*. Baltimore: Johns Hopkins University Press, 2008, 148–169.

"Tragedy and Self-Sufficiency: Plato and Aristotle on Fear and Pity," Amélie Oksenberg Rorty, ed., *Essays on Aristotle's* Poetics. Princeton: Princeton University Press, 1992, 261–290.

Nuttall, A. D. *Why Does Tragedy Give Pleasure?* Oxford: Oxford University Press, 2001.

Nwokeji, G. Ugo. *Slave Trade and Culture in the Bight of Biafra: An African Society in the Atlantic World*. Cambridge: Cambridge University Press, 2010.

Obeng-Odoom, Franklin. "The Informal Sector in Ghana under Siege," *Journal of Developing Societies*, 27 (2009): 355–392.

O'Flynn, Siobhan. "Why the Hunger Games Is not Harry Potter and Why We Should Care," (blog) http://siobhanoflynn.com/why-the-hunger-games-is-not-harry-potter-why-we-should-care/, last accessed Dec. 23, 2019.

Okeke, Romeo I. *The "Osu" Caste System Concept in Igboland*. Enugu: Access Publishing, 1986.

Okwu, Augustine S. O. *Igbo Culture and the Christian Missions, 1857–1957: Conversion in Theory and Practice*. Lanham: University Press of America, 2009.

Olaniyan, Tejumola. "Festivals, Rituals, and Drama in Africa," Abiola Irele and Simon Gikandi, eds., *The Cambridge History of African and Caribbean Literature*, vol 1. Cambridge: Cambridge University Press, 2004, 35–48.

Interview with Phyllis Taoua and Jean-Marie Teno; https://vimeo.com/37670
8021?fbclid=IwAR29UeF8fO7l4eyEcuS-K2PjLpCUxajOijZE0lzzrIQAOc8
OyfbpYuh8-Eo, last accessed Dec. 4, 2019.

O'Neill, Bruce. *The Space of Boredom: Homelessness in the Slowing Global Order.*
Durham: Duke University Press, 2017.

O'Neill, Kevin. *Secure the Soul.* Berkeley: University of California Press, 2015.

Osinubi, Taiwo A. "Abolition, Law, and the Osu Marriage Novel." *The
Cambridge Journal of Postcolonial Literary Inquiry,* 2 (2015): 53–71.

Owens, Thomas. *Wordsworth, Coleridge, and "The Language of The Heavens."*
Oxford: Oxford University Press, 2019.

Parker, Patricia. "Dilation and Inflation: *All's Well That Ends Well, Troilus and
Cressida,* and Shakespearean Increase," *Shakespeare from the Margins: Language,
Culture, Context.* Chicago: Chicago University Press, 1996, 185–228.

Literary Fat Ladies: Rhetoric, Gender, Property. London: Routledge, 1988.

"Othello and Hamlet: Dilation, Spying, and the 'Secret Place' of Woman,"
Representations, 44 (1993): 60–95.

"Shakespeare and Rhetoric: 'dilation' and 'delation' in *Othello,*" Patricia Parker
and Geoffrey Hartman, eds., *Shakespeare and the Question of Theory.* London:
Routledge, 1993, 54–74.

Shakespearean Intersections: Language, Contexts, Critical Keywords. Philadelphia:
University of Pennsylvania Press, 2018.

Parker, Patricia, and Geoffrey Hartman. *Shakespeare and the Question of Theory.*
London: Routledge, 1993.

Parry, Benita. *Conrad and Imperialism: Ideological Boundaries and Visionary
Frontiers.* London: Palgrave, 1983.

Paul, Lissa. "Enigma Variations: What Feminist Theory Knows about Children's
Literature," *Signal,* 54 (September 1987): 186–202.

Phelan, James. "Sethe's Choice: *Beloved* and the Ethics of Reading," *Style,*
32.2 (1998): 318–333.

Pigafetta, Antonio. *The First Voyage Around the World, 1519–1522: An Account of
Magellan's Expedition,* ed., Theodore J. Cachey, Jnr. Toronto: Toronto
University Press, 2007.

Prabhu, Anjali. "Fanon, Memmi, Glissant and Postcolonial Writing," *The
Cambridge History of Postcolonial Literature,* vol. 2, ed., Ato Quayson.
Cambridge: Cambridge University Press, 2012, 1068–1099.

Probyn, Clive T. "Waiting for the Word: Samuel Beckett and Wole Soyinka,"
Ariel, 12.3 (1981): 35–48.

Pullman, Philip. *His Dark Materials Trilogy.* London: Scholastic, 1995–2000.

Quayson, Ato. *Aesthetic Nervousness: Disability and the Crisis of Representation.*
New York: Columbia University Press, 2007.

"Anatomizing a Postcolonial Tragedy: Ken Saro-Wiwa and the Ogonis,"
Performance Research, 1.2 (1996): 83–92.

"Autism, Narrative, and Emotions: On Samuel Beckett's Murphy," *University
of Toronto Quarterly,* 79.2 (2010): 838–864.

Calibrations: Reading for the Social. Minneapolis: Minnesota University Press, 2003.

ed., *The Cambridge History of Postcolonial Literature,* vol 1. Cambridge: Cambridge University Press, 2012.

"Comparative Postcolonialisms: Storytelling and Community in Sholem Aleichem and Chinua Achebe," Special Issue on Jewish Studies and Postcolonialism, *The Cambridge Journal of Postcolonial Literary Inquiry,* 3.1 (2015): 287–296.

"Criticism, Realism and the Disguises of Both: an analysis of Chinua Achebe's *Things Fall Apart* with an evaluation of the criticism relating to it," *Research in African Literatures,* 25.4 (1994): 117–136.

"Ethnographies of African Literature: A Note," *Contemporary African Fiction, Bayreuth African Studies,* 42 (1997): 157–166.

"The Journal of Commonwealth Literature: the 1980s," 50th anniversary issue of the *Journal of Commonwealth Literature* (September 2015): 1–18.

Oxford Street, Accra: City Life and the Itineraries of Transnationalism. Durham: Duke University Press, 2014.

"Postcolonializing Shakespeare: Parables from the Canon," *Postcolonialism: Theory, Practice, or Process?* Cambridge: Polity Press, 2000, 156–184.

"Self-Writing and Existential Alienation in African Literature: Chinua Achebe's *Arrow of God,*" *Research in African Literatures,* 42.2 (March 2011): 30–45.

Strategic Transformations in Nigerian Writing. Oxford and Bloomington: James Currey and Indiana University Press, 1997.

Quayson, Ato, and Girish Daswani, eds., *Companion to Diaspora and Transnational Studies.* New York: Blackwell, 2013.

Quigley, Mark. "Unnaming the Subject: Samuel Beckett and Colonial Alterity," *Samuel Beckett Today/Aujourd'hui,* vol. 15 (2005): 87–100.

Rancière, Jacques. *The Politics of Aesthetics: The Distribution of the Sensible.* London: Continuum, 2004.

Ransome, John Crowe. "Piazza Piece"; www.poetryfoundation.org/poems/49146/piazza-piece, last accessed July 6, 2020.

Ray, Carina. *Crossing the Color Line: Race, Sex, and the Contested Politics of Colonialism in Ghana.* Athens, OH: Ohio University Press, 2015.

Reiss, Timothy J. *Against Autonomy: Global Dialectics of Cultural Exchange.* Stanford: Stanford University Press, 2002.

Richards, David. "*Òwe l'esín òró:* Proverbs Like Horses in Wole Soyinka's *Death and the King's Horseman,*" *Journal of Commonwealth Literature,* 13.1 (1984): 89–99.

Ricoeur, Paul. *The Symbolism of Evil.* New York: Harper and Row, 1967.

Time and Narrative, vol. 2. Chicago: University of Chicago Press, 1984.

Rizzo, Matteo. *Taken for a Ride: Neoliberalism, Precarious Labour, and Public Transport in an African Metropolis.* Oxford: Oxford University Press, 2017.

Roberts, Julian. *Walter Benjamin.* London: Macmillan, 1982.

Rothman, E. Natalie. *Brokering Empire: Trans-Imperial Subjects Between Venice and Istanbul.* Ithaca: Cornell University Press, 2012.

Roy, Arundhati. *The God of Small Things*. London: Vintage, 1997.

Rymer, Thomas. *A Short View of Tragedy*. London: Scolar Press, 1970.

Said, Edward. *Culture and Imperialism*. London: Vintage, 1994.

  Orientalism. London: Vintage, 1979.

Salih, Tayeb. *Season of Migration to the North*. London: Heinemann Educational, 1969.

Samatar, Sofia. "Open Letter to a Late Author: Dear Tayeb Salih," *ArabLit Quarterly* (Fall 2018): 24–30.

San Juan, E. Jnr. *Beyond Postcolonial Theory*. London: Palgrave Macmillan, 2000.

Schelling, F. W. J. "Philosophical Letters on Dogmatism and Criticism" *The Unconditional in Human Knowledge: Four Early Essays, 1794–1796*, trans. Fritz Marti. Lewisburg, PA: Bucknell University Press, 1980, 156–196.

Schlegel, August W. *Lectures on Dramatic Art in Literature*, trans. John Black. Aeterna Publishing, 2011. First published 1815.

Scott, David. *Conscripts of Modernity: The Tragedy of Colonial Enlightenment*. Durham: Duke University Press, 2005.

Seeff, Adele. "*Othello* at the Market Theatre," *Shakespeare Bulletin*, 27.3 (2009): 377–398.

Sekyi-Otu, Ato. *Fanon's Dialectic of Experience*. Cambridge, MA: Harvard University Press, 1997.

Sewell, Mary. *Patience Hart's First Experience*. Sydney: Wentworth Press, 2019.

Shakespeare, William. *All's Well That Ends Well* (Arden Shakespeare Third Series), eds., Suzanne Gossett and Helen Willcox. London: Arden, 2018.

  King John (Arden Shakespeare Third Series), eds., J. J. M. Tobin and Jesse M. Lander. London: Arden, 2018.

  Othello, 2nd edition (Arden Shakespeare Third Series), ed., E. A. J. Honigmann. London: Arden, 2016.

Sheffer, Gabriel. *Diaspora Politics: At Home Abroad*. Cambridge: Cambridge University Press, 2006.

Shohat, Ella. "Notes on the Postcolonial." *Social Text*, 31/32 (1992): 99–113.

Siddiq, Muhammed. "The Process of Individuation in Al-Tayyeb Salih's Novel *Season of Migration to the North*," *Journal of Arabic Literature*, 9 (1978): 67–104.

Smith, Robert. "In Search of Carpaccio's African Gondolier," *Italian Studies*, 34 (1979): 45–59.

Soyinka, Wole. *Death and the King's Horseman*. London: Metheun, 1975.

  Myth, Literature, and the African World. Cambridge: Cambridge University Press, 1975.

  The Road. Collected Plays, vol. 1. Oxford: Oxford University Press, 1973. 147–232.

Spivak, Gayatri. "Ghostwriting," *Diacritics*, 25.2 (Summer 1995): 64–84.

Stasik, Michael. "Roadside Involution, Or How Many People Do You Need to Run a Lorry Park," Kurt Beck, Gabriel Klaeger and Michael Stasik eds., *The Making of the African Road*. Leiden: Brill, 2017, 24–57.

Steiner, George. *The Death of Tragedy*. New York: Alfred Knopf, 1963.

Stock, Brian. *Augustine's Inner Dialogue: The Philosophical Soliloquy in Late Antiquity.* Cambridge: Cambridge University Press, 2010.

Stoler, Ann Laura. *Race and the Education of Desire: Foucault's History of Sexuality and the Colonial Order of Things.* Durham: Duke University Press, 1995.

Street, Susan C., and Charles L. Crow, eds., *The Palgrave Handbook of the Southern Gothic.* London: Palgrave, 2016.

Strickland, Lloyd. *Leibniz's Monadology: A New Translation and Guide.* Edinburgh: Edinburgh University Press, 2014.

Suhr-Sytsma, Nathan. *Poetry, Print, and the Making of Postcolonial Literature.* Cambridge: Cambridge University Press, 2017.

Suleri, Sara. "The Adolescence of Kim," *The Rhetoric of British India.* Chicago, IL: University of Chicago Press, 1992, 117–131.

Suzman, Janet. "*Othello* – A Belated Reply," *Shakespeare in South Africa*, 2 (1988): 90–96.

Szondi, Peter. *An Essay on the Tragic*, trans. Paul Fleming. Stanford: Stanford University Press, 2002.

Taylor, Charles. "Modern Social Imaginaries," *Public Culture*, 14.1 (2002): 91–124.

Taylor, Neil, and Bryan Loughrey, "Murphy's Surrender to Symmetry," *Journal of Beckett Studies*, 11/12 (1989): 79–90.

Tessman, Lisa. *Moral Failure: On the Impossible Demands of Morality.* Oxford: Oxford University Press, 2015.

    When Doing the Right Thing Is Impossible. Oxford: Oxford University Press, 2017.

Thomas, Nicholas. "Becoming Undisciplined: Anthropology and Cultural Studies," Henrietta Moore, ed., *Anthropological Theory Today.* Cambridge: Polity Press, 1999, 262–279.

Trotz, Alissa. "Looking Well to See Well: Lessons from Oxford Street, Accra," *PMLA*, 131.2 (2016): 524–527.

Twain, Mark. *The Adventures of Huckleberry Finn.* Orinda, CA: Seawolf Press, 2019.

    The Adventures of Tom Sawyer. Orinda, CA: Seawolf Press, 2018.

Uchendu, Victor. C. "Slaves and Slavery in Igboland, Nigeria," Suzanne Miers and Igor Kopytoff, eds., *Slavery in Africa: Historical and Anthropological Perspectives.* Madison: University of Wisconsin Press, 1977, 121–132.

Vaughan, Virginia M. Othello*: A Contextual History.* Cambridge: Cambridge University Press, 1996.

Vendrame, Alessandra. "Toni Morrison: A Faulknerian Novelist?" *American Studies*, 42.4 (1997): 679–684.

Vernant, Jean-Pierre. "Tensions and Ambiguities in Greek Tragedy," Jean-Pierre Vernant and Pierre Vidal-Naquet, eds., *Myth and Tragedy in Ancient Greece.* London: Zone Books, 1988, 29–48.

Wafer, Alex. "Informality, Infrastructure and the State in Post-apartheid Johannesburg," PhD dissertation, Department of Geography, Open University, 2011.

Walkowitz, Rebecca L. *Cosmopolitan Style: Modernism Beyond the Nation*. New York: Columbia University Press, 2006.

Wallace, Jennifer. *The Cambridge Introduction to Tragedy*. Cambridge: Cambridge University Press, 2007.

Waterhouse, John William. *Ophelia*. Oil on canvas, 1889; www.john-william-waterhouse.com/ophelia-1894/, last accessed July 6, 2020.

Weinstock, Jeffrey A. *The Cambridge Companion to the American Gothic*. Cambridge: Cambridge University Press, 2017.

Wells, Stanley, Gary Taylor, John Jowett, and William Montgomery, eds., *The Oxford Shakespeare: The Complete Works*. Oxford: Oxford University Press, 1988.

White, Robert S., Mark Houlahan, and Katrina O'Loughlin eds., *Shakespeare and Emotions: Inheritances, Enactments, and Legacies*. London: Palgrave, 2015.

White, Stephen K. "Introduction," *The Cambridge Companion to Habermas*, ed., Cambridge: Cambridge University Press, 1995.

Whitney, Lois. "Did Shakespeare Know Leo Africanus?," *PMLA*, 37.3 (1922): 470–483.

Williams, Bernard. *Problems of the Self*. Cambridge: Cambridge University Press, 1973.

Williams, Raymond. *Modern Tragedy*, ed., Paula McCallum. New York: Broadview Press, 2006.

Wimmer, Andreas, and Nina Glick-Schiller. "Methodological Nationalism and Beyond: Nation Building, Migration, and the Social Sciences," *Global Networks*, 2.4 (2002): 301–334.

Wofford, Chloe A. "Virginia Woolf's and William Faulkner's Treatment of the Alienated," MA thesis, Cornell University Press, 1955.

Wool, Zoe H. "In-durable Sociality: Precarious Life in Common and the Temporal Boundaries of the Social," *Social Text*, 130 (2017): 79–90.

Yeats, W. B. "Easter Rising"; www.poetryfoundation.org/poems/43289/easter-1916, last accessed July 6, 2020.

"Second Coming"; www.poetryfoundation.org/poems/43290/thesecond-coming, last accessed July 6, 2020

Young, Julian. *The Philosophy of Tragedy: From Plato to Žižek*. Cambridge: Cambridge University Press, 2013.

Young, Robert J. C. *Empire, Colony, Postcolony*. Oxford: Wiley Blackwell, 2015.

Empire, the National, and the Postcolonial, 1890–1920. New York: Oxford University Press, 2002.

The Idea of English Ethnicity. Oxford: Blackwell, 2008.

Postcolonialism: A Historical Introduction. Oxford: Blackwell, 2001.

Zimmerman, Michael. J. "Lapses and Dilemmas," *Philosophical Papers*, 17.2 (1988): 103–112.

Index